The Republic of Silence

The Republic
of Silence

COMPILED AND EDITED BY

A. J. LIEBLING

*May this Republic about to be set up in
broad daylight preserve the austere virtues of
that other Republic of Silence and of Night.*

JEAN-PAUL SARTRE

New York

HARCOURT, BRACE AND COMPANY

Contents

v

PART THREE: RESISTANCE BECOMES GENERAL

PART FOUR: THE FIGHT

PART FIVE: THE WAR BEHIND THE WAR

PART SIX: MARTYRS . . . ASSORTED

PART SEVEN: VICTORY!

PART EIGHT: SUMMATION

Argument of This Book

Argument of This Book

One of the most dangerous stories in the French language is LA CHÈVRE DE MONSIEUR SEGUIN, by Alphonse Daudet. It is intrinsically dangerous because of its moral implications. It is dangerous to France because of its effect on world opinion. LA CHÈVRE of the story is a young white nanny goat who refuses to stay tethered. She wishes to go up on a mountain which she can see from the yard of Monsieur Seguin's house, in order to fulfill her destiny. Monsieur Seguin adjures her to play it safe, which he calls being reasonable. "There is a bad wolf on the mountain who will eat you if you go up there," he says, talking as Marshal Pétain used to. "But if you will be a spineless unimaginative nanny goat and demonstrate a will to co-operate I will even lengthen your tether. There is plenty of grass here if you will just learn to adjust yourself to conditions." But the nanny goat slipped her tether and went up on the mountain, and the wolf ate her, which proved Monsieur Seguin had been right. The Messieurs Seguin-Pétain-Daudet and the counterparts they have in every country are always right, if you accept the stories they make up themselves.

In real life, the men of the French Resistance were like the white nanny goat. They refused to listen to Marshal Seguin-Pétain, even though in real life one story-book attribute had been transposed and the Marshal had the quavering voice of the goat. The Resistance men went up on the mountain and met the wolf. But there real life and the story diverged. Because the Resistance men beat the tar out of the wolf, who only has power over those who fear him. Walt Disney wrote a healthier wolf parable than Alphonse Daudet. The Daudet story is particularly dangerous be-

3

cause it ascribes benevolent characteristics to the counselor of caution. *I once intended to call this book* THE NANNY GOAT WAS RIGHT, *or* MONSIEUR SEGUIN WAS WRONG, *but I gave up the idea because it embarrasses people to ask for a book with an odd title.* THE REPUBLIC OF SILENCE, *which is not my own invention, is much better. Nevertheless the book is the story of the refusal of the French to accept a lengthened tether in exchange for a destiny. It is told for the most part in their own words, which I think you will find admirable.*

Looking back it has occurred to me that a good part of the American misconception of the nature of France, where it existed, may have been due to the kind of texts on which students formed their early notions of the language. LA CHÈVRE *is the archetype of these. In quest of texts that would be at the same time simple, not too colloquial, proper and without relevance to life, compilers went too often to writers remembered in France with the same amused indulgence reserved for a Second Empire bibelot, say a stuffed hummingbird suspended by a supposedly invisible wire over a bowl of wax fruit, the whole under a glass bell. The stories were too often sentimental and what the French call* NIAIS, *which means corny. And since our opinion of a culture new to us is likely to be based upon our first contact with it, the American inducted into French via the* NIAISERIES *of Monsieur Daudet and comparable saps is likely to go through the rest of his life believing Frenchmen to be quaint imbeciles. Students who begin French in the first year of high school are less likely to suffer from this initiation than those who begin it in college. Daudet, François Coppée, Edmond About and the rest are on about the same aesthetic and intellectual level as a Greer Garson picture and the pre-adolescent may not notice anything wrong with them. But college men and women are likely to be put off by the disparity between the intellectual content of what they discuss in non-language courses and the dreadful corn syrup they are asked to ingurgitate in the course of learning simple French. I first got this book together for the use of college French teachers, keeping the French parts in French and me in English, or my own approximation thereof. Then I got to thinking that there were a lot of people who had been discouraged from learning French by their* first classroom experiences, but who could be reached by a version with the French done into English.

The idea is succinctly expressed on the title page of my copy of LE MOYEN DE PARVENIR: "A new edition corrected of many faults which were not there in the first place and augmented by several new ones."

The selections that I have tried to arrange in an approximation of a pattern in the following pages were all written by Frenchmen between May 10, 1940, when the German Army opened the campaign that ended with the Pétain armistice, and early September, 1944, a couple of weeks after the liberation of Paris. All the selections, with two or three exceptions, which will be duly noted, were written in France under the German occupation. Some, a number that surprised me when I totted up after making the selections, are by writers who had excellent and well-founded reputations before this war—for example Louis Aragon and François Mauriac. Others are by professional writers like Vercors and Claude Roy whose fame is a wartime development. But many, as you will see, are by complete novices, such as a corporal in an armored division recording his first sight of refugees, or a boy of seventeen setting down his last thoughts before facing a firing squad. "All the same, it's hard to die," the boy concludes. It was only by the fortune of secret war that the corporal too did not wind up before a firing squad. Two years after he saw the refugees he was in the Resistance, running parachuted arms to hidden arsenals.

Some items are anonymous, pieces culled from that great clandestine press which arose under the occupation and waged a war of ideas that turned public opinion completely against the conquerors —who had to aid them in their propaganda only limitless funds, powerful radio stations, all the printing establishments of France, and some thousands of miserable traitors. You will find a great many references to these last in this book. The fact of betrayal is an integral part of the story of France under the occupation, as it is of the New Testament. Incidentally, I wonder whether from a pedagogical standpoint Judas is not the most successful symbol in the Christ story. Not everybody has learned to love Christ, but virtually everybody succeeds in hating Judas.

Many of the writers represented here were such only in that they put words on paper, and not in the professional sense at all. Their writings are simply colloquial speech fixed in ink. The least experienced authors, as you will notice, were sometimes the most ornate. They felt that they had to "take things big." And yet their overblown verbiage fails to conceal the tragic import of what they had to express.

The approximation of a pattern that I have tried to follow in my selections and their arrangement is simple, but hard to classify. It might be called a case history of a sick nation, beginning with the crisis of the disease, and following through to convalescence and recovery. But there is something entirely too passive in the concept of France as a patient. Or it might be called THE AUTO-BIOGRAPHY OF A NATION, 1940-44, except that that is too inclusive. The France Gertrude Stein wrote about in WARS I HAVE SEEN also existed during those same years, I am sure. That was the France of the middle-aged and the old, who appear with relative infrequency in the chronicles of the Republic of Silence. And when, like Marc Bloch, they do appear, they are playing young men's roles.

This certainly isn't an anthology, if you think of an anthology as a selection of the "best" writing of a period, because as I have said some of the pieces have no literary quality at all. And I have omitted many fine things written during the four years that didn't seem to fit into the book, as well as many others that I have not happened to read. I am not a student of Resistance literature; candidates for the degree of doctor of philosophy will have their crack at it later. Then there will be bibliographies, and theses, and monographs of minor writers, and in time chairs of Resistance Literature endowed by the descendants of cartel millionaires and filled by professors exactly like Monsieur Seguin.

The book, the French writers' part of it, that is, begins with the catastrophe. But it is the catastrophe as seen by four or five men involved in it. It goes on through selections that tell how Frenchmen viewed their plight and what they thought about it, and what they thought were the chances of getting out of it. And what they did, and what life and death were like, at different periods of the occupation—for moral and material conditions were very different in 1940-1 from 1942-3, for example. The bits of language show how hope grew, and how the fear and cruelty of the occupant kept pace with it. Finally there are some accounts of how men felt during the liberation and immediately afterward.

In the spring of 1944, when I was in London waiting for D-day, I had the opportunity to see some hundreds of Resistance newspapers of all sorts that were flown out of France to the headquarters of the Provisional Government—which the United States of course did not then recognize as even a provisional government—and from them I made up a kind of mosaic of what life must be in France under the occupation. I compared the process to salvaging scraps of paper dropped from a house where a friend was held prisoner by kidnappers. Each paper might have a word or two written on it, and then one would put the papers together and try to read a continuous message. I wrote three long pieces for THE NEW YORKER, following that scheme, and arrived at a result that I found afterward had been pretty accurate—much more so than that achieved by our own State Department, for example, which had been getting its information from a man at the Brookings Institution looking into a crystal ball. The Department had the quaint notion that there was somewhere in France an anti-De Gaulle, inactive, Monsieur Seguin kind of a collaborationist Resistance movement that would come to light once danger was past and gratefully receive France from the hands of a third secretary. When they sought this alternative group with which to do business they naturally looked not to groups left of De Gaulle, but to his right, not understanding that he was already as far right as any French leader could go without losing his leadership. They talked of a large, inert, conservative mass in France which would manifest itself if given a chance in a free election. Two free elections have been held there since the liberation, at this writing, and the vote cast by elements to the right of De Gaulle have been negligible. De Gaulle himself, in fact, has proved too conservative to stay on top.* This book is the same kind of a reconstruction as those

* Harry Butcher's book, My Three Years with Eisenhower, proves, to my sorrow, that Mr. Roosevelt, if not originally responsible for this error, was even more stubbornly persistent in it than his subordinates. To paraphrase Mr. La Guardia, the President made few mistakes, but when he did they were beauts.—L.

articles, but one on which I have had a chance to check before publication.

Men seldom write as ingenuously ten years after the event as when they are in its grip. This is particularly true when it involves national AMOUR-PROPRE or the apportionment of individual and party responsibilities. Samuel Pepys, writing at Clapham in his retirement in 1680 concerning the years covered in his diary, would have presented a much less veracious record of what had happened, as well as a duller one. He would have written about what, by that time, he thought must have happened, in the light of his own later opinion of himself. So I have a high esteem for history that may be picked out of accounts as contemporary as these, like the sweet meat from the claws of a lobster.

I once knew a school committeeman named Rowland Palmer in Exeter, Rhode Island, who held that it was foolish ever to buy new history-books of the Civil War, because, he said, it stood to reason that the sooner after the war a man wrote the more he would remember about it. The flaw in his argument against buying the books, I think, was that the old ones he had hadn't been written soon ENOUGH after the war. For history written a hundred years after the event is more accurate than the kind written ten years after it. After a hundred years the participants are dead and the historian doesn't have to justify his friends. To form his conclusions he goes back to the contemporary sources and ignores most of the stuff written in between.

In reading the first version of this book, therefore, college students learn not only French, but a better grade of European history than will be academically available for ninety-eight years, and should receive double credits toward graduation, although the volume is sold at a single price. It reminds me of a little Japanese picture-book I have, with text in Japanese, Chinese and English. "By this book," the English foreword says, "you may see all world-renowned sites of beautiful Japan, without making any travel, and spending only a trifle for it."

Perhaps it would be a good idea for me now to explain why I felt impelled to put this book together. A man should have some reason for anything he does. I love France, just as I love New York City or the smell of burning leaves on a Long Island lawn. This does not mean that I love all the French or everything French, but the things I do not like I can often find excuses for. This is a pretty sure sign of an emotional attachment.

In this book I am not an author but a go-between. I try to fill in gaps in continuity and to supply bits of background when it would be difficult otherwise to understand the motivation of certain pieces. I should call myself a master of ceremonies if that term were not reminiscent of night-club and music-hall brashness, and if this were not an extremely serious book. There is a French term, COMPÈRE, for a chap who explains what is going to happen in a revue, and as he goes off-stage often pinches (Fr.: PELOTER) the showgirls' bottoms. But that also has too flippant a connotation. Then there is the narrator of documentary films—like the one who should say, "Time stands still, or so it seems while you are listening to this ominous croak." With him I care still less to be confused.

I am very conscious of the master-of-ceremonies analogy. It is a rôle difficult not to overplay, and I remember with misgiving some of the hams I have seen getting between show and audience instead of bringing them together. I will try not to get in the way of the performance. But it seems I should make some allusion here to what had happened before May 10, 1940, when the curtain rises.

PART ONE

The Débâcle

The Débâcle

It has become a commonplace to speak of France before the war as a sick nation. It is true after a fashion, but it is difficult to name any other nation that at that time presented evidences of glowing health. The struggle against periodic business slumps in the United States, and the officially-proclaimed distressed areas in Britain, scarcely could have been considered indications of high form. The hectic glow of Nazism reflected fever rather than the pink of condition in Germany. The heavy Mussolinian rouge on Italy's face was an attempt to hide her deathly pallor. Nor were the political trials in Russia symptoms of national well-being.

France at that time might have been compared to a man with a touch of flu, something of a temperature, a sprained ankle and possibly a bit of a hangover, none of them an affliction in itself likely to be fatal, but all grave because of the circumstance that he had a date to box fifteen rounds with the heavyweight champion of Europe on the evening of his illness. The Third Republic would have proved viable under ordinary conditions, but it could not win a war. The knowledge that this unwelcome war was inevitable aggravated its domestic conflicts. As war came perceptibly closer the search for an instant remedy for internal troubles became more frantic and more futile. And the shock of war itself sent the Third Republic toppling, as a right hand to the jaw would drop a sick boxer.

François Mauriac, at times a great writer and at times a great man, in spite of his membership in the French Academy, said shortly after the liberation of Paris that the four or five years that preceded the war had been for an intellectual more terrible than

13

the occupation. "There was no danger of arrest, no threat of torture," he said, "but you had the sensation of being a passenger
in an automobile without brakes or steering gear, that dashed on
toward an abyss. And you could do nothing. It was like a nightmare. And then after 1935 there was the sensation of humiliation,
of having been discounted in advance by a world that saw us
yielding to every threat of the fascists." Mauriac, a leading French
Catholic and by tradition a man of the Right, had strongly supported the Loyalist Government in Spain, joining in that the two
eminent Catholic philosophers, Georges Bernanos and Jacques
Maritain. There were at the same period lifelong Socialists like
Marcel Déat and Paul Faure who advocated truckling to the
fascists. These political paradoxes added to the confusion of the
time, but they were atypical.

In general the conservatives favored appeasement, or at least
emulation, of the authoritarian governments in Rome and Berlin,
while the men left of center (a demonstrated majority in all
elections) did not know quite what to do to avert disaster. The
left-of-centers had been anti-militarists and preachers of conciliation
until about the time of the Ethiopian War. They were at best
embarrassed protagonists of a stern foreign policy nor had they
thought sufficiently about national defense to recognize that by
new standards France was almost without any. Unlike Hitler, the
ex-corporals and junior officers who had risen to the control of
French politics retained their awe of their former commanders.
After all THEIR generals had been winners. They trusted their
professional competence. Even for Communists, Pétain remained
a military oracle.

Also they were interested in social reforms like the forty-hour
week, vacations with pay and collective bargaining, which the
conservatives found "untimely." There is no instance in history
of a conservative finding that a proposed reform WAS timely.*

Pierre-Etienne Flandin, a shrewd fellow, once gave me a less
impressionistic picture of the prewar years than Mauriac's. Until
the emergence of De Gaulle Flandin was known and caricatured
as the tallest man in French politics. He was certainly the coldest.

* They frequently claim credit for having originated past reforms, however,
which at the time they were moot they opposed with all their strength.

Flandin, a former prime minister and minister of foreign affairs (the second time under Pétain, at a time when Admiral Leahy was our ambassador to Vichy), had in 1941 bought a thousand-acre estate in North Africa to which he fortunately or advisedly removed just before the Allies landed and cut it off from France in 1942. Since he had been in years before the war considered an Anglophile, he may have expected the Allies to invite him to form a government. But he had had the bad judgment, after the Munich pact, to send telegrams of felicitation to Daladier, Neville Chamberlain and Adolph Hitler. It was one of those incidents that stuck in the public consciousness, and so the Allies passed him over in favor first of Admiral Darlan and then of Marcel Peyrouton, by way of what diplomats consider a compromise with public opinion. Flandin, if he was disappointed, remained affable and hopeful, and during several months before the arrival of De Gaulle in Africa hospitably received Allied journalists in his villa near Philippeville. He passionately loved to talk politics with them, as old jockeys love to talk of horses or old wenchers of their past mistresses.

"The course of the great industrialists was set in 1932," Flandin said calmly in the course of one of these conversations. "In that year they contributed great funds to insure the election of a Chamber of Deputies that would choose André Tardieu as PRÉSIDENT DU CONSEIL.*" (Prime Minister; the* PRÉSIDENT DE LA RÉPUBLIQUE, *under the 1878 Constitution, had so little power that it wasn't worth five francs to have him on your side.) "When they failed they said that democracy was a farce—you couldn't even buy an election. So they began backing French fascist organizations patterned after Mussolini's blackshirts—Hitler wasn't an assured success yet. But the 'leaders' they put at the head of these parties proved ninnies. They attempted a* COUP *in February, 1934, and couldn't carry through. By that time Hitler was firmly established. So the industrialists decided that the only salvation for their version of France was entrance into the German orbit as a junior partner. From then on they were interested in submission, without war if possible, but through military defeat if necessary. 'Better Hitler than Blum,' they said in 1936, but Blum had little to do*

with it. *The Popular Front Government came in a full four years after they had made up their minds."*

While Left and Right wrangled, Mauriac's automobile dashed on.

André Chamson's novel, LA GALÈRE, published in 1939, is an excellent reflection of those prewar times and their reactions on members of the French middle class, which was split as never before in its history. Chamson's QUATRE MOIS, incidentally, is an almost equally good picture of how French soldiers felt during the first months at the front, when there was no activity beyond small raids. It was a winter of severe discomfort on the line and of uncertainty in the rear areas, as well as inaction, but the national morale was decidedly better than it had been for several years preceding the war.

I remember with what apprehension (which I tried ineffectually to hide) I went to Paris at the beginning of October, 1939, when it seemed possible that the Germans would follow up their victories in Poland by a blitz attack on France. But as months went by and nothing happened I took this state of suspended warfare for granted, and actually went poking about France for subjects for articles. I felt a sense of personal outrage, as if at an intrusion, when the anti-aircraft guns woke me early on the morning of May 10. Going out on the balcony of my hotel room, I looked up and for the first time saw a German plane in daylight over Paris. It was part of the wide-flung air reconnaissance accompanying the ground attack, which had already started.

The sleepy people, leaning against their window-sills and peering upward from the buildings on all four sides of the quiet square I inhabited, seemed to sense that the war was on at last, but none of them headed for shelters. I had a luncheon appointment with Captain de Villelume Sombreuil, a friend I had made on the front in Alsace, but he telephoned to say that his leave had been canceled and he was returning to his division immediately.

During the day, although there were vague reports of disaster, the crowds were fascinated rather than panic-stricken. Only a few politicians and their French journalistic confidants, and a few high officers of the army knew what probably impended. They knew how weak the army really was, and how insignificant the ARMÉE DE L'AIR. A few sensitive Frenchmen, intellectuals like Jacques

Debû-Bridel, the author of the fragment of journal which is the second selection in this book, had a presentiment that something was somehow amiss, that Mauriac's automobile was still without steering gear. But the premonition was based on small, alarming details like the one Debû describes rather than upon positive knowledge. As for the army rank-and-file, their feelings are expressed in the short letter sent to me on the morning of the tenth by my good friend Jean-Paul Salen, at that time a CARPORAL-DÉPANNEUR in the Seventeenth Battalion, Chasseurs à Pied, serving as armored infantry.

A DÉPANNEUR is a chap who repairs vehicles EN PANNE, which means out of whack. In an armored division he functions on the battlefield. Jean-Paul was at that time an intelligent good-natured man of twenty-nine, with the equivalent of an American prep school education. He had been an automobile draughtsman in civil life and had played a lot of ice hockey. He had not gone untouched by the economic and political troubles of the late thirties. For one thing his father had lost his money, which had left Jean-Paul a member of the middle class only by courtesy and education. For another, many friends among his contemporaries had joined fascist and pseudo-royalist groups and urged Jean-Paul to come along. There, as in some circles in the United States before the war, it had become a fashion to blame democracy for every personal misfortune or shortcoming. When Jean-Paul declined, his friends had accused him of being VEULE, which means spineless. This is Jean-Paul's letter:

Friday, May 10

Dear Jo,

Thanks a lot for the package. We're doing all we can to stay cool and collected.

We keep on practicing and we're pulling at the bit, but we're still in the same place. But maybe we'll take off pretty soon, especially after what seems to be happening today.

Today we saw a constant procession of vehicles coming from Luxembourg. You could see that the people in it had grabbed their stuff and beat it. Detail: 90 per cent of the cars were American makes.

Myself I am still foreman of the repair crew, and the least I can say is that we're not loafing. I've been reading the newspapers and I feel sure that the United States will come in on our side soon.

I think that the real slugging match, in a certain sense, is going to begin now. So much the better, it will be like breaking an abscess, whatever happens it will bring the end nearer.

I think a lot about my parents who are at Paris and so more exposed than I am.

Thanks again and all the best,

Jean-Paul.

The letter contrasted sharply with a note I had had from him in November, 1939, during the DRÔLE DE GUERRE, the "funny war," when nothing happened. I think "funny" or "strange" by the way is a better rendering of DRÔLE DE GUERRE, than "phoney war." Most Frenchmen felt that the war was genuine enough, but it just didn't proceed like any other war they had ever heard of. The November note had said:

For the last two days I have been at Verdun, and, good Lord, but it's calm; it's true that we hear a bit of ack-ack, but apart from that, it's hard to feel we're at war.

We take things as they come, and with the French soldier's gift for getting by, each of us rigs up a little personal life for himself and we tell ourselves that there are others in worse spots than we.

All the best,

Jean-Paul.

In neither of these letters, however, will you notice any pessimism or unwillingness to fight. As a matter of fact the armored division to which Jean belonged fought well, although it was ordered into a series of retreats that the men naturally had difficulty in understanding. The French High Command, among other whimsies, stuck to the seventeenth century doctrine that a unit must pull out as soon as it is flanked, which the Germans disregarded. The division finished the campaign intact, and earned the nickname of LA DIVISION MALGRÉ, the In-Spite-of-Everything Division.

The armored division to which Vladimir Pozner, a young Russian naturalized in France, was attached did not fare so well, as you will judge from The Battle of the Loire, the long narrative that you will soon read. And yet even there you will note that the protagonists volunteered for what seemed a dangerous duty (although of course they grumbled), and you will see how the tight-fisted and apparently apathetic peasants could still be wheedled into giving up their precious gasoline to help win a battle. The story that the French Army was "rotten to the core" and the men unwilling to fight, even before the breakthrough began, is a lie or at most a small fraction of a truth. Most of the bad things said about the military doctrine, the functioning of command and the degree of preparation, however, are unfortunately true. It was after the promised French airplanes failed to materialize above the battle lines, after the men had lost confidence in their officers, after they had found that 25-millimeter "anti-tank" guns are as effective as anti-tank bean shooters, that morale began to crack.* Tell it not at a Fourth of July celebration, but there were several occasions later in the war when the morale of American units going into action for the first time was uncertain, too. Success breeds confidence.

With Debû-Bridel's little piece, we find ourselves in the sphere where there was foreboding, even at the kick-off. Debû-Bridel, who is about forty years old now, was of course mobilized in 1939. Before the war he had already written several novels, and had won the second most important annual award for novels in 1936, LE PRIX FÉMINA, with JEUNES MÉNAGES. Debû was a Republican of the Right. On the occasion of the award of the Prix Fémina he had got into a violent literary quarrel with Claude Morgan, a young Communist writer who had written a review panning the prize book unmercifully. This is worth mentioning only because later, in the Resistance movement, Debû-Bridel and Morgan became close associates, although neither changed his political orientation.

This fragment of his journal, written in occupied France, was

* The American army psychiatrists, Grinker and Spiegel, writing of soldiers' reaction to such circumstances, say, "The soldier in this case is not ill. The situation is ill."

first published, illegally of course, at Easter, 1943, in LES CHRON-
IQUES INTERDITES, *The Forbidden Annals*. LES CHRONIQUES was a
book gotten out by LES ÉDITIONS DE MINUIT, *Midnight Publications*,
a Resistance publishing house that functioned for two years under
the noses of the Germans. The piece first appeared under Debû's
Resistance signature, Argonne. No Resistance writer, naturally,
dared use his own name. There was a fashion among them of
taking the names of regions or towns (not of provinces or departments properly speaking) as pseudonyms. It is as if in an American
underground men took names like Panhandle or Catskills or
Eastern Shore. A man did not take the name of the district where
he was born, or lived, because that might identify him.* I don't
know why Debû-Bridel chose Argonne. Debû's misgivings because
the newspapers published Hitler's speech without comment, paralleled the disquiet of American correspondents who learned on the
same day that German air attacks on railroad centers had been
virtually unopposed, and precious airplanes had been destroyed
on the ground. The French High Command had had nine months
to study the lessons of the Polish campaign but had evidently
learned nothing.

I had a renewed attack of this feeling—it reminded me sharply
of Debû-Bridel's piece—in Times Square in November, 1945. The
electric sign that moves around the Times Building was flashing
out the message "Nuremberg defendants say Hitler foretold British
attack on Reich." No qualifying comment. New fools seemed to
be taking up where the old had left off.

* There were exceptions. George Adam, who was born in the Belgian
province of Hainaut, wrote under the name of Hainaut. Don't ask me why.

Pages from a Diary *

by JACQUES DEBÛ-BRIDEL (ARGONNE)

Paris, May 10, 1940

Extra!

Profiting by my first day of furlough, I did not go out until late in the day. The blue sky, the fresh Parisian air, the cooing of the pigeons, preening themselves and dipping their coral feet in the water in the gutters, two little girls in white veils on their way to Saint-Sulpice for their first communion, the prospect of leaving soon to join my family in Brittany—all these were enough to efface the painful shock of our brutal awakening. After all, it was spring!

In the street, the grave air of commiseration with which two old carpenters returning from their work seemed to look at me, surprised me. A group of students went by me, talking in loud voices.

"It's impossible, I tell you. It has nothing to do with 1914. Not a thing in the world, you understand."

"Just the same, they are strong. Remember Trondheim!"

"Trondheim? So what?"

Students actually condescending to take an interest in the war! It must be the effect of last night's air raid alarm.

"Frightful! Yes, my dear lady, a frightful thing to go through it all over again at our age," the woman who ran the notions shop, AU PETIT BÉNÉFICE, was confiding from her doorsill to a customer who seemed very wrought up and whose only reply was: "And not a newspaper to be had!"

The morning papers that Jean had bought and left in the lobby merely announced the occupation of Iceland by the English and dwelt at length on the double ministerial crises, in London and in Paris: Chamberlain across the Channel and the undersecretaries of Paul Reynaud here. On the Boulevard Raspail, a mob of men, women and children swarmed about a newsvendor who

* From Les Chroniques Interdites.

was selling special editions, fairly snatching them out of his hands.

Strangers spoke to each other, crowding together to read over each other's shoulders, and discussing the news.

"No doubt about it, last night's bombardment must have done a lot of damage."

I hurried toward the crowd. One detail struck me. The headlines spread in letters an inch high across the five columns of the front page of the first paper I saw; the sub-heads seemed to fill the entire page.

"Oh, yes, madame," a fat man with a white mustache was saying in the crowd behind me: "Last night, Belgium, Holland and the Grand Duchy of Luxemburg."

So that was it!

The invasion of Belgium. Like a very fast movie, memories of 1914 flitted through my mind: King Albert, his photograph with Queen Elizabeth and the two young princes of my own age, the resistance of Liège . . . Without any transition, I saw two uhlans on horseback and with their lances, a picture from a book I had when I was ten years old, a scene from the war of 1870. Then other troopers, with drawn sabers, this time out of a novel by Erckmann and Chatrian.* A squeezing sensation at the lower end of my heart sent the blood pounding to my temples. A stupid reflex set me to giggling, with the unseemly laughter that, even in childhood, used to shake my body when I had been guilty of some misdeed and was afraid of punishment. How many scoldings, cuffs and humiliations this ill-timed laughter had brought upon me! And I was not yet cured of it. Many a sharp rebuke it had earned me.

"Sometime you'll laugh out of the other side of your mouth! You'll see!" a man who had lost a leg in the other war had exclaimed, indignant at my indecent outburst of mirth.

Exasperated at my foolishness, I pushed my way through to the newsvendor and snatched the special editions of the INTRANSIGEANT and PARIS-SOIR. Abandoning all my plans, I went straight back to

---

* French novelists. Collaborating under the name Erckmann-Chatrian, they wrote patriotic historical novels. (Translator's note.)

the apartment, still pursued by the troopers with their drawn sabers out of Erckmann and Chatrian.

Across the entire page in letters an inch high, PARIS-SOIR announced: "This morning the Germans invaded Holland, Belgium and Luxemburg"; and in two-inch type:

THE FRANCO-ENGLISH ARMY
Called Upon for Help
CROSSES THE BELGIAN FRONTIER

The four columns on the right half of the page announced:

Nancy, Lille, Colmar, Lyon, Pontoise,
Luxeuil Bombed by Germans
Dead and Wounded Among Civilian Population

Of course there were! This detail was too idiotic for words. Since when have wars been fought without people being killed?

In view of the situation, M. Paul Reynaud has reshuffled his cabinet. Louis Marin and Ybarnega-ray * were appointed ministers without portfolio and members of the war cabinet.

The right-hand column gave us a rehash of the parliamentary debates of the day before, already stale and belonging to a bygone world. Unequal to the effort of reading this newspaper all in capitals, a veritable billboard, I turned to the other one. Here the headlines sprawled across the entire page:

BELGIUM, HOLLAND AND LUXEMBURG INVADED BY GERMAN TROOPS

French and British Armies
Immediately Go into Action

And in smaller type, this strange repetition:

At the break of dawn the German Armies began their penetration of Holland, Belgium and Luxemburg. The French forces had been alerted during the night.

* Two rightist politicians. (*Translator's note.*)

Then more two-inch headlines:

SEVERAL FRENCH CITIES BOMBED, MANY DEAD AND WOUNDED, MANY BUILDINGS DESTROYED

Finally, lapsing into regular headline type, these details appeared:

German planes flying over French territory last night and this morning bombed a certain number of our cities.

Brief dispatches, giving no other details, state that enemy planes dropped bombs on Pontoise, Lille, Colmar, Nancy, Luxeuil, etc. Dead and wounded are reported at Nancy. Soldiers were killed at Lyon and factories destroyed in the region of Lille. Three bombs were dropped on Colmar.

Further down the page were enormous headlines, divided so that each one filled a third of the page. At the left, in the place of honor:

TIME FOR DECISIVE BATTLES HAS COME, SAYS FÜHRER. HITLER'S PROC- LAMATION TO GERMAN SOLDIERS

By some unaccountable whim of this newspaper, it was a proclamation by Hitler that was to have the honor of breaking the news to the French reader. Hitler was speaking to us. Hitler alone! So I listened to the FÜHRER:

"The hour of decision has come," he says. "For three hundred years the English and French rulers of Europe have done their utmost to prevent any real unification of Europe and especially of Germany. They have kept Europe, and especially Germany, in a state of weakness and impotence in order to attain this end."

Three hundred years. I am not very good at mathematics; I had to count back, 1940 to 1840, 1740, 1640 . . . Ah, yes, the

Treaty of Westphalia, 1648,* "the masterpiece of French diplomacy," the beginning of religious liberty, of German liberties. It started a chain of thought. It was the balance of power that Hitler was attacking, balance of power or the Empire. Once more there was the parade of troopers from Erckmann and Chatrian followed by the file of uhlans from my childhood book. . . .

1815, 1870, 1914 . . .

I went back to the newspaper:

> "France alone has declared war on Germany
> thirty-one times in two hundred years."

Two hundred years, 1940 to 1840 to 1740. Thirty-one times! I tried to gather my memories. Germany? What is meant by Germany in 1740? Austria? Prussia? Bavaria? Frederick the Great. Maria Theresa. Joseph II. The wars of Louis XV. A shifting ground. 1740 . . . the War of the Polish Succession, the War of the Austrian Succession, the Seven Years' War. Then peace until 1792. Louis XVI and his Austrian Queen; then—let's see—the Revolution, 1799, 1802, 1804, 1807 . . . Was it France that had declared the wars in 1810, 1815, 1870, 1914? . . . Anyway, that makes twelve times. No matter how you figure it, I was stumped. He said thirty-one times—exactly, thirty and one. I must make a note to ask Rouvier, the professor, who knows so many things that I do not. But why on earth have printed this proclamation on the front page of this newspaper, without any explanation, without contradiction, without correction and without discussion? A lot of poor devils, men and women even more ignorant than I, would read it. And they would believe it! They were talking about it already.

"Just the same you seen it! It was us that declared war thirty-one times on Hitler—I mean Germany—in two hundred years!"

"Oh, it isn't so! It can't be so!"

"But it is, I tell you. It says so in the paper. Here, look at it yourself."

* The Treaty of Westphalia, between the German princes, France and Sweden, put an end to the Thirty Years' War and gave the princes of Northern Germany religious liberties and the right to make separate alliances. Thus it hindered the Austrian policy of hegemony. It also gave Alsace to France. (*Translator's note.*)

"But, you dope, that's only what Hitler says."

"Sure, I know. But if it wasn't so, if it was bluff, they'd say so in the paper. If they don't say anything, it means that it's true. Thirty-one times. That's a lot."

I could imagine I was listening to my buddies discussing it in the mess. I was listening to the triumph of Antoine, the gun-thug of the P.P.F., the fascist! I could see the hesitant eyes, the unhappy, worried air of our good peasants, the postmen trying to recall the odds and ends of the history they learned in grade school. They didn't want to believe it! Thirty-one times in two centuries we had declared war on Germany! Once every seven years!

Their faith in our cause was a little shaken now. It was printed right there, on the front page of the paper, without a word of contradiction, and at the very moment when the Germans were invading Belgium as in 1914.

Great God! what was the idiot of an editor who featured this proclamation on the front page thinking about? What possible sense did it make?

In as grave a time as this, my thought was distracted from the dangers that threatened our lives, to try to figure out what these thirty-one declarations of war were. Other Frenchmen by the thousands were unhappy over the part that their own country had played or were only too eager to condemn its imperialism in order to justify their reluctance to risk their all to defend it.

What was the use of censorship? Was there really some mysterious force working unremittingly to sow confusion in our midst?

Pozner's piece, which follows, is I think a great picture of the disintegration of an army, the saddest thing a man can see. I like to think that at least a few of the Germans who took part in the campaign of France survived to witness the disintegration of their own.

"Six weeks," the soldier Mirabelle says, "and to think that there once was a time when they fought Hundred Years Wars." The selection is formed out of the third and sixth chapters of Pozner's novel, THE EDGE OF THE SWORD, which he wrote and published in America in the fall of 1942, after escaping from France. In French it was called DEUIL EN 24 HEURES, a title derived

from the signs that used to be displayed by dry-cleaning establishments specializing in dyeing clothes black for bereaved families at twenty-four hours' notice. The novel is formed of several intertwined narratives, of which the history of the last tank is one, and nothing that happens in chapters four or five interferes with the continuity of this particular story.

The Edge of the Sword *

by VLADIMIR POZNER

THE LIEUTENANT'S COMPASS

They smelt of leather, tobacco, and gasoline, and they were attractive to women.

The lieutenant tried to size them up before he spoke to them. Their vizorless helmets, leather-padded in front, with their broad chin-straps, accentuated their features amid which shone eyes reddened by conjunctivitis, an occupational disease of tank drivers.

The lieutenant was young, and he loved fine phrases.

"I need three men," he said, "for a dangerous mission. But it's for our country."

Vandervenne, a little sheepish, was the first to step forward. The officer scanned the others, avoiding the eyes of Moustier, whose loose-jointed gait and perfunctory manner of saluting implied a subtle contempt for the calling to which he was temporarily constrained.

"What's it all about?" Moustier drawled, and after a fraction of a second he added, "sir?"

It's not according to regulations, the officer reflected. But neither was the situation, and he no longer had any secrets from this handful of men—all that was left of their battalion.

"It's about the tank," he said.

The tank rested in the shadow of the trees, enormous and

* By arrangement with Maxim Lieber, copyright 1942, by Vladimir Pozner.

misshapen, triply camouflaged with paint, mud, and green branches. Through the open door could be seen the rows of 47-millimeter shells in their compartments, and machine-gun cartridge belts hanging on the wall. The aerial had been blown off by a shell-splinter, but this did not matter much as the radio no longer worked. Neither did this matter: the tank no longer had combat orders to receive, united combats to participate in. All of its kind had remained on the Meuse, their fuel reserves dried up after a few kilometers, their ammunition exhausted a few hours later. The sole survivor of an extinct species, this one had escaped: its transmitter having become deaf-mute in the thick of battle, and consequently failing to receive suicidal orders, the radio operator had had to fall back on his own common sense. Two days later the crew came upon the reinforcements that had gone astray. They found refueling tanks full of gas and trucks of ammunition. In the course of the weeks that followed, by a phenomenon of capillarity, survivors of the Meuse had collected around the souvenir-tank.

"It's the last tank in the battalion," said the lieutenant. "It must on no account fall into German hands."

He thought to himself: if the major were here he might change his mind about me. But the major was not here, for the good reason that one cannot be in two places at once, and he had fled the day before, with two other officers, in the staff Peugeot car.

"Three of you," the lieutenant continued, "will do the impossible to get through the enemy lines and bring the tank to safety. The rest of us will take a roundabout way north, through the woods."

He was about to add: following the same route as the major's car, but caught himself in time. As for the tank, its gasoline reserve left it no alternative but to flee in a straight line.

"If you are surrounded you will use your ammunition till it is exhausted, and then destroy the tank."

It is asking too much, he said to himself. He suddenly felt sorry for these men whom he was sending to certain death, and for himself, who was also doomed.

"This is not an order," he said. "It's a request—man to man, Frenchman to Frenchman. You are free to . . ."

"We get the idea," said Moustier.

The lieutenant noticed that an unlit cigarette stub hung from his lower lip. He felt an urge to smoke, and was even more deeply moved.

"I need a third," he said.

A soldier who answered to the jovial name of Mirabelle stepped forth from the group.

"I'll go wherever anybody goes," he said, pronouncing "buddy" for "body." Discreet laughter acknowledged the pun.

"You wouldn't happen to have a map, sir?" asked Moustier with the same imperceptible hesitation before the "sir," and without waiting for the answer he added one of his favorite phrases, "But it's of no importance."

The maps were undoubtedly in the pocket of the Peugeot: the major had foreseen everything. I could give them my compass, thought the lieutenant, who knew that the one in the tank was broken. But what about the rest of them? And myself?

"Our maps wouldn't have been of any use to you," he said, in a matter-of-fact tone. "They only went as far as the Somme. We must be some thirty kilometers north of Paris. Drive south," he said, because he had just thought of the compass, "keep driving south."

"A tank," said Moustier, "is sort of unhandy. It's hard to see the stars from inside."

I have to keep it, thought the lieutenant, I have to keep it if I'm ever to get out of this. I don't want to be taken prisoner. The compass was burning his pocket.

"You will leave immediately," he said. "I entrust this tank to you. Save it. The Germans must not get their hands on it. Don't forget that it cost . . ." He had no idea of the cost of a tank, and chose a figure that would impress the men and that impressed himself. ". . . it cost a million." He tried to think of a fine phrase, found none, and repeated awkwardly, "I entrust this tank to you."

"Suppose the Fritzes are already in Paris?" asked Moustier.

Why does he keep bringing things up? What does he expect me to say to him, thought the lieutenant. He had contemplated this possibility and, finding no solution, had avoided thinking about it. He knew that Moustier's question had not been dictated

by fear and resented it all the more. I ought to tell them that
Paris is free. He did not dare to lie. A fine phrase, finally, drew
him out of his perplexity.

"There is still room to fight in France," he said in an unhappy
voice.

The three men had stepped out of the ranks and were making
their packs. They had removed their helmets and again looked
human: the officer covertly observed Mirabelle's round face in
which the eyes were set flush, his jowls covered with prematurely
gray stubble, Moustier's thin lips and sharp nose, Vandervenne's
large head with its shock of mussed hair, his kindly, trusting
eyes which because of the conjunctivitis looked even more than
usual like those of a Saint Bernard. They got up again, put on
their helmets, and once more the three looked alike and like
the others.

"Hey, are you coming?" said Vandervenne, who had not yet
spoken, and he pushed his massive body with difficulty through
the narrow opening in the side of the tank.

"Hay is for horses," said Mirabelle, and followed him.

Moustier was the last to climb in.

"So long, fellows," he said. "We'll meet again some day over
a drink."

The officer marveled at him. Courage is easy for some people,
he thought. He was young, the lieutenant, young and Jewish,
and therefore looked upon askance at the officers' mess, but at
present there was no one to look upon him one way or the
other. He smiled, immediately reproached himself for this sign
of nervousness, pressed his compass into Moustier's hand, and
shut the heavy door himself.

It was night. The tank followed the road, hugging the forest
that edged it on the left in order to be able, at the first alarm,
to make for cover. Seated on the low metal seat, Vandervenne
was driving. Mirabelle was beside him. Moustier was up in the
turret. Three pairs of eyes scrutinized the outer darkness. The
macadam of the road, and the tree-trunks, were ink-black; between
the black tops of the trees that bordered the road, one saw what
might be taken for a flow of dull slate: the sky.

The motor roared. The treads bit into the wet grass, pulverizing the kilometric posts as it went. From time to time a shrub which had strayed with the heedlessness of youth from the main body of the forest rose before the mass of metal, and the driver alone for a fraction of a second would feel the pitiful resistance of the crushed flesh.

By the beam of his flashlight Moustier consulted the compass. The road deviated slightly westward of south. We'll see, thought Moustier. He passed his tongue across his lips, avoiding the burnt-out cigarette stub still glued to them.

Vandervenne leaned over to look at the gas gauge. There was still enough fuel to go another thirty kilometers. We'll find some in Paris, he thought. He did not know Paris. In civilian life he was a teamster and drove trucks in the Anzin mines. The North will be all destroyed again, he further reflected. It had taken twenty years to reconstruct it. It'll take another twenty to put it back into shape. Forty years of war. That's hard. Too hard. He felt a vague desire to talk to Mirabelle about it, but remained silent, as was his habit.

With the base of his spine he felt that the tank had just passed over some tiny obstacle, a small tree no doubt. He saw nothing and kept skirting the forest as a blind man hugs a wall. The lieutenant's words suddenly came back to him. A million, he thought, Jesus, a million.

Suddenly they heard the boom of a heavy gun.

"Stop!" Mirabelle shouted in Vandervenne's ear, but the tank had already veered and taken shelter among the trees. Here we go, Mirabelle said to himself.

The three men waited for the shot that would follow. It did not come.

"Turn off the motor," said Mirabelle.

Silence filled the tank as water does a glass.

"Should I take a look outside?" suggested Moustier.

"You're crazy!" said Mirabelle. He was hot and sick to his stomach. From outside came the sound of crackling branches. Mirabelle saw outlined against the night the barrel of a gun, two, three gun barrels, aimed at the tank door.

"Don't open," he whispered, "can't you hear?"

Rustling sounds rippled the surface of the silence, footsteps, muffled jostlings. Still no sound of cannon.

"They're waiting," said Mirabelle.

A limp body went "plump!" on the roof of the tank. Vandervenne raised his head gravely, said nothing.

"You've got cold feet, you sap," Moustier declared, with laughing eyes, not addressing anyone in particular, and he added, "Me too."

He listened for a few moments; one could not tell whether his attention was riveted on the sounds outside or on his own fear.

"But it's of no importance," he concluded, and with a brusque movement he pushed open the door a little and looked out.

From the depth of his pit Mirabelle heard his comrade's snicker and his voice saying, "Come and take a look."

The forest was as dark as ever, but now each branch was outlined against the crimson sky. Ruddy reflections glimmered on the surface of the wet asphalt of the road.

"A fire somewhere in France," said Moustier, and he jumped out.

Mirabelle cautiously approached the exit, looked in turn. Moustier was leaning over and patting a little calf. Black and white, very young, it stood quivering on its spindly legs. Noticing that Mirabelle was watching him, Moustier abruptly straightened up.

"The incident is closed," he said—another of his favorite expressions.

Mirabelle said nothing; as a child, in his father's barn, he had been allowed to pat the coats of newborn calves when they were still damp.

Back at his post in the turret, Moustier watched the vanishing pink ribbon of the road. Compact little shadows kept crossing it, other shadows bounded amid the trees. In the light of the conflagration he consulted the compass: the road had swerved southward. An owl bumped against the turret. Moustier tried to calculate the distance they had covered since they had started out. A hare came and hurled itself under the tank. Blinded by the headlights, thought Moustier, and immediately caught himself: what headlights? Then only he said to himself, we are the only ones coming down. All the others are heading north.

The animals were heading north. Wild rabbits, a hysterical doe with her fawn, a fox, crossed the tank's path, too panicky to become more panicky at this encounter. Other animals, smaller, grayer, scuttered through the woods: weasels, squirrels, martens. Owls, large and small, beat the air blindly with their noiseless wings, and clusters of day birds, awakened at night for the first time in their lives, broke from the trees like ripe fruit. Bats reeled dizzily, black against the sky in which tawny and orange gleams flashed. Poultry and livestock now mingled with the wild creatures. At one turn of the road the tank flattened a whole barnyard beneath its treads; a horse whinnied; emaciated dogs dashed past without stopping, without barking: they no longer caught the scent of man, and if they did it was only to run away from him. The tank alone was rolling in the other direction, against the current. Moustier felt a mad impulse to turn back. He consulted the compass. The road ran due south.

Springing up to the right, amid the trees, a river—a canal perhaps—appeared alongside the road. Mechanically Moustier looked for a bridge, found none. Suddenly, on his left, the forest ended, and he saw the flames.

Half a mile ahead the river, ablaze, curved leftward, and in the hollow of the elbow a village seemed to be flying skyward in a pyrotechnic display. Roofs buckled, sucked up by the heat, and the walls, smeared with flames, fluttered a moment before crashing into the brazier. A bell-tower reeled, leaned over, hesitated—outlining its black weathercock against the orange sky—and plunged head foremost. Moustier thought he heard the clanging of the bells.

On his left, in the plain, thousands of brand-new trucks were drawn up in rows like soldiers in review. One could make out those in the first line, each one clad in its own flames, but beyond spread a sea of fire, with here and there brighter waves rising from the gas tanks that had blown up. Still farther to the left began the forest, sprinkled with flakes of flame and sparks, and already nests of fire were lodging among the branches.

Mirabelle tugged at Moustier's arm.

"Come, quick!" he cried.

The tank had stopped, and in the silence of the motor one heard the roar of the fire.

"Well?" said Mirabelle.

Moustier jumped to the ground, leaned against the tank, rolled a cigarette, passed his package of "gray" regulation tobacco to Vandervenne who had posted himself in the doorway.

"Well?" he said in turn.

"We might try to turn round and go back?" suggested Mirabelle in a tone devoid of conviction.

He looked at Moustier, who was lighting his cigarette without saying anything, and answered his own question,

"We haven't enough gas left."

Again he cast a sly glance toward Moustier.

"You know how to swim?" he asked.

He waited for the answer which did not come.

"Suppose we beat it?" he suggested in a low voice, half questioning, half affirming. "We cross the river, and once we're over we'll manage somehow," he said hurriedly. "It's no trick at all to cross this river. I'll bet we could get over on foot," he added, relieved.

Moustier seemed to be pondering.

"What about the tank?" he asked.

This was the question Mirabelle feared.

"We've done what we could," he exclaimed with irritation. "Listen, Moustier, do we beat it, tell me, do we beat it, Moustier?"

"Let's see what Vandervenne says," said Moustier, and he swallowed the smoke of his cigarette.

"Oh, him!" Mirabelle shrugged his shoulders. "But you, you agree, no?"

"No fair prompting the player," said Moustier. This was the last of his favorite expressions. "Let's see what Vandervenne says."

"No," said Vandervenne suddenly, and was silent.

"What do you mean, 'No'? 'No' what? What are you talking about, you horse's ass?" Mirabelle was jumping up and down with impatience and rage.

"No," Vandervenne repeated, and he turned away.

Moustier smiled with his eyes and, chewing the burnt-out stub between his lips, began to roll another cigarette.

"You want to get yourself killed?" bawled Mirabelle. "Roasted alive, shot full of holes for this piece of rubbish?"

He struck the side of the tank with his fist. He hated the stupid tank, he hated the lieutenant who had sent them to their death, and Vandervenne who kept obstinately silent.

"Well, say something, you dirty son of a bitch, tell us what's on your mind," he shouted.

Vandervenne felt no inclination to talk. He knew he would not leave the tank, no matter what happened. Mirabelle's voice annoyed him: he craved silence. He finally said, "I like a job well done."

Moustier smiled, and Mirabelle, watching him, became hopeful again.

"There are three of us," he said. "Let's just vote on it. Whom do you vote for, Moustier, for me or that milksop?"

Moustier inhaled the smoke, made a show of hesitating. Little folds formed round his eyes.

"I vote for the milksop," he said.

Without a word, Vandervenne climbed back into the tank, waited for the other two to follow him, and started up the motor.

They advanced slowly, hemmed in by water on their right and fire on their left, straight into the fire—the road ran through the blazing village. Mirabelle was behind Vandervenne; he could see nothing from his post, feel nothing but the slowly rising heat. He looked, to his right, at the rows upon rows of shells. It's stifling here, he thought to himself, I'll unbutton my leather jacket. But he stopped as he fingered the first button: he would offer up his sweat as a propitiatory sacrifice. Way down he strove not to think about the gas tank. If only it doesn't blow up.

With the back of his hand, Vandervenne wiped away the sweat that was blinding him. Through the narrow slit in front of him he could see only the fire. On his pasty tongue he felt the taste of blood. He must have bitten his lips. Behind him he sensed that Mirabelle was taking off his helmet.

"Keep it on," he said with difficulty. His lips hurt.

"We're sunk," cried Mirabelle.

We're sunk, thought Vandervenne. Flaming beams came crashing down on the walls of the tank.

"The gas tank!" screamed Mirabelle, breaking down.

"Shut up!" ordered Vandervenne.

He became aware of a new presence behind him.

"Now what?" said Moustier's voice.

The road had reached a stone bridge. A bomb must have struck it on the side and gone right through it. It rested on its two extreme piers, torn in the middle across the whole width. Vandervenne turned to look through the left slit. The flames were licking the edge of the water.

"You're stopping?" moaned Mirabelle.

He saw nothing except the reflections of the fire on the polished surfaces, and his comrades' faces. Hearing his own voice relieved him.

"Why did you come down, Moustier?" he said. "What's going on? Tell me, what's going on? Hey, you didn't answer me. Tell me, what's going on? It's going to blow up, isn't it, the gas tank's going to blow up? You know it's going to blow up, don't you, you know it is. I want a drink of water, and I got to keep my helmet on. Tell me, what's going on?" A new idea had just taken hold of him. "If we'd swum across we'd have had plenty to drink. If we'd swum we'd have been all right. You didn't want to. Now the gas tank's going to blow up."

"You take care of the tank, I'll take care of Mirabelle," said Moustier. He turned to the latter. "Why did you come along then? Nobody was forcing you."

Mirabelle remembered his pun, "I'll go wherever anybuddy goes"—which at the moment had seemed to him so funny that he hadn't been able to resist the pleasure of making his comrades laugh, without thinking of the consequences. Never had he got used to the power of words, and his tongue had played him such tricks many a time. Anybody goes, anybuddy goes, he repeated to himself with irritation. In the light of the conflagration the pun did not come off quite so well. Seized with an urge to justify himself, he said with conviction, "You didn't think I was going to leave you in the lurch, did you?" He wasn't far from believing this himself, and to increase his own assurance he added, "I thought you might need a good buddy-guard!"

He noticed that he was no longer afraid.

Vandervenne was having trouble keeping his eyes open. Sweat was trickling down from under his helmet, from his eyebrows, down his nose, saltier than blood. The break in the bridge was two yards wide, or three. It was coming closer, and as it came closer the two lips which it formed seemed to part more and more. The tank would never make it. Vandervenne looked through the left slit, perceived the inverted reflection of the fire in the black river. The tank tilted forward. Vandervenne no longer saw the hole in front of him, and thought he was going mad. The tank kept tipping further forward. Here we go, said Vandervenne to himself, having just realized what was happening. He looked down as though he expected to see only empty space. A tingling sensation crept up his legs and his spine, and his blood seemed to have changed into fizz water. Yet the treads were still catching. Do the others know, he wondered. He cut down speed even more. I'm going to count ten, he thought.

The front of the tank was slowly lifting. The bridge hesitated, quivered, did not collapse. On his shoulder Vandervenne felt Moustier's hand. Before him everything went black. I'm going blind, he thought without astonishment. He said,

"Take my place. I can't see very well."

He rolled into a ball. A million! he thought. Then he heard Mirabelle's voice say, "I told you we'd get out of it all right!" and fell asleep.

When he awoke the tank had stopped, and its door stood open. Mirabelle and Moustier had disappeared. Still heavy in the head, he got out.

The night was as opaque as ever. At first Vandervenne could see nothing. Feeling his way round the tank he discovered a man sitting on the roadbank in the circular beam of a flashlight. He was bareheaded, wore a khaki shirt, and his hands were busy with a bundle of cloth, which was likewise khaki. With his albino head bent forward, he seemed absorbed in a task, the nature of which Vandervenne could not determine. He walked toward him.

Moustier's voice broke out from somewhere above the cone of light.

"Is the road clear?" he asked.

The man moved his right hand, and Vandervenne perceived a knifeblade at the end of it.

The man pondered.

"Why, no," he said finally with a childlike smile, "why, no. The Germans are right ahead. They kill off the officers. You won't get by."

"Where is Paris?" Moustier inquired.

"The Germans are in Paris," said the man.

Vandervenne looked at his shirt, which was of silk, at his bright boots. He's ripping off his stripes, he suddenly realized. He's an officer. I must tell Moustier.

"I'm surrounded," said the officer with a little laugh. "And you too. They're everywhere. There's nothing to do but sit down and wait."

The idea appealed to him.

"That's right—sit down, gentlemen," he said. "We'll wait together. You fellows have nothing to be afraid of."

His rabbit head melted into the night: Moustier had lowered the flashlight.

"It's of no importance," he said.

The circle of light shone on three slender gold stripes lying on the ground.

"Thank you, sir," said Moustier, this time not hesitating before the "sir."

"Do we go?" asked Vandervenne.

"What about him?" inquired Mirabelle, nodding in the direction of the spot where they had left the captain.

"Oh, him! . . ." said Moustier. "He can shift for himself."

They got back into the tank.

"Do we try to go through the Fritzes?" Moustier asked.

"If they've taken Paris . . ." Mirabelle was undecided.

"We still have enough gas to go another fifteen kilometers," said Vandervenne, consulting the gauge.

Moustier turned the compass till the needle lay on the north-

south axis. It lay parallel to the tank, in the direction in which
it was headed.

"Let's try anyway," he said.

They loaded a shell into the 47 and checked the machine-
guns. The tank started off.

It was still dark, but the road was beginning to be visible.
Broad and smooth, it was peopled with mute shadows. The tank
would swerve before shadows that looked like obstacles, and rear
before shadows that looked like ditches. He said the Germans were
ahead of us, thought Mirabelle. He was seized with the drowsiness
that follows sleepless nights, and the thought of danger barely
grazed his mind. We should've brought the cap'n along, he reflected. He might hurt himself with his pocket-knife.

An explosion filled the tank and they stopped dead. Here we
go, said Mirabelle to himself. Almost immediately he caught a
glimpse of Moustier's crestfallen face.

"I thought it was the real thing," said the latter, "and I fired.
Like an idiot. On a bunch of trees. If they're around here they've
got us spotted now."

Such a possibility did not strike Mirabelle as too unpleasant.
"So what?" he said.

All three of them were sleepy, and were not quite sure what
they were saying.

"The Germans are up ahead," said Mirabelle, and he burst out
laughing. "What do you think of that, Vandervenne?"

Vandervenne was peering out. The shadows were fading, and the
road which the night had dug full of holes now lay stretched out
flat, wet with dew. A cottage sprang up at their left, then another,
then a whole swarm of small houses, all alike with their entrance
gate and three porch steps. There were more and more of them
on both sides of the road, which had become a street. Vacant
lots separated long buildings with glassed roofs whose chimneys
were not smoking. A livid dawn was rising over piles of slag and
scrap iron, dusty dahlias and scrawny salad greens. Now the tank
was rolling over stone paving, between two unbroken rows of gray
houses with closed shutters. Around the turned-over garbage cans
cats and dogs fought over the refuse.

The tank emerged on a square, circled around a monument, started down a slope. Suddenly Vandervenne stopped the tank.

"Come on, let's get out," he said.

Paris, lighted up from behind, unfurled before their fresh eyes the most imposing succession of avenues in the world, deserted at this hour, while two other soldiers, who knew it by heart, paused in their flight to look at it once more for the last time. The road passed over a half-finished bridge. Farther on, to the right, Vandervenne pointed to a weblike structure outlined against the sky from which the sun, rising in front of them, was dispelling the last wisps of mist. They had seen it a hundred times in moving pictures, photographs, drawings, on ashtrays, mantelpieces, paperweights, and lampstands.

"It's the Eiffel Tower?" he said, a little incredulous.

Only a bridge now remained to be crossed, and it was not guarded. They had outdistanced the Germans.

"Was I in a funk last night!" said Mirabelle, and he let out an admiring whistle.

"Not as bad as I was," said Moustier. "Only I didn't let on. I don't like to show off."

Above the capital, bled of men, in the blue and gold June sky, given over to planes and anti-aircraft shells, the wary birds flew low.

None of the three knew Paris. Vandervenne had spent his life in the Anzin mines, Mirabelle was a native of Périgord, and Moustier of Auvergne.

"And now let's find some officers," said the latter, "hand them the tank, and go and get a bite to eat."

But down the whole length of the Avenue de Neuilly they did not catch a glimpse of a single uniform.

"Do we turn right?" suggested Moustier, consulting the compass. The houses grew more scattered. In the distance the boom of cannon could be heard. Once more the tank entered a wood. It was not like the forests they had crossed farther north, but was cut through by lanes that skirted lakes in which rowboats and swans floated. There were signposts everywhere and, around the lawns, wire that was not barbed. Soldiers passed, singly or in small groups, bearded, some of them helmeted, most of them bareheaded, some toting their guns, all the rest disarmed. They moved slowly, with a heavy tread, without looking right or left, without looking at the tank. There were Frenchmen and North Africans, Senegalese and Annamites, West Indians and Madagascans: the Empire.

Mirabelle got out to try to find some officers. Clusters of soldiers sprawled on the grass. They kept coming and coming. They would first eat and immediately go to sleep. New stragglers would arrive and shout, "What division?" In a group of six men, five different answers would come simultaneously, "The Nineteenth . . . The Thirty-third . . . The . . ." It was never the right one, and in their turn the last comers would drop heavily on the green. "Amiens, Beauvais, the Somme," they would say, and take off their shoes. "This is fine," they would exclaim in astonishment, and sleep would overtake them.

"Where are your officers?" Mirabelle inquired, and one soldier, who had kept only a pair of duck trousers and a shirt, asked him in turn,

"What about yours?"

"This is Paris, isn't it?" ventured Mirabelle.

"Paris, sixteenth district, the Bois de Boulogne," said the other.

Mirabelle ran back to the tank.

"This is the Bois de Boulogne," he shouted from a distance.

They skirted a vast field bordered by a track of trampled earth and enclosed in wooden bleachers, and found themselves back in the city.

"Look," said Moustier, "a gas station."

There was no one around, and the hose dragged on the edge of the sidewalk. They pumped in vain—nothing came.

Along an avenue, between a double row of trees, the tank rolled down toward a square. The vehicle entrances to the houses were all shut, the shutters all fastened. The only creature in sight was a big plush bear, leaning against a tree, its left arm raised in the Hitler salute.

The Eiffel Tower suddenly loomed to the right of them, close by. They stopped to look at it.

"I've got some cousins who've been all the way up to the top," said Mirabelle.

"We haven't got time," said Moustier. "Some other day."

A large truck drove past them, filled with suitcases on which soldiers were perched. A non-commissioned officer cried, "Slow on the turns!"

"That must be the right direction," said Moustier.

The tank crossed the square, turned, and reached a bridge. The quays extended right and left.

"It's the Seine," said Mirabelle, all excited.

They drove along the river, to the left. Palaces succeeded one another, whose names they did not know, and bridges, broad and arched, adorned with statues and lamp posts. At a street corner a gentleman in white gaiters was blowing up with a bicycle pump one of the tires of a 120-horsepower car loaded with suitcases. A hospital unit was coming up the quay toward them. Their eyes sought officers' stripes, but found none.

The quay led into another square. It was vast as a continent, with its fields of asphalt over which stone women wearing crowns held sway, with its dried-up fountains, the cast-iron posts of its hundreds of street-lamps, and in the center, rising up from a huddled mass of sandbags piled up by the Civilian Defense, a stone needle engraved with birds, snakes, and suns. Orderlies on motorcycles, helmeted, with rifles slung across their backs, swept round on the square and vanished down the QUAI.

"A newspaper," said Moustier, and once more the tank stopped.

For two weeks they had been without news. It was only a grimy strip, that had been dropped at the edge of the sidewalk. On one side there were only personals. On the other, a notice in enormous letters.

"WHAT DO THEY NEED?" Mirabelle read. "TANKS! TANKS! TANKS!" And, at the bottom, "BUY DEFENSE BONDS."

"We're fashionable," said Moustier.

Vandervenne broke in, "I'm almost out of gas. What do we do?"

"We stay here," Moustier decided, "and we wait for the tank collectors to come along."

At one end of the square, Vandervenne had spotted some chestnut trees. He drove the tank there, carefully drawing it up under the foliage, sheltered from the planes. Then all three sat down on a bench and waited.

The avenue bordered by the chestnut trees was wide as the Seine, its solemn and unbroken sweep extending to a distant rectangular arch, gleaming in the sunlight, under which it passed. There were neither pedestrians nor cars, only a boy, lost in the immensity of the roadway, who was pushing a wheelbarrow in which an old woman slumped like a sack of flour, her face swept by gray strands of hair. He passed in front of the three soldiers and disappeared under the trees. Then, coming down the avenue, appeared a cart drawn by women and pushed by little girls, loaded with bundles of wash, for all the world like a laundry establishment on wheels. Moustier pondered.

"If that's the ARC DE TRIOMPHE," he said, "we're on the Champs-Elysées."

Fifteen minutes passed. The sun rose higher in the sky and the chestnut trees cast a network of shadows across the asphalt. Black specks appeared in the distance, coming slowly down the avenue toward the spot where the three soldiers sat.

"The Fritzes," said Mirabelle, and he got up.

"We've got time," said Moustier.

They waited. Now they could make out figures and vehicles, too small to be armored cars, too slow to be motorcycles with sidecars.

"Civilians," said Moustier. "They're on foot. But what are they pushing?"

"Another of the Fritzes' inventions," said Mirabelle in a tone of conviction.

They hid among the trees, ready to climb back into the tank at the first sign of danger. Mechanically Moustier inspected the terrain. There were numerous paths of retreat, the bridge was not mined, and when they reached the square the assailants would expose themselves fully to the tank's fire.

"Maybe I'm crazy," said Vandervenne, "I see baby-carriages."

Mirabelle burst out laughing.

"He's right," said Moustier, "I'll be hanged if I . . ."

He suddenly stopped.

A baby-carriage was rolling toward them, its springs sagging under the weight of the old clothes with which it was loaded. An old couple was pushing it, the man in shirtsleeves, the woman hatless, disheveled, as though they had had to get up in the middle of the night and flee in haste. Another carriage rolled behind them, then two others, and still more. They kept coming, more and more of them, landaus, children's push-carts, soap boxes mounted on rollers with a piece of string as sole harness, new silent streamlined baby-carriages whose chromium fenders had been given a coat of blue paint to conform to the Civilian Defense regulations, and still others, very ancient, which had creakingly transported generations of newborn babes, double carriages for twins, black, coffee-and-cream, bright blue, ivory, pink, carriages overflowing with suitcases, packages, bundles, dishes, indispensables, and the things that come within reach of a distracted hand: a watercolor lampshade, a porcelain shepherdess—thirty years of memories, of family life. Only the nurslings were allowed a place in them, wedged between a pile of dishes and a sewing machine; the children who could, walked, even if they only toddled, their unsteady legs dragged along by the weight of their heads, too large for their little bodies. The mothers, sisters, grandparents, the invalids and the exempt served as haulers. They were too hurried, weary, and hot to look at the Champs-Elysées, which most of them were seeing for the first time, and they were only at the beginning of their journey.

Silently the three soldiers observed the stream of baby-carriages flow past them.

"Nothing but civilians," said Moustier, and Vandervenne, "Did you see the kids?"

Moustier meditated, then observed, "In 1914 there were the taxis of the Marne."

A little old man emerged from among the trees, came up to them, examined the tank with indifference as though he had seen it there every day on his way to work, and went on his way. Moustier called him back to ask him where the nearest barracks were.

"The garrison left yesterday," said the old man. "Paris has been declared an open town. Everybody has gone." He smiled. "You can get around in Paris all you want to now," he said. "There's plenty of room."

Bewildered, Mirabelle repeated, "The garrison has left. What'll we do?"

"We don't know anything," said the man. "We don't get any more newspapers, no more news. The last ones left last night on foot."

Vandervenne got up. "Come on," he said, "we'll catch up with them."

"We don't know anything," the old man repeated. "It seems the Germans are around Melun. Anyway you might try the Porte d'Italie."

"Is that south?" asked Moustier.

"It's over that way, I don't know the district very well," said the old man, and he went off, as unconcerned as though he had spent his life giving information to tank crews on the corner of the Champs-Elysées and the Place de la Concorde, at the feet of the Marly horses.

Vandervenne was again driving. Moustier directed him, compass in hand. The tank passed through deserted districts, among hundreds of thousands of fastened shutters, went down broad avenues, lost its way in small streets whose whole width it filled. Sometimes they would run into the procession of pushcarts, and lose it again. Slumped on benches, clusters of old women with gray straggling hair, black woolen shawls round their shoulders, would look at the tank without curiosity. Dragoons on motorcycles would wheel around on the squares. At a crossroad two road-menders were repairing the edge of the sidewalk. A milkman passed, carrying his cans: it was so unexpected that they kept looking after him till he disappeared in a doorway.

They stopped only once, before a large gray house whose marble entrance fascinated them.

"The INVALIDES," said Mirabelle.

A wretched old woman came out.

"What is it?" inquired Moustier.

"A house."

"What kind of a house?"

"Why, a house! A building."

Next to the entrance stood a toy shop.

"Come and see," called Moustier.

The dealer, too, had brought out his stock of second reserve soldiers. They wore the 1914 uniform: the French were sky blue, and there were Americans. One large box bore the inscription: "The Siegfried Line." Moustier read the notice placed beside it: "In this absorbing and original game the two players take turns bombarding the Siegfried Line." A poster was hung in the window, with the words, "Give games to your soldiers and your children."

The streets were becoming narrower, the houses more squalid. There was a great bustle of people, some pushing baby carriages and wheelbarrows, others waiting on doorsteps. Moustier gave directions.

"Right! . . . Left!—Straight ahead!" he suddenly shouted when Vandervenne turned down a side street. The latter had caught sight of a gas station.

The pump, though it had been abandoned, was not out of gas. They pumped with all their might, five liters at a time. Twenty-five, thirty, thirty-five, the indicator moved across the dial with a click, the gas rose bubbling and settled back with each stroke. Then the pump went dry.

The street widened, turned, ran into an avenue. A black sign rose before them, with a white inscription: "PORTE D'ITALIE." The avenue continued beyond. As the tank headed into it, Moustier once more consulted the compass: the needle pointed south.

The road was wide, and edged with sidewalks. A thick jelly of refugees filled it to the brim. Large and small trucks, ambulances, cars, caterpillar trucks, forage wagons, vans, gasoline trucks, field kitchens, tractors, buses, municipal sprinklers were jammed in among immense peasant carts, harnessed to three or four plow-horses, loaded with calves, children, old clothes, big loaves of household bread for the men and forage for the livestock. The smallest interstices between the vehicles were stuffed with baby carriages and pushcarts drawn or driven by dogs, women, old men, children, with tri-cars, with motorcyclists and bicyclists pushing their machines loaded with household utensils. There were pedestrians who, when a twenty-ton truck honked at their backs, did not even turn round and had to be pushed aside with the bumpers. The Paris garrison was on the road, all regiments, all services intermingled—infantry, anti-aircraft, marines, aviators, service corps, commissariat, artillery, engineers, motorized cavalry, cuirassiers—still in uniform, already disarmed. Soldiers clung to the running boards of civilian cars, civilians clung to gun-carriages, filled ambulances. The cars would weave in and out, get stuck sideways, climb onto the sidewalks, pushing the pedestrians into the ditches, into the fields, dashing forward to gain a few inches, standing still for fifteen minutes, starting off again all at once, the heavier ones plowing through the lighter chassis, with a roar of racing motors, a grinding of gears, coming to a stop with a screeching of brakes suddenly jammed on. Then the drivers would get down, gentlemen with Legion of Honor ribbons in their lapels who had forgotten to put on their neckties, mechanics in overalls covered with grease, soldiers with empty revolver holsters dangling from their belts, and they would lose their tempers, shout or wait in silence according to their temperaments and the state of their nerves. Wheel to wheel, fender to fender, old rattletraps which faith alone, or acquired momentum, enabled to advance, bent under the weight of valises, bundles, the mattress lashed to the top to intercept machine-gun bullets, bikes or go-carts perched on front or rear bumpers. The motors spat, panted, coughed, always in low gear, and the entire road was like an immense cemetery of cars resuscitated for the Last Judgment.

Vandervenne was driving. Through the open doorway Moustier and Mirabelle looked out on the road. In the suburban towns the crowd of pedestrians was so dense that they stood in line in order to pass. Most of the shops were closed, and all the gas stations.

A woman passed the tank dragging a packing case on four rollers which was at the same time being pushed by a small five-year-old girl who was running to keep up with her.

"Mama, can I rest a little?" said the small girl, but her mother did not stop walking, and the child had to hobble along, her face scarlet under her white beret.

The tank caught up with a procession of old men—some asylum in flight—one pushed in a wheelchair, the others limping along with an assortment of canes and crutches. No one made way for the tank to pass, and for some minutes Vandervenne had to drive in the midst of this Court of Miracles. Moustier remembered the animals he had seen, the night before, fleeing before the fire.

Two policemen stepped out of a prefecture car in order to open a pathway for themselves through the throng and get away more quickly.

"I don't like cops," said Moustier. "I don't like anything about them. They're stinkers. They don't go to the front, they get others to go, while they stay home feeling up the women."

"Well, what do you expect of a bull? . . ." inquired Mirabelle.

A hearse edged its way past them, crammed with people and baggage. Families, numerous as at a wedding or a burial, surrounded their cars, already out of gas, pushing them from one dry pump to the next. More and more cars were being towed. From all the side roads refugees came streaming onto the national highway. Passing through centers the crowd would assault the bakeries, empty of bread and of bakers. In the fields hastily overturned cars were burning up.

"You see!" said Moustier. "The high command has foreseen all eventualities!"

"It's foreseen heaps," said Mirabelle, and he tilted his head up.

In the blue sky, dotted with scattered clouds, a white fringe uncurled, decorative and innocuous.

"The Fritzes," said Mirabelle.

There was a new jam. The tank stopped beside the little girl in the white beret, whom her mother had finally put on top of the case. The woman looked up at the sky.

"What is it," she said, "a publicity stunt?"

"Yes," said Moustier. "Publicity for Hitler."

The cars got into motion. The tank and the case on rollers moved forward side by side.

"As long as the smoke is in a straight line," said Moustier to the woman, "it's not serious. If the plane makes a circle above us, run over and lie down in the ditch."

Again the traffic was blocked. The road, as far as the horizon, hummed with cars. Their occupants had settled down on the roadbank and were idly observing the sky which became streaked with a second fringe, perpendicular to the first. Tired of waiting, pedestrians began to scurry across the fields. A woman with a baby on her knees unbuttoned her blouse and pulled out a heavy blue-veined breast which the child seized. Cutting across the diminishing hubbub of the road, the roar of a squadron made heads tilt upward. Above the refugees a slender ring of white smoke had just closed in the sky.

From a truck some anti-aircraft soldiers jumped out on the roadway.

"Who has a pair of field glasses?" they cried, looking round.

"They are Heinkels," said their sergeant. "They're beating it."

The planes executed a wide half-circle and swooped low.

"Look out," said the sergeant, and he threw the cartridge-clip of his sub-machine gun into position.

"You take the first one," a soldier said to him.

The planes banked again, ever lower, flew away, banked, returned.

"They're coming," said the soldier.

"They're off," said the sergeant.

"They're coming," repeated the soldier.

The civilians observed them with indifference.

"A bomb is all it'll take," said Moustier, "a single bomb. Fifty thousand dead. Panic. People are stupid."

Diving through the ring of smoke, the planes swooped down on the axis of the road. The sergeant shouldered his sub-machine gun. Tightly packed along the roadbank, the families had pulled out sandwiches and bottles of beer. Only the soldiers and the children looked at the sky, and the soldiers alone were afraid.

"Go to it!" said a reservist to the anti-aircraft sergeant.

The planes scattered fanwise.

"They're off," said the sergeant.

"They're laughing at us," said Moustier.

The planes were pirouetting in the sky.

The sergeant was short, squat, swarthy.

"Say, fellow," Moustier asked him, "where are you going?"

"We're following the movement," said the other, winking his eye. "We're consolidating the pocket."

"You're doing what?"

"Say, where do you come from?"

"From Flanders," Moustier explained.

"Didn't you read the papers up there?"

"Not every day," said Mirabelle apologetically.

"Then you don't know that Weygand, when he took command, announced that the Fritzes had made a pocket in our lines and that he was engaged in consolidating it. We've been consolidating now for three weeks. I was in Flanders, too," he added. "I nearly fell for their racket. But I soon caught on."

"How come?"

"An idiot of a quartermaster put us into a casemate, somewhere around Valenciennes, with orders to hold out to the end. We had our bare hands to defend ourselves with. Not for me."

In the distance the cars were starting up. The families, with their mouths full, made a dash for their cars. The mothers clucked as they pushed their brood before them, administering cuffs right and left. A baby cried.

"We ought to give them battle on the Seine," said the sergeant. "Now all they have to do is to cross it on the bridges of Paris. So we're going to give them battle on the Loire. You know, the Loire." He got into the truck. "Whatever happens," he cried to Vandervenne, "don't push us from behind."

"The battle of the Loire," said Mirabelle. "Which way is the Loire?"

"Well, it's south, I know," said Moustier. "And don't ask me to show you a map. I haven't got one."

"The General Staff has foreseen all eventualities," said Mirabelle.

"But it's of no importance," said Moustier.

At noon they shared their last half ration-loaf of bread, which was as old as the battle of France, and Mirabelle replaced Vandervenne at the controls. Their only beverage was the coolness of the Fontainebleau forest and the sight of a section of pontooners, their boats piled on trucks and drifting among the branches. The town itself was being evacuated. One saw military trucks on the sidewalks, camouflaged with boughs and, in the courtyards, tarpaulin-covered guns. Soldiers slept on the ground, open-mouthed, purple with heat and fatigue. The tank made a detour only to fall back, after leaving Fontainebleau, on the national highway and the convoys.

There were even more of them than in the morning: lines of Parisian buses were unloading refugees, civilians stood in the grass watching the army pass by, a column of caterpillar trucks waited along the edge of the road; on the rails that ran parallel to the road a train, filled with evacuees, was coming down from Paris, a freight train was going up to the front, packed with Senegalese: Vandervenne caught sight of one, in shirt sleeves, a red rose in his helmet, his thirty-two teeth glowing. A third train followed it: flatcars loaded with trucks, large and small, and ambulances, all the drivers at the wheel, and platforms bristling with 13/2 machine guns.

The soldiers who were going up asked those who were fleeing, "Things in a bad way up at the front?" On the off chance, the latter answered, "No."

In a jam an aviation lieutenant got out of his car. "It's a disgrace!" he said. There were many officers doing their own driving, with their wives beside them. Non-commissioned officers ran along the convoys blowing their pea whistles. The tank would advance, stop, start again, and again stop, its sides beaten by a swarm of bicyclists. There was a horde of them, all boys with a bundle or a cheap suitcase.

Voices rang out, "Ambulances are coming! At least let the wounded get through."

The procession started off, without paying attention to the ambulances, wedged between other cars.

Postmen and gendarmes on bicycles slipped between the trucks. A solemn old man was driving a steam roller. The firemen of Sartrouville, in uniform, waited at the edge of the road on their red engines, their families perched on the long ladder, the women below, the children in the middle, and the tots strapped on at the top. At nightfall the tank entered Montargis.

The whole town population was sitting on suitcases, in the great station yard. They must have been waiting several hours, perhaps since the day before. The initial nervousness had given way to indifference. There were no longer any trains, but the people, straight and still on their suitcases, waited for them just the same—for them, or for the Germans. Before the station the procession moved endlessly. Night was falling on the cars, on the station, on the railroad tracks, on the men, motionless in the station yard.

Lost among the convoys a boy in aviation uniform, his girlish face shadowed with down, was desperately attempting to regulate the traffic singlehanded. At every moment he had to jump aside to dodge a car.

"Say, sweetheart," Moustier shouted to him, "do you know another road besides the national highway to get out of Montargis?"

"I'm not from these parts," the boy answered. He shrieked, "No passing! Stay in line!" He disappeared behind a hearse.

At the first crossroad Moustier said, "Turn left." The tank turned. "If we follow the others," explained Moustier, "we're lost. We'll try the side roads."

Suddenly there was emptiness and silence. The narrow road ran between fields. From time to time they perceived a few small houses, or a parked car along the roadside. Its occupants, settled in the grass for the night, chatted and smoked. Moustier looked at his compass.

"At the first crossroad, turn right," he said.

For a time they had been headed east. There were no crossroads, nothing but cattle-crossings between the fenced-in fields, trails that vanished in the meadows. The tank stopped.

Moustier tried to imagine the map of France.

"What is there east of Montargis?" he asked.

"Auxerre," ventured Vandervenne.

"The Fritzes," suggested Mirabelle.

It was too late to turn back. "Too bad," said Moustier. "We'll cut across the fields. We'll find a road sooner or later."

"What about the crops?" Vandervenne's tone was disapproving.

"For all that'll be left of them after this business is over . . ."

The tank crashed through a fence, and the treads dug into the soft earth. They were barely moving, and darkness had fallen, as opaque as on the previous night.

"What do they grow around here?" asked Vandervenne after a silence.

"Macaroni," answered Mirabelle, and he was the only one to laugh.

The tank was drifting in the night. It rolled and tossed, broke through hedges, crossed ditches, pierced haystacks. Through the open door the cold air entered. They cut across a road which also ran east, climbed hills, rolled over shrubbery. Vandervenne had passed the controls to Mirabelle. They had not eaten, had hardly slept for twenty-four hours. At last they noticed that they were almost out of fuel.

"What do we do?" asked Mirabelle.

"We sleep," said Moustier.

They went on another dozen yards or so to a haystack, which they spilled across the tank to camouflage it. They in turn stretched out in the hay beside it.

"My brother is in the class of 1911," said Vandervenne. "He fought all the way through the last war. He went off to join his regiment when he was twenty-one and got back at twenty-eight: three years of military service, and the war. When the armistice came they let them keep their helmets. He got back home, came into the house, to the forge, put his helmet on the anvil and began hammering it. I thought he'd never stop. He was crazy. It took him a year before he could go back to work."

"Is he the one who keeps the smithy?" asked Mirabelle.

"He must have left now. We're from the North."

He went to sleep. Mirabelle was already snoring. The Battle of the Loire, said Moustier to himself. He tried to get his bearings. We started off yesterday or the day before yesterday, or yesterday. He too fell asleep.

THE BATTLE OF THE LOIRE

Moustier became hungry and woke up.

Day had risen. His comrades were still asleep, half hidden in the hay; lively dream-shadows, the kind that precede the moment of awakening, fluttered over their faces. Gray stubble had sprouted on Mirabelle's chin. Vandervenne's lips opened imperceptibly to let out all the words he had not spoken while he was awake.

The tank, buried in the haystack, was coated with dew, with flowers and wisps of dry grass. Clumps of black earth had lodged in the treads, incrusted with pebbles and ears of wheat of a green already turning yellow. Gossamer hung on the tank's flanks, and a spiderweb stretched between the mouths of the machine guns was specked with tiny iridescent drops.

A quarter of a mile from the spot where they had spent the night Moustier made out a village. It wasn't there last night, he thought, it must have evacuated from the North.

"Do you think we'll find something to eat here?" said Mirabelle's voice, behind him.

Vandervenne woke up.

"And gas," he said.

"And a map," said Moustier.

The turret where he had taken up his post reached the level of the second stories. As they rolled by he heard through an open window a familiar voice, which he almost immediately recognized.

". . . our troops," said the voice, "are retiring in good fighting order to positions prepared in advance . . ."

The radio.

No one was to be seen in the single street, except for several dogs which contemplated the tank with respectful suspicion. They saw men emerge from it and, relieved, barked in chorus.

The soldiers set out in search of gasoline and bread. The two bakeries in the village were closed, and there were no pumps. When they came back, empty-handed, toward the tank, it was surrounded by a crowd of peasants. There were only old men, women, and children, who were gazing at it, silent and hostile. They barely moved aside to let the soldiers pass, and a woman brusquely pulled back an urchin who had ventured to run his fingers across one of the treads.

Moustier watched them study him furtively, with sly, sidelong glances.

"Where do we find bread in your town?" he asked.

Silence.

"We're hungry," said Mirabelle.

"The refugees and the soldiers have eaten everything," said one woman, "we haven't got enough left for ourselves."

"We'll pay," said Moustier. "We're hungry."

"I'm telling you we haven't got any left for ourselves."

"Is there a garage around here?" asked Moustier.

Silence.

"No!" a little boy shouted finally; a hand, emerging from the crowd, caught him by the shoulder, and he disappeared among the skirts.

"What they ought to have," murmured Mirabelle, "is a good spraying with a machine gun to teach them manners. We're Frenchmen, what the hell!" he pleaded. "We'll pay."

The village remained obstinately silent, full of disapproval.

The children solemnly sucked their thumbs. The end, thought Moustier. A lot of good it had done to cross the flaming village, the bombed bridge, Paris, a quarter of France. There was nothing left to do but get out and walk, and just keep on walking.

"How much gas is there left?" he asked.

"Not enough to bother starting her up again," Vandervenne replied.

Mirabelle took them aside.

"We could always find something to eat," he said.

He thought to himself, We're armed, after all; did not dare to say this; and added, "Of course it wouldn't look so good."

"And then what?" Moustier inquired, and he explored his pockets for the package of regulation tobacco—it was empty.

He's caught on, Mirabelle reflected with embarrassment.

"Sure," he said, "that wouldn't start our tank. It seems that pretty soon we'll be able to use sea-water instead of gas."

"Let me have the recipe," said Moustier, "and slip in a bit of sea along with it."

So many words for nothing, Vandervenne ruminated. So many words.

Moustier again rummaged in his pockets, and pulled out an old piece of paper which he unfolded. It was the page of newspaper he had picked up in Paris in which everyone was enjoined to subscribe to the defense bonds because "they needed tanks."

"Without flowers or fanfare," he said, and he tore up the paper. Gray shreds fluttered in the air.

"Oh, s——!" exclaimed Mirabelle. The blood had rushed to his face. "The hell with it! We're not going to get up there and haul the tank. We've done what we could, and maybe just a little more. I'd like to see what the lieutenant would do if he was in our shoes. He talked nice, the lieutenant, but otherwise! I'll bet you my balls . . ."

"You'll bet what?" Moustier broke in.

"What'll I bet?" Mirabelle noticed with irritation that Vandervenne was not listening to him. ". . . That we'll have to get the hell out, that's what."

"Nobody's holding you back," said Moustier in a gentle voice. "What?"

Dumfounded by this lack of resistance Mirabelle looked at his comrade incredulously. "Where do you expect me to go all by myself?" He calculated that if Moustier was willing to let him go it was because he had yielded, and he added in a persuasive tone, "Come on, let's beat it together. We'll get along all right, you'll see," he reflected aloud.

"I don't like to walk," said Moustier nonchalantly. "It tires me."

Mirabelle realized that he had made a mistake. He spat on the ground. "You give me a pain! All right, stay here with this dear treasure." He waved his arm violently toward the tank.

"You can feed your face with shells, and maybe those screws'll sell you a little well-juice to drink. I'm leaving. You can say hello to the Fritzes from me when they come and pick you up here." He was sputtering, seized with a buffoonish rage. "If they ask you who you are, tell them, 'We're a couple of poor bastards who've taken in a tank to nurse, only we can't leave it seeing as it can't walk yet.' Not for me. Just look at that other calf, with his balmy stare," he cried, pointing to Vandervenne, who without seeing him had fastened on Mirabelle his meditative gaze. "But you, Moustier, I thought you were smarter. All right, all right, I was wrong. Anyway I'll be on my way! I'm leaving. I'll send you post cards. I tell you I'm beating it. Good-bye!"

He did not even make a move to leave. The three men remained silent. The villagers had not stirred, mutely contemplating the soldiers as though they had just dropped from the moon with their leather jackets, their helmets, their thirst for gasoline. The children peered at the tank, disappointed at not discovering fragments of meteors or tails of comets caught between the treads.

Above them, in the street, the radio was shouting itself hoarse. It too finally became silent.

"Wait," said Vandervenne.

He had removed his helmet; and his rumpled hair, with wisps of hay caught in it, looked like a fur cap.

"Balaam's she-ass!" Mirabelle exclaimed, sarcastically.

"Shut up!" Moustier ordered in a hard voice, and they watched Vandervenne walk toward the crowd.

Massive, broad-shouldered, he towered above the villagers. They eyed him in silence as he approached. He stopped, looked straight at them, slid his tongue across his lips. In the distance the radio sent forth its six familiar notes.

"We don't give a damn about the bread," said Vandervenne. "It's the tank. It's the last one of the battalion. It costs a million. We mustn't let the Germans get it."

"How much?" asked an old man.

"A million," Vandervenne repeated.

He thought a moment. He was alone, with the refrain of "The Marseillaise" that burst forth, suddenly choked, and then broke out again, insistent and monotonous, like a fixed idea.

"We started out day before yesterday," he said ponderously. "We've been moving ever since. It was . . ." He gave up attempting to explain. "It's the last tank in the battalion," he repeated. "We've got to take it down to the Loire. They're fighting on the Loire." He remembered the newspaper Moustier had just torn up. "What do the boys need?" he asked, in a compelling and passionate voice. "Tanks. Tanks for the battle of the Loire." He became silent.

What's the use! thought Moustier as he surveyed the crowd: faces cut out of wood, seamed with lines, like grooves, the piercing eyes beneath bushy eyebrows of the old men, the pale, drawn lips of the women.

The woman who had first answered that the village no longer had enough bread to feed itself, said in an incredulous tone, "I think I have a small can left. If you can use it . . ."

Already the children were scattering in all directions.

The woman came back carrying a can with the paint almost entirely gone.

Mirabelle shrugged his shoulders.

"What do you expect us to do with five liters?" he said.

Vandervenne took the can, said gravely, "Thank you, madame."

Other cans appeared, big and small, round and square, mended with pieces of wood, stopped with rags, covered with dust, spiderwebs, manure. The gasoline gurgled joyously in the reservoir.

"Right this way," Mirabelle cried, "right into the gas tank—who ever said gas stank? Say tank you, thank, for all the cans of gas, if you can—and I gas you can."

Old men smiled with amusement, and Mirabelle said to Moustier, "What do you think of our she-ass? When she begins to talk, you'd think it was Solomon himself." He dropped his voice, "Say, did I give you a scare a minute ago? Did you think I was going to chuck you and scram?"

"Hell, no."

"It just relieves my nerves."

"And then you like to talk."

"By Jesus! I'm not a dope!"

There was bread, too, in the village, and eggs, and soup, and wine, and even tobacco. They received as many invitations for the noonday meal as there were hearths on the main street, but they were in a hurry to leave. They lost five minutes, however, shaking hands with everybody, and the whole village population accompanied them to the end of the village, and the dogs and the youngsters, even the tots, those who would keep this as their first memory, followed them beyond.

What had seemed at night to be charged with menace and with the unknown revealed itself in daylight to be almost frivolously commonplace. There were, to be sure, hillslopes and a few tufts of trees, fields of wheat giving way to meadows, brambles and honeysuckle along the whole length of the dusty road that twisted and turned without apparent reason, forming the north and south, the east and west boundaries, according to its fancy, of Peter's or Paul's parcels of land, passing over bridges with stone parapets that straddled trickles of water with blue-green dragonflies hovering over them, traversing ten different landscapes—the landscape with dandelions hemming a ditch, the landscape with nests of mistletoe in the branches of the oak, the landscape with a wheelbarrow turned upside down next to a pile of pebbles, without counting the rest—between two kilometric posts, on the first of which one could barely decipher, "La Chapelle, 6 km 3," and on the second, "La Chapelle, 5 km 3," La Chapelle, thus announced for ten leagues around, being composed of two farms and one tiny abandoned house, which would long since have fallen into ruin if on one of its walls there had not been an advertisement of a brand of apéritif, in white against a blue background and badly in need of a coat of paint.

Along the little roads of France, bordered with hedges, with flowers that bloom in the hedges, with birds that sing in the hedges, along the crayfish-streams and the pike-streams, amid the flowers of France—poppies, bachelor buttons, daisies—France was going to the dogs. Towed cars, broken-down cars, abandoned cars, cars in the ditches, cars piled high with rags, with soldiers clinging to a running board or lying on a fender, with a cage inside the spare tire in which two green parrots calmly perched, cars with weeping children, cackling hens, yelps, curses. The small roads, the medium small, and the tiny ones, with traffic congestions in every hamlet, every junction, that Moustier and Mirabelle had to untangle by dint of shouts, curses, and their tankers' helmets. People would stop without knowing why and start off again likewise, with no idea of where they were going.

Toward eleven o'clock, they again ran into the Parisian buses scattered through the villages and serving as dormitories. Some of them had kept their name-plates—BASTILLE, GARE DE L'EST, OPÉRA.

"We ought to be on the Loire by this time," said Moustier.

They had just come out on the square of a small town, black with refugees. Before the town hall a colonel was chatting with a lieutenant colonel.

"Stop," said Moustier, "we'll get some information from them."

With his shuffling walk he went up to the two officers and waited to finish his cigarette before talking to them.

"I come from Evreux," said the lieutenant colonel, who wore the acanthus-leaf insignia of the commissariat. "We were bombarded several times."

"So were we," said the colonel.

"Yesterday I shipped three hundred and seventy-five employees to Toulouse," said the lieutenant colonel, "and I'm expecting three hundred more here this evening, but I can't find any place to billet them."

"I've got four thousand fellows to assemble," said the colonel, "and I don't know where they are."

"I have three evacuation orders, the Pyrenees, Bordeaux, and the Massif Central," said the lieutenant colonel.

"Excuse me, sir," said Moustier, throwing away his cigarette butt as he addressed the colonel, "our lieutenant entrusted my comrades and myself with a tank to save it from the Germans. We were supposed to drive it to Paris, but Paris was evacuated. What are we to do with it now?"

"I have no idea what you're talking about," said the colonel. "Have you, colonel?"

"Not the slightest idea," said the lieutenant colonel.

"You have no orders?" the colonel asked Moustier. "Well, neither have we!"

He had turned to his fellow-officer, and the two exchanged a well-bred smile.

"You might as well go on south of the Loire," suggested the lieutenant colonel, "unless . . ."

But Moustier, at attention, was already saluting. Behind him he heard one of the officers saying, "Tell me, colonel, didn't you know Colonel Pilavoine in Evreux? . . ."

All the refugees made a rush for the baker's where a fresh batch of bread had just been taken from the oven. Pilavoine, Pilavoine, fumed Moustier, and to his waiting comrades he said, "What do you expect? They're officers!"

"You missed your chance at one last night," said Mirabelle to Vandervenne. "We didn't see him either, but his driver came and woke us up to find out what street he should turn down to dodge the Fritzes. We explained to him that he couldn't miss it: it's a one-way road. Poor France! Fellows like that trying to run an army!"

"The driver seemed to be a good guy," said Moustier. "I don't think he liked his job much."

They set out in search of provisions. The bakery had sold every loaf of bread. It must have been the last baking, for a "No

Bread" sign hung at the entrance. Mirabelle finally found a piece at a bicycle dealer's who refused to accept the money he offered her for it. With Vandervenne he went into a grocery. The woman sat knitting among the empty shelves. She smiled to the soldiers.

"You wouldn't happen to have any sandwich spread," said Mirabelle timidly, "or some sardines, or anything?"

"All I have left is mustard," said the woman, as she stopped her knitting and laughed. "It's all I have—mustard."

"All right, let's have the mustard," said Mirabelle, and she served them, laughing all the while.

On their way out they met Moustier.

"I went into a stationery shop," he said, "to try to get a map. Do you know what they offered me? A map of the Balkans, the only one they had left."

He pulled the compass out of his pocket, lovingly rubbed the glass with his sleeve and said, "But it's of no importance."

"We've got bread and mustard," Mirabelle announced.

"No importance," Moustier repeated. "We haven't time to eat. I've made inquiries. We're not as far south as I thought."

They saw more and more towed cars, and others in the ditches. Along the edge of the road women with a pail or a jug in their hands were begging the soldiers for some gasoline. In the grass large families waited.

"You can say what you like," said Moustier, looking at a family —father, mother, kids—pushing a stalled car, "human meat is cheap."

"You believe we'll win the war?" Mirabelle asked him.

"I believe what I see," said Moustier.

"The English have always won their wars," said Mirabelle wryly, "ever since the Romans . . ."

"The best Englishmen," said Moustier, "are the Canadians be-cause they're not English."

"What I'd like to see just once," said Mirabelle wistfully, "is a French plane."

"Now I know what pilots are like," said Vandervenne with sudden violence. "They're not men. They spend their time pushing it into the women while we get ourselves shot."

"A pilot can sure pile it on!" decreed Mirabelle.

"Pilots and officers," said Moustier. "It's lucky there are the mud-sloggers."

All three were agreed on this point, and the conversation died for lack of contrary opinions.

A line of civilian cars had stopped on the highway, and Vandervenne got around them by driving off the road across the grass. The automobilists watched the tank pass with bleak resentment. A sergeant sprang up before them, saluted, and shouted to Moustier, of whom all he could see was his head and helmet, "You have the priority, sir, but you won't get by—the bridge has just been blown up a little farther on."

"How do we get through then?"

"I don't know, sir."

"Let's try anyway," said Moustier. "We'll see."

The road had been cleared at the approaches to the bridge which rested, in broken pieces, on the two banks and in the river, a slender thread of water which an officer, wearing a trooper's outfit on which he had sewn his three captain's stripes, was contemplating with a critical eye. Half a dozen soldiers were busily engaged around a broken-down delivery truck, without headlights, without a hood, mounted on antique studded solid-rubber tires, and that bore the motto, written in chalk along its side, "Just drifting along, but we'll get there."

The tank stopped. Mirabelle jumped down, went toward the officer while hastily buttoning his leather jacket.

"Pardon, sir, do you know if there's another bridge around here to get to the other side?"

The officer was smoking avidly. He was lean, dark, and in his bony snub-nosed face two vacantly staring eyes swam in the depth of their dark rings. He did not answer, and Mirabelle repeated his question.

"Leave the captain alone!" cried one of the soldiers, and Mirabelle, speechless, looked at him.

Moustier went over to the delivery truck where the soldiers were piling up shovels and picks; by their insignia he saw without astonishment that they all belonged to different regiments, only one of them being an engineer.

"Having fun?" he asked.

A small colored cuirassier looked at him from head to foot, and said nothing. The others had not even turned round.

"You know the region?" Moustier asked. "Is there another bridge not too far from here?"

"There must be another one upstream, and one downstream," the cuirassier answered, "you'd better hurry."

The soldiers laughed in chorus.

"Are the Fritzes in the region?" Moustier insisted.

"Maybe so. They might be on the other side of the water, and it wouldn't astonish me. It wouldn't be the first time it happened to us."

Moustier had just been struck by an idea.

"Why didn't you go over to the other side before you blew it up?"

"It must be that there's still work to be done on this side," the cuirassier answered, and again his comrades burst out laughing.

Behind him Moustier heard Mirabelle's playful voice, "I say, Moustier, you got a cigarette to give me?"

Mirabelle did not smoke. Moustier looked round and saw his companion winking at him.

"I left them in the tank," Moustier lied, and the two men went off.

"I don't like this," Mirabelle whispered, stammering with excitement. "That private with captain's stripes who doesn't know the region. I'll bet you my balls," he burst out, and turning round to see if he had been heard, he concluded with a murmur, "they're parachutists."

"But they talk French," Moustier objected.

"Not the officer. He didn't say a word. And even if they talk French that doesn't make any difference."

They had come back to the tank. Why not? Moustier thought. He remembered that only the cuirassier had talked, and the others had merely laughed.

"We'll see about that," he suddenly decided. "Get inside and hold the machine guns ready. I'm going to talk to them."

He retraced his steps.

"What the hell you doing here?" he said, rolling his cigarette stub between his lips.

"Are you interested?" asked a fair-haired, slender soldier who wore the insignia of the medical service.

"Yes, I'm interested."

"Well, we've blown up the bridge, in case you hadn't noticed it."

"I'm not joking. Who are you? Where are your papers?"

They burst out laughing.

"All right, all right," said Moustier, "you don't have to talk the language to laugh. Only," he added, weighing his syllables, "if I were you I'd answer," and he cast a glance toward the tank whose machine guns converged toward the group. "There's nothing fake about that," he said meaningfully.

The laughter ceased.

"You'd better watch yourself," said the cuirassier. "We're loaded with dynamite. Captain," he cried, "come over here, this fellow's trying to make trouble."

Interrupted in his meditation by a familiar voice, the officer approached and said in a tone of exasperation, "What's the matter?"

"With your permission, I'd like to see your papers," said Moustier. If he makes a fuss it means Mirabelle is right, he thought, but the captain asked absent-mindedly, "What papers? What for?"

He headed toward the truck.

"Are we leaving?" asked the cuirassier.

"Not if I've got anything to say about it," said Moustier and he took a few steps toward the officer.

"Leave the captain alone," the medical orderly snapped.

"We're late," said the officer, and his soldiers looked at one another with the knowing smile of pupils who hear their favorite teacher use his pet expression.

"You're not leaving before you've shown me your documents," said Moustier obstinately. "If your captain doesn't understand French all you've got to do is translate it for him."

"Leave the captain alone," the orderly repeated.

A boy with a doll-like face, his plump chin pricked with a dimple, the only one to wear the black sappers' insignia, said in a conciliating tone, "Why do you want to see our papers?"

"Because I don't believe you have any."

"Why, of course we have. Look."

He pulled out a grimy military record book that Moustier read attentively. "Dandeau, Robert, Marie, Pierre, born in Pontgibaud . . ."

"We're in order," said the sapper. "We'll show you our record books, only don't bother the captain."

"You're from Pontgibaud?" asked Moustier. "Then we're almost neighbors. I'm from Clermont way."

"I worked there before the war," said Dandeau. "I'm a harness-maker. You know the Touillac outfit?"

Moustier turned toward the tank and shouted, "The incident is liquidated. You can come. What's the matter with your cap?" he asked the sapper.

"What makes you think anything's wrong with him?" said Dandeau, aggressive.

"He's not very talkative."

"He's got other things to do besides talk. We've got work on our hands."

"What work?"

"The bridges."

Five weeks before, a company of engineers, commanded by the captain and to which Dandeau belonged, had been stationed in Belgium, on the Meuse, ready to blow up a railroad bridge as soon as the order came.

"We're still waiting for that order," said Dandeau. He and the captain found themselves, the only ones in their unit, in the Ardennes, to learn that the bridges on the Meuse had not been blown up. "It was pathetic," said the sapper. "He kept saying that he shouldn't have waited for orders. If you had seen him then, as I saw him, you wouldn't be asking me what's the matter with him. And with all that, very simple."

This matter of the Meuse bridges not having been blown up must have assumed in the officer's mind the proportions of a fixed idea. Having decided once and for all never to wait for orders again, he had recruited a few stray soldiers picked up at random in the course of the retreat, and resolved to avenge the fateful railroad bridge whose metallic parapets mocked his dreams with their persistent solidity.

"There were fifteen or so of us at the beginning," said Dandeau contemptuously, "but some of the guys got cold feet."

Those who remained felt themselves really live only at the approaches to a bridge. It was their bread, their passion, it made them forget about the war.

"What do you do for grub?" Mirabelle asked. He and Vandervenne had come up to the sapper and were listening to him talk.

"We manage," Dandeau answered vaguely.

Although they had to get along without the melinite and the cheddite which they had had at the beginning and be satisfied with dynamite, and the captain's cigarette applied to the fuse had replaced the electric detonators, the officer did not have his equal for getting hold of explosives; on the other hand he never concerned himself with the quartermaster's department. Chance had favored them: two Parisian furriers whom they had helped to get across the Marne, in Lagny, had made them a present of a sack of furs. "It's not much—dyed rabbit, but the peasants like it," Dandeau explained hastily, as this question did not interest him. "He's a prince," he said, returning to the subject close to his heart. "You see that truck? We found it along the side of the road, going to Nemours, completely broken down, with an old madwoman jumping around it as though she had lost her fortune. Well, he got it going right away. He crawled under it and got it going! Then he stood up again, lit a cigarette, and said, 'Dandeau, now we're motorized!'" At that time he never stopped smoking, but now that cigarettes are scarce, he keeps them to light the fuses. He finishes the cigarette while the bridge blows up." The sapper's voice expressed admiration. "Do you know what they call him?" With a theatrical voice he announced, "Captain Dynamite."

The cuirassier came toward them.

"Hurry up, Dandeau, we're leaving."

Vandervenne disapprovingly contemplated the blocks of stone that bathed in the shallow water.

"It costs work, all that," he said.

The cuirassier spat noisily.

"We're not masons," he said, "we're dynamiters."

"You coming, Dandeau," cried the captain, and the sapper, radiant, ran over to the truck.

"Parachutists," said Moustier, smiling, and turning to Mirabelle he asked, "You still want your cigarette?"

The old rattletrap coughed, quivered, and chugged off.

"One single commissioned officer who hasn't run away, and he's mad," observed Mirabelle.

They got back into the tank and forded the river, whose water barely wet the treads, as easily as they would have crossed on the bridge whose scattered fragments offered the only and a futile obstacle to their passage.

Thanks to Captain Dynamite they had outdistanced the bulk of the civilian cars, bottled up at the approaches to bridges that were becoming scarcer. In the Nièvre the fleeing people were only just arriving. Seated on straw chairs before their houses, old women in peasant headdresses observed the strangers pass. Farther on, entire villages were on their doorsteps to watch the rising tide, and the children, on seeing the tank, would come to attention. Still farther on, they again ran into the military. There were Madagascans, Moroccans, Annamites. At the entrances to the tiny towns obstacles made of stone and tree trunks had been placed, but there was no one to stop the cars. In the dip of a valley some balloonists had moored two blimps. A Paris bus was abandoned along the roadside—on the red sign-plate that indicated its itinerary, from the Bastille to the Madeleine, someone had written in chalk, "Out of gas."

It was still daylight when they came upon the farm. Surrounded by trees, it was vast and well kept, and from the yard rose cries of men and the lowing of cattle. The sight of the tank caused a general running for cover. A little girl alone remained where she stood, sucking her thumb. The three soldiers jumped out into the yard, and on seeing French uniforms the farmers came out of hiding.

They were on the point of leaving, the grandfather, two women —an old and a young one—two adolescents, and a flock of youngsters, all in black, in their Sunday best, with hats on their heads, as though they were going to mass.

"Is the Loire still far from here?" inquired Mirabelle.

"You're on it," said the old man. He added, "We were about to leave."

"Leave?"

In the middle of the yard stood a large carriole, piled high with household utensils.

"You're leaving for good?" asked Moustier.

"Sure we are," said the young woman, "we're doing like everybody else."

"And where are you going?"

"We're crossing the bridge. After that, we'll see."

"And all this?"

He pointed to the newly stuccoed house, to the stable that had recently been reroofed, the cattle, the field of wheat, the hens that were pecking for food between the legs of the horses harnessed to the carriole.

"We're not the only ones," said the young woman with a guilty smile. She was redheaded, and her blue eyes did not smile. This would be the place to stay, thought Vandervenne, forever, with her.

"We've let the animals loose," said the old man, "they'll find fodder."

The children, full of awe and wonder, were contemplating the tank.

"Does that thing weigh a lot, monsieur?" one of them asked Vandervenne.

"Yes, young fellow."

"How heavy? As heavy as the house?" And becoming steadily bolder, "And your helmet, monsieur, is it heavy?"

"Kids like to know about that sort of thing," said the old woman apologetically, and to the child, "Jeannot, don't bother monsieur."

"That's all right, madame," growled Vandervenne. He had lost the habit of talking to women and children.

"If you want to take anything along," said the old man, "don't hesitate. Some hens, or even a cow. I saw service in 1914," he added, "in the artillery."

The redheaded young woman disappeared in the house. The soldiers' eyes followed her. She returned with a bottle and glasses. "You must be thirsty," she said with a slow smile.

"Don't stand on ceremony," said the old man.

"Your health," said Mirabelle politely, and they drank avidly.

"Your wine is good," said Moustier, wiping his mouth.

"Madeleine, go and get a few bottles," ordered the old man. "I'm leaving two barrels," he explained. "If you'd like to . . ."

"You have people in the war?" Moustier ventured.

"My oldest son and my son-in-law, Madeleine's husband. They were in the North."

Married. Vandervenne's heart contracted.

"We've just come from the North," said Mirabelle. "It was calm up there."

"We've had no news," said Madeleine. "My husband is in the motorized cavalry. I have the number of the postal sector."

Vandervenne looked at one of the boys, redheaded too, and asked, for the pleasure of hearing Madeleine's voice, "Is he your brother, madame?"

"He's only sixteen," she said.

"Almost seventeen," the boy protested, turning beet-red.

"He's too young for the army," said the old farmer's wife, "but he's helped us a lot here."

"Isn't it true, monsieur, that you can volunteer at seventeen in time of war?" the boy asked Moustier in a voice that was too loud. He blushed to his ears.

"Be patient, Lucien," said the farmer. He winked his eye at the soldiers. "You're too young, and I'm too old."

Vandervenne sought the boy's eyes and smiled at him, not daring to smile at his sister.

"You think my husband would get my letter if I wrote to his postal sector?" she asked.

"They left long ago," affirmed Moustier. "Everybody's left."

"Rinse the glasses, Madeleine," said the old woman, "and put them back in the cupboard."

"So won't you take anything?" said the old man. "A few chickens?"

"Thanks," said Moustier.

"You're not standing on ceremony?"

"No indeed. We have no room. We're going to fight."

"I understand," said the old man with an air of importance.

"The battle of the Loire," said Mirabelle.

"I understand," said the old man.

Before starting off they turned round once more to look at Madeleine. With her mouth half-open, her eyes grave, she nodded her red head in a last greeting.

The road led to the Loire and ran onto a bridge. There stood an abandoned sentry-box on which someone had written in chalk, "Places without love." The river was wide, and slow, and slack, fringed with willows and hazel trees.

"We got here in time," said Moustier. "They've left no one to defend this bridge."

The tank maneuvered round so as to obstruct the approach, its cannon and its machine guns pointing north.

"We have only ten liters of gas left," said Mirabelle.

"Where do you want to go?" asked Moustier. "We've arrived."

Now there was nothing for them to do but wait, and they waited, in the dark, not daring to smoke, barely daring to open their mouths.

They said they would cross the bridge, thought Vandervenne—he didn't know why, but the Loire had reminded him of Madeleine. He waited, but no one came. They must have taken a different bridge, he thought. It was better so. They had arrived.

No sound reached them save, at intervals, the hooting of a night bird, the roar of an invisible plane, and, in the distance, strings of explosions. In the past two days they had slept five hours, but none of them was sleepy. The moon rose in the sky, was reflected in the Loire, outlined the bridge and the tank. The sound of a plane swelled in jerks, there were several explosions near by, and then silence returned.

"Oh, the swine!" said Mirabelle.

Moustier had rolled a cigarette which he chewed without lighting it. Through the slit a slender ray of moonlight entered the tank, lighted up Vandervenne's nose, a machine gun belt, made the dashboard gleam. Again the roar of a motor in the sky, the rending of explosions.

"Oh, the bastards!" said Mirabelle.

"Well, you sap, was it worth it?" Moustier suddenly asked.

"What?" said Mirabelle, and understanding immediately, "You

mean, all that?" With his hand he pointed to the shells, Vander-venne, motionless, his eyes shut, the ray of moonlight. "I'll say it was."

Dry branches crackled, a voice said, "There they are!"

There was a metallic click, and the same voice said, "You have the hand grenades, Duval?"

"Look out," said Moustier, "here are reinforcements. And the Germans must be just ahead. Get ready."

He started to open the door, and at the same instant a round, heavy object came and struck the side of the tank, next to the opening. The night became illuminated with red stars, and Mou-stier fell backwards, pulling the door with him as he fell.

If he had done more than open it ajar he would have been dead on the field of honor, and with him his two comrades and those who were outside, too, most likely; exploding among the shells, the grenade would have transformed the tank into a scrap-heap. They owed their salvation to a fraction of a second or a fraction of an inch, or simply to the pampered childhood of Cadet Officer Gévelot whose arm lacked that precision which is acquired only in the street, between the ages of eight and twelve.

Burned in the forehead and the right hand, Moustier had merely been knocked unconscious. Outside, the assailants were holding a consultation. Mirabelle, in a fury, yelled through the side slit, "You goddamn lousy bunch of stinking bums! You're too stupid to recognize a French tank!"

There was a silence, then an embarrassed voice said, "Are you hurt?"

"Sure we're hurt," groaned Mirabelle. "What did you think you were throwing? A bouquet?"

He opened the door. A cadet came up, crestfallen, followed by a sergeant and a few men. "I didn't . . . ?" he asked, pointing to Moustier, who did not move.

"Yes, you've killed him," cried Mirabelle. "That's all we needed. What are you doing here?"

"We're defending the bridge," said the cadet. "We were told there was a German motorized column in this vicinity."

Moustier groaned, and sat up, careful not to lean on his burnt hand.

"Why, he's alive!" said the cadet. "We must transport him."

"It's of no importance," said Moustier.

His head ached, and he couldn't find his words.

"Where are you defending the bridge?" he asked finally.

"On the other side of the Loire, on the south bank," the cadet explained, voluble now. He had had a bad scare.

"On the south bank?"

"Yes, a corps of engineers mined it this morning, but they left without telling us how to light the fuse. The major sent a motorcyclist to get the information."

He removed his glasses and wiped them.

"You don't light a fuse," said Moustier. "There's an electric detonator, and no fuse. Unless you've had a visit from Captain Dynamite. But then there wouldn't be any bridge left. Where's your major?"

"Across the river. You're not too badly hurt?" the cadet inquired. "You know, I'm terribly sorry and all that. Mistakes like that are common in wartime."

"Let's go, boys," said Moustier without looking at him, and, tossing the words over his shoulder, "and be sure you don't touch anything. You'd be just as likely to run the tank into the river."

He staggered a little as he started across the bridge. Vandervenne came up close to him, slipped his arm under his, being careful not to touch his burns.

"I could carry you," he said casually. His own strength embarrassed him.

"Thanks, sweetheart," said Moustier mockingly, and Vandervenne felt himself blush.

We got here just in time, thought Moustier, and as though he had heard him, Mirabelle said, "Who knows—but for us the Fritzes might be crossing the Loire."

He meditated in silence.

"Do you think we'll get the War Cross?" he asked.

"As if I gave a good goddamn," said Moustier.

They had straightened their helmets, buttoned their leather jackets, tightened their belts, and were walking slowly, arm in arm, kicking pebbles before them as they went, joyous and grave, drunk—Mirabelle with pride, Moustier with pain, Vandervenne with satisfaction over a job well done, and all three with fatigue and sleeplessness.

The command headquarters were set up in a shack. A gasoline truck was parked before the entrance, and the driver, leaning over the wheel, was snoring. The major was asleep on a camp cot, fully dressed.

"Well, is it all set?" he said without opening his eyes and, waking up, he examined the three soldiers with astonishment. "Were you sent about the mine?" he asked more dryly. "Where is the motorcyclist?"

Moustier tried to stand at attention, lifted his burnt hand to his helmet.

"Sir," he said, "we bring you a twenty-two-ton tank, armed and with its full stock of ammunition. At your disposal, sir, for the defense of the bridge."

His head felt as if it was going to burst. I must take off my helmet, he thought vaguely, but instead of doing so he began to roll a cigarette.

"A tank . . . the defense of the bridge?"

The major was at a loss. One point alone was clear: these men were not here to blow up the bridge, the motorcyclist had not returned, he would have to remain still longer, to wait, wait . . .

"What are you talking about?" he asked.

Moustier tried to explain. As he spoke it seemed to him that his tongue was swelling in his mouth, the words got through all twisted.

"What the hell do you expect me to do with a tank?" the major finally said.

"It's the last one in the battalion," explained Vandervenne.

"So what? Wake me up in the middle of the night about a thing like that! I never heard of such a thing!" The major was furious.

Moustier finally found the phrase he had been looking for from the beginning. "It's for the battle of the Loire," he said.

The major looked at him as though he were mad. "What battle of the Loire?"

They were ridiculous, these three soldiers, who had come out of the night, with their tank which they wanted to sell at all costs.

"Orléans has been declared an open town and evacuated this morning," he said, "so you can just keep on running after your battle of the Loire!" He was fed up: he had enough troubles of his own. He looked at Moustier. "Take that cigarette out of your mouth before you talk to me," he yelled.

They went out in silence. Outside, Moustier was the first to recover his wits.

"Discipline is taking a hair of the dog that bit it," he said. "We'll win the war."

They came back to the tank, got into it without paying any attention to the cadet and his men, and Mirabelle started up the motor. The tank described a half-circle and headed across the bridge. When they reached the gasoline truck, Moustier snapped out to the sleeping driver, "Fill up the tank. Major's orders."

They rolled on in silence. At the end of fifteen minutes, Vandervenne, whom the others thought asleep, began to swear. He swore for a long time, putting into it all his truck driver's experience, all his man's passion. There was silence once more. Finally Mirabelle asked, "Orléans is on the Loire?"

"Sure," said Moustier.

"Then all the Germans have to do is cross it?"

They were silent again, for ten minutes. Vandervenne had an aversion to regrets, but not to rage. He had sacrificed Madeleine—to what?

"Where do we go?" Mirabelle asked again.

"Now that I know what the score is, I'm going home," declared Moustier.

"What do you mean?"

"The incident is liquidated. It should at least be good for that," said Moustier, pointing to the controls.

Mirabelle reflected. "It's a go," he said. "We're headed my way, too."

"And you, Vandervenne?" asked Moustier.

"I can't go home. I'm from up North."

"I'll take him along," said Mirabelle.

"No, he's coming with me," said Moustier.

Before a pond that shimmered in the night he had the tank brought to a stop.

"Get out, fellows."

He pulled a shell from its compartment, passed it to Vandervenne.

"Catch it, sweetheart!" The shells went "plump!" as they sank into the water. Frogs darted about, terrorized by this bombardment, circles spread on the surface of the pond. When the tank was empty of ammunition Moustier said, "And now we smoke a cigarette." They had removed their helmets, leather jackets, and blouses, rolled up their sleeves. The night was balmy and peaceful. Springing back out of prewar days, lavender suspenders resumed their place on Mirabelle's shoulders, the tattooings re-emerged on Vandervenne's forearms.

"Here we are promoted to the status of veterans," said Mirabelle. "Beaten veterans," he added.

They rode all night without stopping. While one drove the other two slept. In the morning they came once more upon the convoys and the civilians.

No longer were all cars going south. Bewildered caravans jogged in every direction, crossing and recrossing one another's paths, going in circles, like a hen that still scurries about a little after having its head cut off, and then, having run out of gas, they collapsed and died alongside a field or a village junction.

The tank rolled on gently, and through the wide-open doorway Moustier and Mirabelle joshed with the women, on whom Vandervenne cast only a hopeful glance, each time disappointed, and paying no further attention to them. They stopped once to pick up some unsuspecting hens, and another time to give a ride to four girls, workers from a Parisian factory, who told them that the day they left the capital, some Gardes Mobiles had come into the shops to protect the machines which the personnel wanted to destroy rather than leave for the Germans.

The inside of the tank, littered with cigarette butts and spattered with wine stains, looked like a bar-room table after a long card game.

Once only Mirabelle asked Moustier point-blank, "What do you say now? Was it worth it?"

Moustier saw again the night on the Loire, the ray of moonlight caressing the shells. "No fair prompting the player," he said. He

thought awhile before adding, "But sometimes you feel like breaking his neck." He said nothing more.

"When I think that it's less than six weeks since we came to
the Meuse," said Mirabelle. "And in the old days there were
Hundred Years Wars!" He became silent in turn.

The road zigzagged upward. Long unmolested by roadmenders,
the meadows had crept right up to the macadam. Vandervenne,
who was driving, gazed as they passed at the episcopal-purple
flowers, clusters of little bells on long stems, that grew on the
road banks, in Flanders, on the Somme, around Paris, from
Fontainebleau to Montargis, in the Nièvre, along the Loire, and
here on the Central Plateau, flowers whose name he did not know
and which he had never seen at close range, not having had the
time to stop and look at them, flowers which had bordered the
flight of the French army. I'll stay a few days with Moustier, he
thought, and then I'll try to see her again. It was not going to be
any more surprising to find Madeleine again than to have met
her the first time.

The road continued to climb, there were fewer villages, fewer
cars, and presently there were no more fields, only meadows reaching to the horizon where blue mountains shimmered. Never had
the meadows of France, with no one to mow them, been so
beautiful, so brimming with flowers. There were meadows all white
with daisies, meadows all purple with wild pansies, meadows all
pink with foxgloves, as though, on these immense expanses freed
of men, there were at last room for every flower to grow.

"Stop," said Mirabelle suddenly.

They were no longer in a hurry. The treads became motionless,
and Moustier asked, "What's the matter?"

As far as the eye could see, hills bared their gentle, flowery
slopes. Lost amid their undulations, a cow standing with its feet
far apart was oddly swaying. Mirabelle pointed to her with his
finger.

"So what?" said Moustier.

"Take a good look."

Moustier gazed at the landscape. His urban eyes noted nothing
unusual. "I don't catch," he said, "I don't see nobody."

"Animals aren't like we are," said Mirabelle, "they can't take care of themselves."

He got out of the tank and walked toward the cow.

She stood and waited for him, motionless, and only a little quiver shimmered on her white, black-spotted flanks. She stretched out her neck, raised her muzzle, uttered a long mooing. Mirabelle went up to her, tickled her between the horns, looked around as though he were looking for something, scratched the back of his neck and returned toward the tank.

"We don't happen to have a bucket?"

Moustier was puzzled even more by his seriousness than by the question.

"Of course not," he said, "but there are some empty wine-bottles. Why?"

"It won't do."

Mirabelle meditated, his eyes explored the inside of the tank. "I've got it!" he exclaimed. "Vandervenne, slip me a helmet."

They had piled up their veterans' souvenirs in the turret. Vandervenne caught a helmet by its broad chinstrap and handed it to Mirabelle.

"Can we come and look?" Moustier asked.

"If you don't make any noise."

Vandervenne looked at him: he wasn't joking.

Followed by his comrades, Mirabelle went over to the cow again. She had not budged, her quivering had become accentuated, her tail beat the air with jerky little movements.

"If you're thirsty, we've got wine," said Moustier, guessing what Mirabelle was about to do, and he began to roll a cigarette.

Mirabelle crouched down and tore off the lining of the helmet, which he braced, upside down, under the cow's rosy teats, to which clung wisps of green grass. His fingers pulled the dugs, lightly, rapidly, regularly. Short jets of milk squirted, bubbling, against the steel walls. Without looking at his hands, Mirabelle raised his head toward Moustier and said, "It's not for me, it's for her. They're as delicate as women. She's still very young, look, you'd almost say she was a heifer. It can't be very long since she calved. So if you leave her without milking she'll croak sure as fate."

Moustier lit his cigarette, said, "If that's the reason, all you had to do was spill it on the ground. It's good for the rugs, they say."

"And let the milk go to waste!"

The helmet was three-quarters full, and through the two holes pierced in the sides to give ventilation slender white trickles fell into the grass. Vandervenne pulled two matches out of his pocket and kneeling beside Mirabelle plugged the openings. The latter said, squinting toward Moustier, "Don't smoke. Or else move away."

"Why?"

"They don't like it."

Embarrassed, Moustier withdrew a few steps.

"I didn't know," said Vandervenne, and Mirabelle understood that he was not talking about cigarettes.

"I know all about cows," he said with a little laugh.

"There's nothing to be ashamed of," answered Vandervenne. His voice expressed consideration.

The cow, quieted, was browsing, her head in the flowers. Mirabelle lifted the helmet and holding it with both hands drank long drafts.

"Go ahead," he said.

Vandervenne was not thirsty, and Moustier did not like milk. They both drank some, not to offend their companion.

"There were six of them at home," said Mirabelle. "Milch cows."

They climbed back into the tank.

The sun was just beginning to go down when Moustier, at a crossing, made a sign to stop. "I've arrived," he said, pointing to the little road that led to the right. "And Vandervenne too. You coming, Mirabelle?"

But Mirabelle was also anxious to get home.

"I'll wait for a car that'll take me further west," he said, "and then I'll be able to manage. They must be waiting for me back home."

"What do we do with the tank?" asked Vandervenne.

"Drive it into a meadow," suggested Moustier. "No use holding up the traffic."

The tank turned sharply, crossed the ditch and rolled with its treads half hidden in the flowers that lay crushed in its wake.

"We'll write each other," said Mirabelle vaguely. Each one was becoming absorbed in thoughts of civilian life.

"Since you're going on," said Moustier to Mirabelle, "I'll make you a useful present." He stuck his hand in his pocket, pulled out the compass, examined it for the last time before handing it to his comrade. "Now you're all set," he said, and he took a few steps down the narrow road. Then he suddenly turned round.

"What do they need?" he droned.

"Tanks," buzzed Mirabelle.

"Tanks," barked Vandervenne.

"Tanks!" shouted Moustier.

They parted at the crossing, before a wooden shack on which, next to a poster of the illustrious Amar circus covered with animals, a woman's hand had written in chalk, "Yves Ollivier, 8 years old, of Givet (Ardennes) is wanted by his mother, who has taken refuge in Villeneuve."

Covered with dried mud and rust, its twenty-two tons sunk in a bed of wild pansies and gentians, its door swung open, through which could be seen the empty shell compartments, the last of the tanks of the Meuse remained alone, enormous and misshapen, in a setting of dead volcanoes.

The Old French Army

There isn't much to be added to Pozner's account of the great southward flight of soldiers and civilians, but it is to be remembered that the whole story is told from the point of view of three baffled tankmen. It is true, for example, that every single soldier in the ground forces was disgusted with the ARMÉE DE L'AIR, because he saw only German planes above him during the horrible six weeks. But the pilots were not, as Pozner's soldiers say, "less than men." With the few passable planes they had, mostly American-built Curtiss P-36's, and even with others so obsolete they were grotesque, the pursuit groups attacked German bomber formations, fighting one or two planes against ten or fifty. They lost all the planes issued to them. The only pilots who survived were those who were grounded because they had nothing to fly in. There were, it seems, a couple of hundred new planes in southern France and North Africa that were never committed to combat. There was also rifle and machine-gun ammunition in various warehouses while troops in the field had nothing to shoot with. These were phenomena of inefficiency or sabotage, like poor Debû-Bridel's newspaper that seemed to be doing German propaganda. But the pilots had courage.

I remember one fighter group at Saint-Dizier on June 6 that was down to three planes fit to fly. The surviving pilots were battling for the chance to fly them and be killed. Commandant Murtin, who commanded them, said that up to then his men had shot down eighty-eight enemy planes and lost thirty-five of their own. "But we would have to get six for one to hold them even," he said frankly and hopelessly. I was to meet Murtin two and a half years later in North Africa, where he fought again, and lost a leg. "All France has embarked on a parachute jump," one boy said to me, "—if we come out of it, good." The Gethsemane of the ARMÉE DE L'AIR has been recorded nobly in Antoine de Saint-Exupéry's PILOTE DE GUERRE, widely popular in America as FLIGHT TO ARRAS. Saint-Exupéry survived until August, 1944, when he was lost flying a P-38 over southern France. But few of his comrades lived so long.

Moustier's condemnation of officers is also far too sweeping, although his attitude was typical in those days. I did see the "self-detached" officers and their women on the roads, and I know one division at least, in which the men developed the habit of shooting all officers they did not recognize, because they might be German spies giving false orders. But there were officers who acquitted themselves like men. Years later, in Brittany, I met a Resistance chief, a Parisian himself, who had come down into Brittany at the entreaty of the men of the battery he had commanded in 1940, to lead them in their new war. His name was Juteau. He had not abandoned his lot, but had brought them through the retreat as a unit, without losing a gun. His Bretons had a very ample vengeance in 1944.

Most of the French Army was made up of reservists. Soldiers

up to about forty years of age were called to the colors, but officers were called up much older than that. The army was dead-weighted with thousands of lieutenants, captains and majors whose bodies were, like their technical knowledge, obsolete. Moreover, these men had been thoroughly absorbed into civilian life as business men or members of the professions. They had been affected by the social struggle of the thirties and feared the proletariat, a term which in their minds roughly corresponded with the enlisted men. Many of them must have secretly sympathized with the fascist groups. The younger reservist officers, the under-thirties, were better, although much of the theory they had been taught was archaic. But promotions in the French Army were so slow that young officers had little responsibility unless they were of the professional army.

The young regular officers, the captains of thirty-five and the majors of forty, were best of all, but there were not enough of them. The most dangerous for France, because they had the most power, were the generals of seventy. There was no massive transfusion of officers direct from the colleges or civilian careers as in the United States. The reserve officers, even if they had wanted to learn about modern war, would have had too much to unlearn. They didn't have to work hard to earn their commissions, as our novices did, because they had had their commissions for years, tucked away in camphor with their uniforms. After the liberation, when the fighting seemed to be virtually over—although the optimism of September, 1944, was not completely justified—thousands of these reserve officers came out of the cracks in the walls asking to be reinstated with seniority over the younger officers of the F.F.I. who had been out in the streets or the hills fighting. They were labeled derisively by the Resistance press, "LA PROMOTION DE NAPHTALINE"—the camphor-ball boys—because of the odor exuded by their uniforms.

Self-satisfied to begin with, in 1939, many of these reserve officers panicked in 1940 when they realized their inadequacy for a kind of war they had scarcely dreamed of. So a greater proportion of officers than of men failed in the crisis.

The shadow, or better the moldy smell, of this reserve system hovers over the officers' mess into which we are introduced in

"Despair Is Dead," the next piece. But you will note that even in this repugnant group three of the officers are good types. And although the story does not carry us beyond the summer of 1940, I would like to bet that by 1942 or 1943 several of their messmates, recovering from the apathy of shock, had joined the first three in the Resistance.

The story, like Debû-Bridel's, is from LES CHRONIQUES INTERDITES. Its author, who signed this one Santerre, is far better known as Vercors, which is the name of a plateau in the mountainous southeast of France. He was in ordinary life a painter named Jean Bruller, but it was as Vercors that he began writing. He made the nom de plume famous at the risk of his neck, and he has retained his second identity now that the war is over. He had been moderately well known, as an artist, for drawings with subjects like frustrated people walking down lonely streets pursued by a little yellow devil. But as the writer Vercors all France knows him. One of his other pseudonyms (for poetry) was Jean La Dolée. It was thought advisable for a writer as prolific as Bruller-Santerre-Vercors-La Dolée, under the occupation, to use several names lest the Gestapo concentrate on catching such a one-man fountainhead of propaganda. He finished this particular story on Christmas Day, 1942. By that time, as you will see from the first paragraphs, despair was indeed dead in France, although the most severe phase of the occupation had just begun. But the Allies had landed in North Africa, Montgomery was driving the Germans through Libya, and the Russians had already won a great victory at Stalingrad. Vercors and his colleagues were therefore certain that liberation was on the way.

Despair Is Dead *

by VERCORS (SANTERRE)

Even now I do not quite understand how the miracle happened —in me and in us all. Nor do I care to. Certain miracles seem

* From Chroniques Interdites.

very natural; I mean to say, very easy to accept. I accept them only too gladly. And this was such a one. I often think of it, and a soothing glow of happiness and tranquillity comes over me. I know that there must be some explanation. But why seek it? This semi-ignorance, I confess, suits my mood.

How quickly even the sharpest torments fade! Three months ago I longed for death. And I was not alone in this. As far as we could see, before us stretched only a foul abyss. Why live waiting only to be smothered in its slime? Oh, for some lonely rock, some desert island, far from the hateful turmoil of mankind!

How strange all that seems today when we have so many reasons for hope! But hope and hopelessness are neither reasoning nor reasonable states. Despair had us beat down. And what we had seen, what we still saw about us, it must be said, was not calculated to help us shake it off.

For not all of us were hopeless. Oh, no! In the mess, where the disaster had thrown together a dozen officers from all over France, with nothing in common except not having done any fighting, the dominant note was not hopelessness. Each officer was first of all concerned for his own welfare and, if only he himself could make his way, worried little about anything else. In that month of July, 1940, the Laval-Talleyrand myth was in vogue: after Waterloo, one rascal had in a few months rebuilt a mighty France; this time another rascal would do the same. It was only a matter of time.

There was one man in the mess whom I shall call Captain Randois. I didn't like him. Even before the defeat, everything about him had repelled me—his haughtiness, his royalist views, his contempt for the masses. I avoided him. I was afraid that in some word he might reveal the gloating that he must feel over the overthrow of the Republic and the triumph of tyranny. I could not have stood it without flaring up. My nerves were not very solid in those days. Fortunately he didn't talk much either. He ate in silence, his great hatchet beak bent over his plate. The idiotic political arguments that were the incessant accompaniment of our meals drew from him only a disdain that I should have considered insulting—if I had not taken the same attitude myself.

Our poor old rogue of a major, CONSEILLER GÉNÉRAL of the Department of the Gard, presided over these tilts, gloating over them with his big lifeless eyes. He resembled, by his accent and his face, a Raimu gone soggy, or one of the Fratellini clowns—the one who died, who used to hide his sardonic capers under the guise of a solemn family lawyer. He scrutinized the future uneasily, wondering what place his fatty unctuousness could find in the new scheme of things.

"Randois," he said one day, "did you see? Your Maurras has come out solidly for the Marshal." When he spoke, his words seemed to be drowned in a mouthful of water that one half expected to see dribble from his shapeless lips. "I am an old Radical Socialist myself, but when our country is in difficulties, one should forget one's convictions. Good for Maurras, I say; that's fine. What will our conquerors think of it, in your opinion?"

Captain Randois raised his nose from his plate; and his eyes, his cold, blue eyes that I had thought cruel, fixed themselves on me. Yes, on me and my neighbor, Captain Despérados; and he replied, "The krauts? They'll swallow us alive."

There was infinite sadness in his voice. I was surprised—by the look he had given us, even more than by his words. He was on our side; he had broken through to join up with us, the solitary and the silent. He had come to understand me better than I had him. Looking back, I see how lacking I was in perspicacity. For this mess was a replica of the entire country, where only the cowards, the schemers and the wicked still found words, and the others could answer only with their silence. You could recognize them by this silence. Randois had recognized us.

I was taciturn, but Captain Despérados was even more so. For he had taken part in "our" battle. In that shameful pretense at fighting which had taught us more, in the three days crowded between the two armistices, about the petty infamy of certain men covered with honors, than the experience of an entire lifetime. He had been through the cruel and shameless comedy from beginning to end. He had had in his hands, brazenly laid before him, the unspeakably filthy proofs that, in the blackest days of our disasters, a certain leader had been guided by no other thought than furthering his own sordid ambition. It was as if this experience had drained the color from Despérados' face—drained it forever. He

was pale and stiff, stiff from an old wound that kept him from
turning his head without turning his shoulders too; and even paler
from an old scar that divided his handsome face, like that of a
graying matador, and kept his right eye pried open as if he were
wearing a monocle. It gave him a sort of double expression,
shrewd and dominating. During all those weeks he never smiled.
I never knew him to laugh—but once.

Yes, it is almost an effort for me to understand today, as I did
then, that a man could be so mortally depressed that for weeks
on end it was impossible for him to smile. Yet I was the same way
myself. In our heavy boots we shuffled idly up and down the
single street of the sun-scorched village where we were billeted
after the armistice. We could not leave it. Our only choice lay
between two BISTROS, a garden bench that some kindly citizen
had put at our disposal, and our rooms. I had chosen my room. I
seldom left it. My depression battened on itself and flourished
on the deadly monotony of idleness. I imagine that Randois and
Despérados must have led the same intolerable sort of existence.
Perhaps that would explain the hellish silence that walled us in
in spite of ourselves.

My room was small. I had chosen it because it was. A single
narrow window high in the wall opened out over the roofs. Thus
it was a little like a cell—a cell that some girl had brightened by
her touch. I spent long hours cooped up in this tiny room, a
prisoner of these walls as I was of the thoughts, simple and horrible, that I could not put aside. I enjoyed feeling the walls close
in upon me as one enjoys prodding with a nervous finger a sore
spot on one's gums. It was certainly not good for my morale, yet,
on the whole, no worse than wandering from one BISTRO to another,
contemplating the moral let-down of my messmates.

I got so that I almost never left my room except to go to the
mess. I did not have far to go. The house where our mess was
installed was opposite my own, across a narrow alley strewn with
stones. The meals were lively and noisy. I found them lugubrious.
We were stuffed like Christmas geese. Our supply depots had not
yet been touched by the defeat. At every meal we had several
kinds of meat that an arrogant cook, holder of a diploma from an
army cook school, disguised with filthy tricked-out sauces that

had the mess gaping in admiration. One of our officers had discovered him and we congratulated ourselves on our acquisition.

A hearty good-fellowship reigned among these officers who tore each other's reputation to shreds as soon as they separated. They were all jealous of each other for one reason or another. The débâcle had not lessened their regard for the prestige of the military rank which they were soon to lose. Their rivalry was also on a more material plane. Some of them had quickly seen that there were profits to be made out of the general disorganization and the difficulty of checking up on their manipulations. The most hated man in the mess was the very one on whom, at meals, they all lavished the greatest signs of devoted respect—our Major-Fratellini, whose rank allowed him to get away with the most profitable swag. We knew that his attic was stocked with chocolate, macaroni and rice. I suppose I too ought to have hated the man. For some reason I never quite could. Perhaps it was because his knavery was such a part of his nature that it amounted to artlessness. Perhaps also because I knew—before he himself did—that he was going to die. He had arrived at such a stage of uremia that a fatal attack could not be far off. He fell asleep, not only after every meal, but after every dish and even, for a few seconds, with his fork in midair, in the midst of every mouthful. I saw the others laugh. It was pitiful and tragic. Good Lord, I thought, let him stock up his attic. Yet I blamed myself for my tolerance.

I was glad that Despérados was with me. I felt less lonely. Not that we had ever exchanged a single word of any importance; but sometimes when I felt my own heart swell with disgust at some new revelation of the sinister complacency of the men whom our country looked upon as leaders, I saw him turn his stiff neck toward me. Our glances met, and we felt better. That was as far as our confidences went.

One morning, however, he went a little further. When I came in to drink my cup of coffee, Despérados was sitting there alone with his own cup on the table before him. He was reading LE PETIT DAUPHINOIS. It was one of the first newspapers we had seen since that terrible fortnight. Suddenly he thrust it toward me in a silent fury, his thumbnail marking the editorial. While I read it, he kept his glowing eyes fixed on me. Yes, this article that he pointed out went beyond anything that I could have expected, beyond anything that even the most cynical contempt for humanity would have made me believe possible if I had not seen it. It served us up, no less (don't forget that it was for the first time), the burning of Joan of Arc, Saint Helena, and "perfidious Albion," in the same column and under the same signature where three weeks earlier the same man had told, with sadistic glee, of the thousands of Teuton savages whose mangled, bloated corpses the Somme and the Lys were washing down to the sea.

What could I have said? I said nothing. I tilted back my head and laughed. Despérados leaned his elbows on the table, rocked back a little in his chair, and laughed too, with a long, raucous laugh. It was not pleasant to hear, this hilarity without mirth in this dismal room, rancid with an odor of moldy bread. Then we were silent again. We left the table because it was time for us to go to a mass that was to be said in the little church for the souls of the men who had been killed in the war.

It might have been simple and moving. It was odious and grotesque. A young soldier-priest, pedantic and ambitious, and glad of the chance to show off his eloquence, preached the sermon. He dished us up an oration, empty and pompous, yet inept and unredeemed by any sign of talent.

I left the church more depressed than ever. I walked along dejectedly between Despérados and Randois, who had joined us. As we made our way down an alley overgrown with grass between two high garden walls, I could not quite hold in the pent-up sigh that ached in my chest. Randois turned his head toward me and gave me a sympathetic smile.

"It gets a man down," he said, and moving in between us, he took us each by an arm.

We went back to the mess. It was not yet time to eat, but for the first time, instead of each going his own way, we sat on the edge of the narrow sidewalk together, and once more silence weighed upon us.

It was then that the four little ducklings came along.

I knew them. Often I had watched one or another of these very comical balls of yellowish down, splashing about in the gutter or in the tiniest puddle without ever ceasing for a second to quack in its frail and innocent voice. More than once, the sight of them had helped me to pass a little more quickly, a little less wearily, a few moments of those interminable days. I was grateful to them for it.

This time all four of them came along in a single file, after the manner of ducks. They turned in from the main street, waddling and solemn, smart, vigilant and military. They never stopped quacking. They made one think of a gymnastic society on parade, carrying proudly their banner and singing earnestly and very off key. I said that they were four. The last one was younger—and smaller, and yellower and more of a baby chick, but determined not to be treated as such. He quacked louder than the others, managed by using his legs and the stubs of his wings, to keep up the regulation distance; but the pebbles that his elders managed to clear, clumsily but still with assurance, were for him so many hurdles where his eagerness came a cropper. There is absolutely no other way to express what happened to him than to say that he fell on his face. Every half-dozen steps he fell on his face again and got up and, scrambling to catch up, started off again with a martial and anxious air, quacking with unflagging profusion and punctuality—only to land on his beak in the dust. Thus they filed by, all four of them, according to the immutable order of duck parades since time began. Seldom have I seen anything quite so comical. Suddenly I heard myself begin to laugh, and Despérados too—but no longer with the ghastly laugh of that morning. This time Despérados' laughter was deep and wholesome, and pleasant to hear. And even Randois' dry chuckle was not unpleasing. The little ducks turned the corner of the lane, and we saw the tiniest one take one last belly-whopper before he passed out of our sight. The next we knew, there was Randois clutching our shoulders to help himself to his feet and, as he did so, he tightened his fingers affectionately but hard enough to hurt a little. "Chow time!" he said. "Come on, m' lads. We'll get out of this."

It happened that that was exactly what I was thinking: "We'll get out of this." Oh, it would not be true to say that I thought it in exactly those words. I didn't—any more than I actually thought of the centuries, even more somber than the very ominous period that loomed before us, when it had required the desperate courage and superhuman determination of a handful of monks, in a world full of murder and pillaging, fanatic ignorance and triumphant cruelty, to pass down a flickering light from hand to hand through almost a thousand years. Nor did I actually THINK that such a task made it worth while to live if that were to be OUR destiny, our only duty henceforth. No, my thought did not take so precise a form; but it was like seeing the outside of a book that one knows well.

How did those four little ducks lead us suddenly to understand that our despair was wrongheaded and sterile? I do not know. Today, as I am writing these lines, I might feel tempted to invent some satisfying and facile symbolism. Perhaps I should not be wrong. Perhaps, as a matter of fact, I did unconsciously think of the other baby ducks who, even in those days, must have paraded just as comically before the eyes of the first Christians—who had even more reason than we for believing that all was lost. Perhaps I considered that those four ducklings, so swashbuckling and artless, were an effective parody of both the worst traits of the mass of humanity and the best that is in us: and that it was worth while to live because we could hope some day to wipe out that worst and see that best flourish again. Perhaps I thought all this. But it is rather more likely that it is pure rationalization. The truth is, I prefer the mystery. This much I know: I owe it to these little ducks, so perky, martial, touching and ridiculous that, in the darkest hour of a black day, I suddenly felt despair slip from my shoulders like too heavy a cloak. That is enough. I shall never forget it.

PART TWO

The Beginnings of Resistance

The First Call to Arms

We will never know how many Frenchmen, in how many different parts of France, said at approximately the same time, like Randois—"Come on, guys! We'll get out of this," or only said it to themselves. Nor can we award the honor of having been the very first Randois. But the resurgence of France began at the precise second that the first Randois said it for the first time.

The most illustrious claimant of the honor of having been the first Randois of France is of course, General Charles de Gaulle, who on June 18, 1940, not many hours after Marshal Pétain had said he was requesting an armistice, spoke from London to give Pétain the lie. The speech, printed in the form of a poster, has become so familiar that anybody who has been in France can identify it by the shape of the printed paragraphs. It is a historic utterance and a great one, and it heartened millions of French men and women between 1940 and 1944. But I wonder how many it convinced? De Gaulle was already outside of France. "We'll get out of this," is a conviction that must come from within. I do not think De Gaulle created the thousands of Randois, who in turn created the Resistance. Rather, the Randois created the Resistance, which in turn adopted De Gaulle as a symbol. It was his reward for not having despaired of the Republic, and he proved that he merited it by standing up for the Republic against the Foreign Office and the State Department. This is the speech that French school children will be memorizing for several centuries to come:

To All Frenchmen

FRANCE HAS LOST A BATTLE!

BUT FRANCE HAS NOT LOST THE WAR!

The men who happen to head the government may have capitulated, yielding to panic, forgetting honor, delivering the land over to servitude. Yet nothing is lost!

Nothing is lost because this war is a world war. In the free universe, tremendous forces have not yet made themselves felt. Some day these forces will crush the enemy. On that day, France must be present at her victory. Then, she will recover her liberty and her greatness. Such is my aim, my only aim!

This is why I invite all Frenchmen, wherever they may be, to join me in action, in sacrifice, and in hope.

Our country is in mortal peril. Let us all fight to save her.

VIVE LA FRANCE!

General de Gaulle

Within a period of months after the armistice, thousands of French soldiers escaped from German prison camps. The Germans had naturally made no preparations for handling nearly two million prisoners acquired in one swoop. Pétain by the armistice terms had turned over to the Germans a whole block of armies still capable of resistance, in addition to the hundreds of thousands the invaders had already scooped in.

The means they adapted for transporting their human catch were summary and brutal—men were herded along the roads on foot or packed into any available vehicles, and slept in improvised stockades. But they were necessarily inefficient. A great many prisoners got away, and a Frenchman who evaded his immediate guards while he was still in France was virtually safe from recapture. He would discard his uniform, acquire civilian clothes, and simply walk on home. The German police system was not as yet established in France; there was nobody to check on the escaped soldier after he reached his native place, even if it was within the Occupied Zone.

The Germans were interested in saving the French harvest in 1940, since they proposed to remove a large part of it to the Reich. Also they wished to leave enough food in France to keep her people quiet until the conquest of Britain. They therefore kept large numbers of French prisoners in the eastern departments even through late summer and early autumn, and allowed them to work on farms. During this period the escapes continued. After the prisoners had been removed to Germany escapes became harder and less frequent.

Escaped prisoners played a great collective rôle during the Resistance; a surprising number of the leaders who emerged had been in the 1940 stockades. This is not difficult to understand. It took initiative and nerve to escape, since the prisoner risked at least the guards' bullets. More, the prisoner was completely disillusioned with the Germans. He had seen them at their most brutal and sergeantesque, and could not be taken in by their "correct" attitude toward the civilian population, or by their professions that they wanted to set up a European brotherhood. And he could never feel completely safe, no matter how well he merged in the daily life of his home town. There was always a possibility he might be betrayed and recaptured; the possibility worried him more as the Germans tightened their hold on local government. So he was a no-compromise man from the start.

Great numbers of people also began their careers of resistance by spontaneously helping their escaped countrymen. It was for a while the only thing they could do.

In Lorraine, on the border between the Reich and France, it began in July, 1940. "To receive and shelter escaped prisoners, and even, at first, to find food and civilian clothes for them (while it was still simple to purchase things at shops) was easy. But an organization was needed to guide them on their way home," the leader of Lorraine, a Resistance group in Nancy, has written. "Building up contacts in towns along the route was a delicate job. When it had been accomplished, the skeleton of a provincial Resistance organization was in being." The Nancy group passed on 6,781 prisoners in a year and a half. The hamlet of Champagne-sur-Loue, in the Jura Department, four miles from the "line of demarcation" between the frontier zone under German military government and Vichy France, "handled" 150 escaping prisoners every night, slipping them across the line. The population of Champagne-sur-Loue was 145.

George Adam, the author of this story of one of those harvest-time escapes (his own), was thirty-two years old in 1940. Born in Belgium, he was a naturalized French citizen and before the war had been a reporter on the newspaper CE SOIR. He looks about thirty now. A chipper, incorrigibly young man, he wears Harold Lloyd glasses and shiny black hair à l'AMERICAIN, serves as managing editor of LETTRES FRANÇAISES, and is one of the few French writing men who gets practical things done fast. That, he explains, is the Belgian in him. This practical quality was to prove of great value to one sector of the Resistance.

"At Liberty's Call" is a part of a longer novel, THE COMPELLING SWORD, written during the years of occupation. The section of this longer work known as "At Liberty's Call" was published "under the oppression" by the secret EDITIONS DE MINUIT. It was signed Hainaut, Adam's Resistance name.

At Liberty's Call

by GEORGE ADAM (HAINAUT)

All afternoon Antoine loitered around the entrance to the camp. When he was tired he leaned against a tree and watched the continual come and go of the interpreters between the French company office and the German headquarters. About four o'clock, a heavy truck driven by two civilians came through the gate and headed toward the cook huts. As it went by, Antoine noticed that the driver's cab had high doors. By squatting on the floor a man could hide beside the chauffeur. Yes, but how could he know the chauffeur would enter into the scheme? Already the truck was coming back. The German sentry held the gate open to let it pass. By supper time nothing had happened. After the meal Ferrand came up to him.

"We haven't seen anything of you all day."

"No. I've got a little headache. I think I'll go to bed."

Ferrand took the hint. "All right. I'll be off then."

Antoine undid the strap of the musette bag which he had fitted into the small of his back under his overcoat. It contained only the duck pants rolled into a tight roll. As it had the night before, it took Antoine hours to get to sleep.

The next morning found him back at his position by the camp gate, between the office and German headquarters. At noon, he swallowed his soup hurriedly and returned to his post again. About two o'clock he saw an interpreter come out of the guard house, followed by a German corporal. "A work detail of thirty men!" he heard the interpreter call out to the clerks in the French office.

Antoine glanced at the sleeves of his coat. He had ripped off his sergeant's stripes with his pocket knife. He picked out a piece of gold thread that still remained in the cloth. Nothing distinguished him now from a private except two narrow traces lighter than the rest of the khaki cloth. A top sergeant had started at double time toward the barracks on the other side of the parade ground.

Shortly he came back, a group of prisoners, their hands in their pockets, shuffling listlessly at his heels. It was a gray sort of day; the low sky was heavy with rain.

"Come on! Let's get going!" the interpreter shouted. "We're ten men shy. Hey, you over there, come here. Yes, you. . . . Nine more."

Antoine eased himself away from the tree he was leaning against and fell in at the end of the line. He unbuttoned his overcoat and put his hands in his pants pockets. It revealed his gray sweater, but the musette bag on his back was completely hidden by the fullness of the coat. "Now, if only they don't search us at the gate," he thought. More prisoners had fallen in behind him. A German soldier, his tommy-gun on a sling under his arm, was getting impatient.

"Three more!" the interpreter bellowed.

Then another German soldier began to count. "DREI . . . SECHS . . . ZWÖLF . . . EIN-UND-ZWANZIG . . . DREIZEHN! STIMMT! . . . ALLEZ, ALLEZ, MARCHEZ!"

The little column left the camp, German soldiers heading the way, German soldiers on their flanks, and two German soldiers bringing up the rear, their thumbs through the slings of their guns. The time to unsling the gun, cock it and aim would give a man a start of a hundred yards or so, and at that distance it takes a really crack shot to hit a man running at full tilt; but the street was full of German soldiers. You met them in groups of two or three at a time. Not a chance! Duck into the open door of a house perhaps and bolt for the back yard? Yes, but then there's the garden wall, and I'm trapped like a rat!

There are a lot of civilians in the streets of Bar-le-Duc. They hardly ever turn their heads to look at the detail of prisoners. There are women and children and old men. Once in a while, one or another of the prisoners calls out a joyous BONJOUR to a passer-by. "I join work details for a chance to do that," said one of the prisoners at Antoine's side. "Just to see people. It cheers a man up."

Antoine did not even think how strange it was that there should be a town with civilians, young women, and shops in it. Yet it was months since he had seen a city street. His hobnailed boots skidded on the paving stones; he was no longer used to paved streets. "I wonder where they're taking us to work," someone behind him said.

At the end of the street was the railroad station. They headed for it. A gate, guarded by a sentinel, opened to admit them. They were in the freight yards. Behind a sort of palisade made of old railroad ties driven side by side vertically into the earth, was a street.

What a lot of cars there were! And Germans all over the place. Beside a shed, a group of infantrymen in heavy boots and helmets, their knapsacks at their feet, were talking and smoking. What a racket those babies could make! The fatigue detail marched between two lines of freight cars and came out at the end of a raised loading platform. They climbed up on it. Detail, halt! Alongside was a train of flatcars. Further on, beyond the train were tracks, more tracks, a passenger train with soldiers leaning out the windows, and civilians looking at them. The platform was jammed with old 75s all falling to pieces.

"Here," the intepreter said. "You're to load these cannon onto the flatcars."

Languidly they set to work. They laid boards across for gangplanks. The cannons rolled slowly and came to a stop. With ropes and pieces of baling wire, the wheels were made fast to the stanchions of the cars.

"Say, you," the interpreter said, grabbing Antoine's arm, "go get some chocks over there." He pointed to where some prisoners with a saw were cutting a beam into triangular pieces. A German soldier, his rifle between his knees, was looking on.

Antoine went toward them. It was about twenty yards. He passed close to the freight cars; some of them were open. With luck he might be able to hide in one of them. Yes, but then what? When the fatigue detail was over, there would be a roll call. Someone missing. If he was still in the freight yard, they would find him easily.

One of the prisoners loaded the chocks into his arms. They had a good smell of newly cut wood. It made an awkward load to carry, but it was not very heavy. Antoine started back toward the platform where the others were waiting for the chocks. However, instead of taking the same route, he followed the track. Suddenly he found himself between two uncoupled trains of cars. Parallel to the right of way there was a paved road. On his right was a train with locked carriages; on the left little wheelbarrows, their shafts pointed skyward, were lined up between the tar-painted palisade of ties and the paved road beyond. He continued on, slowly and naturally, waiting for the moment when the German soldier guarding the men who were sawing should yell at him. Nobody yelled. Antoine turned his head slightly and looked over his shoulder. He saw nothing but the cars that hid him from the sawing detail, because the track curved and the cars were between them now. He kept on walking, still carrying the chocks. Slowly and naturally. He had gone perhaps two or three hundred yards. At his left, the barrows were spaced out, and he was only a couple of steps from the high, tarred palisade. On the other side, the street no longer followed the barrier. In the space that widened out between the palisade and the street, two houses raised their leprous walls. Between the houses and the palisade were a courtyard, two courtyards, a small garden and a bigger one. Antoine had almost reached the limit of the freight yard. The black shining rails ran under a high foot-bridge that crossed the tracks. At that moment a woman, two men and some little girls were crossing the bridge. Look, there, to the left, the ties were not planted so close together; a couple of feet from the ground there was room to squeeze between them. And just beyond was a garden with trees and bushes. If he were to drop the chocks and . . .

He heard a sound behind him. He edged slowly away from the opening in the palisade and very slowly turned around. From between two cars, almost at the end of the yard, a German soldier emerged. He had a board in his hand. Antoine went up to him, the soldier waited for him to approach. "Lost," Antoine explained to him. "Lost."

The German looked at him and tried to understand. "JA, JA," he said at last. He made a sign for Antoine to follow him. Behind a car, he picked up a bicycle.

His hobnails scraping the pavement, Antoine kept abreast of him. In no time at all, they were back where the men were sawing chocks. The soldier got astride his bicycle and, his board in one hand, steering his bicycle with the other, went toward the exit. He gave Antoine a broad smile as he rode away.

Missed it! Missed it completely!

And, back on the platform where the loading was still going on, the interpreter was going to be sore because he had taken a hell of a while getting those chocks! But the interpreter wasn't sore. In the meanwhile another prisoner had been sent to get some chocks. So Antoine dropped his chocks beside the platform and, as if it were the most natural thing in the world, wandered back to the men who were sawing them.

The German guard was visibly bored. You could see that he would like to take the saw and get some exercise himself. Antoine waited for the beam to be cut up into triangular blocks. When he had his load in his arms, he backed slowly away. Nobody paid any more attention to him.

Then, without hesitation, he started off on the same route that he had taken before, between the rows of cars. Once more he was on the paving between the train and the barrows with their handles pointing skyward. Then the barrows were spaced out, and the paved road ran alongside the tar-painted palisade. Antoine kept going, slowly and naturally, like any prisoner working reluctantly at a job. He arrived at the same point that he had reached before. For a moment he watched the rails slipping under the foot-bridge. Now he was opposite the opening in the palisade.

He stooped and carefully deposited the chocks on the russet grass beside the tracks. Still stooping, he raised his head. On the foot-bridge, two women had stopped. They were looking at him. One of them was pointing at him. The idiot! She was pointing at him. Still stooping, Antoine angrily waved at them to move on. As if at that distance they could understand what he was gesturing about! In one bound he cleared the distance from the spot where the chocks lay scattered on the sere grass to the breach in the palisade. He squeezed through. Another bound and he was in the garden. He made for a tool shed. Hell! it was locked. There was a low wall a couple of feet high. Still crouching, he put his hands on the top and vaulted. God damn! the garden was built on a terrace. It was at least ten feet from the top of the wall down to the vegetable patch where his feet sank heavily into the earth. The time to get up and look around and—hup! There was a little shed on the other side. He sprang into it.

The shed was jammed with tools, wheelbarrows and kegs. At the level of his eyes was a small window barred with chicken wire, but he could not see the railroad yard because of two trees and the wall. I've got an hour and a half, two hours before they notice anything. Until the detail's job is done. The overcoat first. The musette bag. The puttees. Hell! got to take off my boots; the pants will never go over them. Bastardly pants. Well, here goes. The boots first, the pants. And the other pair in the musette bag all wrinkled up. Now to put the boots on again. There!

The next thing is to get out of this yard—through the house. Nobody in that kitchen window anyway. If only I don't run into some woman who will take me for a burglar and start yelling. I'll come right out with it: "I'm a prisoner, trying to . . ." Here's hoping she won't start screaming her head off. The kitchen door isn't locked. Not a soul. A long hallway with a floor of black and white tiles. No use trying to be quiet with these hobnails. Still not a soul. The front door. The knob turns. The door is going to open. If only she is not on the other side of it, to start screaming. The door is open. There is nobody on the doorstep.

The street is there, quiet and calm. To the left is the railroad station. I'll take the right then. But that leads toward the center of the town. I'll cross the foot-bridge. After that it ought to be the country.

All right, hands in your pockets. And above all, don't run. Don't run. Walk naturally. Don't run. Don't . . .

Although he kept telling himself that it was silly to give a thought to such minor considerations, Antoine could not help thinking of the warm overcoat that he had left in the shed in the garden near the station. The escape had gone off without any trouble at all. He hadn't even felt any fear. Already the fleeting instants were beginning to take on the definite shape that they would have henceforth in his memory: a corridor black with gloom, at the end of which rose the dazzling sun of liberty. But before arriving at it, before earning it, there would be many more trials to undergo: the long journeys in the forest, the food problem. . . .

His courage running low, Antoine leaned against a tree. He felt the first stirring of hunger deep within him. Dressed only in the duck pants and sweater, he shivered. The wintery silence of the forest conjured up menacing phantoms in this twilight glistening with rain drops as sharp as needles. Lost among these stark branches of oaks, poplars and elms, without warm clothes and with no food to put strength into his wobbling legs, without map or compass, everything seemed to bristle with obstacles that in his daydreams back in the camp had seemed so easy to overcome. In the first hours, he had pushed on straight ahead, guided by a single idea—to get away as fast as he could from the city and frequented roads where he might run into a patrol. He clenched his fists in his pockets and tried to hide his anxiety, shortness of breath and the shifty, furtive look he felt he must have. He had succeeded. The few people he had passed had scarcely given a second glance at this man walking right along, the collar of his sweater turned up to his ears. His boots sounded on the wet macadam. Between its double border of trees, the road wound peacefully across the newly plowed fields.

Suddenly alarm sent his heart to his throat. His mouth filled with a sickening flow of saliva. The hoarse voice of a klaxon sounded behind him. He glanced over his shoulder. God! A gray car! That does it: it's all up with me. A dozen yards further on, the car slowed down. It stopped at the edge of the road. Nothing to do but brazen it out. I can't stop. Look surprised if they speak to me. Ten yards can be long when the whole weight of a captivity, lifted for a moment, suddenly drags at your legs, like the leaden soles of a diver emerging from the sea. Finally he came abreast of the stopped car. Out of the corner of his eye, he saw two officers inside, bent over an outspread map. It's silly, my heart is pounding as if I had committed a crime. They are going to yell at me to stop. What shall I tell them? I'm caught. But the car was on its way again, the motor purring cheerfully. With a smooth sound of shifting gears, it shot by the fugitive and disappeared around a curve.

Antoine stopped a moment to laugh nervously at the shock he

had felt. For the first time since his escape from the station he felt how greatly his situation had changed. HE WAS FREE. Free! There would be no mess call at six o'clock, no curfew at nine, and no roll call tomorrow morning. When he met a German soldier, he would no longer feel humiliated.

But to continue walking along the main roads was to put his head in the lion's mouth. At the first dirt cross-roads that he came upon, he turned off to the left. He made a wide detour to avoid a village and came to the fringe of a forest. Resolutely he plunged into it, hoping to keep his bearings and cross the forest in an unwavering line toward the west. He left the dirt road, took one path and then another. It was a labyrinth of paths. Through the stripped branches the sky looked as if it were hung with dirty white rags. When night fell, not a star would be visible. Such notions of orientation as he remembered from the infantry field manual turned out to be woefully inadequate. A dank silence stuck to the rotting tree trunks, the moss and the grass. Antoine began to understand that he must get out of the forest before nightfall and ask for help at some farmhouse. Beside a brook he stopped to drink a swallow of icy, insipid water from the hollow of his hand. Little by little, he felt hunger taking hold.

More paths. Wood roads whose ruts were filled with muddy water. Still more paths. And finally a wide prairie like a vast lake, still green in the middle of the forest. Antoine followed the edge of the meadow for an hour and finally came upon a sunken road. Wearily he sat down on the bank beside it.

He shivered. Come on, too much time lost already; he must keep going. But as he was about to get to his feet, he pricked up his ears. Close at hand, a man's voice suddenly rang out. "Gee! Gee!"

With one leap, Antoine plunged into the thicket. On the sunken road two horses shortly appeared. A man, enveloped like some sylvan deity in the faint steam that rose from their shining hides, walked behind the powerful animals. Squatting under the bushes, Antoine watched him draw near. With a single glance at his stubble-covered cheeks and little mustache, Antoine knew him for what he was. His mind was made up. Pushing aside the branches he jumped down into the road. The man gave a start, stopped his horses with a sonorous "Whoa!", and waited.

"Hey, say . . ." Antoine began.

"Yes?" the peasant said unperturbed. He was short and stocky. His right hand gripped a long, supple whip. With his other hand he pushed his cap back on his head.

"Say," Antoine went on, "am I still far from the road?"

"The road? Which road?"

Antoine made a vague gesture. The man looked him squarely in the face, and the ghost of a smile flickered under the short gray mustache.

"You wouldn't be . . ." he began slowly.

"Yes," Antoine said timidly, nodding his head.

"Well, now! You should have said so right away. So you gave them the slip? Good for you! And where are you headed for?" (He used the familiar "TU" instead of "VOUS.")

Antoine shrugged his shoulders. He felt suddenly weak, defenseless, incapable of expressing the unaccountable dejection that had come over him, and ashamed to admit that he was hungry and cold, and dreaded spending the night outdoors dressed as lightly as he was. The man still looked at him in silence. His eyes glazed with the strain of thinking.

"Look," he said at last. "Night is coming on. You must be hungry. You can't stay outdoors. Here's what we'll do. I'll go home first. In fifteen, twenty minutes, you start out. This road will take you to the national highway. Cross it. On the other side, you'll see a village at the end of a dirt road. Don't take that road. Follow the highway two or three hundred yards. Then take a path to the right that goes down toward the brook. Cross the bridge at the foot of a stony road. You'll see the church in front of your nose. Stand beside the road and wait. If you hear anybody coming, hide. When it gets good and dark, I'll come fetch you. I'll whistle twice—like this. . . . I'll take you to the farm and give you some grub and a bed. After supper, we'll talk things over."

The horses stood quietly, their great heads drooping. Their velvet eyes gleamed behind the blinkers. From time to time there was a metallic click of the bits as one of them nuzzled against the other.

"I can't take you there directly, you understand. First place, there are the neighbors. People are suspicious in a small village. They'd start talking if they saw me with a stranger. Then, I've got kids in the house. Tomorrow at school they wouldn't find anything better to do than blab the whole story. So we'd better wait till they're through supper. All right?"

"Yes," Antoine said, his heart swelling with gratitude.

"Good," the man said, "I'll be going. See you soon."

He touched the steaming croups of his horses with the whip. "Gee! Gee!" Antoine sat at the foot of a tree to wait.

Some ten kilometers after Bar-le-Duc, the Ornain flows through a narrow plain hemmed in by low hills. At the right of the river one of these hills, a fairly steep one, is crowned by a plateau from whence there is a view of the sad and gentle countryside of the Meuse. Above the sinuous silvery thread of the river, hidden among trees is a village consisting of a few houses and a rather ugly church with a square tower. The village is transected by two streets, of which one is merely the road connecting the national highway with another village between the canal and the railroad.

The Météniers own one of the three farms among which the land of the plateau and the valley is divided. Their property is assuredly the richest in the village.

It was not until he had become, quite recently, proprietor of his own farm that Louis Méténier had ever given much thought to his place in the world and begun to formulate rules of conduct that already existed in his mind, in a confused and general way, so that they formed a sort of rudimentary philosophy whose precepts were to take on more shape as he grew older. This cogitation went on imperceptibly. Méténier never suspected that thought could dwell in him. If he had been more educated, more accustomed to using words, he would have explained that it came about through the force of circumstances, during the long hours of working by himself perhaps, or when, on the seat of the McCormick reaper, his body shaken by the vibration, absorbed in steering the team over the golden flank of the wheatfield, he allowed one corner in his brain to mull mysteriously over a small stock of simple ideas.

Thus, the ideas of Louis Méténier were not limited to his

practical knowledge, extensive and long to acquire as it was, of the secrets of his craft. To know exactly at what moment of the year the hay or the wheat must be cut; keep a general idea of the pace of the season; choose the propitious day to begin sowing or reaping; and so manage to bring a few more wagonloads into the barn—all this is a part of the great gamble against Earth and Weather that is the life of a shrewd farmer.

With his wife or with Durbec, who had been his buddy in 1914, he often discussed all these details and many another too, in the course of those slow, thorough conversations in which one is not afraid to repeat the same phrases in order to be sure that they reflect the truth exactly. But it often happened that, after having explained to Durbec his views on the price of that year's calves, he found himself involved in considerations as far from his subject as they were fascinating.

Méténier, unlike Mathilde, his wife, who had filled out with age, was small and wiry. Physically he was almost the same man as the twenty-year-old-infantryman, whose photograph—retouched with crayon—hung on one of the panels of the dining room (that was never used for dining). He had a firm, clear voice that became shrill when he was excited. At these times, even if his listener agreed with him, he would repeat automatically the last phrase that he had said. "At that price a hundredweight, it doesn't pay for your work . . . it doesn't pay for your work."

The farmyard, surrounded by buildings, some of which had recently been rebuilt, was a spacious one. Its latticed doors opened onto both the streets of Vouzy. The yard itself constituted a sort of additional village street in which ducks and chickens quacked and squawked. Louis Méténier had acquired the house, and the stables and barns that went with it, only recently. Before that there had been a long job to attend to, a job that had spread out over fifteen years. A job that had amounted to the gradual realization of the secret dreams and the general direction of the farmer's life: raising three children, saving up capital, buying cows, horses, and agricultural machines. Maurice, his oldest son, had just passed his school diploma and it was on a farm belonging to his own family that he had begun following in his father's footsteps.

Including Mathilde, that made five pairs of hands—enough to handle forty hectares of wheat, oats, beets and potatoes—but just enough. Méténier never had any spare time on his hands. After the soup at noon, he might sprawl for a moment on a pile of hay in the barn; but hardly had he relaxed before he was up on his feet again, fidgeting to be at work. He never got away from his work. You should see him in summer urging his horses on, from the seat of the reaper. If the field was not finished when noon came, he preferred to let the soup wait and get cold. "What is done is finished with." Sunday, after mass, he would stroll across the barnyard, restless in his leisure. Often he would sneak out and harness the horses to "get in a couple of licks" in the wheatfield.

In August, 1939, he had thought that he was going to be called up again, and he would have gone without too much grumbling, though he was far from being fool enough to like war and all the servitudes of military life. HIS job henceforth, his only function in life, was to cultivate his land. Yet at the memory of Verdun or the Chemin-des-Dames his chest swelled with a feeling of nostalgia. Not that he had any warrior soul; but since the cruel years of his youth he had learned that it was sometimes necessary to give material expression to the real and living bond that united him to the multiple reality of his country. If he had attempted to explain this feeling, nebulous as it often was in his mind, it would have given a sudden insight into the value that he attached to his liberty, to his rights as a citizen, to the greatness of France— realities of which he seldom thought, but which were, nevertheless, almost as much a part of himself as his fields, his horses or his crops.

But because of his three children he had not been mobilized after all. He had continued his work until the first days of June, but he was never very satisfied with himself during those months that the war lasted. The news that he gleaned over the radio or from the columns of LA CROIX MEUSIENNE worried him. It sometimes occurred to him to wonder if there were not dark forces secretly at work within the country itself, trying to undermine the will to win the war.

The débâcle came at the moment when the wheat was ripening and it was time to harvest the hay.

"Leave the farm? We had never thought of it! We'd seen so many of them going by, you see—all the refugees from the Ardennes or Belgium. We decided, my wife and I, to stay put, no matter what. Hein, Mathilde?"

Her arms crossed over her voluminous bosom, standing before the black stove—a little round opening in the door reddened with the dying glow as the wood burned out in the grate—the farmwife nodded her head.

A lamp with a pink shade hung from the ceiling and lit up the oilcloth of the table, the brick-red tiles of the floor and the bench where Maurice, the oldest of the children, sat listening to his father retell the days of the exodus. The farmer had kept his cap on his head. Antoine pushed back his plate. A welcome warmth crept gradually into his legs. A peasant soup, a thick slice of salt pork with potatoes and two glasses of a sharp tangy wine—what a wonderful meal! A meal the like of which he had never even dreamed of in the days of his captivity! A little drowsy with so much unaccustomed food, he began to reflect that tomorrow he would have to be off, avoiding main roads, being careful about taking strangers into his confidence. What of it? Never again would he feel alone, a stranger in his own country, a hunted animal hedged in by forests murky with November mists and menacing shadows.

When Méténier had pushed him into the kitchen, the pitying look that the farm woman gave him had embarrassed Antoine at first. They had seated him at the table, put a plate and a glass before him. "We have eaten already, before we put the young ones to bed. Go ahead, eat! Don't be bashful; we know you are hungry. Now then, don't let me catch you leaving a bit of it!" The gruff cordiality had moved him almost to tears. His immediately saying TU instead of the formal VOUS was the symbol of their brotherhood.

"I was down in the meadow—the one you came across—loading a wagon with hay. The first I knew, there was Mathilde hollering down to me, 'The mayor says we've got to evacuate the village!' I finished loading the hay just the same. I came back to the barn and we unloaded it, too. I wasn't going to lose that hay. Then we loaded up, the whole rack full. The droves of folks that had been going by all night on the road in front of the house! And was it raining! All night long, right up till morning, you could hear them swearing—'NOM DE DIEU!' 'Hey, keep moving!' Then it cleared up. So I hurried to get the hay in. We left in the early afternoon."

From the sea to the Rhine there stretched a strip of land from which all life had ebbed. It was like a sandy beach, naked and deserted, but strewn with black shingle, scorched by a hail of bullets. A shifting beach. For the wave approached at the same time that the dry land withdrew. And all this took place in a few days, as if this belt of silence and nakedness had always existed between the implacable advance and the slow withdrawal.

This zone cut across fields where the wheat was already high, across meadows where abandoned cows were lowing. It crossed roads whose black-top was cracking in the sun, ditches where a dead horse, its four legs stiff in the air, lay bloating. It flowed down over hills, and into ravines full of springs and flowers. It overwhelmed villages whose streets were quieter now in broad daylight than during the summer nights, white beneath the moon, when at least the snore of some sleeper might be heard from some open window. It wound the length of Picardy, across the north of Champagne, and through Lorraine, and even cut into the Ile-de-France. Sometimes it was several kilometers wide, sometimes hardly a hundred meters separated its edges.

Wide or narrow, the same silence dwelt there. Stray dogs, their tails drooping, slunk along the walls of houses whose doors stood ajar. They would trot a little way through the alfalfa and clover, but suddenly they stopped short and, ears pointed toward the vast forlorn summer sky, began to howl. The highways and dirt roads, even the forest paths, seemed to have existed throughout eternity, as if there had never been automobiles, wagons and carts to justify their existence. In the fields, it might have been Sunday. Yet there was something in the air that said that the bells in the steeple on the horizon would not ring for mass or vespers for a long time to come. So it was not Sunday. There were no more Sundays, or weekdays either. There was only silence. For one night or two days.

Strange odds and ends littered the earth. They belonged already to the shapeless destiny of inanimate things. Along the edges of the roads especially. Ripped handbags from which a sock, a pantie, a pad of writing paper escaped, guns still loaded with cartridges, a shovel, a heap of shovels, a light truck tipped up on two wheels, the hood of the motor lifted, a neat pile of 75 shells already eaten with rust beneath the branches. At the edge of a wheatfield were carefully laid a periscope-case in pigskin, a pair of heavy wire-cutters, a gas mask, a Lebel rifle, model 715, a bayonet and two magazines—as if the person who had laid them there intended to come back for them later. In the woods, at the entrances of dugouts roofed with logs, the earth was caving in. The straw had begun to rot around the clumps of bushes. A mattress, abandoned as too bulky, and swollen by the last rain, was ready to burst.

Here and there, as if on an island that the flood had missed, a few men, hollow-cheeked, unshaved and grimy, their eyes agleam with weariness, lingered patiently beside a machine gun. At a crossroads, beside a patch of woods, behind a hedge, they waited, finger on the trigger—an hour, a day. Suddenly, because something stirred in the distance, because there was a glint of metal in the sunshine, through the leaves, they fired. They fired in quick, irritable volleys. They fired, they fired. Still one magazine; it's the last. Je-sus! it's all up with us. They're pouring it in from every side. We'd better beat it if we don't want to be cut off. It was true, the Germans were firing back. The bullets ricocheted on the road, slashed the branches, smacked against the wall.

In another place a great beetle ambles up a road, spitting and rumbling, its antennae feeling before it. It is alone. The big apple trees along the edges of the road spatter it with sun and shade. Its shell gives out a metallic rattle, and the bug lurches from side to side, unsteady on its legs of rubber and chains. The men lie in wait for it, their fingers on the trigger. Behind a blind of leaves a sort of blunderbuss with a funnel-shaped muzzle, like those used by the bandits of Calabria, lies dull and black. The silence is hardly troubled by the three or four shots. The beetle slumps, its armor pierced through and through. But it has had time to lower its antennae and spit—once, twice. The leafy blind is pulverized. The island is wiped out. Only a few fragments attest its momentary existence: the beetle's carcass, toppled into the ditch, the blunderbuss with its funnel-like muzzle, a few huddled bodies. The men take to their heels, stooping as they run. Already other beetles are appearing on the road, under the apple trees.

And yet life began again.

The tide before which the desert zone retreated and which drove it ever toward the South, gnawed at its edges and submerged it more and more. It was a race between the two shores, between the wave and the dry land. The men on the rare islands, their eyes gleaming with weariness, counted for less and less. In the beginning, when it still covered only Picardy, Champagne and Lorraine, the zone was wide: silence and solitude thickened over kilometers of ground under the summer sun. As it drifted toward the South, it grew thinner. At first its southern fringe was groups of men in khaki, armored cars, batteries of 75s, weapons-carriers. The further the zone withdrew toward the South, cutting France in two from the sea to the Rhine, the more these groups mingled with civilians. Soon there were as many wagons loaded with furniture and mattresses as there were field kitchens; as many cows, goats and Percherons as motorcycles; as many old women burdened with packages or young women carrying babies as there were men dragging their rifles by the muzzles.

Now the last farm wagon, the driver lashing his horse, was scarcely over the horizon toward the South, before the first of the enormous beetles appeared on the road. They lurched between the apple trees; and the further the zone spread toward the South, the faster the monstrous insects could move. They caught up with the last wagon loaded to the canvas top with chairs, bird cages, tables, valises and invalid grandmothers. They lunged into the convoy of refugees, splitting it in two and forcing it off into the ditches.

The man who looked over his shoulder, his mustache grazing the broadcloth of his coat, slackened the reins as he saw them thunder up behind him and heard the clatter of their armor. It isn't worth while going any further; they have caught up with us. The man helps his wife down from the wagon and hitches his horses at the edge of the road. He sits down in the field, his legs

stretched straight before him, and begins to eat, watching the
steel beetles rumble by. Thus, little by little, the convoy came to
a halt. The zone of silence and solitude was no more.

The surrey loaded to the awning, the hay-rick covered with
furniture and mattresses, the wheelbarrow full of valises, the baby
carriage filled with a three-year-old child, a loaf of bread and
bottles of wine, do an about face and retrace their steps toward
the North. They encounter armored motorcycles, bicyclists with
tricolor badges on their helmets, high-wheeled trucks crammed
with FELDGRAU uniforms. They leave them the middle of the
road. Temporarily at least, let them push on toward the South, as
fast and as numerous as they wish. We are on our way back to
our homes in the North.

The villages are no longer deserted. They are overflowing with
FELDGRAU uniforms. On the walls, these new bills have been
posted: "DESERTED POPULATIONS, HAVE CONFIDENCE IN THE GERMAN
SOLDIER!" The man who is leading his horses and who has stopped
for a moment to read the bills, spits on the ground in a gesture
of incredulity and scorn, tugs at the halter and moves on. He is
going back to the North. There is no more evacuated zone.

Life began again. It would never again be the same.

Méténier's story came to an end; but under his bushy brows
his eyes still flashed with the contradictory sentiments that he
felt: humiliation at having been a straw carried away on the
troubled torrent of the exodus, and rage at his impotence to place
the blame for the sudden breaking of the vital dikes of his country,
a physical need to place the responsibilities for the disaster, to
establish in his concept of history the alignments of cause and
effect.

He remembered times when, with the far-sighted understanding
of the men who had been through the "other" war, he had
watched in alarm the breakdown behind the lines. While the last
companies in the North yielded slowly to the pressure of the
numbers that were thrown against them, disengaged themselves,
retreated ten kilometers, held for an hour or half a day, then
disengaged themselves once more—while these men were fighting,
the unwieldly mechanism of the non-combatant army suddenly

went to pieces, each of its cogs turning in the opposite direction from the others.

"The whole tragedy was there," Antoine said. "Against a formidable battering-ram, well mounted on perfectly greased wheels, we could oppose only a wavering curtain of troops, and behind them nothing organized, nothing solid."

Instead of the Météniers' kitchen, tranquilly set in the midst of the Lorraine night, he saw for an instant the vision of the lines that his own regiment had held for a month along the Ardennes canal—vague positions, hastily consolidated by hedgehogs of resistance, lines like patched linen.

"What's more," the farmer went on, "our heart wasn't in it enough." (During his whole recital, he had leaned motionless against the buffet in the rosy half-light of the lamp shade. The pictures that his rather shrill voice evoked were all the more striking because they seemed to come out of the mouth of a statue. Suddenly he took a step forward and leaned over the table, his head surmounting a lean neck whose sinewy cords stood out now in the circle of light.) "We didn't understand what it was all about yet. We had listened too well to the laddies who told us that this war should never have broken out. Good God! Do you think that it was any fun for us in 1914? When you start to empty a cesspool, you finish the job, even if, once you get started, you see that maybe you ought to have put it off a few days. We were in the war; we should have kept at it."

His voice choked with indignation at times. Each time that it broke out Méténier's anger swept over Antoine like a purifying wind. He went on to say that to find the root of the disease that in a few days had brought the country to the brink of death, you had to look back many years.

"When Hitler came into power, he didn't lose any time in telling us that he was going to settle our hash. And yet there were people in this country ready to explain that he didn't mean anything by it, that we mustn't attach too much importance to speeches. But when the day came to fight this war that the enemy had wanted for such a long while, even the most ardent among us had begun to have their secret doubts about whether

the cause was worth defending. Nobody—or almost nobody—
wanted to fight."

Antoine objected, "Fight with what? So many officers were the
first to set the example of funk and dragged their men into a
stampede! What did we have for arms?" He was searching his
heart, anxious to prove his sincerity to this judge standing behind
the table in a peasant kitchen. Were we so much to blame? Yes,
probably; but only to the extent that each of us gave himself up
to the inevitable and accepted the disaster as an accomplished
fact. Should we not rather have denied it, denied it with all our
beings? But it was too late; what was there left of France?

"France? A fine state France is in!" the farmer scolded. "Given
up to the hypocritical thieving of the victor! Bled like a pig!
Before the year is out, if it goes on this way, she'll be down to
her last sou. And meanwhile they want us to believe that Hitler,
Mister Hitler, asks nothing better than to save us, that he is going
to help us rebuild our ruins. There are nitwits who say, 'After all,
maybe the Fritzes aren't so bad as all that! All they want is our
own good.' But just wait till the skin of their bellies sticks to the
skin of their backs! Then they'll understand! When the skin of
their bellies sticks to the skin of their backs! Oh, the nitwits! The
Nazis in this war, you see, are like the Kaiser's bullyboys in the
other one. We know it, we folks here in the East. . . . Above all,
don't go saying it is too late!"

Oh, if this could be true! Antoine asked nothing better than
to lose himself in this absurd faith his host revealed and, sharing
it, to find a reasonable justification for the vague urge which,
beginning with his daydreams in the camp at Bar-le-Duc, had
driven him to risk escape. Once more he was a part of the world.
The catastrophe had not only left its mark on himself and his
companions in captivity; it also continued to crush with all its
weight the civilians of the invaded land. Antoine had imagined
that regaining his own liberty would efface the nightmare. Now
he knew that he had been mistaken. He was not returning to a
world where at last peace and happiness could be plucked—however surreptitiously—like a fine fruit from the tree of suffering.

"No, above all don't go saying it's too late!" Méténier repeated.
"You are going to hear something that will prove that I am right."

He took a thick nickel-plated watch from his vest pocket. "Hell, we are going to miss it!" Turning to a shelf that supported the varnished case of a radio, he began turning the knobs. After a few minutes of whistlings, belches and twitters, a voice broke through clearly, so close at hand they heard its human breathing: "Frenchmen are speaking to Frenchmen . . ."

So everything that Ferrand had said when he came back to the camp after the harvest was true! Open-mouthed, Antoine listened, his whole being straining toward this voice so calm and poised, so near and so strangely familiar. Confidently it asserted that the hour of deliverance would someday strike, and that everything that seemed irreparably lost today would be regained. It said also that it would be a long and bitter struggle. It urged the humble virtues of patience and endurance and yet, by some miracle, appealed for highest ecstasies of heroism to celebrate. Without Méténier's saying a word, Antoine understood what a rebirth of hope it had been for the peasant, humiliated and wounded in his deepest feelings, the day when his groping fingers had brought out of the nothingness of the ether one of these messages from a world that had remained friendly. Into the dark and mucky pit where defeat had plunged him along with millions of his compatriots, someone had lowered a rope, a rope that he must seize with both hands and cling to with all the might of his manhood.

This voice had brought him face to face with the inexorable demands of war. For a few hours, in this Lorraine farmhouse, the monologues of Pétain had evoked the bleakness of an accomplished reality, a war terminated by defeat. It had seemed as if it was still possible, in spite of everything, to acquiesce to a precarious peace, a happiness as tenuous as a blade of grass beneath the snow. Everything pointed that way: the mistress of the house, stolid and calm, her back to the stove; her son, leaning his elbows on the table in silence; the circle of light in the center of the room; the heavy oak furniture; the red tiled floor.

But now this isle of refuge was no longer anchored firmly in the rural night. It was drifting toward a tumultuous ocean, lit with a bloody glow and streaked with the pitchy clouds of the débâcle. Beyond the village, tossing in restless sleep, were the billets of the victor's army. There were munition trains and airdromes, casemates crouched like beasts of prey on the beaches, and the cannons. The war was not a finished reality: It was still going on. It needed men—this farmer, this prisoner who had just accepted the implications of his escape. He must slip through this enemy-held terrain, slip through the war, to go in search of his OWN war.

A dry click: Méténier had turned off the radio.

"Well? Puts heart in a fellow, doesn't it?" he said in a changed voice. "You see that we'll pull through in the end, and better than you'd have thought. We aren't alone any longer, each in his corner eating his heart out at not being able to do anything about it. Oh! I know it won't be easy; we've all got to get together to boot them back where they belong. But that day will come, and we'll be in on it, you and me. In the meanwhile, we'd better see about putting you up for the night."

"And none too soon either!" his wife laughed. "You talk and talk and the poor man is tired. That's enough of your talk tonight. Tell monsieur what you think he ought to do and ask him his plans. Then we'll see."

The farmer turned toward Antoine, who was looking at Mathilde, a smile of confidence lighting his face.

"I'm not too sure," Antoine faltered. "I'd like to keep on toward the South, cross the line of demarcation, and reach the unoccupied zone. If only I had a map!"

"Yes. Yes, of course," Méténier mumbled, raking his bewhiskered cheek with his black, broken fingernails. "But you told me a while back that you were from Paris and you are married. Has your wife probably gone back there? Well, then?"

"What?" Antoine asked, not daring to understand.

The farmer burst out laughing, slapped his thighs and gave his wife a poke in the ribs.

"You hear that? He thinks that they stop folks at every street corner to ask for their papers! Why, my lad, you'll be safer right there in Paris than anywhere else. Naturally, remember, the Fritzes have your address; they'll probably go take a look there. But you've certainly got some other place you can go?"

"Of course," Antoine said. The words opened new vistas to him.

"Well then, this is what I suggest. Tomorrow you'll stay here quietly and rest. You won't leave the room that we are going to put you in tonight. The kids mustn't see you. And you, Maurice, you won't go talking in the village either, you hear? I'll scout around to find out where the best place to cross the line is near Revigny. You can be sure that every path isn't guarded. Mathilde, you must have an old suit of mine around somewhere?"

"We'll find something."

"Good! Then you'll set out before dawn. About twenty kilometers' walk and you're in the Marne.* There, at Sermaize, you can quietly take the train. You'll inquire around first, of course, to make sure they aren't asking for papers and that there's no patrol in the station. And that same evening you'll be at Paris! How's that!"

"Oh!" Antoine exclaimed, overwhelmed. "You think that I could . . . I don't know how to thank . . ."

"Bah, it's nothing. And now how about bed?"

Shortly, Antoine found himself at the foot of a bed in a large room. Méténier and his wife stood beside him. White sheets and a soft mattress! The farmer gave a hearty laugh.

"And in two days, my lad, it'll be your own bed you'll be getting into, with a little woman in it! That'll be still better, hey?" (He gave a wink that he meant to be confidentially suggestive.) "Come along, Mathilde!"

When they had gone, Antoine undressed and slipped between the sheets. Ah, the rough smoothness of the fresh linen, the marvelous softness of the mattress! It was as if his body were afloat in a clear cool brook. He closed his eyes. Gently, the bed began to sway.

The station at Bar-le-Duc, the camp, the milling drove of prisoners under the horse chestnut trees, the stunned hours of the retreat, the firing, the ambush in the Argonne forest, the ten-foot drop in the garden, the German automobile on the road . . . And roads and roads along which men in work clothes walk, a hoe

---

* The department, not the river. The line of demarcation that Antoine had to cross before taking the train at Sermaize-les-Bains was not the line between the North (Occupied) Zone and the South (Unoccupied) Zone, but a line between the frontier territory of the East that the Germans intended to incorporate into the Greater Reich and the rest of Northern France. (Translator's note.)

over their shoulders, but their furtive eyes showing that they escaped from some camp in France or some STALAG in Germany: men who took advantage of the confusion in some railroad station, the solitude of a field, the inattention of the guard on some work detail, to escape. Men who had slept under hedges, swum rivers, dodged enemy patrols. Men who had answered the call of liberty.

In the false dawn of a November morning a sharp little breeze whipped through the apple trees along the road. It stirred a faint odor of moldiness from the brown pulp that rotted on the ground beneath the trees. Sometimes a German car sounded its klaxon and swept by the man walking on the brown grass along the edge of the ditch. Soon it disappeared into the pearl-gray mist. But no one paid any attention to the early traveler. Two horses emerged from a dirt road, and the boy sitting sidewise on one of them shouted, "Gee, Blanchette!" A flock of crows flapped heavily away at their approach; their caws answered each other from one clump of woods to another.

Antoine walked fast, his blood quickened by the damp cold of the dawn. Happiness thumped in his chest like a drum. Under his his arm he squeezed the newspaper bundle in which Madame Méténier had wrapped some food for him. After a while he would find a stone to sit on in some orchard and eat. Then he would set out again, the fine gravel creaking under his hobnails. He carried in his head a map of the roads and paths that Méténier had described for him that morning in the kitchen as they drank the piping hot CAFÉ AU LAIT before he started out. Dawn was beginning to bleach the light of the lamp under its pink shade. Méténier repeated his last instructions.

"It's a farm in the middle of the fields. Good-bye, my lad, and good luck. Write to us when you get there. And remember, there's no hurry about sending those little things back."

Little things? A suit of heavy black broadcloth, a faded raincoat, a béret and three hundred francs. For Méténier had not hesitated to ask if he had enough money. "Only a hundred francs? You couldn't even pay for your ticket. Here," he said, taking his pocketbook from a drawer of the buffet, "you can send it back by money order when you get there. . . . Sure, take it, don't worry. We trust you!" Antoine finally took it.

Twenty kilometers on foot through fields and woods, what did that amount to after the year that he had gone through? Yet it was not a simple interlude that would end tonight or tomorrow at the GARE DE L'EST, in that same railroad station where, for so many men, it had begun a year ago. It was true that during the monotony of the "phoney war," during the hours of fighting along the Ardennes canal, in the bewildering whirlwind of the débâcle, throughout the long desolate days of captivity, the frail little flower of a fond hope had never altogether faded. Once in civilian clothes again, his former life with Germaine in the little apartment in the Rue Monge might start up again. But the simple act of furtively abandoning his khaki coat beside the freight station had not sealed, as for a long time he had thought it would, his return to the comfortable, carefree world of liberty.

While Antoine was working his way through the maze of the line of demarcation—(Look close now, you mustn't miss the dirt road. . . . There it is . . . and the farmhouse that Méténier described . . . and, further on, the steeple that you must head for)—the camp at Bar-le-Duc awoke in an unaccustomed excitement. The barracks leaders were ordered to report to the German office with the list of their men.

"Barracks 1 to 20, Tents A to L, fall in in the courtyard at 8:15," the interpreter said. "Baggage packed and ready to move. Barracks and tents should be completely empty and cleaned." . . . Slowly the train began to move. While it went by the camp, the men who were leaving had a chance for a last look at the buildings of the military hospital. In the courtyard, behind the gates and the barbed wire, they saw for the last time the comrades they had left behind and who tomorrow would be shipped away in their turn.

Fortunately, here and there on the roads of France, a man is walking slowly along, his face set toward the West, toward Paris or toward some small country village.

✦

Toward noon that same day, Antoine arrived at Sermaize. He had had no trouble crossing the line of demarcation. At the station he learned that a train left for Paris every day and that the German control at Châlons was not very strict.

He bought his ticket and went into a small café opposite the station. After engaging a room, he ordered a half-bottle of red wine. On a marble-topped table, with workers all about him eating their lunches, he unwrapped his package and began to eat.

Epernay, Château-Thierry, Meaux, Paris!

The third leg of his clandestine travels had begun, and everything was turning out easier than he had imagined. Walking alone on the national highway through the gray haze of a wintry afternoon and later by twilight in the silent underbrush of the forest, he had felt more lost, more cut off from the world, than Hop-o'-my-Thumb in his ogre-haunted wood. But once emerged from this misty mid-region of ghosts, the friendly handclasp of Louis Méténier had drawn him gently toward a shore where he had found fellow beings bound to him by a link of secret complicity. . . . Epernay, Château-Thierry, Meaux, Paris! . . . Among the crowd, burdened down with bundles and children that swarmed aboard the train at Châlons-sur-Marne, he had become a civilian once more, taciturn and suspicious, but inconspicuous in the faded raincoat and broadcloth suit that gave him the air of a peasant in his Sunday-best. He was no longer the hunted fugitive whom the crackle of a twig or the sudden apparition of an unfamiliar silhouette threw into a panic. If he did not yet enter into the conversation of his fellow travelers, if he kept a watchful eye on the compartment door where at any moment might appear a soldier in FELDGRAU with a military-police badge suspended by a chain about his neck—still he no longer shrank, as if to make himself invisible, in his corner. This crowded train made it easy for him to pass unnoticed. It was Sunday; he had as much right to be going to Paris as any one else. In the waiting room at Châlons, he had walked right past many a uniform with the outward appearance of assurance and unconcern. That proved it: he was no longer in any danger.

The train rolled across the country with an honest clank of

iron wheels and rails—Epernay, Château-Thierry, Meaux, Paris!
. . . His liberty began to live for him again, like a faithful helpmate that he had never left. The compartment hummed with
conversation. Two girls sitting nearest the door were exchanging
sprightly repartee with a pimply lad. Only the woman sitting
opposite Antoine—a middle-aged woman with too much make-up
—locked her thin scarlet lips. Disgusted at having to share the
promiscuity of a third-class coach, no doubt. (There's a war on, of
course—and after all that we went through in this terrible exodus!)
And who knows if perhaps in her heart might not also be locked
the heavy clot of some unspoken grief? An elderly couple sitting
next her opened a package of food and began to eat. . . . AND
HERE IS EPERNAY! Epernay, Château-Thierry, Meaux, Paris! The
young people followed the elderly couple's example. Now they
were sucking hard candies that they shook out of a white cardboard box.

"These are becoming scarce at Châlons."

"Everything is becoming scarce, mademoiselle," the old man
said sententiously, between two mouthfuls. Like Antoine, he was
dressed in a black peasant Sunday-best suit. He drank his wine
directly from the bottle. Antoine tried unsuccessfully to take an
interest in what they were saying. His brain mulled over and over
again an endless flow of questions.

He did not want to think of Germaine any more, because he
had superstitiously decided, last night in his dusty room in the
little inn at Sermaize, not to tempt fate by forming too precise
a picture of his arrival at Paris. According to what he called "the
law of universal vexation," that would be the surest way to make
everything go wrong. There was only one chance in a thousand,
anyway, that she hadn't left Paris during the general exodus in
June. Yet you never could tell. He knew her: it was enough that
all the people around her should lose their heads for Germaine
to become as imperturbable as a block of wood. She was the kind
of woman who is always on the spot when there is a traffic accident,
a fire in a movie theater, a railroad wreck—the woman who calmly
sets about doing the right thing, saying the proper words, finding
the nearest drugstore (which everybody else has overlooked in the

excitement), remembering to telephone for the police and the doctor. But the exodus from Paris had surpassed in stupidity anything that could be imagined, it seemed. Perhaps she had been forced to leave. In any case he would find her. He would go to the Rue Monge first. Even if she had left Paris when the others did, she must have been among the first to return, knowing that it was there that he would write to her as soon as he could. . . . Château-Thierry, Meaux, Paris! Château-Thierry, Meaux, Paris! How they chattered! What pleasure could they find in this senseless babble of words, all running together like a flock of sheep in a narrow lane!

"But, yes, indeed, madame, the MÉTRO is running! Fortunately! There are no more taxis or autobuses. This is the second time I have gone to Paris since the troubles. You may be sure that . . ."

The troubles! So that was the demure euphemism that they used to designate the tornado that had devastated the country. The troubles! Exodus had become too much of a reminder of panic, of roads blocked with refugees, of bombardments and general collapse. So they had come to speak of its as the troubles! Impersonal and neutral. This was at least the twentieth time that it had popped up in the conversation. "The troubles!" he snickered to himself. "A funny name for it!"

If he could only tell them about his own exodus, how they would open their eyes! Tell them that he was an escaped prisoner who had known the cruel hardships and hunger of the retreat, one futile stand after another, from the Ardennes canal to the prison camp at Bar-le-Duc; and that his escape had enabled him to triumph over the slough of despond in which his brain was bogged down: that to strike for liberty is to regain one's human dignity; that Louis Méténier had shown himself to be just such another as the peasant that Ferrand had told him of, the one who every night pressed his ear to the cloth of the radio amplifier; that one must never lose hope, even when overwhelmed by the blackest of defeats; for even this is not yet the full measure of the cataclysm— nor yet the moment when, as Méténier had said, "the skin of their bellies will stick to the skin of their backs." The days of famine and slavery, he could have told them, were drawing near.

Our only chance is to start working together today, to link up with the Météniers of France.

Meaux, Paris! Meaux, Paris! . . . The childish amazement that he had felt so acutely as far as Epernay, at being once more in a civilian train, gave way to impatience. At the left of the track, the Marne wove in aimless meanderings beyond which the French countryside spread its meadows, fields and villages and stations. A pale late autumn sun moved behind the clouds, spotting the landscape here and there with clear, luminous brush strokes of light. They had passed Meaux. The train rumbled on toward Lagny. It was no longer the country. Little railroad stations clicked by in rapid succession. There were fewer and fewer trees to be seen by the window. Small factories and sheds with rusted metal roofs filled the landscape. Red brick villas, with gardens the size of pocket handkerchiefs, huddled together. Gas tanks. Apartment houses several stories high.

"Too bad we don't stop at Bobigny," the elderly couple grumbled, lifting down their suitcases from the rack. "Just think, having to take the MÉTRO with all that baggage, and a long walk after that."

Paris! Paris! What are they stopping here for? There's a light against them. What are they up to, for Christ's sake?

It seemed to Antoine as if the suburbs would never end. His eyes devoured the sad, dark picture that unfurled with scant variety in unending length. He was like a provincial seeing Paris for the first time. For this was already Paris: bedraggled fronts of buildings, iron blinds blackened by smoke, shops along the sidewalks, and all the BISTROS blinking from afar . . . Ah! Paris! Just as he was saying to himself again that the suburbs would never end, the train pulled into the station, coasted along a cement platform, and came to a stop.

"Are you getting off or not! Make up your mind! We're in a hurry if you're not!"

Standing on the lower step of the car, Antoine's head swam before the compact sheet of faces already massed on the platform. He could not resent the man behind him jamming his valises into his back. He was overflowing with good-will toward all his compatriots. Surly and selfish as it was, what a joy it was to rediscover the impatience of the crowd. Stoutly, like an inexpert swimmer steeling himself to plunge into a cold pool, he swung down to the platform.

"I must be something to look at," he thought, as he gave himself up to the swirling currents that swept him toward the exit, "with this black suit and these heavy boots!"

Nobody paid any attention to this lone traveler without baggage. He reached the gate and gave up his ticket. He found himself on a sidewalk. He walked nonchalantly by several groups of German soldiers. Before approaching the outer gate of the station, he made sure that the German guard there was not examining the travelers' papers.

Oh, the first exhilarating lungful of Paris air! How breath-taking it was! He stopped. He wanted to make sure whether the city still had that same unforgettable scent that had made his heart quicken whenever he thought of it back in the prison camp. It did; there was no mistaking it. It was the same subtle blend of smells that he would have recognized anywhere, as a man recognizes among a hundred thousand the distinctive animal scent of the woman he loves. He had not yet decided what his first act as a free man should be. His eyes wandered from one building to another. They were so tall, so tall! In a kiosk there were newspapers, and the posters that had hung on the billboards since before the war were bleached and faded. The cafés were swarming with customers. Only the center of the streets was empty—not a bus, not a taxi, not a car.

Then Antoine decided to act as if he were not in any hurry to get to Rue Monge. He entered a café and ordered a small beer, which he drank in little swallows, standing up to the zinc bar.

It was only then that he began to notice the German soldiers. They were seated at the tables, thick as flies in summer, clustered about the round marble table tops loaded with beer and cognac. It's true, the krauts drink them both together, a swallow of beer and a swallow of cognac. A queer custom! They were laughing, gabbling. Their guttural voices dominated the indistinct murmur of the crowd. Antoine suddenly remembered the gray-headed soldier with whom he had shared a bar of chocolate and a hunk of bread somewhere along the roadside a few kilometers the other side of Vavincourt. "Imagine it! The KRAUTS at 'CHEZ-DU-PONT-TOUT-EST-BON'! * I couldn't bear it!"

Antoine decided not to take the MÉTRO immediately. He must kill a little time before starting to look for Germaine. It was not quite noon yet. It would be better to reach Rue Monge about one o'clock to be sure of finding her home having her lunch.

He walked down the Boulevard Magenta. Then, slowly, like a man out for a Sunday morning stroll between his APÉRITIF and lunch, he followed the boulevard toward the GARE DU NORD.

He had expected to find traces, still fresh, of the war. He knew that Paris had not been defended, that the city had opened at the enemy's approach. Why then did he imagine that he would see, if not ruins, at least a few house fronts scorched here and there, a few broken windows? Nothing! The body was intact, with its bones and flesh and veins. But the blood in its arteries was no longer the same. People walked peacefully through the streets, without seeming to notice the groups of soldiers in FELDGRAU uniforms that they encountered. From the way they looked right through them, the soldiers might have been made of the impalpable stuff of specters. What was it then that was gone from this city that had been the Paris of liberty and pleasure? Antoine tried to define his uneasiness, to find a word to fill this emptiness. Suddenly, in spite of the shuffling of passing feet, the vast silence of the invaded city struck him with the force of a blow. That was it: the living sounds of the city were hushed, the symphony of singing motors, honking of horns, street cries, the news-vendors: "PARIS-MIDI! Buy the PARIS-MIDI! L'INTRAN, latest edition!" The voice of Paris was dead, killed by the presence of the enemy.

The doors of almost all the hotels were plastered with red and white posters printed in German. A German soldier stood guard at the entrance. What would a hotel turned into a barrack be like? A hotel where all the guests knew each other and which was not a caravansary of anonymity whose every cell, once closed, gave passing shelter to so many mysteries, so many loves, so many crises of human life? Those rooms where, the key turned, between

* Dupont: the name of a chain of popular cafés. Their trade slogan is: "At Dupont's everything is good."

the washstand, the wardrobe and the bed, in one's solitude, one suddenly became conscious of being a living molecule, frightfully personal, of the great body of Paris.

As far as the Boulevard Barbès, the street was an unbroken front of hotels and shops. The dairy shops alone were open—because it was Sunday perhaps, but here already was the first sign of the famine that could only get worse. Milk can or shopping bag in hand, women were still waiting in lines, although it was noon. In lines! Antoine called up his remotest memories: when he was a child, he had heard about standing in line for food during the other war.

He continued his stroll, carried along slowly by the crowd. At the Barbès station, the MÉTRO emerges from under ground. A train went by with a deafening roar of metal. Come now, not everything is lost—since the MÉTRO still rumbles along! He took the MÉTRO. Instinctively it all came back to him: sliding the money in at the narrow ticket window, the iron bar at the level of his thighs, the click of the ticket punch, the stairs, the gate to the platform that invariably closes just as you get to it. And the train roaring out of the tunnel like a scenic-railway at an amusement park. The first-class coach was full to bursting. German soldiers were jammed around the doors. The enamel plaques bearing the Alexandrine line that the company had dedicated to its passengers, "THE TRAIN CANNOT DEPART UNTIL THE DOORS ARE CLOSED," were still there.

The buildings on the Boulevard Rochechouart flickered behind the iron beams. The train was swallowed up in the tunnel beneath the heights of Montmartre. It passed the station of Anvers without stopping, Place Pigalle, Clichy . . . and up above, on the street level, Place Blanche, the vanes of the windmill of the MOULIN ROUGE, the cafés, beer halls, the whores—all this world that does not begin to come to life till later in the day, when the mauve twilight has descended, when the lights used to begin to glow and the cold fire of neon signs proclaimed the glory of Paris. But there are no more lights, neon or otherwise, and no more night life. . . . Rue de Rome, Villiers, the respectable, stuffy residences of the Parc Monceau quarter, the Ternes (a melancholy name) and the Etoile!

In a few quick leaps he was out of the MÉTRO station, as if

propelled into the midst of Paris by a happiness too powerful to
be restrained. An old man with gray hair whom he collided with
on the escalator was on the point of giving him a piece of his
mind, but already the unmannerly fellow was out in the open air.
Anyway, he was so badly dressed that his lack of manners seemed
normal to the old gentleman, whose dignity not even "the troubles"
had shaken.

Antoine felt like thrusting out his chest, making his hobnailed
boots ring on the pavement, shoving aside, like foam under the
cutwater of a ship, the German soldiers before whom he passed
haughtily.

He did none of these things, however. He walked along as if he
were out for a Sunday stroll. Through eyes alight with joy, he saw
the familiar vista that once he had never expected to see again.
Never had the sunlight caressed the roofs and the gray stone more
delicately. A gentle winter sun laid a reddish glint on the window
panes and the moist pavement, lit a pale and fugitive gleam afar
on the blue-hooded top of a street lamp, and swept, from a vast
pure sky, down toward the CONCORDE and the TUILERIES. And his
memory, immediately preparing before him sumptuous feasts,
intact images of a sentimental past: the afternoon of a holiday
coming back from the Bois de Boulogne with Germaine, borne
away in the happy indolence of the crowd with the taxis and
autobuses rolling toward the MADELEINE; a morning of the Fourteenth of July with bandstands decorated with greenery and
pennants at the street corners, and families hurrying toward
their favorite vantage points with cardboard periscopes in their
hands. . . .

Precarious happiness. He had only to walk a hundred yards
farther down the street to measure its fragility. Opposite the
MÉTRO station George V, he looked up. Over a business block
floated an enormous red flag, its swastika rippling in the crisp
air with a sarcastic jauntiness. He was obliged to stop to grasp
the import of this "sign" that was given him.

He was still stunned and sick at heart from the shock, when
he heard the confused distant sound of a shrill, piercing music.

"Look. The circus is on parade again!"

It was a man beside him who spoke these words in a voice

choked with bitterness and scorn. The woman on his arm bit her lip and made no reply. Already motorcyclists in iron-gray slickers draped in wide folds down over their machines were clearing the avenue before them, obliging the rare vehicles to draw over to the cement curb and stop. Once more Antoine felt the same horrible sensation that he had experienced when, with his comrade Hirschfeld, he had discovered that he was lost in the no-man's-land of the retreat. What was it? Anguish? Dread of the future that opened before him? He could never give a name to the feeling.

He wanted to run; he could not. He stood there, fixed to the spot, spellbound, like the couple beside him, who had also stopped and stood there sullenly. The military band drew near. Snare drums and the shrill whistle of fifes. The glockenspiel red and black, with a horsetail floating from the top. Then, mounted on a sleek, restive horse, an officer—his saber held stiff and rigid against his body. Then came the company which, in ranks of three, was only a single pair of boots. Their heels thudded on the asphalt and their tread echoed lugubriously in Antoine's brain. They carried their rifles very low, the butt at the level of their hips.

In the pit of his stomach, Antoine felt once more the mysterious and unbearable tension. But over the horrible spectacle a veil had fallen. He hardly saw the motorcyclists who brought up the rear of the parade or the car in which a German soldier stood keeping a watch on the silent pedestrians.

The woman tugged at her husband's elbow. With a jerk of her head, she indicated the man standing beside them. He was still young, dressed in a shabby raincoat, hobnailed boots, and an ill-fitting suit of black broadcloth. She opened her mouth to speak, then she blushed; her glance had crossed with that of Antoine, who was trying vainly to hold back the tears that filled his eyes and rolled slowly down his cheeks to the bitter line of his mouth.

Embarrassed, the man led his wife away just at the moment when Antoine, unable to stomach any more of it, turned his back on this cheap display of the conqueror's vanity. The couple walked along a few steps, abreast of him. As if to excuse himself at first, the man began to talk. His rather quavering voice trembled with a suppressed rage, like an animal straining at a leash. One felt that he would have liked to roar his words loud enough to shake every window in Paris.

"They don't understand. They will never understand. They have no conception what men who cherish their liberty are like— men who, sooner or later, are bound to find a way to regain it. . . . And who will do it, I tell you! They will do it!"

How It Began

Historians probably will debate for a long time about when outward manifestations of resistance began, and here they will have a better chance to offer proof than on the more important question of when it began in men's minds. Probably it will come down to an issue of split seconds. Between June 17, when Monsieur Seguin in the person of Marshal Pétain asked 'for an armistice, and June 23, when the Germans granted it, fighting continued. There is a natural disposition on the part of soldiers whose chief has acknowledged defeat to accept his verdict. But some units permitted themselves to be decimated for the sake of their honor and despair. The official cease fire went out on June 23.

The race among historians will be to find out who first violated it. The records of the German military courts may furnish evidence.

My own candidate for the honor of first armed resister has no dossier in the archives of the Gestapo, because he was never caught. If you follow his story, you will understand how these things begin.

The Conscience of Monsieur Boivin *

My friend Monsieur Boivin (that is not his real name, for he is shy) is a carver of RETABLES and altar chairs, and since many

* Permission *The New Yorker*, Copyright 1946. The F-R. Publishing Corporation.

churches in his native Lorraine were damaged during the first
World War and many during the second, he has seldom lacked
employment. Indeed, in some instances he has had the economic
privilege—he would scarcely call it a pleasure—of carving three
successive sets of chairs for one parish, his first two creations with
the churches they adorned having been destroyed by German
shells. Monsieur Boivin, never having been completely satisfied
with any of his carvings, has relished the opportunity to improve
upon them, but he wishes his earlier pieces had survived for purposes of comparison. It is not a happy thought for a wood-carver
that his work will prove as ephemeral as a journalist's.

Despite his vocation, or perhaps because of it, since a large
acquaintance among clerics is seldom conducive to awe, Monsieur
Boivin is not much of a churchgoer. He inherits his politics from
Poincaré and Clemenceau, who were less than punctilious in their
worship, and he is inclined to rate priests simply according to
their stature as Frenchmen. His wife has sometimes reproached
him about this, but he has never gone into the matter deeply
with her, having an old-fashioned belief that to be happy, a
husband must keep many of his thoughts and experiences to
himself. He is a tall, spare man, who was already thirty-seven in
1914 but who nevertheless served through four years of the war
that began then. He won the Croix de Guerre with star twice, and
refused a third award, in 1918, because, he says, by that time they
were sending up the decorations with the rations as morale
builders. One of the citations he did accept was for holding a
section of trench for an hour and three-quarters, alone, against a
German attack, serving and firing his machine gun after all his
companions had been killed.

At the end of that war, Monsieur Boivin set up an atelier of
wood sculpture at Nancy, and when, in the thirties, the number
of churches to be restored had diminished, he even constructed a
bit of secular furniture, mostly accurate copies of old pieces. The
beginning of the recent war found him spending the summer in a
two-room cottage he owned in a village which will here be called
Poires, and which is in the Vosges about fifty miles from Nancy.
He had with him his wife, their daughter Odile, who is an un-
married schoolteacher getting on toward forty, and a grandniece
ten years old. Knowing that Nancy, which was the headquarters

of an Army Group, was almost sure to be bombarded by the Germans and that it is always easier during a war to find goods in the country than in the city, he determined to stay in Poires for the duration. It was there that I met him in December, 1939. The encounter was not an accident. Monsieur Boivin has another daughter, Céleste, who is married to a friend of mine in New York, and she had sent her parents' address to me in Paris, asking me to look them up if I had a chance. After the Germans occupied France, Céleste worried a good deal about her parents and heard little from them, but in the winter of 1944 letters began to arrive regularly and she learned that they had survived in good shape.

Last spring, Céleste was able to get over to France to see them. When she came back, she brought with her a document enclosed in an envelope addressed to her husband. It consisted of six four-page sheets of letter paper, each page marked off by faint lines and crosslines into seventeen columns and ninety-six horizontal rows. The paper was covered with the strong, precise, vertical hand-writing of Monsieur Boivin, now sixty-nine. Each letter was exactly two rows high and filled precisely one-third of a column, and between every two lines of writing two rows were left blank. The letters were as distinct as if Monsieur Boivin had cut them out with a whittling knife. They seemed to have a third dimension.

Céleste said that her father had written this out in one after-noon, when, troubled by arthritis, he had been unable to walk around and had been so cross that it was a question of finding him something to do. So Céleste, who said that during her visit he had often told her anecdotes about the German occupation, had sug-gested that he write out a connected narrative of his most memor-able experiences, that she might take home to her husband. The old man likes his American son-in-law. The son-in-law showed the manuscript to me because I knew Monsieur Boivin. I began to read out of politeness, and continued, I think, because I was hypnotized by the letters marching across the page like wooden legionaries on a carved Stations of the Cross. Also, the opening of the narrative recalled a time that I vividly remember but seldom think of nowadays, the time when our side was down and the others were up.

In the little Vosgian town of Poires, the Mayor's secretary had been mobilized early in 1939, and when I visited there that year, Monsieur Boivin, who, since he fixed his own working hours, had a more flexible routine than most of the residents, had taken over the secretary's duties temporarily.

"After the sixteenth of June, 1940, we at the MAIRIE got no more orders from the local prefecture," the story begins. "The gendarmes had been ordered to be ready to evacuate their barracks at any time. We didn't know or understand anything of what went on outside our immediate region; we just heard rumors. On the evening of the sixteenth, the artillery headquarters of the Fifth Army arrived in Poires with four or five trucks loaded with equipment and set up its telephones and tables in the ballroom of the MAIRIE—but not for long. It left next morning, abandoning most of the gear. So we knew that the retreat was really on and that the artillery general had no hope of an improvement. Until then, we old sweats of 1914-18 had been unable to believe that the French Army had retreated as quickly as the radio said—all the way from one big city to another in one day, sometimes. In the last war, we had so often held out in small groups, under the command of a corporal, or with no command at all. The Germans never moved more than a few meters at a time through us.

"Next day, the gendarmes got their orders and left in the direction of Dijon, moving southwest along the only main road that was not already barred by the enemy. On the same morning, the tide of refugees, moving in the same direction, reached our village. We learned from some of them that a German Army, driving south from Champagne, had already reached the Haute-Marne Department, while another, which had broken through at the south end of the Maginot Line, was advancing to the northwest, with the object of encircling the French Army of Alsace and the Vosges. If they succeeded, our town probably would be by-passed and there was a good chance there would be no fighting in the immediate vicinity. Just the same, everybody who could leave began to prepare to join the refugees. People who owned any kind of vehicle got together the most valuable portable possessions they had. It is a sad sight, an exodus.

"Sitting on the bench in front of the MAIRIE, I could see the whole population of the Meurthe-et-Moselle Department—easy to identify by the license plates of their vehicles—passing along this one free road. Often, I would hear my name called by somebody in an automobile, without being able to make out by whom, because the cars were packed so closely together that I couldn't see everybody. Women, children, men, some on foot or riding bicycles, others crowded into vehicles of every kind, pressed against one another, hampered one another, were loaded down like donkeys with all they could carry. I went back into my house feeling very low.

"I wondered if I should yield to the contagion and get out too. There was still a train in the railroad station that would leave the next morning for some indefinite destination. I felt it was my duty to urge my wife and daughter to take this last chance and leave with our little orphan niece. As for myself, I determined not to leave no matter what happened.

"That night, neither my wife nor my daughter nor I slept, but none of us said a word. The prospect of parting and the difficulty of ever getting together again kept us awake. Morning came, and with it the time to part. The hand luggage was packed. Everybody had something to carry and a parcel of food for the journey besides. My little niece was even carrying her straw hat with her. Odile begged me to come along with them. I still said no. Then she said, 'Well, if you won't go, we won't go either.' And they all put down their bags. 'If we are going to be killed,' she said, 'we'll all be killed together.' I was happy. I was glad that I would not have to be separated from them, and at the same time felt that I had done my duty as head of the family by suggesting that they leave. Odile's decision turned out to be lucky; it saved us a great deal of trouble and an unknown amount of suffering.

"The next day, the escape corridor was cut off by the Germans at a point about sixty miles south of our village. All the sad crowd that had fled toward Dijon had to turn back, and since other thousands, not knowing what had happened, continued to push south, the road was soon choked. The Boche were reported within a day's march of Poires. At about 1:30 that afternoon, while on my way to the MAIRIE, I turned a corner and found myself nose to nose with an armored car which had stopped. Its machine gun was pointing straight at me. The front of the car was draped with a great red cloth ornamented with a white swastika. No mistake, the Boche had arrived. And ahead of schedule. I walked on, trying not to show any emotion, and once I had passed the car, restrained myself from looking back at it. There were two other armored cars in the village, an advance element of a motorized column. They took a turn through the town and stopped for a considerable time in front of the wine cellars of a wholesale liquor dealer, whom they made give them drinks. Then, after loading their vehicles with sufficient reserves for the road, they headed back toward Bourbonne.

"Next morning, the Germans arrived in force, and marched through the principal street all day, heading northwest. It was an armored division, impressively disciplined, impeccably equipped, a formidable unit of picked men of uniform age, uniform height, uniform courtesy. Doubtless by command, they saluted the monument to the dead of 1914-18 in front of the MAIRIE as they passed. Those who paused in Poires were polite, modest, and invited friendship, but nobody was taken in for a minute.

"Now I began to understand why our army had had to retreat so quickly. I could see that our enemies had studied everything out and left nothing to chance, while we had napped, relying on our treaties. Every bit of mechanism well oiled and every man at his post. I didn't despair altogether, but I doubted that we would ever be able to get rid of this terrible army, twice the size of ours and infinitely better armed.

"On the day after that, I learned that the Germans had passed Mirecourt and were pushing rapidly toward Nancy. I made up my mind to keep pace with them and get to the city at nearly the same time they did so I could save our house from being requisitioned or looted. I made ready my little motor bike, wrapped up some bread and meat to eat on the road, and got going. As far as Mirecourt, all went well, but between Poussy and Diarville, to judge by the look of the road, the abandoned military gear, and straying animals, there must have been pretty heavy fighting on the previous day. Useless fighting, since the French Army was surrounded. Hundred of dead or straying horses encumbered the road. Most of the strays were wounded; one lay dying upside down in the middle of the road, with an enormous, gaping wound in his chest, his glazed eyes indifferent to the pitched battle between two Arab stallions, now at liberty, who were fighting around the spot where he lay.

"I feared that I would not be able to go much further, for on the far side of Diarville, the cannon thundered and there seemed to be a serious battle. I got through the village without being stopped, but the inhabitants advised me to go no further. I am stubborn, however, and I hoped to drive along side roads, so I pushed on. But after I had traveled a couple of miles, I was passed by two Germans mounted on one motorcycle. They stopped soon after passing me, and when I caught up to them, halted me and by signs ordered me to dismount from my little motor bike. The loss of it would have stranded me at an equal distance from Poires and Nancy. I protested as energetically as I could and clung to the handlebars, pulling the bike my way while they pulled it theirs. To cut the argument short, one of them drew a grenade from his musette bag and made a motion as if to throw it at me, crying 'KAPUT!' There was no good resisting further, so with a heavy heart I let go my grip. I saw them ride away, one on the motorcycle, the other on my bike, and I was sad. How could I reach Nancy on foot? I walked on, nevertheless, not giving up hope, and in a few seconds I saw that the two thieves had stopped again and were making motions to me that I didn't understand. I did understand, though, when I saw them abandon my machine by the roadside, then both again mount the big motorcycle and depart at high speed. I concluded that they had found my bike too slow to keep up with the motorcycle and so of no use to them. Rejoicing, I hurried to take possession of my property again. After this scare I made a couple more attempts to get through to Nancy, but since the battle seemed to be moving in my direction, I gave up. I decided to go back to Poires for the night, happy that I hadn't lost my bike.

"But I could not stay home. I filled her up with gas next morning and this time I swore I would get to Nancy, no matter what happened."

✦

The picture of Monsieur Boivin, his trousers held above the ankles of his long legs by bicycle clamps, trundling his mechanized Rosinante out onto the cobbled street to begin again his trip through the whole German Army, made me pause at this point the first time I read his story. He must have known that even if he could reach his home in Nancy, he could do no more than protest against the seizure of his house and wood-carving shop, just as he had when the soldiers had taken his motor bike. He was sixty-three years old, and the journey, as he had discovered on the previous day, was not without danger. It reminded me of those Norman peasants who, in 1944, used to return to farms that were in the middle of battles to milk their cows—"because otherwise the beasts would fall ill." Monsieur Boivin, in 1940, I suppose, could not accept the idea of a society in which a man had no rights; he believed, like many Frenchmen, that a right unasserted lapses. He had to go to Nancy to make an assertion. The courtesy of the German soldiers in Poires had not fooled him; if their discipline and sobriety had made any favorable impression, it had been erased when the motorcyclists had pinched his bike.

"I left early in the morning," the manuscript continues. "This time, I got as far as Tantonville without being stopped. I saw some German supply troops there, but went right by them and on through the town. Beyond it, though, I had to take a roundabout road because the German Military Police were now patrolling the main roads continually, watching over the rear elements of their steadily advancing column. I met some refugees who told me that the head of the German column must be at Nancy already. This news spurred me, but the difficulties were becoming serious, as I perceived when coming out on the main road again, at the top of the slope at Ceintrey. There I was stopped almost immediately, and in spite of my papers, which were in order, forced to go into a cattle pen. There were already a couple of dozen other civilians there, all guarded by a sentry who walked a post that ran the length of the pen. I left my bike leaning against a tree outside, thinking that I might soon have use for it again.

"I passed about an hour in that place. I went in dry, but

emerged soaked, because a thunderstorm came up while I was there. It didn't last long, but the water came down hard for a while. My fellow-captives told me that we were to be let go after the passage of a big convoy of prisoners which was being sent on to Nancy. Without waiting any longer, profiting by the sentry's absence at the other end of his post, I lay down on the ground and, wrapping my arms about my chest, rolled under the barbed wire and bumped against the rear wheel of my faithful bike. It only took an instant to push it out on the road and mount it, shielded from the view of the sentinel by an embankment. I coasted down the slope without using the motor, and didn't start it up until two hundred yards further on, at the beginning of the almost impassable little side road that leads to Clairey."

At this point, I must confess, my old acquaintance, Monsieur Boivin, began to astonish me. I had not thought of him either as so agile or, from my point of view at least, so reckless. He was not bound upon a mission of great public importance, nor were his loved ones in danger. In his place, I should have stayed in the pen. I can ascribe the increasing vigor of his reactions only to his increasing sense of injustice. After all, his papers were in order!

"I took the little side road without hesitation," the narrative goes on, "to avoid two German military policemen on a motor-cycle with a sidecar, who, I learned, were patrolling a triangular beat from Ceintrey to Tantonville to Vézelise, coming around once every seven or eight minutes. The triangle has two long sides, of about two miles each, and a short base, of about a mile. The side road cut through the triangle near its tip, by-passing Ceintrey. On this bad road, fortunately not very long, but muddy after the downpour, I had to dismount and walk several times. This delay threw my timing off, and I foresaw that I would be overtaken when I emerged from the side road, for I knew that I would have to take the Ceintrey-Vézelise road as far as the village of Omelmont. But I pushed on as fast as I could, all soaked with rain and sweat. I got to the Ceintrey-Vézelise road and reached Omelmont safely. There I asked whether I could get over to the Vézelise-

Pont-St. Vincent highway without going all the way to Vézelise, where I feared there would be a post of military police. As I was receiving directions, I heard the sound of the motorcycle with the sidecar. I had just time enough to skip into a barn—a close call. I again had seven or eight minutes' grace.

"According to the directions given me, there was only one way to get to the highway I wanted without going through Vézelise. This was to go down a goat path as far as a little stream, carrying my bike on my back; cross over the stream on the trunk of a tree that was left there to serve as a footbridge [but not for old gentlemen carrying motorbikes!]; and so reach the little village of Houdreville, which is on the highway. I took the chance without hesitation and succeeded in crossing over the tree trunk without mishap. How I managed it, I hardly know. I marvel every time I have another look at the place. Happy at my exploit, but dead beat, splashing through puddles, badly shod with rubber soles that had no grip on the clay soil of the vineyard slopes, I pushed my motorbike along with difficulty, falling to my knees many times. I tried to use the motor to get up the slope of the ravine on the Houdreville side of the stream, but the narrow path, slippery with rain, made it useless. I still had a hundred yards to go, when all at once I heard that blasted motorcycle behind me. It was passing on the road that I had left to cut across country, about three hundred yards away. I immediately tried to hide in some vines, but I had been seen. The vines were not high enough to conceal me, or perhaps I had been seen from farther away, before I started to take cover. Whatever the case, the motorcycle stopped, the fellow in the sidecar took aim with his carbine and loosed off a clip of bullets at me that hit all around, but didn't wound me. Instinctively, I let myself fall limp, abandoning my motorbike. I saw the butchers on the other side of the ravine looking at me and wondering, probably, how they could get near me. They must have thought it too much trouble, for presently they drove off in the direction of Ceintrey.

"Some minutes later, believing them definitely gone, I resumed my Calvary and finally got onto the highway I had been trying to reach, but I had scarcely put foot on it when I saw my pursuers on the other side of the ravine again. They had turned and were traveling in the direction of Vézelise this time, doubtless meaning to come around on the Vézelise-Pont St. Vincent road, where I now was, and take me alive.

"I lost no time, but got going, knowing that their heavy machine was a great deal faster than my poor little putt-putt. But in spite of my best efforts, after leaving Houdelmont, the next village after Houdreville on the way to Pont St. Vincent, I heard the noise of their powerful motor once again and knew them to be getting closer and closer. The race being unequal, and I having no place to hide, I felt myself lost. The road along which I was driving, like several I had already been on, was littered with the debris of an army in rout. Gear and arms of all sorts lay strewn along the ditches, scattered among dead men, and this abandoned road, on which, for the moment, I and my pursuers were the only living beings, seemed sinister in its loneliness. I fled, but like a hard-pressed beast I felt myself about to be taken. I expected the impact of a bullet against my spine at any second.

"Going down a slope, I saw that the road turned at its foot, and that there was a thicket in a ditch just by the turn. I heard the danger behind me, and I decided to throw myself into the thicket to hide. I hadn't looked about for a weapon, but at my feet, as I dismounted, were several rifles. I grabbed one of them, and automatically, without thinking what I was doing, I checked it to see that there was a cartridge in the chamber. Then, jumping down in the ditch, I crouched behind a sapling, on one knee, awaiting my pursuers. A few seconds passed. They appeared, and raced into easy range—thirty or forty yards, perhaps—undoubtedly thinking I had gone on around the turn. Calm, aiming right at the torso, I fired at the man driving the motorcycle. The machine went on for ten or fifteen yards and crashed into the ditch beyond me. It burst into flames instantly."

Here, when I first read the manuscript, I paused. When I reread it, I still pause. To say that I had been surprised by Monsieur Boivin's action would be an understatement. But there was, on reflection, an inevitable quality about it. You start pushing around *people who aren't used to being pushed around and droll consequences are to be expected.*

"I was half crazy, I believe," to quote from Monsieur Boivin's account again. "I jumped on my bike without worrying about the Boches and made off as fast as I could. I got to Xeuilley, the next village, very quickly, completely exhausted, and terribly thirsty. I couldn't refrain from stopping for a drink in the local inn. I was the sole customer, because the countryside was virtually deserted. The young woman in charge of the place looked at me with an astonished air. She must have wondered where I came from. I was hatless and unshaven, and my hands, knees, and elbows were covered with red mud. I must have looked like a poilu of 1914 who had been buried by a shell and dug out alive. I asked her for water and did a summary wash job on my face and hands. I then heard her say, 'Aren't you Monsieur Boivin? I thought so when you came in, but I couldn't believe that you could be in such a state. My name is Poirot. I used to live with my parents in Nancy, near your house, but I was very young then, so probably you don't recognize me. But I recognize you very well.' I explained my appearance by telling her I had got caught up in the battle and had had all kinds of trouble to get out of it. She served me a Pernod, diluted with plenty of water, which helped quench my thirst, and I admit (I hope I'll be pardoned for it) that I immediately ordered another one, which I drank, this time, with no water at all. It was already late, and, still hoping to get to Nancy that same day, I said good-bye, and a quarter of an hour later arrived at Pont-St. Vincent, where I found part of the town in flames and the big bridge over the Moselle completely destroyed. One more difficulty for me, since I had to get over to the other side. I decided to cross the bridge at Maron, a few miles downstream, and I was driving along the towpath by the bank when I saw the Boches building a temporary bridge to replace the destroyed one. A boat, which they had commandeered, had just unloaded some materials on my side of the river. One of the Frenchmen in it, seeing me with my motor bike, quite evidently looking for a way to cross over, called to me and offered me a place in the boat. He set me down on the other bank.

"My cup of joy now flowed over. I was sure to arrive, for now there was not a road or bypath where I would not be perfectly at home. I put my leg over the bike and struck off on the main highway. An hour later, at about eight in the evening, I arrived at my house—sore, crookbacked, hungry, but happy. I was not to begin to worry until the next day, for I went to sleep almost immediately and slept as if I had nothing on my conscience.

"Very early in the morning, I was awakened by the sound of marching troops. Looking out of my bedroom window, I had the pain of seeing a great convoy of French prisoners passing. I stood at a ground floor window and watched the prisoners march past all day and part of the next night. What a humiliation! Our Army of the East, surrounded and betrayed, had surrendered to the enemy. All the men complained of having been sold out and abandoned by their generals. As they went by, many gave me money, wallets, letters, and keepsakes to send back to their relatives. I was destined to have considerable trouble in delivering them all. The day, depressing for everybody, was especially so for me.

"I began to think of the horrible consequences my hasty act might have had. I could have been arrested, and in that case it would have been all up with me. The consequences for my family would have been something I was afraid to contemplate. I wasn't sure, for that matter, that I had not been seen. In my excitement I had seen nothing, noticed nobody; I had acted without the least precaution. And then, too, I began to feel a kind of remorse. Had I had the right to kill? And then to abandon my victims! I argued with myself, unsuccessfully, that this was war and that I ought to consider it a legitimate act of self-defense. But I had not been in uniform. I could not regain my calm. The night was restless and full of nightmares. I felt tired when I got up next morning.

"I decided I ought to go back to Poires to reassure my family, but my true reason was a desire to know what had happened to the two Germans. Like an assassin, I could not stop myself from returning to the scene of the crime. I decided I would pass by Pont-St. Vincent and retrace the route I had followed forty-eight hours earlier. I hoped to learn the details of what had happened, either by going over the terrain or by questioning people who lived near by. I had no trouble traveling this time. The war had passed over us. There were few Germans left in the countryside, and in any event an armistice had been declared. When I got back to the thicket at the bend in the road I stopped and pretended to putter with my motor. The first thing I noticed was the burned-out wreckage of the motorcycle. There were also a few shreds of burned clothing. That was all. Much moved, I tried to reconstruct the scene. Nothing had been changed, and a rifle I saw lying in the ditch was probably the very one I had used. My conscience was less and less easy. I wished I knew what had happened to the two men. Were they dead or alive? Had they suffered much? I left this silent place, hoping to learn a little further on that my victims were not dead.

"I went on as far as Houdreville, and as I entered the village I saw a priest, with a cane in his hand, who seemed to be out for a stroll. He was coming toward me, walking briskly, and he didn't have the look of a village priest about him. As we approached each other I saw that he was still relatively young and a wearer of the Legion of Honor, and I felt sure that he must be the chaplain of some army unit. I stopped and asked him if he had any news. We talked about the catastrophe and exchanged a few ideas, and then I had an inspiration. Perhaps this man would be able to tell me what I wanted to know. I thought I could have confidence in him because of his rank, his calling, but above all because of his affable, honest air.

" 'Monsieur Chaplain,' I said, 'for that's what I'm sure you are, I have something serious to communicate to you, and a great service to beg of you.'

" 'Do you want to confess to me?' he asked.

" 'When you have heard me out, you may call it a confession or a confidence, whichever you please.'

" 'Come with me,' he said. 'As you have guessed, I am not the curé of the village. Only the turn of events has forced me to remain here, in the house of an old lady, for a few days or perhaps a few weeks. If, during that time, I can be of any use to you, I will do my best. Now come with me and tell me what it's all about.'

"So, confidentially and without any third party present, I got rid of my load of care, in telling this man, without omitting a single detail, all the events of that terrible day and the way I now felt about them.

"After listening to me, he attempted to raise my spirits, endeavoring, by touching words, to demonstrate that my scruples were exaggerated, that war was a sad business, but that it was a duty to defend oneself when in danger. Finally, he assured me that he would do everything possible to find out what I wanted to know. He had already heard something about the affair, he said, but had not paid much attention to it because it hadn't seemed important. Now circumstances were changed and he would make inquiries. We agreed that I would come back that way in a few days, on my return from Poires to Nancy, and that if he had to go away before, then he would leave a letter for me with his landlady. He would mark the envelope with the numerals of his military class, '14, and of mine, '97. To obtain the letter from the landlady, I would have only to repeat these numerals.

"Having reached this agreement, we parted, and I continued toward Poires, where I arrived during the afternoon. I stopped at the MAIRIE, where Odile had been doing my work during my journey. I met the Mayor there. Noticing my look of exhaustion and distress, he asked me what in the world had happened to me. I told him. He said I had done well, but underlined the risks I had run. The Mayor and the Chaplain were the only ones I ever took into my confidence about the matter until today. Not even Odile and her mother know the whole story. Thirty-six hours after my arrival at Poires, I set off for Nancy again, promising myself to see the chaplain at Houdreville and find out what he had learned. He had had to leave the village early that morning, I was told, but I found the letter waiting. I wasted no time opening it. To my joy I learned that I hadn't killed anybody. My conscience was lightened. It is no slight thing to think one has killed another human being, even in self-defense.

"To conclude this narration, I enclose a copy of the chaplain's letter:

Beloved Friend,

Listening to your story and feeling the great distress of your
conscience, I was unable to find the word of consolation equal to
the circumstance. My priestly heart perhaps blamed you, but my
old soldier's heart beat in unison with yours. I prayed God to
inspire me, that I might bring comfort to a great soul in pain, and
He has granted that, from today on at least, you shall have the
moral solace you so much need. Without delay, as we agreed, I
write out the following information (not the fatal sort you feared).

I located the place of the accident you described without any
trouble, especially as boys playing near by gave me some useful
information, without even knowing that I was especially interested.
There remained on the spot only some twisted metal, a knapsack,
and two charred waterproofs.

Mme. Petitier told me that the Thouvenin boy had brought the
two injured Germans to her house at about six forty-five on the
evening you remember so well. He had been on the way home
from the fields when he saw the motorcycle and sidecar in flames.
One of the wounded men, the motorcyclist, had received a bullet
in the shoulder, and his left arm was badly burned. The other,
badly burned about the face and neck, seemed to have either a
fracture or a bad sprain of the right leg; in addition both had
abrasions and cuts on their heads. An ambulance came at about
eight o'clock to pick them up. By that time, they had already
been bandaged by medical soldiers from the dressing station at
Omelmont. According to the medics, neither was in danger of
death.

As to the wounded, there is no doubt that somebody fired at
them. The motorcyclist lost all control and ran into a tree, the
gas tank took fire, and the men had a hard time getting clear of
the burning machine. There was no search for their assailant,
because they hadn't seen anybody and, as many French soldiers
were still scattered through the forest on that Saturday, the shooting was attributed to some straggler.

I think that your exaggerated regret will find a palliative in the
reading of this message. Your scruples, which I respect, were due
to a fine sensibility, but should now be dissipated. They will give
place completely to the peace of mind that you must already

have partially recovered if you have prayed to God, as I advised you.

Next time you come by, stop and see me; I have a number of things still to tell you. We will chat like comrades, soldiers of '14, before a bottle of excellent local wine; we will talk especially of the not so distant time when we were happy, when we hoped that the age of atrocities had passed forever, and that the sacrifices we had made would permit us to hope.

Your friend,

M. Albert

"But I have never seen the good man again," Monsieur Boivin wrote. "He never returned to the region of Poires. The incident had no sequel, and I am writing it out for you now only because I have the gout and I thought it might interest you.

"Affectionately,

"Your father-in-law,

"Boivin"

I have heard a French lecturer * in the United States in 1945 say that there was no Resistance before the Germans invaded Russia in June, 1941. This sounded like a reverberation of the old Vichy charge that all active members of the Resistance were Communists, Jews or "terrorists," (like M. Boivin, no doubt) and that their love for Russia, not France, governed their actions. I wondered why the man was lecturing under the auspices of an institution friendly to France.†

I cannot furnish a definite answer to the question of when Resistance started. But I do remember what I was told, in the small town of Antrain-sur-Couesnon, in northern Brittany, early in August, 1944, after the Americans had broken south through Avranches. I asked the local Resistance chief when it had begun in his part of the country. He was the tax collector for the surrounding district and at the same time the leading poacher, two remarkable qualifications for his post. As collector he could visit a lot of people without causing suspicion, and as poacher he knew

* Jacques de Lacretelle of the Académie Française.
† Columbia University.

every occult path through the forests. He was a fine man and by the time the first Americans arrived there he had rounded up four hundred German prisoners and locked them in a barn. So I had confidence in what he said. He told me the people in the district had killed a German in July, 1940, that the Germans had shot hostages, and there had been a guerrilla war ever since. Brittany is a province where people have hot tempers, but I hardly think that I stumbled upon a unique case.

A month later, in liberated Paris, I asked the same question of three officers of the FRANC-TIREURS ET PARTISANS DE FRANCE, often referred to as F.T.P., the great Leftist segment of the F.F.I., or FORCES FRANÇAISES DE L'INTÉRIEUR. They told me that they had returned to Paris after being demobilized in the summer of 1940 —all three had served in the ranks in THAT army—and had found Resistance functioning already.

"There were even chaps in the streets selling anti-German newspapers openly," one of them said. He was a Negro from Martinique, a teacher in a primary school. "They were so green they didn't know it was an offense, and they were surprised when they were arrested. But they caught on very quickly."

These men had all belonged to labor unions the Germans had abolished—which in practice meant forced underground. So they found themselves members of illegal organizations by the time they returned from the Army. These clandestine labor organizations furnished the framework for one large and important portion of the Resistance. The Communist Party, which had been dissolved at the beginning of the war, following the Moscow pact of August, 1939, had been functioning illegally for almost a year already. It also was converted into a Resistance organization. Despite the fact that the Soviets were officially at peace with Hitler, French Communists went into action against the Germans immediately.

The commander of all the Resistance forces in the Parisian region during the insurrection of August, 1944, was a former automobile worker named Tanguy, known in the F.F.I. as Colonel Rol. He was a graduate of the F.T.P.—all the Resistance organizations had been merged for the final struggle—and he had as direct subordinate a former aviation mechanic named Jung, in the

Resistance Lieutenant Colonel Rochet. The basic unit of the
F.T.P. was a group limited to eight men. Rol and Rochet belonged to the same group in August, 1940. They were its sole
survivors in 1944. The others, one by one, had all been executed.
One man in each group, at the beginning, had contact with a
higher unit in the detachment. A detachment consisted of four
groups. Later, detachments were linked in battalions—four of
them made one battalion. Some of the groups were drawn from
the Communist Party, some from the labor unions. But most
were mixed, since many Communists were union members too.
The groups had to arm themselves at the expense of the enemy.
Rochet told me how he and a comrade, since executed, had
followed the German non-coms from a hotel in the Place de la
République in August, 1940. The Germans wore beautiful automatic pistols. The Frenchmen carried rubber blackjacks under
their shirts. "The result was positive," Rochet said, showing me
a fine German PARABELLUM pistol in the top drawer of his desk.
"This pistol is the first firearm we ever had, the nucleus of the
arsenal of a battalion."

Breton peasants and Paris workmen were then about as different
in politics and mentality as two groups could be. Yet spontaneously and at about the same time each in its own way had begun
the battle. In dozens or hundreds of other spots in France the
same process must have been beginning. I therefore think that
the theory of a Resistance movement beginning only after June,
1941, is an invention of all the little Messieurs Seguin who
could not make up their minds until the autumn of 1944. Paris
had a word for them—"LES RÉSISTANTS DE SEPTEMBRE."

It was to take nearly four years, after the dispersed beginnings
of Resistance, however, to convert most of France to violence and
to merge all the streams of Resistance into one great flood. It was
a constant process of unsteady speed. There were times when it
went very slowly and others very fast. And only at the end were
all the streamlets of Resistance aware of one another's existence.
It was, on a large scale, the story of the mess in "Despair Is Dead."
Only gradually did the collective Santerres recognize the collective
Randois and Despérados. Even then, it has been said, only a
minority of the French people was "in the Resistance." That is

as pertinent as saying that here, even during the war, only a minority of the population, ten millions out of 140,000,000, was in the armed forces.

In the first year that followed the Pétain armistice little of this nascent, scattered dissidence appeared on the surface. France lay stunned under the blow, trying to understand what had happened to her. And the Germans made some attempt to win her over, employing in the process their usual mixture of intelligence and stupidity, with the stupidity, as always, predominating in the end. The German troops who first entered France were, as you have probably read, an impressive lot, calculated to create the impression of a race of athletes. Their attitude toward the civilian population was "correct" with even a hint of cordiality. The famous poster of the handsome, virile German soldier with a couple of French children playing in his arms appeared on hoardings all over France. The invaders were extremely helpful to refugees returning to their homes. They wanted to restore a normal economy so they could milk it. But even then, while they were trying so hard to impress, the brutality and disdain with which they handled the prisoners of war were antagonizing the French. For they had seemingly forgotten that in a country of 40,000,000, practically everyone must be the relative or friend of at least one prisoner—when there are two million prisoners.

The selection of top-grade troops for the first occupation did not work out so well either, for since it was impossible to keep the best troops always there, the population soon began to notice a deterioration in the quality of the Army of Occupation. The same thing was true of matériel. And where the physique and equipment of the first Germans in France impressed a stunned country, the timid, ill-clothed, limited-service troops, boys and old men, who in large part replaced them, symbolized for the French the decline of Hitler's fortunes, as did the horse-drawn transport that replaced the tanks.* The myth of the master race was exploded long before the armies of liberation landed.

As for the German soldier shielding French children, the steadily increasing difficulty of feeding the children soon taught

* See p. 158 of "In Our Prison."

French mothers what the poster really meant. The milch cows and the eggs and meat and wheat that should have fed the children were being shipped off into Germany. And the individual German soldier soon became known as a shameless grafter, re-selling the requisitioned foodstuffs at black market prices when-ever he could.*

With their confidence that countries can be controlled by "élites," and their belief in the power of the lie, the Germans naturally made a great effort to enlist French intellectuals. They went all out on the aesthetic and intellectual plane, inviting French writers and artists for tours of Germany and subsidizing publica-tions that paid high rates for contributions. Independent literary magazines were unable to find paper.

Writers are peculiarly susceptible to flattery. They are also peculiarly unable to withstand economic pressure, since there are so few outlets for their work. There had been a small pro-Fascist clique among French writers before the war, among them the talented but increasingly mad Louis-Ferdinand Céline, who wrote novels of black despair, and the snarling false pedant Charles Maurras of the newspaper L'ACTION FRANÇAISE. Maurras had de-voted fifty of his seventy years to profitable abuse of the Republic. He habitually referred to the Republic as LA GUEUSE, "the drab." Now there were accessions. Some were weak sisters, easily shaken, others bandwagon-jumpers. One French writer—also of the ACADÉMIE FRANÇAISE—whose reputation had been gained as an interpreter of Anglo-Saxon culture stood poised with one foot on the bandwagon and the other in the United States, where he told everybody he met that the Germans were invincible. A few hundred others were simply venal, running eagerly to spew filth on the "terrorists," as they always would have spewed to order for anybody who paid them. Prewar French journalism had been infested with cynical blackmailers; these men did not change. All together they made a great noise, and the overwhelming majority of intellectuals, honest and patriotic, were precluded from using the public prints to refute them.

Such a propaganda, continuous and unopposed, could influence

---

* Some American soldiers later sold on the black market, but they at least sold American goods.

many of the timid or the merely isolated. So the organization of a medium for counter-propaganda was one of the first necessities of the Resistance.

By far the most powerful lever with which Hitler tried to move French opinion during the first years of occupation was the politico-geographical fiction known as LA ZONE LIBRE, the Free Zone, usually referred to in the United States as Vichy France. Instead of occupying all France in 1940, Hitler took over only the northern two-thirds of the country plus the coastal strips. A line running roughly from Geneva on the Swiss frontier to Poitiers in the Loire was the border between Occupied Zone and Free Zone.

The Free Zone, although it contained only one-third of the area and much less than one third of the food of France, was overpopulated because of the great number of refugees from the North who remained there. It was, as you perhaps remember, administered, at least officially, by the dreary old Marshal, who did exactly as the Germans told him. He cried and dug his heels in now and then, as when he dismissed Laval, the Reich's favorite French traitor, in December, 1940, but he always ended by yielding, as when he took Laval back in the following April. And his gestures of protest—petulance would be a better word—grew progressively feebler and less frequent. The Marshal preached, as only an old man in fear of damnation could, that France had brought all its troubles on itself by deserting the principle of authority, both religious and secular. His doctrine was guilt, repentance and self-abasement. He was therefore well qualified to keep France on her knees.

If conquered France collaborated loyally with Germany, the Germans might even "restore" the northern zone (i.e., permit the Vichy Government to move there), the Marshal used to say in the first months of the occupation. (Monsieur Seguin offered to lengthen the nanny goat's tether if she would be a good nanny goat.) Only Britain's unreasonable resistance prolonged the war and prevented Hitler from showing his generosity. But if the French acted in a manner to displease Hitler, the Germans would move south and take over "Free" France. (The wolf would eat the bad nanny goat.)

This reiterated warning had a certain effect. Millions considered the Marshal a wise old man who had saved one third of a loaf, minus the coastal crusts, for his countrymen; "While look what had happened to those stubborn Poles and Norwegians, MA CHÈRE —they lost everything!" Dissidence was much stronger in the North, from the beginning. People there figured things couldn't be much worse. "No hope can know no fear."

In the Free Zone the police of Vichy had the aid of uniformed proto-Nazis like the LÉGION DES ANCIENS COMBATANTS and the SERVICE D'ORDRE DE LA LÉGION. These were "veteran's" organizations, encouraged by the government, which accepted as members veterans and non-veterans alike. The police and these sinister clowns harried "political criminals," a term which included Spanish Republicans, De Gaullists, Communists, or just people who called the Marshal a fossil. The concentration camps to which Vichy sent these people offered accommodations no more luxurious than those in Germany or Czechoslovakia, although there was not so much systematic torture of the prisoners. In place of torture there were callous brutality and short rations. LE RADEAU DE LA MÉDUSE, by Leon Moussinac, is a fragment of the diary * that Moussinac, a poet and critic, kept at the Camp of Gurs, in the Pyrénées Orientales Department. The title is taken from the name of a painting in the Louvre known, through reproductions, to every French schoolchild. The painting, which is by Géricault, shows the survivors of the shipwrecked frigate MEDUSA dying of starvation on their raft, in the middle of the South Atlantic.

The Raft of the Medusa

by LEON MOUSSINAC

Autumn 1940 at the camp at Gurs

September 21. Petit-Louis has served out his sentence (his twelfth condemnation I think). He leaves the camp followed by

* Since published as a book, under the same title.

the farewells of all the "old timers." Someone yells after him, "See you soon!" It is hard to tell whether that means he hopes to join Petit-Louis in liberty or to see Petit-Louis back in prison.

I am on the potato-peeling detail. It helps to kill time. The kitchens are set up all along the main camp street. There are 100 pounds of potatoes, meant for the soup, not "eating potatoes." We never have potatoes to eat. And 100 pounds for a thousand portions of soup (since there are still a thousand of us in the camp) leave hardly a trace in the soup kettles when mealtime comes.

We received over the ever mysterious grapevine a copy of PARIS-SOIR. It contains an article on Block B that provokes general indignation. The whole paper is full of nothing but lies. Monsieur Nicolas Mouneu affirms that the only prisoners in Block B are "swindlers, crooks, shady business men and general bad actors." Speaking of our food, he says that we are wakened in the morning by "the good odor of coffee that is served to us (sic) and the sound of the guitars of the Spaniards across the road." This same person assures his readers that our "re-education" is progressing nicely. Monsieur Nicolas Mouneu, it is to be hoped, will not be surprised some day at receiving a certain number of swift kicks in the pants. That is how the new press of the new state keeps the new Frenchman informed.

September 22. Clearer today. It is almost as warm as a day in summer, but where are the swallows? I am very weak and can't stay on my feet for long. Yet I set about doing a serious job of delousing myself, out in the alley between the barracks, and naked. It has become a routine job with a technic of its own but I have neglected it a little these last days. Any repugnance I ever felt has long since vanished.

Without noticing it, I began to whistle. For a long time nobody has paid any attention to the camp regulations. But why should I whistle? For the same reason that one sings. Perhaps to get something off one's chest or to express something. I haven't sung for a long time, because now my voice is cracked. But I still whistle on key, and yesterday it was an old Ukrainian song that I had on a record in Paris. I fell into the rhythm of the melody absolutely unconsciously. The first time I heard this song it was in a garden at Kharkov where a group of writers were giving a reception for me in 1934. It was just such a Ukrainian night as one imagines through the poems of Gogol. Yet this memory meant nothing to me at the time. Absorbed in examining the seams of my underwear, I was gradually conscious that something strange was happening. A group of men had come out of the barracks one by one and gathered about me. Noticing only that all of them were Ukrainians, I finally recognized the song myself. These men did not move but looked at me with curiosity and surprise— and emotion too. Then I smiled at them and imagined what my own sentiments would have been if a prisoner far from my own country, among strangers, I had suddenly heard someone whistle JEANNE D'AYMÉ or LE BOUVIER, folk-songs of my native Quercy. A far-off fatherland had called to these men, had gathered them together around a naked stranger as destitute as themselves who was delousing himself while whistling the song so out of place in this Pyrenean landscape, all criss-crossed with barbed wire.

I exchanged a few words with them. I don't know for what reason they were arrested. They also are a little suspicious of me. But for an instant the lovely Ukrainian night, all golden and blue, was before our eyes, the infinite plain where poetry and music took on the voice of love and death.

Daniel R. was taken to the infirmary. His course on the age of Pericles has therefore been postponed. One of the prisoners is very sick. We sent in a hurry call for the doctor. This affair has depressed us all. Many of us are afraid of death. I dread the outbreak of panic.

October 9. I am feeling a little better this afternoon. I decided at last to give the lecture that I have promised to our clandestine "university." I addressed an audience of about thirty of my comrades, old and young, assembled in Barrack No. 6, while some of the others kept watch outside. I had been asked to talk on the origins of the French language. It was very moving. I was struck by these attentive faces that seemed to lean toward me. Using an elementary grammar and a school anthology of the classics of the French language which I had brought along in my exodus from Paris, I chose as illustrations for my lecture the text of THE

OATH OF STRASBOURG, and excerpts from THE SONG OF ROLAND and THE CHRONICLES of Froissart. I quoted from memory some verses of Villon and, to finish, Ronsard's sonnet, LA MORT DE MARIE. When I reached this point, the emotion rose to such a pitch that every eye in the audience was filled with tears. I felt all the greatness—I might say the human grandeur—of this scene that I was living.

"Pour obsèques reçois mes larmes et mes pleurs,
 Ce vase plein de lait, ce panier plein de fleurs
 Afin que, vif et mort, ton corps ne soit que roses . . ."

I talked for an hour and a half. I was exhausted and almost fainted. I went to lie down in my corner. Never shall I forget this day, those faces, all that beauty in the midst of our rags, our misery, and dominating everything else, our pride at being men and speaking French.

October 14. This afternoon lying on my bunk I noticed D. walking nervously back and forth. Each of us has his own way of suffering hunger, of course. I quite understand that for some it must be terrible. I have succeeded in imposing a sort of discipline on my own stomach. But the looks in my companions' eyes often hurt me. For example, when the bread is being issued each day, and when the soup is being measured out by the ladle. But to get back to the look in D.'s eyes a moment ago, what was he expecting? What was he waiting for? I didn't question him. I have gotten into the habit of talking as little as possible. Talking tires me. The thing is to save one's strength. It must also be said that there are times when silence has a soothing charm of its own. But this continual pacing back and forth, which lasted for an hour and a half, kept me from dozing off. D.'s features were drawn and hard. The way the gaunt muscles stood out in his neck recalled the drawings in Leonardo da Vinci's notebooks. At every instant his anguish grew more acute. What was going to happen? What was D. spying on so intently through the shutters of the barrack? I waited. Suddenly D. came to a stop. Slowly a hard smile spread over his lips, and I heard him muttering to the shadows, "There is the smoke! there is the smoke!" Then

I understood. The fires of the cook shed had just been lighted. This was what D. was waiting for to give him patience to live for a little while longer. "There is the smoke!" He was reassured, once more there was a glimmer of hope in his life. Ah! that gray smoke rising to the sky was lovelier than dawn breaking over the world. It also symbolized a victory of his will, since he had not given in. But how would he ever reach the end of his two years unless something changed, for him, and for all of us? Hunger makes us dream of sumptuous meals. Sometimes I wake up to find my mouth watering with the savor of meat. In Hutment 13 one of the prisoners, a cook by trade, spends the whole day making a collection of cooking recipes. As soon as a chapter is finished, he reads it to his companions, and each of them gives his suggestions and opinions. Each of them talks of his own tastes as if to see who can make the others drool the most. "And I, when I get out, I am going to set myself up to a thick steak with French fried and a bottle of beaujolais." I have often tried to change the subject of these rather cruel conversations. It is no use. We even exchange addresses of restaurants.

The men in Hutment 5 are the lucky ones today. It is their turn to divide up the bones from the soup. Two big baskets full. Their turn to be the "zoo at feeding time."

Since they had no public outlet for their thoughts, some French writers during the earliest period of the occupation confined their writing to their diaries. Among these records one of the most moving is that of Jean Guéhenno, man of letters, who defined his vocation in one of his pages, which follows:

Voltaire originated the phrase, "man of letters," to designate a new duty and a new honor. Just as in other centuries there had been men of arms, and men of the law, to carry on the social ceremonies, henceforth there should be men of letters, free and makers of free men, and liberty would be their weapon and their honor.

A man is free or a slave according to the measure of his soul. A true man of letters is not a purveyor of diversions. His liberty

is not the liberty of his laziness or of his musings. Idle contemplation of himself is not enough, nor are the subtleties of his mind.
For any man of principles, liberty, even more than his own liberty,
is the liberty of others. He cannot feel himself free when two
millions of his compatriots are hostages in the prisons of the
conquerors, when forty million of men around him preserve what
remains of their dignity only by silence and cunning.

*Guéhenno is a frail sage with parchment-like skin, lank black
hair and prominent white teeth. He looks unworldly—an intelligence held to earth by the exact minimum of the corporeal required to keep him from volatilizing and disappearing altogether.
The parts of his diary given here cover a period from 1940 to the
spring of 1944. If the arrangement of this volume were strictly
chronological, I should break the diary up into small bits and run
them in separate sections of the book. But in that way you would
lose some of the feel of Guéhenno. The diary as he wrote it would
make about nine hundred printed pages, but only a portion was
published during the occupation. It was to be published in its
entirety in 1946.*

*Soon after writing up the first part of the diary Guéhenno made
effective contact with certain colleagues and with them succeeded
in finding a medium that would reach the public. Portions of the
diary, including all those translated here, were published "at the
expense of some literate patriots, at Paris, under the Oppression,"
on August 1, 1944. That made it one of the late publications of
the Midnight Press, for on August 18-19 the insurrection began,
and on August 25 the German military governor of Paris surrendered. It was published under the title of* DANS LA PRISON, *and
signed with the author's Resistance pseudonym, Cévennes, a
range of mountains in the southwest of France.*

In Our Prison

by JEAN GUEHENNO (CEVENNES)

June 17, 1940

Well, it is all over. An old man who has no longer even the voice of a man, but speaks like an old woman, informed us at twelve-thirty today that last night he sued for peace.

I am thinking of all the youth of France. It was cruel to send them off to war, but is it any less cruel to force them to live in a dishonored country?

I shall never believe that men are made for war. But, also, I know that they are not made to be enslaved.

June 18

At nightfall I walked up the road to the plateau that overlooks the city. It was so strange. The Germans are only a dozen kilometers away. They will probably enter the city tomorrow morning. . . . Yet it was an evening like any other evening! People were standing in front of their doorways enjoying the evening air. The rout has swung off toward the South, and we were alone on the road. At long intervals a cannon boomed like a warning. We could still make out the red roofs in the plain below and the white fronts of the houses, dominated by the weird silhouette of the cathedral. The moon rose behind the steeples, and far in the background the glow of burning gasoline dumps reddened the horizon. The smoke shrouded the whole sky as far as the mountain, like an immense black flag.

June 27

The military philosophy of history: It is the valor of armies and their generals that wins battles; but it is of course, "the fate of battle" that loses them. (See General Weygand's address to the troops.)

I am trying to take a calmer view of things.

(1) Once again MY country, the country that is only an idea, has not been invaded and never will be.

(2) Pétain is not France. Pétain and Laval do not speak for us. Their word is not binding on us and is powerless to dishonor us.

(3) The only valid measure of the disaster must be on a world scale. On the world scale, France is not beaten.

This is the February PUTSCH all over again.* They failed in the Place de la Concorde. Then they had one river to cross—the Seine—and the Chamber of Deputies to take by assault. This time to succeed, they had to flee across five or six rivers, the Meuse, the Marne, the Seine, the Loire. The whole thing is nothing more than an ignoble settling of old political scores.

July, 1940

Victory would not have changed my thoughts on any subject of any importance. Why should defeat change them?

Proud of the battles they lost, our new masters are organizing silence. But there is silence and silence. In the silence of his heart, every man is his own master.

What efforts they make to force a word of recantation from us! If you do this, they promise, you will be born again, you will rise again. A trick for stealing souls. They count on our weariness to wring a lie from us. They urge us to repent, but we have nothing to repent.

Our only right henceforth is to comment on the messages and laud the wisdom of a marshal of the other war who is now too senile to count the stars on his own sleeves, an old stockholder in the army who repeats whatever his prompters whisper in his ear. We wanted to believe that military servitude had done with this old soldier long ago. But, since we were not prompt enough at beating our own breasts, the exploiters of defeat pushed him

* February 6, 1934: the fascist element in France, led by the *Croix de feu* and reactionary veterans' association, attempted to overthrow the government. Massed in the Place de la Concorde, they attempted to cross the Seine and capture the *Palais Bourbon* where the Chamber of Deputies was in session.

forward and selected him to read the act of contrition and submission that they had already drawn up for us.

Stupidity and hypocrisy are enthroned—"moral order," the
virtue of the rich. The ladies of the upper classes hug themselves
with joy. No longer will they have to compete for chickens in the
market against women in cotton dresses. At last everybody will
eat according to his social standing.

The defeat of France is only one episode of the European civil
war. Beneath the conflict between nations lies a deeper social
conflict. Each nation is so sharply divided within itself that some
one of the parties that compose it can think that their country's
loss is their gain. Thus, for some groups of Frenchmen, the misfortune of France is such a victory as they no longer dared to
hope for.* The Republic has lost; therefore they have won.

These days that we are passing through reveal men as they are.
Looking back over the history of the past fifty years, over the
extraordinary effort of so many Frenchmen to achieve some degree
of well-being and self-respect, it is easy to understand what a cruel
blow such progress must have been to the selfishness of the old
"first families." What pleasure is there in having what everybody else has? Some people are so made that they feel less happy
and less free as soon as others are as happy and as free as themselves. The happiness of others seems to cheapen their own. The
liberty of others seems to them to be license, anarchy, not to say
a menace. They are filled with hatred for these upstarts, these
thieves. And that is how things stand. Today, fifty years of hatred
thinks it has its revenge at last. Undoubtedly our tribulations
weigh on these "first families"; but they have compensations.
Once more they think that henceforth they alone shall be free
and happy. Fools! They speak of our unhappy country as a master
speaks of a sick domestic servant; they accuse it of malingering.

The common people, always ready to believe what they are
told, all stunned by the disaster, rub their eyes and wonder if,
after all, it may not be true that they are more guilty than
unfortunate.

Is it really so necessary to upbraid those who are suffering? Must
they be further degraded and covered with shame? Is this the way

* A "divine surprise," Maurras called it. (Author's note.)

to restore their courage? I know now what it means to be a people. I feel it more clearly in our distress than ever in our glory. To every person of my country, I should like to make a sign of brotherhood.

WE are not of the "first families." Our country is only an idea. It is a country that cannot be invaded. It is our impregnable refuge where shame cannot touch us. What connection can there be between this idea and the shortage of airplanes and armor-plate, the blunders of generals, the baseness and scheming of traitors? It is their nature to degrade all things and to turn every-thing to their own petty advantage. We know that their crimes will bring great sufferings upon us. We accept the sufferings, but we reject the dishonor.

Then too, we know only too well what history is—its im-morality, its cruelty. It misses no chance to avenge itself on legend. It seems to be jealous of the gods a people carries in its soul. It seizes on every inadvertence, on every one of those moments of slumber when we lose sight of these gods that guide us. Then it makes us stumble and fall. But the very fall itself awakens us. We recover our deep faith.

Should we cease to love France the way we love her, and love another France in another way? But France has been here for centuries! As well try to level off her mountains, shut off her rivers, change every aspect of a meadow. One is as hopeless against an idea as against the sky and the stars.

We will not admit that France for these last fifty years has been so ugly and ignoble. The envy of the entire world would testify against this calumny. If it is true that she was happy, is happiness such an ugly thing? Some Pharisees pretend to scorn it? We have, it is true made great efforts to achieve it. But it is safe to say that everyone is French to this extent, and that envy alone inspired the German critic * who accused God of having Himself naturalized as a Frenchman.

* Friedrich Seiburg, whose book, *Gott in Frankreich*, translated into English and French as *Is God a Frenchman?*, conceded France a higher degree of material and spiritual civilization than other countries had attained, but mockingly insisted that the very perfection of her way of life made her out of step in a world of discontent and change. Seiburg subsequently joined the Nazi propaganda department. (*Translator's note.*)

God, the eternal spectator, if He exists, if He is neither absurd nor cruel, if He does not believe that men should toil for toil's sake but rather to make His earth more beautiful, if He likes men sometimes to raise their heads and look at the heavens— God, looking down between two clouds on France when she was herself, must not have been too dissatisfied with us on the whole.

The domain of the French, the part of the earth that God had allotted to them, was fairly well cultivated. Here and there a mountain top lay fallow. But they have made up for it by enriching the plains. They had more bread than they could eat, more wine than they could drink. They fed their wheat to the chickens and distilled their wine for fuel. The villages, not yet models of neatness, were nevertheless cleaner than they had ever been before. New roofs of slate or tile glistened in the sun. Between the church and the MAIRIE, God could pick up buildings where little children were learning to read and write and figure—and think. To think— what an ambition that is! Each one of them aspired to become a person. What aristocrats these French democrats were! Across the wheatfields, the vineyards, the forests, the meadows, from village to village, from city to city, gleaming between the rows of plane trees, went the roads, a web spread out over the whole land, a network of sociability. Automobiles, blue Peugeots, black Renaults, ran toward each other like the thoughts of friends. The cities expanded, the suburbs spread, as if drawing the country to them. It is true that these new suburbs lent themselves to criticism. City-planners tore their hair. What disorder! What anarchy! Would these Frenchmen never learn! A race of villagers, each of whom wanted to have the whole horizon to himself. They planted their city houses like farms, contrived to turn their backs to their neighbors, each bent on his own snug privacy. They would sooner have renounced the sun itself than submit to any regimentation.

Out of these motley agglomerations that they built up in the towns where they lived, together and yet alone, great disputes rose, like clouds of dust that here and there obscured the landscape. New prophets for a while might make brains reel; but when the dust had settled, these impenitent individualists returned to their own hearths, dreaming of bread and ways of earning it— bread and liberty. For this was their device: they never separated the two. Bread and liberty. Nor was it for themselves alone that they wanted them, but for all men. It was their mania never to dream, never to think, for themselves alone. Self-centered in little things, but generous in big ones. A people of faithful servants of the mind and of humanity at large.

In summer, in front of tents pitched like those of a caravan, little children used to play at the edge of the sea; at the edge of the world. In their childish meditations, they knew that France did not end there, where it seemed to end, at that first wave that swept away their sand castles, but that she reappeared again beyond the sea, that she was an idea among ideas and therefore, like a star, owed her light to all the world.

But what I imagine moved God most of all, when He looked down between two clouds on France, were those diligent artists that He saw working in houses of glass, carving stones, painting canvas, or perhaps, before shelves loaded with books, covering white paper with black lines. There were perhaps no men on all the earth who better knew how to love His creation. They were attentive and subtle, and so skillful at unraveling meanings, finding the exact tones, delineating mystery with a clean line. When things had passed through their masterly hands, they seemed to become at once clearer and more precious. Stone, colors and words took on a fresher glow, till God Himself looked with quickened interest on His world. He did not know that He had created such great marvels. Grateful, He said, "All this must not perish."

But what is the use of these fables? A game to help a prisoner while the time away . . .

What I know with an ever increasing certitude is that all dignity consists in seeking one's own order within one's self, in searching out the truth, as our old Montaigne says, and when one thinks one has found it, in holding to it regardless of what errors may have passing triumph. The thought is not devoid of melancholy; and it is rather presumptuous perhaps, in the midst of this storm that is sweeping our lives away, not to be satisfied merely to exist without trying to explain and understand one's being. In this involuntary retirement of mine, I often think of myself as an abandoned guitar. It no longer sings; but if by accident one of its strings is struck, a pure sound rises, proving that all music is not dead and testifying to an eternal order.

Why should I keep on writing? It is no longer possible not to see something ridiculous in the exercise of so personal a profession. The times call for modesty. Man is seeking the new conditions of his mere survival as a species. Poor species! Aghast at its own discoveries, lost in a world that it has transformed, victim of its own creations.

We are still the same great apes, greedy and lascivious, who, when the glacial era caught them by surprise and threatened to exterminate them, somehow managed to survive, by becoming men. What shall we become this time? What is happening today is probably of little concern to the conscience of the individual and only makes man's delusion—the impression, that every one of us has, of existing by himself and being the magic and predestined mirror in which the shapeless universe achieves its order and beauty—seem the more fantastic.

All France, all Europe, is in prison. Over the whole countryside, at the doors of schools and MAIRIES, at bridges and crossroads, men in green are standing guard, legs planted wide apart, eyes staring unseeingly before them. From time to time, there is a sharp click of one boot against another. As if by clockwork, one of them moves his joints, brings his heels together, presents arms; and there he is, as wooden again as ever and miraculously even more immobile than before.

He has saluted the New Order, a general in high-peaked cap passing in his car. This puppet show is taking place here and there all over Western Europe thousands of times a day; and we are supposed, it seems, to look at it with reverence. It is practically a scandal for the landscape itself not to snap to attention when the general passes. But the gentle wind goes right on blowing over the eternal hills and fields, the birds sing, and the foliage rustles. We too shall escape from this mechanical nightmare. We shall not snap to attention.

Each of us must paint the walls of his own prison. I do not know what I shall paint on mine; but I am sure that all my old dreams, all the symbols of my faith will be there. This is not the time to change one's faith, but rather the very time to be danger-ously loyal to it. In the sky of my painting, the goddess of liberty will still float. Our imprisonment may last a long while. I shall work unhurriedly. The time has come to write for no aim, for my own pleasure. We are reduced to silence and solitude, but also perhaps to seriousness. Whether or not our cells be full of light depends, after all, only on ourselves.

We should feel honored. A tyrannical power, by attributing so much importance to our thoughts, obliges us to recognize how untoward and irrepressible they are. It gives us back to ourselves. We did not dare to believe we were so important. We were getting old, and our best thoughts were becoming too familiar to us, and liberty made them too easy to come by. Now they are going to begin to cost us something. That is good. The chances are all against these pages ever being published. All contact with living beings is cut off. Abolished are the hope of reaching them immediately and the vain aspiration to change them, which often strains the voice and makes even the most sincere writer lie. To write like a dead man with nothing to look forward to except the Last Judgment is not, all considered, such an unfavorable condition under which to work. I am as free on paper as in my own mind. Nothing now forbids my being my true self. I know—this can be the most difficult and the trickiest of obstacles. Yet what an opportunity to arrive at an intimacy and a depth that no one has ever reached! To work!

*　　*　　*

I wanted to see with my own eyes. We followed a path along a garden plot, climbed over a little wall, and crossed a road. There it was. The property had been "requisitioned for military purposes." It was a fairly deep hollow in a grove of sparsely planted trees. The bullets had buried themselves in the bank. People who had come out from town were walking around the shattered stump of a tree, such as I had seen twenty years ago in the Ardennes. We approached. This was the spot. The tree had been cut off, hacked to pieces by bullets at the level of a man's heart. It had been used all through the winter, four or five times a week. At the foot of the tree, the ground was trampled hard. The bark had peeled off. The tree itself was black with the blood that soaked into it. It could no longer be used, it was too shot up. It had finally toppled over too. The people from near-by farms had carried away the upper part of the trunk and the branches. I stood before it lost in contemplation. In the stump itself a V, yes, a V, had been gouged with a knife. By whom? By the Germans, as a signature to their crime? Rather, I should guess, by some French boy, as a tender salute of friendship and hope to the men who had come to die there, and as a promise that they should be avenged.

A few paces further on was the tree that is now in use. It is a beech. There are only a few bullets in it as yet. Its splintered bark already reveals, however, its white flesh spotted with streaks of blood, always the same height, at the height of a man's heart. There is no trace of bullets below that. The executioners are good shots.

I was filled with grief, disgust, and horror.

* * *

UNOCCUPIED ZONE. The chief concern of the men of Vichy is to keep the people in this zone from knowing what is going on in the other zone.

In order to be more free to carry on their treason, they have to keep public opinion here in a state of ignoble complacency. Above all, no one must learn what the requisitions have been like or the thousands of Frenchmen that have been shot. By relating things as they are and passing around the copy of L'ŒUVRE that announces the new measures taken by the chief of the SS, not only have I rendered myself suspect and become the target of all the spies in the village but I am considered as a troublemaker by everybody. People hesitate to believe me. The figures have become so enormous as to be also incredible. People prefer not to know. By now they are used to it. The men of Vichy have made two Frances, and they have degraded one in order that the Germans may more quietly slaughter the other.

Paris is in the war. Here we are merely in filth. The grossest kind of stupidity reigns. Last night the president of the Vichy Legion, the druggist of the village, who in the last two years has been making up for never having had any influence before in his life, went from house to house asking people to join him in a ceremony before the war monument, where he proposes to collect a little bag of "consecrated earth" to send to Gergovie.*

The same ceremony is to take place in all the villages of France. This morning I decided to go to see this parade of heroes and arranged to cross their line of march. It was not much of a success. Very few people. But the mayor was there, and his deputy, and the schoolteacher—all of them militant Radical-Socialists or Socialists two years ago—and the presidents of local organizations and a few important personalities of the region. Altogether about fifty men, abased by fear, greed or vanity. The mayor wants to make sure of his Legion of Honor. The schoolteacher is afraid of losing his job. The presidents of organizations are always proud to have a chance to march in a parade. Here and there an old invalid had joined the parade for fear that, the next time he had an attack, the druggist might let him die. It is from such fine enthusiasms as these that the new régime draws its support.

But the common people were not there. They have kept their good sense and their sense of honor. The remarks of even those who WERE there warrant some hope. One man was complaining that he had finally been obliged to join the soup line. The deputy said that all that these little bags of earth sent in by all the villages of France really amounted to was so many shovels of earth on the corpse of the Republic. But . . . There were people within earshot so he didn't finish his sentence.

* * *

1943

TO THE GERMAN THAT I MEET IN THE STREET. I cannot quite say what I feel when I meet you. I do not hate you, I no longer hate you. I know that you will never be my master. I pretend not to

---

* In 1941 Vichy inaugurated the scheme of having little bags of "consecrated earth" collected from various war monuments all over France and sent to Gergovie. This actually was an attempt by Vichy to apply to France the Nazi idea of folklore worship. It meant the destruction of the old administrative divisions (departments) created after the French Revolution and a rejuvenation of the pre-Revolution concept of the province. Added significance is given this scheme by the fact that Gergovie is both in the center of France and the site of the defeat of Caesar by the Gaul, Vercingetorix. (*Translator's note.*)

see you. I act as if you did not exist. I have resolved never to
speak to you. I understand your language, but when you address
a word to me, I wave my arms in the air and pretend I do
not understand. The other day however—it was in the Place du
Châtelet you came toward me. You were wandering about like any
other soldier lost in a city, looking for Notre-Dame. Then I con-
descended to understand and, with a gesture, without a word, I
pointed out to you the towers standing out against the sky on the
other side of the river, staring you in the face. You felt like a
fool, you blushed, and I was pleased. That is where we stand.

What are you doing here with that green livery of yours, in our
streets and in our squares? In Paris, in France, a soldier is blue or
khaki. You are too buttoned up. And those swank gloves that you
wear? You are too polite. And your dagger? And your revolver?
An executioner with gloves. And your boots? How many pairs of
shoes one could make out of all that leather for people who now
go barefoot!

I do not hate you. I do not know how to hate. When you get
into the MÉTRO, we crowd together to make room for you. You
are the untouchable. I lower my head a little so that you cannot
see what I am looking at and to deprive you of the pleasure of
exchanging a glance with a fellow human being. You are there in
the midst of us, like an object, in a frozen circle of silence. I
look you over from head to foot, in your uniform now getting a
little shabby and somewhat threadbare at the knees and elbows,
with, in the middle of you, above your navel, your brass belt
buckle with this inscription that I always read with the same
surprise: GOTT MIT UNS!

It gives me pause: GOTT MIT UNS! I try to imagine what this
God who is with you is like. A funny God! Is He still with you
when you shoot hostages? Was He there when you pinned that
heart of white paper on the chest of my friends as a target—for
you like a workmanlike job. But you understand why I cannot
look at you. For after all it might be you! And what if I were
to recognize in your eyes that little gleam that makes you so
good at shooting? There are not so very many of you at Paris, and
six hundred and seventy Parisians have already been shot. Count-

ing ten men to a squad, that makes six thousand seven hundred executioners. How do I know that you are not one of them?

I know that there are many different kinds of men among you, just as there are among us. Some of them rather low types. There are the officers one meets around the Madeleine and the OPÉRA, in their elegant greatcoats, with their high vainglorious caps, that look of conceited stupidity on their faces, those nickel-plated daggers that dangle against their behinds. There are also those busybody little females of your species, those postal clerks, and telephone girls that look like Valkyries and seem so fatuous and vapid. The other day in the Place de la Concorde, in front of the Ministry of the Navy, I had stopped to stare at the sentries, these two puppets who stand motionless on each side of the door. They have been there for two years, without drinking, without eating, without sleeping, like the symbol in the heart of Paris of your lugubrious robot order. I watched them for a while going through their marionette routine. But one eventually tires of the mechanical clock of Nuremberg, and I was leaving, full of disgust, when, as I turned away, I unintentionally bumped into somebody. I apologized, looked up. Who was before me? It was one of those Valkyrie telephone girls, red with rage, frothing at the mouth, ready to call the guard to complain that she had been insulted. But my excuses had put her out of countenance. She pulled herself together and exclaimed with a triumphant air, "Ach! . . . So . . ." How I regretted that I had begged her pardon!

But you are not all alike. I see you every Wednesday morning on my way to work, in the square in front of my office. For what organized pillage do you gather there every week? When I arrive about eight o'clock, your wagons are already parked under the trees along the sidewalk. The men are in the near-by factories gathering up merchandise. Only a few stay behind to guard the wagons and the horses. I sit on a bench a little way off, waiting for my office to open. Most of the men of the detail are peasants, reservists. There are a few young men also, but they are misshapen and deformed. Among them is a sort of dwarf. The seat of his pants almost drags on the ground, and he seems to be the scapegoat of the squad. They stand around talking among themselves, but I am too far off to hear what they say. There hangs over them an air of sadness and homesickness that makes it a pleasure to look at them. But it is not the dwarf who interests me most. It is an old man who, for at least six months, has been there every week, minding the horses, exactly opposite my bench, so unvarying is the routine. I note the signs of wear on his blouse, his trousers, and his boots. He stands at the head of the team of horses, leaning against a pole. He seems so alone, so resigned, so desolate. "ZU BEFEHL," I hear him cry, clicking his heels together every time a sergeant speaks to him. "ZU BEFEHL," without end. He smokes a porcelain pipe like the legendary Germans of the past. Sometimes the dwarf exchanges a few words with him but never for very long. He has only one friend. His friend in exile and in war, during these many years that they have plodded together over the roads of Europe, from the east to the west, under sun and rain, in dust and snow, for so many years when they have marched together without knowing why—"ZU BEFEHL, ZU BEFEHL"—is a horse, the horse on the left-hand side in the team, an old black horse who also has long ago lost track of the sufferings and victories of war. Every Wednesday I watch them exchange signs of affection. The old horse strains at his collar until he succeeds in touching his friend with his muzzle. He nibbles gently at his shoulder, until at last the old soldier turns and strokes the muzzle of the contented beast with his clumsy fingers.

The old man, reduced to himself and to this friendship for his horse throughout the endless sufferings of war and exile, helps me think of you with some pity still and to envisage you as men. We are almost of the same age, this old man and I, and I meditate on our common history as lost Europeans trying vainly for the last forty years to reconcile the demands of our honor and of our hunger. It seems that the hunger of one of us cannot be assuaged except by the starvation of the other, and the honor of one of us must be paid for by the humiliation of the other. This is not true.

But, old man, why don't you go back home? Go back home.

Vercors' Silence of the Sea

Vercors, whom we have already encountered (under the spare alias of Santerre) in "Despair Is Dead," symbolizes the literature of the Resistance for more Frenchmen than perhaps any other writer. This is not only because he was one of the most talented and prolific of the Resistance authors, but because his SILENCE OF THE SEA was the first book to issue from the Midnight Press, in February, 1942, and made a consequent sensation in a country where for nearly two years no other volume had appeared without the official stamp of the German censor.

The very fact that the clandestine press was now able to print books, and very well-made ones, under the noses of the occupants indicated to the public how well the dissidents must be organized and how firmly they must be established. In Britain, Switzerland, South America and the United States, wherever the book arrived, it was a tangible proof of the survival of French intellectual life.

The riddle of Vercors' identity—"the best-kept secret of the Resistance," one of his colleagues called it—added to the author's fame, for readers the world over continued to argue about who he was. Even insiders in the French literary world failed to identify him, because he had written little before the war and there was no mannerism by which he could be recognized. This was not true of several Resistance writers, whose styles were so marked that any well-versed reader had a shrewd suspicion of who they were, no matter how mysterious their pseudonyms. François Mauriac, one of the constant lights of contemporary French literature, was particularly vulnerable. Hundreds of thousands of readers knew how he put words together, and since he had been writing for thirty-five years he found it impossible to change his mannerisms. Mauriac wrote a Midnight Press book called LE CAHIER NOIR over the nom de plume of Forez, but he did not trust his pseudonymity. Shortly before the book appeared he left his elegant apartment on the Avenue Théophile-Gautier in Paris and lived in hiding from then until the liberation. He acted wisely; a day or two after his departure the Gestapo was in his studio going through his papers.

But Vercors was a mystery even to his colleagues in the Resistance. Not more than three of them knew who he was. His wife, incidentally, was one of those who remained in ignorance. The best of the jest, although it could not be told until after the Liberation, was that the strong, resourceful organization that got out the first book consisted primarily of two men, Vercors and a boyhood friend, the novelist Pierre de Lescure.

Jacques Debû-Bridel tells the story of the founding of the Midnight Press in a little book called LES EDITIONS DE MINUIT printed last year by AUX EDITIONS DE MINUIT, which with peace has blossomed into a leading Paris publishing house. The artist Bruller-Vercors-Santerre-Dolée-etc. had after his demobilization been so depressed that he had gone to work in a small town as a journeyman carpenter. He lacked the heart to paint pictures. On a visit to Paris in 1941 he bumped into an old friend, Pierre de Lescure, and they had dinner together. De Lescure was already in contact with other intellectuals who were editing a secret revue, LA PENSÉE LIBRE. He asked Bruller-etc. to write a long short story for the revue. Painfully, for he was not used to writing, the painter complied. But by the time he had finished his story the revue had "fallen," a Resistance euphemism for "been raided." The editors had been arrested, the printing press confiscated. De Lescure and Vercors then decided, quite simply, to publish the long short story as a book. And since they wanted to impress public opinion abroad, they determined it must be well-printed.

Three thousand francs, borrowed from another friend, served as initial capital. Vercors called on Monsieur Aulard, one of the best printers of Paris, whom he knew well, having illustrated books for him. It was not practical to print at Aulard's plant because it was too large, too many people would have to be let into the secret. But Aulard promised to furnish a fine Garamond type and good paper. He found them a printer named Oudeville, proprietor of a one-man job shop that specialized in wedding and funeral cards. Between batches of wedding announcements, Oudeville printed pages of LE SILENCE. He had just enough of the Garamond to set eight pages at a time, and when he had printed them he would break up the type and set eight more, by hand, for he had no linotype machine. Another old friend, Yvonne Paraf, known also in the Resistance as Yvonne Desvignes, stitched the pages together. It is not customary in France to issue books ready bound in cloth or leather, so the lack of a cover did not detract from the elegance of the slim volume.

Vercors did not inform Madame Paraf-Desvignes who "his" author was. She subsequently guessed. Madame Desvignes (like Vercors she has retained the Resistance name) is now his associate in the direction of the post-liberation publishing house AUX ÉDITIONS DE MINUIT, the continuation of their Resistance venture. Oudeville finished printing LE SILENCE in February, 1942. De Lescure and Vercors then set him to work on a clandestine edition of Jacques Maritain's A TRAVERS LE DÉSASTRE, which the Catholic philosopher had published in the United States in the fall of 1940 but which was a forbidden book in France. Lescure owned one smuggled copy. This second book was coming off the presses when they began to take a few other writers into their enterprise. After all, now that they had established a publishing house they had to have manuscripts!

By then Aulard had found excuses to get rid of the workmen he was not sure of. LES ÉDITIONS had the use of his good plant. And in the course of the occupation the Midnight Press actually built up the astonishingly efficient organization that they had been credited with.

LE SILENCE DE LA MER, received as a happy portent in the outside world, to which copies penetrated soon after its appearance, has had British and American editions in both French and English. Mr. Henry Luce's LIFE, a picture magazine with a circulation of several millions, many of whom can read, carried a translation in the United States in 1943. Because of the length of the story and because it is already known to so many American readers, the book is not reprinted here.

It is a story told in the first person. The narrator, an elderly gentleman and a scholar, living alone in a country house with his niece, tells how a young German officer, named Werner von Ebrennac had once been billeted on them. Von Ebrennac, an uncertain, apologetic sort of German with aspirations to be considered a cultured "European," has made efforts to fraternize with his unwilling hosts. Most of the efforts have taken the form of long monologues about his love for France—he claims descent from a French Huguenot family that emigrated to Germany after revocation of the Edict of Nantes in 1685—and even of his dislike of other Germans. His ex-fiancée in Germany, for example, lost his love by pulling the wings off a mosquito. He feels sure the Frenchman's niece would not be like that. He rips off long catalogues of French writers whom he has read, and he plays Bach on the family piano to show art is international. He also recites from MACBETH.

But all his talks are monologues because neither the old man nor the niece ever speaks to him. The job-printer, Oudeville, after setting up most of the story, said to Vercors, "You should not call it 'The Silence of the Sea,' which, if you will pardon me for saying so, means nothing at all. You should call it 'The Silence of the Niece.'"

All he wants of France is a kind welcome, this remarkable (and slightly implausible) German says. Finally, he tells them he is going to Paris for a couple of weeks, "the happiest of his life," to take part in a cultural union of France and Germany, when the German authorities are going to take France into equal partnership. He implies that when he returns the old man and the girl will recognize that he has been right all along. But in Paris more knowing and cynical Nazis tell him that the policy of conciliation is all a lie. Disillusioned, he comes back to tell the girl (who still says nothing) that he has volunteered for service on the Russian front, where he is killed.

A number of critics, both in France and outside, have found this libretto too kindly toward the German character, and by implication toward all Germans. Jean Paulhan, himself illustrious in the Resistance, took a dig at it in his parable, "The Bee," which is included in this book. When it reached the United States, via Luce, nearly two years after its publication, it seemed remarkably indulgent.

The situation had justified this line when it was issued, however, because LE SILENCE was an appeal to intellectuals to disregard the approaches of the Germans, with their specious program of European cultural solidarity and their flattering deference to "élites." In its hour it was effective. By 1943, when it was published here, the Germans had abandoned all pretense of conciliation, and LE SILENCE seemed as archaic as a Hudson bomber (a very effective aircraft, too, at the time Vercors was writing his tract). Nothing, perhaps, is as dead as yesterday's newspaper, but year before last's propaganda line can sometimes be pretty dead too.

The Resistance, even intellectual resistance, was not a game. There is in France now an important weekly, LES LETTRES FRANÇAISES, which began as a clandestine publication ("What a contradiction in terms," one of its editors once said: "to make public in secret!") Every issue carries on its front page the line: "Founders: Jacques Decour (shot by the Germans) and Jean Paulhan." Decour was the ordinary, peacetime pen name, not a Resistance sobriquet, of a young man of letters named Daniel Decourdemanche. This young man, of a wealthy stock-broking family, had written several novels of promise, but he was primarily a pedagogue—professor of modern German literature at the LYCÉE ROLLIN, one of the great Paris secondary schools for young men.

French schools are part of the national university system. Teachers move upward through them to chairs in the provincial universities and in time, if they are lucky, return to the University of Paris. Decourdemanche was a young man with a future. The faculties and student bodies of the universities had a proud and honorable part in the Resistance from the first, and the number of scholar-martyrs was out of all proportion to their relative rank in an occupational census. Since the liberation, the LYCÉE ROLLIN has been renamed LYCÉE JACQUES DECOUR. The best possible introduction to Decour is his last letter, written in prison before his execution on May 30, 1942.

The Falling Leaves

Saturday, May 30, 1942, 6:45

My dear Parents,

For a long while you have been expecting a letter from me. You did not expect to receive this one. I too hoped to spare you this grief. Always remember that I remained worthy of you and of our country that we love to the end.

You see, I might very well have been killed in the war, or even in the bombardment last night. So I am not sorry to die a death that has some significance. You know that I have committed no crime. You have no reason to blush for me, I have done my duty as a Frenchman. I do not think of my death as a catastrophe. Remember that at this moment thousands of soldiers from all the countries in the world are dying every day, swept away by the same great wind.

You know that for the past two months I have been expecting what is to happen to me this morning; so I have had the time to prepare myself for it; but since I have no religion, I have not given myself up to any meditation on death. I consider myself rather as a leaf that falls from a tree to become mold nourishing its roots. The quality of the mold depends on that of the leaves. I am thinking of the youth of France, in whom I put all my hope.

My darling parents, I shall probably be buried at Suresnes. You can, if you wish, ask that I be moved to the Montmartre cemetery.

You must pardon me for having caused you this sorrow. My only concern during the last three months has been your worry. At this moment what troubles me most is the thought of leaving you without your son who has brought you more grief than joys. But, you see, in spite of everything, he is pleased with the life that he has led. It has been a beautiful one.

Here are a few requests. I was able to send a word to the woman I love. If you see her—soon I hope—give her your affection. This is my dearest wish. I also wish that you could keep an eye on her parents who need help badly. Tell them how sorry I am to desert them this way; I find some consolation in thinking that you will take my place and be something of a "guardian angel" to them.

Give them the things that are in my apartment and which belong to their daughter. The volume of the PLÉIADE, the FABLES DE LA FONTAINE, TRISTAN, LES QUARTRE SAISONS, two water colors (Vernon and Issoire), the menu of the inn LES 4 PAVÉ'S DU ROY.

All these last days, I have thought a lot about the good meals that we should have together when I was free. You will eat them without me, all the family together, but not sadly please. I don't want your thoughts to dwell on the good times that we might have had but on those that we really have shared. During these two months of solitude without even anything to read I have run over in my mind all my travels, all my experiences, all the meals that I have eaten, I even composed the outline of a novel. The thought of you never left me, and I hope that you will have, if it is necessary, a great deal of patience and courage, and above all no bitterness.

Give all my love to my sisters, to the tireless Denise who was so devoted to me, and to the pretty mother of Michel and of J. Denis.

I had an excellent meal with Sylvain on the 17th. I have often thought of it with pleasure, as well as of the New Year's supper with Pierre and Renée. Questions of food, you see, have taken on a great importance. Give Sylvain and Pierre all my love, and the same to Jean, my best friend, whom I thank for all the happy moments that I have passed with him.

If I had gone to his house on the evening of the 17th, I still would have ended up here, so there is nothing to regret.

I am going to write a note for Brigitte at the end of this letter. You will copy it out for her. God knows that I have thought of her! She has not seen her father for almost two years.

If you have a chance, ask my successor to tell my seniors that I have often thought of the last scene of EGMONT *—with all due modesty.

* The final scene in Goethe's play Egmont in which the Belgian Count d'Egmont is beheaded by order of the Spanish Duke of Alba for leading an insurrection against the Inquisition. The night before his execution, a vision appears to Egmont assuring him that his death will secure the freedom of

All my best regards to my colleagues and to the friend for whom I translated Goethe faithfully.

It is eight o'clock. It is almost time to go.

I have eaten, and drunk my coffee. I think I have attended to everything.

My darling parents, I kiss you with all my heart. I am very close to you and the thought of you never leaves me.

Your Daniel.

Jacques Decour

Decour was a Marxist. Jean Paulhan, his partner in founding the clandestine LETTRES FRANÇAISES, is not. Paulhan, who looks a little more literary than an American writer could afford to look, with a Barrymore profile and graying hair, has a bit of the tart precision of a professor in his manner, too, joined with a superior wit. Before the armistice of 1940 he was editor of LA NOUVELLE REVUE FRANÇAISE, the undisputed leader among French literary revues. When the Germans decided that they needed the NRF for their cultural propaganda, Paulhan resigned. Otto Abetz, the German ambassador to Pétain's Government, installed Drieu La Rochelle, a well-known collaborationist writer, as editor in Paulhan's place. Shortly before the liberation Drieu tried to kill himself, but was prevented. After the liberation he tried again and succeeded.

Paulhan joined one of the first Resistance groups—which had as nucleus a number of anthropologists on the staff of LE MUSÉE DE L'HOMME. The group was discovered and Paulhan disappeared for a time. When he returned to circulation he joined Decour in the attempt to establish a National Committee of Writers which would channelize the intellectual Resistance. The members, besides Decour and Paulhan, were Guéhenno and Debû-Bridel, whom we have already met, Charles Vildrac, the poet and dramatist known in the United States for his play PAQUEBOT TENACITÉ,

the Netherlands provinces, hailing him as a conqueror, and extending him a laurel crown. (Translator's note.)

Jean Blanzat, a young novelist and critic, and the Reverend Father Mäydieu, a Catholic priest and writer. The committee was to have as organ a clandestine review that the intellectuals of France could call their own. Decour and Paulhan were assigned to found this review. Decour called upon an old friend, Claude Morgan, to assist in the work. But Morgan did not know Paulhan. Decour was the only link between them.

The team of three—a type known in the Resistance as a TROIKA, from the Russian three-horse hitch—got out a couple of mimeographed numbers. Then Decour was "burned"—spotted by the Gestapo.

Morgan had gone to a café to wait for him one winter evening. But he did not appear. Morgan divined what had happened. It was months before any of Decour's acquaintances in the outside world heard from him directly. Then his family received the last letter.

Decour had been tortured, but he had not named Paulhan or Morgan. Morgan carried on alone until he could re-establish contact with the committee, of which he had heard only through Decour. He was confident, he said later, that if he could get out only one number, other writers would "come to the sound of the cannon." And he did it. The committee got together again; constantly enlarged during the Resistance, at the liberation it united all the patriot writers of France, and maintains its importance in peacetime.

Twenty numbers of LES LETTRES FRANÇAISES appeared under the German occupation. The first were crude jobs mechanically, but the last eleven were well printed eight-page publications that look good in any newspaper kiosk. This technical improvement was due to the escaped prisoner of "At Liberty's Call," George Adam, who found a printing plant for it. Adam, until the liberation, was the only member of the editorial staff of LES LETTRES FRANÇAISES who knew where it was printed—a knowledge he shared only with the bicyclist who carried the copy. The plant was directly across the street from a garage requisitioned for German military vehicles, and the type for LES LETTRES' permanent head came from the fonts of the PARISER ZEITUNG, the official German newspaper in Paris. A patriotic compositor had stolen it.

POUR L'ELOGE DE JACQUES DECOUR, *Paulhan's tribute to his old comrade, appeared in the first number of* LES LETTRES FRANÇAISES *published after the liberation. The mimeographed sheet had at last grown to a fine illustrated weekly, with a list of contributors that included every great name in France, except those on the blacklist of collaborators. But Decour's had become the greatest name of all. By his death he had secured an immortality far beyond the gift of the* ACADÉMIE FRANÇAISE, *which creates conventional literary "immortals."*

In Memory of Jacques Decour *

by JEAN PAULHAN

Three months after the armistice, I met Jacques Decour in the Rue de Vaugirard. He was going by on a bicycle, seemed to be in a hurry, and did not give me his address. He stopped only long enough to say, "After all, France only got what she deserved," and, "Pétain? What's the difference? One shame or another." We agreed as for the shame. Then he pedaled away.

Decour believed that a country whose laws are unjust can rely on the devotion of neither the privileged classes, whose only concern is their privileges, nor the victims, who have nothing to defend except—what? What they know only by hearsay, some vague hope. To me, it seemed, on the contrary, that the obverse of privilege, its concomitant, might be a boundless abnegation. But it was he whom events were to justify.

Later I saw Jacques Decour four or five times a week, at the CAFÉ DE LA FRÉGATE, at Jean Blanzat's, Debû-Bridel's or my own apartment, and even once at the NRF. We were preparing to get out our newspaper. One evening I turned over to him ten thousand francs that Robert Debré gave us. He seemed pleased, and it occurred to me that I usually thought of him as being rather cold.

* From *Les Lettres Françaises*, September 9, 1944.

Decour was tall and thin, with sharp elbows. His wide mouth wore more than one smile at a time, so that one often did not know how to take him. His eyes were gentle, but there was an intransigence about his face as a whole. He was one of those men of whom one could not help feeling, "He wouldn't hesitate to . . ."

There were twenty years of friendship between us. I liked his novels—which he did not. I felt more reservations about his political essays. (But they dealt with questions on which I am no authority.)

We exchanged news about the war. Very few general observations or predictions. He did happen to say to me, "When the Allies land, the strangest thing will be to learn it from abroad."

What a true and subtle remark that was to make in '42! I never realized it (so to speak—and badly) until two months ago—when I saw, from my disappointment, that I had been stupidly expecting something quite different, like newsboys shouting the news in the street perhaps, gatherings in the street and, in every house, progressive parties from floor to floor. No, nothing. And we were so perplexed (though delighted) that we were at a loss to know what to call the event. The INVASION? That sounded as if we were sore about it. The LANDING? But they weren't going to stop at that! The LIBERATORS? That was vague and rather on the sentimental side. No, Decour was right. The thing itself was so strange that it didn't seem to have a name.

We were not always very grave. Yet he said to me one night, "Now, I know that they can take me and do whatever they want to me. I shall not talk."

It was a few days later that they arrested him. They did do whatever they wanted to him. And he did not talk. But I return to what I was going to say and which is of a general order. One's country is not an easy concept to grasp—as we have seen. We need everything we have; and we should be lost if, in our next ordeal, there were Frenchmen—and among the best—who deemed that France deserved to be punished.

Thucydides has Pericles say something like this. "If I prove that Athens has just laws," he says, "I shall have pronounced sufficient eulogy of our heroes." But for us, it is just the opposite: the day when France has just laws, we shall have given Jacques Decour the eulogy he deserved.

Paulhan's parable of the bee, which follows, dates from the same period when too many Frenchmen continued to hesitate. It became celebrated throughout France after an inauspicious start. LES CAHIERS DE LA LIBERATION, the clandestine review in which it first appeared, was the organ of a group of Lyon intellectuals. The number containing "The Bee" was confiscated almost in toto, and only fifty copies reached the public. "The Bee," however, was reprinted in many clandestine newspapers, and also in L'ETERNELLE REVUE, a Resistance prototype of our digest books. It reprinted articles from other Resistance journals, and in the latter days of the Resistance, when the Silent Republic was a well-organized State within a puppet official State, L'ETERNELLE REVUE attained a circulation of 20,000.

The Bee

by JEAN PAULHAN

If we had been occupied (as the polite phrase runs) by the Swedes, we should retain perhaps a dance step or a vogue for blue and yellow ribbons. Occupied by Javanese, we might acquire a way of wriggling our fingers. Hottentots, Italians, Hungarians, might leave behind them a song, a certain way of smiling or tossing the head. In short, any one of a number of those absurd mannerisms that have no particular significance—that mean merely that one is glad to be alive, that one prefers living to not living at all, and that (specifically) it is amusing to have a body capable of such whimsies.

But from THEIR occupation, it is clear to everyone, nothing will remain. Not a song, not so much as a grimace. It never occurs even to the children in the street to imitate the goose step. In the MÉTRO, which has become, along with the grocery store, the only refuge of any sort of community life, they never shove anybody—as we, alas, are apt to do. They even pick up the bundles some fumbling woman drops. Yet they inspire us with no desire to imitate their politeness in this matter. They are not animate. They will have come and gone like a great emptiness—as if they were already dead. Except that this death of theirs they spread around them. It is the only thing they seem to be capable of doing.

That they seem so diaphanous to us, it is sometimes said, is the result of our dignity. It could be. I see it said in books * (put out by the best publishing houses at that) that a respectable French girl may lodge the noblest of the occupants under her roof for six months (and even fall a little in love with him) without ever saying so much as "good morning" to him. But she was probably an exceptional French girl. As for me, I do not discover quite such a fund of dignity in my make-up (nor any such promptitude at falling in love). And, in general, Frenchmen have NOT been as dignified as all that.

It must not be forgotten that France is not, so to speak, at war. It is a sort of neutral country whose capital is Vichy. We show no hesitation—fortunately—in speaking the truth about the men of Vichy: to wit, that they are a lot of swine. That does not prevent us from being somewhat at one with them. There is in each of us—unfortunately—something that understands them, that does not dismiss them as plain ordinary madmen, that even goes so far at times as to wonder whether perhaps Vichy was not just a trick to save Algeria, and Pétain a monster of cunning (and to hate ourselves at the same time for thinking of it); something that finds itself obliged to make allowances for them. For after all, the man in France who does fight today, does so without being obliged to. He does so with all the merit and all the pure grandeur of the soldier—which official wars are apt to make us forget exists.

So then, those of us who are not fighting might be content to be amused (if "they" were amusing)—or to learn from them (if there was anything for them to teach us). But even in those

* A jibe at Vercors' Le Silence de la Mer, which was published by the clandestine Editions de Minuit, enjoyed a tremendous vogue in France, but was looked on with some suspicion in certain quarters of the Resistance because its hero was a "good" German, who in spite of a genuine love of France and things French, found all his efforts at fraternizing with the French girl in the house where he was billeted, repulsed. (Translator's note.)

ways—though it is nothing for us to pride ourselves on—they are a disappointment. It is exactly as if they were already dead. But—I come back to the point—this death of theirs is something that they spread.

When I was a child, it always surprised me (as it does all children) to find in the daily chronicles much more news of deaths than of births. (The explanation—but one never thinks of it until later—is obviously that, except for kings, it is rare for a man to be very well known at his birth; while for a man already famous, all that remains is to die.) I also had a feeling that all this had been changed, that the tide was more toward births and people died a lot less.

It was an absurd concept, yet vaguely I think that I have always clung to it and that it is a fairly common feeling, and that it accounts to some extent for the pain we feel at a time when a month seldom passes without our learning of the death of one or another of our friends. One had taken to the Maquis; his body, already bloated, was found in a field. Another wrote leaflets, still another carried messages; they were riddled with bullets with a song still on their lips. Others, before they died, underwent tortures that surpass in horror the agony of cancer or tetanus.

I know that there are people who say, "They died in vain. A simple bit of information (not always very accurate, at that), a leaflet or even a clandestine newspaper (often poorly gotten out) was not worth the price they paid."

To such people the answer is: "You see, they were on the wrong side of life. They loved insignificant things like a song, a snap of the fingers, a smile. You can squeeze a bee in your hand until it smothers. It will not smother without having stung you. It stings in vain, you say. Yes, it is in vain. But if it did not sting you, there would long ago have been no more bees."

The sting is the bee's only form of franchise. It is its only way of voting against tyranny. I heard the same thought expressed in Oran in 1942 by a man distinguished in a rather different sphere from Paulhan's: Major General Terry Allen, then commanding officer of the First Division. Major General Allen said that if the politics of El Paso, Texas, were corrupt, the citizens who abstained from voting had themselves to blame. "It's the same for nations," he said. "Sometimes a country has to fight just to put itself on record. But if it won't fight, what right has it got to kick about anything that happens?"

In his third paragraph Paulhan registers a playful (but stinging) criticism of THE SILENCE OF THE SEA, which he evidently considered, even under the circumstances, too kindly in tone toward the German character.

I like the piece particularly because I myself, without ever having read it, wrote a kind of pendant to it in September, 1944.

"But from them, anybody can see that nothing will remain to us."—Paulhan.

"Paris has been liberated for only four weeks, but an American arriving now would find it hard to believe that the Germans had been here for any considerable time. The Germans build nothing. In Paris, because of the fortunes of war, they were also prevented from destroying anything. Culturally sterile, they have left no imprint on thought or on manners here. The children have forgotten the Germans already, I am sure. The rest of us will forget too soon."—THE NEW YORKER, September 26, 1944.

Before he was Marxist or martyr, Jacques Decour was a teacher, and this last excerpt from LETTRES FRANÇAISES completes the portrait of one whom the Monsieur Seguins called a terrorist. It is a letter to LETTRES from one of Decour's old boys:

Jacques Decour as Seen by His Students

by JEAN-LOUIS D'HOURSELLES

LE LYCÉE ROLLIN has been renamed. On the pediment over the main entrance, where the French flag floats once more, a broad panel reads: "LYCÉE JACQUES DECOUR." Pinned to the door below is a sign with this brief phrase: "He died for France, May 30, 1942." That is all, and it is enough for us. All the pupils of the LYCÉE ROLLIN remember meeting Jacques Decour, tall and smiling, in the corridors between classes. All of them had heard of the community of purpose that existed among his students and the excellence of his teaching. Those of us who saw him every day, knew him even better. So it is almost a duty for us who were in his classes to pay this final tribute to our teacher.

We shall long remember his German classes. Avoiding bookish learning and hackneyed texts, he treated his subject as a living thing. We had note-books filled with notes—more notes than text perhaps—which constituted a thorough basis for an artistic and intellectual culture.

Decour enjoyed a reputation in the LYCÉE that amounted to a local fame. At the beginning of the term three years ago, we found our class invaded by a group of five or six pupils who, deserting the classes of an old professor too disconcerted to protest, had their hearts set on "doing their German with Decour." Decour smiled and made the necessary arrangements for them to remain with us.

In summer, through the open windows of his classroom, the quadrangle echoed with phonograph records of LIEDER and symphonies. And painting! How many of the masters of German art Decour brought us to know! His comments on Holbein, Cranach and Dürer were marvelous. He brought in post cards and reproductions of pictures to show us: "Franz von Sickingen," "The Knight and Death," "The Philosopher and the Lion," and the divine "Melancholia." His lectures on literature—the NIBELUNGEN, HANS SACHS, DIE MEISTERSINGER—filled us with the heavy perfume of these old legends. Then we would talk of Wagner, the RHEINGELT, TANNHÄUSER, and LOHENGRIN, and compare the operas and their source. Decour excelled at bringing us to appreciate the poetry of the storytellers and folklore—everything that had remained simple and pure in language and in thought. Another time he would take up Eichendorf and the Romanticists; and a whole period would be conjured up before our eyes—universities, students and beer gardens. How many topics that might have been dull and colorless Decour endowed with reality and life for us! In our junior year we translated WILHELM TELL, and in our senior year EGMONT. Decour had the gift of pointing out in the works of Goethe and Schiller passages that restored our hope.

More than that, he insisted that each pupil take an active part in the course. One student, because he was an Alsatian, was called upon to give a talk on Strasbourg, its cathedral, and the ancient city all a-flutter with flags on the the 11th of November. Another gave a résumé of a modern book that he had read. Or in epic contests, one half of the class asked questions of the other, to see which side could "spell down" the other.

Then one day in February, the pupils lined up to wait at the classroom door, but Decour's lean silhouette did not appear. The following week a substitute professor took the class for one week, two weeks, and finally seemed to have taken over permanently. We were told that Decourdemanche was ill, that he was on leave, and then, that he had retired. Finally his successor confided to us that he was in prison. "Yes, he has been arrested. For political reasons, probably." We were stunned. Never in any of his courses had he spoken a word on any subject that might be considered political. None of us could have said whether Decourdemanche had carried on propaganda for or against communism; nor that the wrote for the clandestine press. Moreover, everything was done to keep the truth from us. It was only many months later that we heard the news: Jacques Decour, our professor of German, had been shot by the Nazis on May 30, 1942.

Others will tell of the teaching of his books, since he was a fervent writer. We had the teaching of his presence. We knew nothing of his writings, and he never mentioned them. It was his example that won us to him, the example of his lively but profound mind, the example of his calm and unshakable faith in the future of France, the example of his courage and his death. The tortures that he underwent left him unmoved. In the presence of his torturers, we have been told, he maintained a scornful silence. From beyond death, from beyond time, his message has reached us: "I think of myself somewhat as a leaf that falls from a tree to become humus. The quality of the humus depends on the quality of the leaves: I am thinking of the youth of France, in whom I place all my hope."

The young forget quickly; but I assure you that those who have won their admiration and kindled their enthusiasm remain indestructibly present in their hearts and in their memories.

Resistance in the Two Zones

The first Resistants were in large part men who preferred death to defeat. But most men need at least a glimmer of hope before they will fight. The glimmers were fitful during the first weeks after the armistice. At Granville in Normandy, only a few miles north of Brittany geographically but temperamentally a world away, the stubborn, mocking, cautious natives saw the light in September, 1940, when a large number of German troops held an invasion exercise, putting to sea in collapsible rubber boats. Most of the boats turned over as they reached the mouth of the harbor. The Granville fishermen, who knew a thing or two about the Channel, concluded the Germans were simply dangerous lunatics, who had no chance of getting to England. Hope spread as Britain resisted. It grew fast when reports began to come back from the Russian front in 1941. German soldiers from Russia, sent back to rest areas in France, were its most effective propagandists. Their terror and pessimism were unconcealed.

In August, 1941, the Germans in Paris ordered the preparation of thousands of posters announcing the fall of Moscow. Workmen employed in the print shops spread the news among comrades in the city. But as day after day went by and the posters remained unused, the Germans' spirits fell and the workmen's rose. By the winter of 1941-2 the people of France knew that the Russian campaign was a wound through which Germany might well bleed to death.

The Resistance movements grew along with hope. But in the Free Zone there was a school of thought known as ATTENTISME, or "wait-and-see-ism." Its exponents used the German reverses as an argument for doing nothing. "By being nice little nanny goats and complying with the German orders—only the ones we cannot get out of complying with, of course—we may be able to sit this one out," they said. "We will come through the war less damaged than any other power after all. Let the Germans and the Russians and the Anglo-Saxons knock each other's brains out." At the time this ATTENTISME suited the German game as neatly as an America Firster editorial in THE DAILY NEWS. A quiescent France was certainly less trouble, while they were fighting the Russians, than one in active revolt. They could settle with France later. As far as they were concerned it made no difference whether the Monsieur Seguins professed to like them or not, as long as they made no trouble.

The French, by the way, have a disconcerting habit of referring to Britons and Americans, lumped, as Anglo-Saxons, which is annoying to non-Anglo-Saxon Americans. They do not mean any harm by it.

In the North the Germans already were having a difficult time with sabotage. The owners of French heavy industry had gone to work for them quite happily, but the products were proving to be distressingly unreliable. "By getting the factories working at once and restoring employment, the Germans, in the beginning, had a chance of creating a favorable impression," Lieutenant Colonel Rochet, the rubber-billy man, once told me. "It was necessary to create a climate of dissidence. So in aircraft factories we would cut one vital rivet almost through with acid, and then when they flew the plane it would fly to bits after a few vibrations. Or we would go to the stockpiles, where steel of different tensions was marked with paint of different colors. We would change the colors, and the poor steel would go into machine tools, or tank armor. Then the tools wouldn't cut, and the men in the tanks would be killed. We would put incendiary devices in new trucks, which would burst into flames when they were driven. Soon the Germans began to shoot our fellows. Then of course the final result was certain." The sabotage spread to the railroads and the coal mines. British planes, after the summer of 1941, were operating over France more often than the Germans over Britain, and the pilots who bailed out offered a new method of serving the Allied cause. A great underground organization grew up to save them from the Germans and get them safely home.

In the South there was an inferior moral climate. The divergence is illustrated by the following extracts from LIBÉRATION, a Resistance newspaper that, incidentally, was to survive the war, like

LES LETTRES FRANÇAISES, and become a great Paris daily. It is dated January 20, 1942, and was, I should think, printed at Montélimar in the central Rhône Valley, in the southeast of France. It carries news of the wholesale executions to which the Germans were already resorting in the North, but its message is directed to readers in the ZONE LIBRE. Thousands of these papers, printed in the South, were of course carried across the line and distributed in the ZONE OCCUPÉE, where there were at the time fewer Resistance newspapers.

Notes from the Zones

Libération
January 20, 1942

OCCUPIED ZONE

NANTES. A pale, chilly dawn. Fifty men, fifty Frenchmen, are led into a near-by quarry. They are herded against the quarry wall. An armored car, already there in position, opens fire. With a little click, like a ghostly mechanical finger tapping at the door of fate, the spray of bullets sprinkles the living bodies. A few seconds. Fifty dead.

There are old men among them, cripples, heroes of 1914—Jost, the president of the National Association of Veterans. Moquet, seventeen years old, son of a Paris deputy. A physics student whose hobby was radio: he had set up crystal sets in his garden—mere toys without any range.

An hour later, trucks carried off the bodies in coffins hastily nailed together. A trail of blood marked where they had passed. In the silent quarry, there remained only a dark red puddle and splashes of blood against the wall.

The next day thousands of bouquets wilted on the stone. Laid there amid the blood by the widows, orphans and friends, they were a pledge of the oath of vengeance, of the oath of death, that

France took one murderous morning and that she will shortly fulfill.

A few days later the German headquarters at Nantes published a list of forty-eight names. Two names were missing and will remain unknown. The Germans were ashamed: the two names were the names of women.

PARIS. DECEMBER. A thousand men are herded into prisons and concentration camps. Eight hundred of them are packed off to the typhus zone of Poland, where Jewish doctors, considered fit only for working in epidemics, have already been sent and where reigns a distress that it is difficult for French minds to imagine.

Of the other two hundred men, one hundred were shot officially. The rest were shot unofficially. All that will remain of any of them is an anonymous grave here and there, scattered throughout the five cemeteries of Paris, a heap of earth and a number.

Yet a few whispered details pass from mouth to mouth. Among the Resistants, there is rage; among the cowards, remorse; among the temporary victors a bewildered anxiety.

A German officer admits, "They die with extraordinary courage, singing patriotic hymns or shouting a last farewell to their country."

One of the widows managed to find a person who had seen her husband die. "Gabriel Péri * was tubercular. The months that he had spent in prison so weakened him that he had to be carried. Yet he was singing."

Another witness says, "Professor Hollwech was arrested in his laboratory in the Pierre Curie Institute. As he was leaving the building, he knocked down his German guard and escaped. He was recaptured. Three days later his wife received a message asking her to come to the morgue of the HÔPITAL DE LA PITIÉ to claim his body."

"I have just been moved to another cell," one of the prisoners in LA SANTÉ writes. "We hear the guillotine working all day. The wardens are full of admiration for the courage of our fellows."

A widow whose husband had been executed unofficially was summoned to the KOMMANDANTUR to collect her husband's

---

* The Communist leader Péri was the man who gave the world the phrase, "*Je meurs pour les lendemains qui chantent*", uttered as he was about to die. (*Translator's note.*)

papers. She reported to the French authorities, who calmly informed her that she was not entitled to the privileges of a widow, since her husband's death had not been officially certified. Hence no death benefits, no probation of his will, and no chance to set up a guardianship for her children. (Must a Frenchman wait to be killed twice before it becomes legal?)

Who says that the French cannot laugh in the face of death? At Drancy, the saying goes, "When your name is called it is either for a shower bath, release, or death." One day thirty names were read off. One of the prisoners recognized his family name with the wrong Christian name. "Go ahead," his buddies urged. "Heads or tails. This time it's to be released."

"Here," he answered. The thirty men were taken to the CHERCHE-MIDI prison. A big feed (that much was ominous—like the last cigarette) and then, after the dessert, they were told, "You are to be shot tomorrow."

The man made a fuss, got in touch with the authorities, and finally persuaded them that his was a case of mistaken identity. It had been a near thing.

But the whisper grows louder, becomes a murmur that will some day be the roar of millions of voices, living and dead. Here is what that whisper says: "The moment they begin to weaken, what a slaughter there will be!"

In the meantime, this is all we have to say, "The sons, the brothers, the wives, the friends are keeping the reckoning. For EVERY French life that they take, we shall kill THREE."

UNOCCUPIED ZONE

Here they have not dared to use fire and sword. Here they destroy underhandedly, by means of cold, sickness and privations. And it is those whose slogan is, "Labor, Family, Country," who have filled the concentration camps and prisons with laborers, heads of families, and patriots.

At Lyon, the SAINT-PAUL prison has room for two hundred persons (and the penal system of France is not famed for its humaneness or sanitation). There have been as many as nine hundred prisoners there at one time.

At Saint-Etienne, for one hundred twenty cells there are three hundred fifty prisoners. Laws and legal safeguards no longer exist.

At Toulouse, the authorities show particular zeal. Veterans, workers, and intellectuals are thrown into prison and maltreated. One veteran, severely wounded in 1940, is suffering from wounds that have re-opened and are running with pus. People are dying of cold.

The death notices in the JOURNAL DE PERPIGNAN are all out of proportion because of the proximity of the camp of La Nouvelle, where children and adults are dying like flies.

At Lyon, in the course of a recent political trial, one of the accused complained that he had been beaten up. The police commissioner, named Pigeon, denied it, but the other defendants, men and women both, confirmed the statement.

For a word of criticism, a young girl was kept confined for six months in a filthy cell without being allowed to communicate with her lawyer or her family. Another girl, on an unsubstantiated charge of distributing leaflets, was placed in a cell twelve feet square, with forty tubercular and syphilitic prostitutes. The doctor is not interested. He waits for rigor mortis to set in before mentioning hospitalization. And the judge waits for a confession. . . .

And the chief of state is a paternal old man. And we are governed by a lot of bourgeois stuffed with moral conventions—and the black market.

Yet Vichy is not satisfied with being the purveyor of prisons in the Unoccupied Zone. It also undertakes to see that the anonymous graves in the Occupied Zone are filled. Men have been turned over to the firing squads. Others have been denounced through the good offices of the prefects and the administration.

But the time will come when the purveyors will pay just as dearly for their crimes as the executioners.

Growth of the Underground Press

The execution of fifty hostages at Châteaubriant, near Nantes, on October 21, 1941, was a reprisal for the killing of a German lieutenant colonel named Hotz, shot down in the streets of that city on the previous night. The Germans did not accuse any of the victims of complicity in the shooting of the officer. They simply took the fifty from among prisoners held at the near-by fortress of Châteaubriant for "hostile actions" or for "crimes against the state." That meant being De Gaullists, or Communists, or labor organization leaders. Many of the hostages had been arrested in 1939, at the outbreak of war. The Nantes episode was the first in a series of attacks on German officers and whole-sale reprisals that continued through the fall and winter. Marshal Pétain and General de Gaulle were for once in accord: both made radio speeches ordering Frenchmen to stop killing Germans. The Marshal said that the attacks were inspired by Russia and Great Britain. De Gaulle was against them on tactical grounds, since they opened the way to such disproportionate reprisals. He advised that Frenchmen await the landing of an Allied army before re-commencing open hostilities. But many Resistance leaders in France felt that the way to create a "climate of combat" was to fight, and they ignored the General's instructions. It was impos-sible to keep up a spirit of resistance without resisting, they argued. This was the same debate that was going on in Yugoslavia between the Partisans and the adherents of General Mikhailovitch, who wanted to save up weapons and wait. In France, as in Yugo-slavia, the ideas of the immediate-action people prevailed.

The executions in Paris were part of the series that started at Nantes. Gabriel Péri, the newspaper editor whose end is briefly described in LIRÉRATION, died on December 23, at MONT-VALÉRIEN prison. He wrote a last letter as celebrated and almost as poignant as Decour's. In one of its phrases he said that he died "in order that France might know singing tomorrows." Guy Moquet, a boy of seventeen, became one of the martyrs of the Resistance.

In the Free Zone the Germans had left to Vichy a vestigial army, with a deficit of equipment and a surplus of senior officers, and a fleet of powerful war vessels that were forbidden to leave port without German permission. Officers of this army had secreted each other they would use them "when the liberators landed," an eventuality that seemed comfortably distant then. Whether, in that eventuality, they would employ the arms principally against some arms in caches scattered about the countryside; they told the Germans or against Frenchmen who believed in a democratic form of government was never very clear.

The naval officers, narcotized by an unrealistic tradition, were the most virulent anti-Allied element in France. French admirals for more than a century had dreamed of avenging Trafalgar, rather than Sedan. Now Mers-el-Kebir rankled worse than the Battle of France. Most of them denied they were pro-German, but they saw nothing incompatible in their two attitudes. They had rationalized the comfortable position in which they found themselves; they were heroically not going to fight anybody. But the ships, they kept reminding lesser Frenchmen, were France's only remaining military asset. If the Germans were offended, they might attempt to take over the ships.

The French naval officers were confused, bitter, and romantic in an opium-impregnated Pierre Loti sort of way, authoritarian by quarterdeck tradition and by family background. They included a high proportion of aristocrats—and an even higher one of imitation aristocrats. They were sufferers from a mass schizophrenia, a withdrawal from the real world. Darlan was their leader, and perhaps the only sane one of the lot; a sane bad man influencing the hallucinations of gold-braided lunatics. Land-bound admirals filled a number of ministries and administrative jobs in the Free Zone; admirals like Robert in Martinique, Decoux in Indo-China, Estéva in Tunis and Michelier in Morocco defended the far-flung interests —of the Axis. Godefroy in Alexandria refused the aid of his ships and crews to the British. Abrial and Platon held important Vichy jobs.

The poison seeped down from the quarterdeck. In the spring of 1943 a pair of fine young sailors in a wineshop in Algiers told me in good faith that the British had attacked the French at Mers-el-Kebir because they knew that the French Navy was then the strongest in the world, which made them jealous. It did not seem incongruous or shameful to them, even then, that this "strongest navy in the world" had been unable even to leave its home ports without German permission.

Within the Free Zone, therefore, the clandestine press had a double task—to arouse Frenchmen against the Germans, and to oppose the arguments of the government of thieves and admirals at Vichy.

LIBÉRATION was typical of illegal newspapers of that period, some of which survived and most of which didn't. The editorial office was an apartment in a working-class district in Lyon. The editor and two colleagues lived and worked there. Roger Massip, editor of the present, legal, LIBÉRATION, edited it for twenty months under the occupation and once told me a bit about it, so I can use it as an example. But it was not unique.

The editors had a mailbox in another tenement house where they received reports from regional correspondents. These correspondents supplied news of the underground struggle in their territories. At another box, LIBÉRATION received communications from its political and diplomatic correspondent, an official in the Vichy Ministry of Foreign Affairs. Many Resistance newspapers had correspondents in the government who furnished them with the most intimate details of Pétain's and Laval's court intrigues. LIBÉRATION's political correspondent was eventually arrested and interrogated by the Gestapo. He got out of it alive and without betraying any of his colleagues. But his body is covered with a tattoo of cigarette burns.

The staff members sifted the news and wrote editorials and articles. When they wanted something that called for special knowledge or a satirical touch, they called upon some journalist they knew to write the piece, even though the man might be outside any organized Resistance movement. Naturally they avoided known collaborators. No newspaperman ever gave them away. When they had decided on the contents of a number, they made a dummy, of two or four small pages, with perhaps four hundred words to the page, and a Resistance railroad man or traveling salesman carried it to Montélimar, where a sizeable job printery worked for the movement. The printery would set the type and print twenty or thirty thousand papers for distribution in the immediate region. But it was not judicious to print a whole number at one plant, since distribution over a large area was a difficult problem. There was also the danger that the Gestapo might capture a whole printing if it should happen to make a raid. Montélimar would therefore send back to Lyon carefully printed proofs on good paper, and technicians would photograph them and make half a dozen sets of zinc printing plates from the photographs. In this work, the Resistance papers had the wholehearted aid of the photoengraving staffs of the Lyon collaborationist newspapers. The plates were distributed to little printing plants from Toulouse to Marseille. These plants were operated by partisans. Each printed an edition of a few thousand. Some of the papers were loaded in packing cases deceptively labeled and shipped by train to stations where Resistance railroad men were waiting for them. Others were carried in suitcases by ostensible VOYAGEURS DE COMMERCE, who risked their lives every time they traveled, for Vichy agents rode many trains searching for contraband black-market food and Spanish cigarettes. If the agents found contraband they confiscated and sold it. If, in searching, they found a suitcase full of newspapers, they turned the carrier over to the GESTAPO. They were hard on newspaper carriers, presumably because they were angry when they found nothing to steal.

One of Massip's printers was a priest who had a press in his church. The authorities allowed him to have electric power in church only on Sundays, when he had services. This was to conserve fuel, since the Germans carried off nearly all the fuel of France. So the priest would print between masses. The priest was caught, arrested, and immersed repeatedly in a bathtub of water just above freezing to make him talk. He didn't talk. He was then given intravenous injections of ice water. He still didn't talk. The Germans next tried to see how long they could hold his head under water without drowning him. They miscalculated and drowned him, but he hadn't talked.

At last the Gestapo smuggled a German officer into the Montélimar plant. He was a linotyper provided with a card in the illegal union and a complete set of Resistance identification papers, and he spoke French with the accent of Saint-Etienne. The plant was raided and put out of business, but all the personnel escaped except the foreman of the photoengraving department. He was tortured to death, but he didn't talk either.

Some of the papers received some of their funds from the De Gaulle government in London. The money was brought in by agents who were dropped by parachute. Other money came in lump sums from patriots who could afford it, and still more in small contributions of from ten to two hundred francs. The journals bought their newsprint from regular dealers, but they always had to pay a black-market price for it. The dealers asked no questions and in fact preferred not to know the answers.

Traffic between the two zones was stringently regulated. Gestapo men checked on all travelers entering or leaving the Occupied Zone, but a certain number of newspapers went over the border in the clothing and baggage of passengers, as did some of the zinc-plate jobs for printers. Passengers who had permissions to pass and repass regularly, for business, were often couriers for a number of different Resistance enterprises simultaneously. De Gaulle's London government, for example, had early established an office in Paris. There was a representative there who got into relations with De Gaullist groups in the various parts of France and maintained a liaison with London. Not until late in the occupation, however, was this office in touch with all of the large Resistance groups.

One of the regular weekly couriers between the Paris and Lyon De Gaullists was a professor of law at the University of Paris who gave one lecture a week in Lyon. Among his running mates was an attractive young woman who was the mistress of a high German officer in Paris. She was so devoted to her family in Lyon (she told the German) that she had to visit it every week. Another courier, a magnificent white-haired woman dewy with diamonds, operated a chain of fancy houses, and was allowed to travel for business reasons (this was a type of business for which the Germans had great consideration). After the liberation the professor returned to his courses, the madame to the ordinary cares of administration, and the young woman to the Frenchman who had been paying the rent of her apartment in Lyon.

The madame was introduced into the De Gaullist group by an overhandsome young man, a merchant of women. As a Resistant he specialized in obtaining weapons from German soldiers. This usually involved killing the soldiers. He was successful many times, but in the end, as the little man who told me the story said, "He died a hero's death."

The Gestapo, as one means of counteracting the secret newspapers, sometimes issued false "Resistance journals" and tracts of its own, and tried to pass them off among the unsuspecting. Two examples from LIBÉRATION follow:

The Fake Underground Press

Libération
July 20, 1943

"THE LITTLE RABBIT BREEDER"

This is the title of a publication that a number of Parisians have recently received through the mail. A very innocent periodical indeed to judge by the first page, which is entirely devoted to hints for the tyro of the rabbit-hutch. But, turning the page, we find hints of quite another nature. They are presented as directives emanating from "the French Resistance organizations" in preparation for an Allied landing, which they claim to be at hand. Mixing the true and the false—directives issued via the B.B.C. by the Allied High Command and forecasts calculated to throw the public into consternation—the publishers of this phoney clandestine pamphlet hope to upset the minds of the uninformed public.

Our readers are requested to denounce this trick.

Libération, Edition Z.O.
July 27, 1943

A CLUMSY TRICK

Citizens of the Parisian region have recently received in their mail a mysterious appeal sent out by a so-called G.A.C. (GROUPE ACTIF DE COMBAT) and entitled POUR LA LIBÉRATION. After recalling the heroism of Frenchmen wherever landings have taken place, this document goes on to urge that this example be followed everywhere, and concludes:

"H-hour for the liberation of France has struck. We appeal to all and we count on you. If you are willing to give us your support, mark your door with blue crosses, and three comrades of the G.A.C. will call on you without delay and give you precise instructions.

"It goes without saying that, in case of any betrayal on your part, your life will answer for it."

As AGENTS-PROVOCATEURS go, it would be hard to be any stupider than this. If the GESTAPO and the followers of Doriot and Déat have no brighter tricks than this for ferreting patriots they have much to learn.

Not all the contents of the illegal newspapers were as tragic as the first sample given. The story of the manifestation of the students of the University of Lyon against the Berlin Philharmonic proves it.

Libération
June 3, 1942

A FINE TIME FOR MUSIC!

No! Truly, it was not an appropriate moment! While dozens of hostages and combatants are falling under the German bullets, while Frenchmen, starving and oppressed, clench their fists with rage, while the rumbling of revolt is heard in the land, and liberation is drawing near, the Nazis and their collaborationst friends request our presence at a concert given at Lyon by the Philharmonic Orchestra of Berlin.

While our brothers were being assassinated, we were invited to applaud the representatives of the executioners.

Lyon took up the challenge.

It is true that music is international, and nobody thinks of making German music responsible for the Nazi crimes. But the Germans are in our country, they have us by the throat, they are pillaging and slaughtering. Therefore, the students and workers of Lyon staged a riot on the 18th of May in the streets surrounding the SALLE RAMEAU to greet the Germans, musicians and others, and the public that came to hear them, with cries of "Down with the assassins! Down with the traitors! VIVE LA FRANCE! VIVE LA LIBERTÉ!"

The hangdog look of the "guests" slinking into the hall through a triple guard of police and soldiers, amid the boos, jeers, and catcalls and cries of vengeance of thousands of patriots who had turned out for the demonstration, was something to see.

The chorus of boos that greeted the procession of German cars that drew up before the hall was real music to the ears. It lasted for an hour. The whole quarter was in a state of siege.

But it was to be repeated that evening at 8:30. A parade of demonstrators gathered at the Place Bellecour and once more marched toward the SALLE RAMEAU singing "The Marseillaise."

The music of the assassins received the welcome it deserved!

And two days later what a triumph was accorded to the great orchestra leader Paul Paray! The enthusiasm of the audience expressed itself in burst after burst of fervent applause. And what frenzy when, as his last encore, Paul Paray called on the orchestra to stand and play "The Marseillaise," and then, turning toward the audience, lifted his baton to lead them in a spontaneous chorus galvanized by its patriotic strains.

The prefect, Angeli, and the mayor, Villiers, had prudently slipped away before the end, to keep from hearing that "Marseillaise."

As for the German musicians, before leaving the hall, each one was given an automatic pistol loaded and cocked.

Such was the reception given the Philharmonic orchestra sent by Berlin to France to blend art with firing squads.

PART THREE

Resistance Becomes General

The Scuttling of the French Fleet

On Armistice Day, 1942, the Germans restored the unity of France. After that it was impossible to withhold its liberty. For two years they had worked to break France into two inimical fragments, one inhabited by prisoners, the other by vassals. Now they made France one by the simple act of marching their troops across the "line of demarcation" between the northern and southern zones and abolishing the fiction of the latter's "freedom." Everyone was now in the same boat and Pétain was completely discredited. Nor was it longer possible for sensitive (and cautious) residents of the southern zone to put the Germans out of their minds because they did not see them. The German uniform was everywhere.

The United States and Great Britain deserve a share of the credit for this unification, because the Allied landings in French North Africa on November 8 served as a precipitant. One by one the Germans, as if bent on re-creating the greatness of France, removed the obstacles to united action. They ordered the bleating old Marshal to disband the remnant of the old army, which they had already rendered harmless. The Marshal obeyed. Patriotic officers who had hung on in the honest hope that some day this army could be made the nucleus of armed resistance now went into more active and effective forms of dissidence.

The old humbugs who had stayed on to protect their jobs and pension rights disappeared into civilian life, where they were at least harmless. Meanwhile in Africa Admiral Darlan, second in command of the French Government, had gone over to the Allies by prearrangement, having a shrewd eye for a winner. Most of the

French fleet lay in the harbor of Toulon, the great naval base on the Mediterranean. The Germans did not know whether Darlan could induce the fleet to fight for the Allies, or even whether he really wanted to. But they were taking no chances. They took measures to prevent the fleet from leaving and sent German crews to Toulon to take over. The fleet then committed suicide, the predestined end, it seemed, of this pathological armada. By orders of Admiral Delaborde, the commanding officer, the crews sabotaged and then scuttled their own ships. The account that follows first appeared in the eleventh number of the clandestine LETTRES FRANÇAISES on the first anniversary of the scuttling. The author, it is now known, was Yves Farge.* The circumstances of the suicide were brave and spectacular, but it is well to remember in reading this eyewitness story of what happened that resolute action any time during the preceding twenty-nine months might have saved the whole fleet for co-operation with the Allies. It might also have shortened the war.

There were some worthy men in the French Navy. A few, like Vice Admiral Muselier, went to Britain at the same time as De Gaulle. Officers and men fought brilliantly, for the most part in small units borrowed from the British. They were condemned to death as traitors by the Vichy government. Commander Estienne d'Orves, a naval officer of an old naval family, was parachuted into France as a De Gaullist agent, betrayed, arrested and shot. But the Hamlet mentality of the navy tinged the thinking even of many men who became sane as soon as they took off its uniform.

I think particularly of the Count Jean de Vogüé, who was French naval attaché in London during the first year of the war. All his sympathies and his instinct told him to stay with Muselier and the British, but when the British destroyed the French squadron at Mers-el-Kebir in Algeria in July, 1940, de Vogüé returned to France, refusing to accept the British explanation of military necessity. After a few months at home under the German occupation, however, he straightened out and got back into the war. He joined a Resistance group, then became its leader, and within a short while was doing a more effective job for the Allies as a guerrilla than he could have done as a commander of a cruiser. Eventually he became chief of one of the largest Resistance organi-

* The present (November, 1946) Minister of Food Supply.

zations in the country, CEUX DE LA LIBÉRATION, and finished the war as a member of the three-man committee that directed the whole Resistance effort in 1944: the COMAC, or COMITÉ D'ACTION MILITAIRE. In the process he had adopted the Resistance name of le Commandant Vaillant, and since more political prestige now attaches to Vaillant than to De Vogüé, has retained the Resistance name in his public life.

A Year Ago—Toulon

by YVES FARGE

It is now a year ago since the roar of explosions at Toulon showed the world that all France had thrown itself into the Resistance. To celebrate this historic day of November 27 which was decisive for the unity of our country, we publish below notes jotted down by one of the witnesses of the scuttling of our fleet. Stripped of any effort toward emotional effect, this hitherto unpublished document is only the more gripping because of its very sobriety and conciseness. It glorifies the heroic dead of our sailors who, preferring combat to dishonor, set a final seal on the shame of the Vichy government.

I

Friday, November 27, at three o'clock in the morning, motorized columns coming from the west set out on the coast road which leads to the center of Toulon. With perfect timing, German tanks appeared on the quays and fired the first shots, intended, it would seem, to intimidate the crews. Simultaneously, a score of planes flew over the basins and the harbor and dropped flares. Further out to sea, German planes began to lay magnetic mines in the channel in order to threaten any French ships that might try to leave the harbor. It was then (at five o'clock in the morning) that the order to scuttle the fleet was given.

Most of the testimony gathered from those who watched the

fight from shipboard or on land agree on one point: A formidable explosion awoke Toulon at about five o'clock in the morning. It came from the blowing up of the turret of the STRASBOURG. Our great 26,500-ton cruiser was under the command of Commander Seyaux who, a few days earlier, had professed his confidence in the "correctness" of the Germans and his faith that they would keep their pledged word. The STRASBOURG flew the flag of Admiral de Laborde, commander-in-chief of the French forces of the high seas. On this 27th of November, 1942, at five o'clock in the morning, Admiral de Laborde was at his battle station in command.

Other explosions followed. The French fleet was being scuttled. It should also be stated, to avoid erroneous conclusions, that except for a few destroyers like the BAYONNAISE and the TAPAGEUSE, the French ships were moored at the QUAI, which explains why they could not be sunk. (Under certain of them, there was less than three feet of water.) In these conditions, the larger units could not be wrecked except by destroying the engines and armament or by capsizing the ships where they lay—operations which necessarily required a certain amount of time.

The fire of the tanks was answered by the machine guns and cannon of the ships. They were fighting to gain the few minutes, and in certain cases the few quarters of an hour, necessary to destroy the ships. On the DUPLEIX one officer was seen aiming his machine gun and firing on the enemy until he himself was wounded. The fighting was bitter aboard the JEAN DE VIENNE, the LANSQUENET, the COMMANDANT TESTE and the ALGÉRIE, whose armored deck blew up with a terrific FRACAS, and aboard all the other units of the fleet, where the engineering officers were flooding the engines, the gunners and gunners' mates blowing up the guns, and as a final step, setting fire to the magazines. Great fires broke out on the STRASBOURG, on the FOCH, which was foundering, on the AMPÈRE, which was listing badly, and on the VAUTOUR, already partially capsized. The aviation of the WEHRMACHT hovered tenaciously over the channel and amphibious tanks advanced on the drydocks. At the CROIX DES SIGNAUX, a searchlight began to probe the darkness. A burst of machine gun bullets from the coastwise fleet put out the beam of light. At La Seyne, in front of the ironworks and shipyards, German soldiers managed to board

the ships and take the crews by surprise. "Hands up!" the attackers
shouted. The submarine crews resisted and continued their work
of destruction. Only the heavy destroyer LA PANTHÈRE fell into the
hands of the enemy intact. The French anti-aircraft guns filled
the air with shells.

The submarines submerged. Six of them took to the open sea
pursued by German bombers. All the tugs and all the small craft
were scuttled. Only two new tankers remained intact. No destruction was effected aboard the CONDORCET, the useless old cruiser
where the WEHRMACHT was to install its kitchens. In the berth
beside the CONDORCET, the PROVENCE went down by the bow. The
COMMANDANT TESTE had a dangerous list. In the drydock where it
was laid up for repairs, acetylene torches in the hands of eighteen
French workers ruined the engines of the DUNKERQUE.

The dawn broke on a harbor echoing with detonations, explosions, and the rattle of automatic weapons—a dawn blackened
by the smoke of fires and by the thick clouds of soot that rose
from the fuel oil depots.

II

At Cap Brun, the explosions died away. The batteries had been
put out of action. A mighty chant arose—"The Marseillaise," in
which the voices of the gunners mingled with those of the civilians
massed along the road to Le Pradet.

Everywhere the population of Toulon gave free rein to its
delight. Now that the moment of decision had come, everywhere
popular enthusiasm in these tragic hours spontaneously seconded
the sentiment of a duty stronger than all the resentment and all
the aberrations fostered by the Vichy propaganda.

German trucks appeared on the Quai de Cronstadt and on the
Quai La Sense. For the first time, sailors, petty officers and
officers mingled in a brotherly disregard of rank. They were loaded
into the trucks. As the vehicles began to move, the crowd—silent
and tense at first, pale in this dawn whose air was heavy with
powder and disaster—began shouting at the top of its lungs: "VIVE
LA MARINE! VIVE LA FRANCE!" The sailors saluted; the officers came
to attention. Machine guns under their arms, the Germans surrounded the convoy. The work was finished. Toulon had ceased

to be a great naval port. Friday evening, Saturday and Sunday the smoke of fuel oil rolled across the sky over the port now guarded by the WEHRMACHT. A glance was sufficient to show what had become of the French fleet. Great skeletons of steel, their decks awash, were all that remained of the STRASBOURG, the PROVENCE, the DUNKERQUE, the COLBERT, the ALGÉRIE, the FOCH, the DUPLEIX, the JEAN DE VIENNE, the MARSEILLAISE, the COMMANDANT TESTE, and all those other wrecks. The fact was there: all the ships were scuttled; all the guns were demolished. The crowd was silent. Pensively it gathered on the QUAIS. The pilgrimage had begun.

Germany's Man Power Drive

The elimination of the differential status of the zones, of the Vichy army and finally the navy, were important steps in creating unity, but the Germans surpassed themselves with their insistence on S.T.O.—LE SERVICE DU TRAVAIL OBLIGATOIRE, or forced labor. By this measure Hitler became Churchill's and Roosevelt's recruiting sergeant.

The French whom we found in North Africa when we landed were never affected by these measures. Consequently the Vichy "moral climate" survived longer in Africa, behind our lines, than in France, under the Germans. This may have accounted for a small part of our State Department's failure to gauge feeling in continental France. The "experts" were listening to the Peyroutons, the Flandins and Noguèses, cynical opportunists who had changed sides only by force of circumstances. They had no time to find out what the people, any people, thought.

If they had really wanted knowledge, they might have spent a few days with the common soldiers of the CORPS FRANC D'AFRIQUE in the forests north of Sedjenane, or with the Zouaves in the mountains in southern Tunisia. The soldiers were not wealthy landowners, but workingmen. They had minds more nearly attuned to France than those of the politicians. But conditions at the

front did not attract the high policy-making boys, although some
of them were disguised in uniforms.

You will remember that on Christmas Day, 1942, the writer
known usually as Vercors had felt able to write, "Despair Is Dead."
And yet France's most bitter trials were still to come. We barely
held French North Africa. Montgomery was beating the Germans
in Libya. The Russians had won a great victory at Stalingrad—
hundreds of miles within their own frontier. Admiral Darlan had
been assassinated on Christmas Eve, but Vercors must have begun
his story before that happened. The battle was just beginning.
But hope swelled so strong in France that it was sometimes painful. The people of France were like miners trapped by a fall of
rock who hear the pickaxes of their rescuers on the other side of
the barrier. It was one of the tasks of their leaders from then on
to moderate their optimism. The people expected a landing any
day.

In Germany, meanwhile, the realization that the second campaign against Russia had failed started a great wave of fear,
swelled by the Allies' move into Africa which forced the Germans
into a "two-front war," their bogey ever since 1914. Soldiers were
needed for the Eastern front. Soldiers were needed for Africa.
They had to comb out their factories for cannon fodder. They
had to have foreign workmen to replace the Germans they took
for the army.

This was not a wholly new or unforeseen condition. For a long
time the Germans had been "recruiting" workmen, particularly
skilled mechanics, in Western Europe to enter Reich war industries. They forced down the level of living in the occupied countries
and lured the workmen away with promises of good pay, copious
food and excellent living conditions. The German labor-recruiting
service put out illustrated brochures that read like advertisements
for summer resorts rather than labor camps. But they found so
few dupes that they had to resort to conscription. As usual, they
put the onus on the "French" government at Vichy by ordering
it to order the forced levy. Laval had entered into an agreement
with the Reich in the summer of 1942 to deliver 400,000 workers.
The men were to be called up as if for military service. Laval tried
to get as many volunteers as possible by pretending that the Ger-

mans would release a war prisoner for every man who went to work in Germany. This fraud fooled nobody. It was not until the winter of 1942-3 that the drive to round up Frenchmen for labor service got really under way. The reaction was immediate. This excerpt from LE FRANC-TIREUR (a Resistance paper which like LIBÉRATION has survived in the form of a Parisian daily) describes it.

Labor Resists

Le Franc-tireur
January 20, 1943

HUNTING DOWN THE WORKERS

They come before dawn like criminals: "Get up . . . take your work clothes. Get going." It is the French police that are doing that to thousands of workers all over France. That's what things have come to.

Already we have seen refugees hunted down, arrested and deported.

Now it is open season on French workers. Four hundred thousand of them are needed. Laval has promised them to Hitler. They don't report voluntarily? Then the police come to grab them, herd them into camps, and track them down like wild beasts. Never in the history of any people have we had the spectacle of the rulers and their henchmen showing such baseness and such servility. In a frenzy of ignominy, they are selling and delivering their country, wholesale and retail, persons and property, soul and body, men and things. All the factories it appears will soon be obliged to turn over 12 per cent of their personnel. Fourteen aviation plants in the Lyon region are sending their machinery to Germany. Labor contracts are signed in the workers' names, and they are forced to leave. It fairly rains requisition orders on every hand. The whole police force is mobilized to round up the thousands of new hostages that Hitler has obtained from Vichy.

And the truth is that this labor draft is only a pretext. It is the first step in France toward such a transfer of populations as has been carried out by the barbarians throughout the rest of Europe. At Lons-le-Saunier, for example, 6000 people were called up for the labor draft, 6000 men from twenty to forty-five years old, chosen by alphabetical order. Among them were teachers, lawyers and even a priest.

The man-hunt is on. Today the workers are the prey; tomorrow it will be all Frenchmen. And except for a few decent people who do their best to sabotage these infamous orders, the prefects, the servile chiefs of police, and their inspectors stand ready to accept and to carry out any order they may receive. If Hitler, through the intermediary of Laval, should ask them to spit publicly in the faces of their mothers, they would do it. What can you expect? Orders is orders! They spit in the face of France.

Once more it is the workers, who have nothing—it is the unarmed mass of the people—who furnished the example of courage and dignity for the rest of the nation. From every train of workers that starts out for Germany these cries are heard: "Down with Laval! Down with Pétain! VIVE LA FRANCE! ON LES AURA!"; and the workers' voices rise in "The Marseillaise" and "The International." At Montluçon a fortnight ago, on the 6th of January, an imposing demonstration was organized. Five thousand people gathered at the railroad station, singing "The Marseillaise" and "The International," to block the train that was about to carry off 300 drafted workers. They uncoupled the locomotive, and young women lay down across the tracks. The train finally succeeded in getting under way with the aid of the police. But two hundred yards further along the railroad workers themselves took a hand. This time did it. The train of slavery did not leave. In the excitement everyone piled out. The Vichy police charged; the BOCHES came running; but it was too late. Out of the 300 drafted laborers, 270 succeeded in escaping from the train and avoiding the draft.

What a lesson! And what an example was also afforded us by the strike of the miners and metal workers of Saint-Etienne on the 5th, 6th and 7th of January! A crowd of 4000 manifestants shouted: "Down with Laval! Down with Pétain! We shall not leave!" There was a riot and arrests, but the blow had told.

Yet all these men who dare to fight know what reprisal they may incur and that starvation may be the price of their refusal to be slaves. What an obligation to stand together their courage imposes on combatant France and all her allies! Not a single worker would leave if the working class knew that we stood behind it with material and efficient help. In 1923 the Germans were able to organize a passive resistance against the French occupation of the Ruhr (a rather mild and limited occupation, it must be said) with the help and consent of all the great industrialists of the Ruhr, who subsidized the workers who refused to work in the factories. The Reich paid the striking railroad workers. All the political parties, from the Communists to the Nationalists, united in their efforts. Today, to prevent total enslavement, cannot France make a similar effort toward unity?

But patience! Let those who are forced to leave and who start out with their hearts filled with a sacred hatred of the enemy and the traitors, be assured that there, as in France, some day they will rise against their temporary masters. In the worldwide uprising that is even now brewing against the Nazis, as the victorious march of the United Nations takes shape, they will once more become Frenchmen and free.

La France
March 20, 1943

FRENCHMEN! STAND AGAINST SLAVERY

The movement is launched.

By the thousands, young Frenchmen are refusing to leave for Germany. By the thousands, the "deserters" from deportation, who tomorrow will be the soldiers of liberation, are taking to the mountains of Savoie, the Massif Central, the Jura and the Var. It is a magnificent stand, an awakening of our people to shout "No!" to the Nazi tyrants.

The whole population of France must participate in the fight against deportation.

Census takers and officials in all government services should do everything possible to hold up the registration of workers. Make mistakes. Mislay the documents, sabotage the checking of lists.

Policemen, members of the GARDE MOBILE, and gendarmes should use passive resistance against the infamous orders that are given them and oppose the force of inertia against the punitive orders that they receive.

Peasants, farmers, and city dwellers who have villas in the country, proprietors of agricultural enterprises, should give shelter to the men who are trying to evade deportation.

The families of those who are selected to be sent to Germany should do everything in their power to support them in their determination to resist.

You risk less by hiding in France than by being sent to the slaughter camps of the East. Women—mothers, sisters and fiancées —should make a row when the police come to round up their men. Shout, scream, lie down on the railroad tracks as the women of Montluçon and Romans did.

The railroad workers should give their utmost support to those who are resisting slavery.

When the police come to your house, do not open the door, let them batter their way in (if they dare), rouse the whole neighborhood, rouse the whole quarter.

Make for the mountains. Organize yourselves into centers of resistance for liberty.

The work of drawing up the lists for deportation is in a hopeless mess, now that the French have begun to resist. The proposed listing of men from thirty-one to forty-one years old cannot be carried out if resistance continues and spreads at the present rate.

Vichy and the BOCHES do not know which way to turn.

Take advantage of it. Do as the other peoples of Europe are doing. They can't arrest and deport an entire nation.

And the day of liberation is drawing near!

A SINGLE CHIEF: DE GAULLE!

A SINGLE FIGHT: FOR FREEDOM!

The Doctors Resist

One group that did all it could to sabotage the forced labor scheme was the doctors. The scheme, incidentally, called for a mass deportation of young physicians. The doctors had had their own Resistance periodical, LE MÉDECIN FRANÇAIS, since early in the occupation. The two shorts that follow tell of their first reaction to S.T.O., of what they did and of how the Germans and their servants tried to counter:

Le Médecin français
April 15, 1943

DEPORTATIONS AND DOCTORS

At this moment we are witnessing a general mobilization for the benefit of Germany. All social classes are affected. The students and interns of hospitals are to be sent to Germany in September. Germany is asking for 5,000 French doctors, and everything indicates that they will shortly be called up. The BOCHE is bent on the physical destruction of our people. Taking away our doctors is one of the means to achieve this aim.

Doctors, if you do not resist now, tomorrow you will be mobilized in Germany and soon, on the battlefields of the East in the German uniform, you will have the privilege of dying for Greater Germany.

This is your duty: to help in the resistance against deportation by rejecting as physically unfit as many Frenchmen as possible in the course of those physical examinations in which you may be obliged to participate, by giving material aid to the RÉFRACTAIRES and to the combat organizations which are organizing and assisting them. Begin preparing now to remain in France and fight any other order you may receive. Try to rouse the public to protest against the dangers that the drafting of doctors will entail.

The deportation of all its sons is the most terrible menace that has yet threatened France. Every possible means should be used to combat it.

La France
August 15, 1943

DOCTORS AGAINST SLAVE TRADERS

"Frenchmen have lost their sense of professional integrity," the quavering voice of the sinister Pétain bleats. "It is by honest toil, and by toil alone, that France may rehabilitate herself."

If there is any one group that has endeavored to keep its professional integrity, it is the doctors. They have gone so far as to reject as physically unfit the undernourished or tubercular young men who are called up for the physical examination for the S.T.O.*

Such a scandalous state of things should not be allowed to go on. A circular from the prefects gives the doctors precise instructions as to how they should proceed in the future: "Examining boards should understand," it reads, "that it is not a question of giving a complete physical examination such as is required for men entering military service nor of any such thorough examination, supplemented by X-ray and laboratory reports, as is required for workers selected for a given type of employment in Germany, but simply of a cursory examination such as used to be given to conscripts [sic]." †

That is to say that in general there should be no rejections and that, except for such persons as are actually invalids, everybody, including those whose general physical condition is poor, can be and should be accepted.

Although they are appointed by Vichy, the National Medical Council has protested.

"The council," it states, "believes that the doctors should have complete freedom to exercise their own judgment as to the fitness

---

* *Service de Travail Obligatoire.*

† The Vichy circular implies that physical examinations for the Army under the Third Republic were no more than superficial check-ups—which is a gross misstatement.—L.

or unfitness of examinees. It is the privilege of the government administration to disregard their findings if it so desires."

In contrast to the shamelessness of Vichy, the medical profession affords a splendid example of professional integrity.

The attempt to browbeat the doctors failed. They continued to reject all candidates except obvious cripples, whom LES NÉGRIERS *"the slavers," rejected as soon as they saw them. In the end* LES NÉGRIERS *dispensed with the formality of medical certificates. But by that time evasion was so well organized that precious few boys fell into their hands.*

As professional men, doctors had to be constantly on the alert against German-inspired moves to debase the practice of medicine. One of the objects of attack was medical education. The Vichy Government tried to reduce pre-medical studies to such an extent that future physicians would be little more than a superior kind of male nurse. It introduced courses in racism—in medical schools! By measuring children's skulls and testing their blood they pretended to tell whether they were Aryan or not. Jewish doctors were of course forbidden to practice. Exceptions were made at first for Jewish physicians who had been decorated in World War I, but these were later withdrawn. The Jews continued to practice unofficially until, menaced by mass deportation, they had to leave their homes. They went underground in many cases to become the physicians of the Resistance.

The gentile wife of one such physician described to me, in the summer of the liberation, a "scientific" inquest at her apartment following her husband's enforced disappearance. The couple had one daughter, eight years old, and the child was likewise subject to deportation if ruled officially non-Aryan. Mother and daughter were in the living room of their apartment near the Eiffel Tower when two Gestapo men and a German doctor presented themselves to search the premises and investigate the little girl. The doctor was a real Heidelberg professorial type—close-cropped iron-gray hair on bullet head, gold-rimmed glasses, black frock coat—the whole bag of props.

He began by asking Madame L. how a nice woman like her had ever married a Jew. "Neither of us had any religion," she said. "I never thought race made any difference." "Ah," said the HERR DOKTOR, fortunately misinterpreting her thought, "but now you know, you poor woman. You see what they are like, these Jews. He goes off and deserts you. He took advantage of your ignorance. But how could you help yourself? Your education had been deficient. You had never had the opportunity to read anything decent. Is this the child of the Jew?"

"She is my child," Madame L. said. The German doctor led the girl over near a window, put his hand under her chin and regarded her in profile. Then he looked in her eyes, which were luckily blue-green. Next he placed the tip of his middle finger on her forehead and the tip of his thumb on the point of her skull. Finally he said, "She is pure Aryan." He removed his glasses so that he could wink more ostentatiously, replaced them, bowed, and waited until his Gestapo men had finished their search of Dr. L.'s effects. Madame L. tacitly accepted the imputation of infidelity in order to save her daughter.

This was the sort of scientific procedure the Germans were encouraging in the French medical schools. French doctors carried on a biting counter-propaganda in LE MÉDECIN FRANÇAIS.

Le Médecin français
April 15, 1943

RACISM AT THE *FACULTE DE MEDICINE*

The course taught by René Martia, professor by the grace of Hitler, is usually held in the utmost privacy. Early in February, however, it was overrun by students who came not to be initiated into "Nazi racial anthropology" but to boo the "professor" vigorously. The dean, called upon to preserve order, rightly chose not to interfere.

The students are resolved to bar access to the university to agents of Hitler.

NAZI CIVILIZATION

We pass on to our colleagues without comment these extracts from German medical journals which illustrate perfectly the state of medical science under the nazi régime:

PUBLIC HEALTH AS SEEN BY THE NAZIS

"The healthiest nation in the world is not the one which has the fewest cases of tuberculosis, syphilis, arthritis, or cancer. No, it is the nation whose racial heritage is constantly augmented by a high birthrate."—WIENER KLINISCHE WOCHENSCHRIFT, 1942, page 842, DR. FEHRINGER.

NAZI POLICY

In the ZEITSCHRIFT FÜR GEBURTSHILFE, Dr. Stive publishes the results that he obtained from autopsies performed on women killed in accidents, and women condemned to death and beheaded. In these latter cases, he observes an arrested follicular development at the level of the ovaries. This "man of science" attributes this condition to the shock to the ovaries caused by the fear experienced by the accused before their execution.

The Railroadmen Resist

French railroadmen had perhaps the hardest task of all. They had to furnish information of troop or munitions movements by rail. Then they had to run the trains onto dynamite or into ambushes that were the consequences of their information. They had to call down air bombardments on their own railroad yards. Then they had to trust to luck to survive. Perhaps the bitterest thing they had to do, for French workmen, was to sabotage their own equipment. Frenchmen like to make material last. They are patchers and conservers to an almost ridiculous degree. But every locomotive that continued to function was an aid to the German war effort.

The BULLETIN DES CHEMINS DE FER was a railroaders' journal, published as a subsidiary of FRANCE D'ABORD, one of the big Resistance papers.

Bulletin des Chemins de fer
November 1943

ATTENTION! RAILROAD WORKERS
TO BE INVESTIGATED

A note from the Central Information Bureau of Vichy, dated August 14, orders that an investigation be made in railroad circles, which it describes as "hotbeds of radicalism." The following topics are prescribed for special investigation:

"(1) Complaints and grievances now being presented by the railwaymen concerning the hours, labor conditions, vacations, salaries, food, etc.

"(2) A study of the rules and regulations concerning the personnel of the French State Railroads, the attitude toward the Charter on the part of trade union leaders of the following three tendencies: Members of the C.G.T., Catholic Labor Unions, and the P.P.F.; applications already carried out in accordance with the provisions of the Railway Charter.

"(3) Political propaganda carried on among the personnel of the French State Railroads, especially in the workshops and engine sheds, both by the Nationalist parties and by the clandestine Communist and Gaullist organizations; themes of propaganda, their effectiveness, scope and results.

"(4) Railroad workers and forced labor in Germany.

"(5) Present attitude of railroad workers in regard to: (a) the interior political situation; (b) political steps decided by the government; (c) those determined by exterior, military and political events; (d) the probable attitude of the railroad workers in case of an uprising. Will they obey directives emanating from underground organizations or from abroad?"

Railroad workers, you are warned. Watch your conversations, conceal your opinions, reveal nothing concerning your plans.

ON THE PILLORY

At 3.55 p.m. on July 29, fifty political prisoners, of whom about twenty-five were women, coming from the concentration camp at Montluc, were embarked for Châlon-sur-Saône under a guard of German soldiers, in the special train 4,122 from the Lyon-Perrache station.

The assistant station master, Dureaux, after having cleared the third platform of all the people who were waiting there, undertook to seize the letters that these unhappy prisoners were trying to smuggle to the rare bystanders. He did this on his own initiative, without any urging on the part of the BOCHES. Notably, he pointed out to the Gestapo two letters that a prisoner had thrown from the door and that a patriot had covered with his foot.

His disgraceful conduct earned him the scorn of all who saw it.

The railroad workers have decided to pillory friend Dureaux. Let us lose no time in showing him what this means.

A CRIMP IN THE KRAUT-LOVERS

We must begin right away to punish those who, out of greed or congenital idiocy, persist in believing that the liberation will come like a young bride leaning dreamily on the be-starred arm of the old jerk from Vichy, with the Auvergnat—black teeth, white tie and all—for best man!

There are a number of effective days of cooling the untimely zeal of these village idiots. A good heavy crate dropped on the toes while unloading a freight car, or a conk on the noggin with a suitcase, for example, may put a momentary crimp in their activities.

There is also the "war of nerves." In dealing with these individuals, their superiors should be on the lookout to crack down on every slip they make. Their subordinates will find sheer inertia an effective weapon against them. When such a man gives an order, execute it as slowly as possible or manage to misunderstand it in such a way as to cause the maximum prejudice to the service. When the suspect approaches a group, stop talking suddenly. Surrounded by hostile silence and general contempt, he will soon begin to crumple. No man, experience proves, can long hold out against unanimous scorn. Follow these suggestions and soon the stool pigeons will come down from their stools.

Bulletin des Chemins de fer
May, 1943

NEWS ITEMS FROM FRANCE

MARCH 27, 1943. Locomotive workshops at Saint-Joseph near Nantes were bombed. The attack took place in broad daylight, which means that serious damage was done to these shops, which are very important to the German transportation system. A stick of bombs fell on the large shop at the corner of the factory. The explosion blew the roof off the southern half of the factory. Several bombs hit the assembly plant and the locomotive repair shops. Two bombs struck the steel works and the rolling mills. Mosquito bombers dropped bombs at low altitude.—LONDON, MARCH 28, 1943 (2115).

On April 4, Allied pursuit planes attacked the marshaling yards at Saint-Brieuc.—LONDON, APRIL 5, 1943 (0830).

Yesterday (April 4) the R.A.F. attacked troops, railroads and German truck convoys in the region of Dieppe and Le Tréport. —LONDON, APRIL 5, 1943 (1330).

On April 9, British fighter plane forces continued their attacks against the railroad yards of Northern France.—LONDON, APRIL 10, 1943 (0830).

During the day of April 13, the R.A.F. attacked occupied territories over a breadth of 1,000 kilometers. Among the principal objectives were the freight stations of Abbeville and Caen.—LONDON, APRIL 13, 1943 (2115).

On April 17, American aviation attacked railway installations at Abbeville and Caen.

On April 18, the R.A.F. bombed the railroad between Paris and Le Mans.

On April 20, in broad daylight, the R.A.F. raided the freight station at Abbeville.—LONDON, APRIL 21, 1943 (0830).

FROM TUNISIA

On April 15, Allied bombardment planes carried out large-scale raids on enemy communications. The road between Tunis and Enfidaville was one of the main objectives. A German commentator, speaking of the battle of Tunisia, asserts that it is because of the disorganization of transportation that the Axis has lost the initiative in this theater.

DAY AFTER DAY

On March 30, on the Saint-Etienne-Lyon line, between Saint-Chamond and Rive-de-Gier, the wrecking of a German supply train blocked the tracks.

On April 1, ten cars of German munitions exploded near the station at Le Mans. Six other cars were burned in the marshaling yards. Several tracks were damaged.

On April 2, a rail was removed between Gary and Châlon-sur-Saône. Between Cartonnières and Cauchy, on the Paris-Cambrai line, a rail was unbolted and a train derailed. Saint-Nazaire was bombed. The Le Croisic line was cut. At Belleville-sur-Saône the tracks were damaged by sabotage.

The German authorities have arrested two teachers assigned to compulsory guard duty along the tracks. They have been incarcerated in the house of detention in the Rue d'Autun at Châlon-sur-Saône.

On April 4, bombardment of Paris-Boulougne. Bombs exploded in the station of the Pont de l'Alma. A woman and a child were killed. Six civilians and five German soldiers were wounded. Tracks

1 and 2 from Puteaux to Issy were cut at Bas-Meudon and at Moulineaux-Billancourt. Tracks 1 and 3 of the Versailles-Chantiers line were also cut. Passenger service was re-established the following day at noon. Normal circulation was re-established on April 5 at 6 p.m. On the Paris-Strasbourg line, an explosion of munitions set fire to a train between Bar-le-Duc and Longueville-Masse.

It was not always easy for relatives of civilians killed in these induced accidents to be philosophical, and the counter-agents of the Gestapo did all they could to cash in on this resentment. This short gives a glimpse of their methods.

Bulletin des Chemins de fer
November, 1943

THE ORDER IS: "SPARE FRENCH LIVES"

Recently attacks have been made on passenger express trains. In less than a fortnight, two trains, train 110 at Châlon-sur-Saône, and train 103 at Collognes, have been blown up.

The Resistance groups in charge of sabotage have absolutely nothing to do with these disasters and have been deeply upset at the thought that Frenchmen acting without discernment have been running counter to their prescribed aims on sacrificing the lives of our compatriots.

It is clear that these attacks are the work of isolated groups or gangs acting without discipline, for their own personal account and without considering the results.

Resistance organizations must do their utmost to run down these mercenaries who are perhaps in the pay of the Germans. They must be prevented at any cost from going on with their infamous work. Special care and vigilance should therefore be exercised to make sure that none but trains carrying enemy troops or material be destroyed and that French lives be protected.

Obey these orders strictly and in case of the slightest doubt, refrain; do not act except in cases of absolute certainty.

We have but one enemy and it is at him that we must strike. VIVE LA FRANCE!

Finally we have a picture of the railroadman as he thought of himself. It is oversentimentalized, of course, but they were really up against it. It is much better to blubber and fight than to keep a stiff upper lip and pretend not to notice there is a fight going on.

Bulletin des Chemins de fer
November, 1943

I AM NOT AN ASSASSIN

My locomotive, my dear old bus, I loved you dearly. . . . For many months, for years, I tended you and coddled you. To me you were not an inanimate thing, a mere monster of steel that human genius had created. You had a soul, a heart, a brain. I suffered when you panted on the grades. My joy was to hear your deep regular breathing when, oiled and polished till you shone, you bore me, your black poet, on toward the horizon. The rails seemed to fade away before you, and the red kiss of your fiery hearth was ample recompense for all my toil.

And yet I killed you, deliberately, savagely. In a spurt of steam, like a soul set free, your life gushed forth after the crash that shattered your boiler. . . .

Before your great ruined body I ought to weep. And yet a wild joy fills me. Dear old girl, they were going to turn you over to the enemy! Understand me. You would have served the enemies of our country, they whose harsh voices give orders in the stations. You would have carried their soldiers, their bloodthirsty wolf-pack. That could not be: it was unthinkable.

So I killed you.

Now you lie there helpless and inert. With one last look in which I put all my tenderness, I say "farewell."

You will forgive me. You have forgiven me—for both of us are French.

First Skirmishes

The mounting number of young men in the mountainous and wooded departments was bound to bring on a sort of open war.

Le Franc-tireur
August 25, 1943

RESISTANCE IN THE CORREZE

According to secret information from a reliable source, the number of RÉFRACTAIRES who have taken refuge in the forests of the Corrèze is said to be in the neighborhood of 20,000 men. They are, for the most part, natives of the department. In fact, according to the admission of the prefecture of the Corrèze itself, only 48 per cent of the young men called up actually leave for Germany—and this is a very optimistic estimate. In certain regions of the Corrèze, around Tulle for example, those who leave are not more than 15 per cent.

In the Corrèze MAQUIS there are also young men from Paris and Marseille, and especially Bordeaux. The organization of these RÉFRACTAIRES is constantly being improved. Their number includes specialists in military engineering and communications. They are adequately supplied with arms, ammunition, tools, transport and food. Their supply problem is further facilitated by the local population and especially by the State foresters.

Thus far, the authorities have not been able to dispose of forces strong enough for any large scale attack. Each time that limited operations have been attempted by the gendarmes or the GARDE MOBILE, the young men have easily been able to escape. Frequently they have even been so successful in disarming the officers of the law that the prefect of the Corrèze has recently ordered that any public official who surrenders his gun shall be suspended from his functions. This situation is causing much ado in the department. On an average, there are three or four attacks each day on members of the MILICE and on MAIRIES and GENDARMERIES.

Thus at Tulle, in the course of an operation carried on by the RÉFRACTAIRES, 18,000 semi-monthly ration sheets were taken from one MAIRIE in spite of a very effective alarm system.

The prefect never travels in the department except with a motorcycle escort.

Bureaucracy and Red Tape

The French as a nation learned to read and write at a period when literacy was a distinction. They were so impressed by their own novel accomplishment that they have been in love ever since with little pieces of paper that have something written on them— no matter what. At times the weight of accumulated paper has threatened to break the back of the State. Robert Stern reported in the New York HERALD TRIBUNE late in 1945 that the new French nation was trying to strangle itself on red tape. The French have a special word for this addiction and submission to paper—LA PAPERASSERIE, which might be translated as papermania, or papyrophilia. A particularly papermaniac official is said to be PAPER-ASSIER; it is an adjective with only one degree as far as French officials are concerned. They are all PAPERASSIER in the superlative. Frenchmen accept LA PAPERASSERIE, but they do not defend it. Their attitude is that of the hunchback toward his hump. It is an irrevocable aspect of life; they react to it with exasperation, with gentle philosophy, with mocking humor, but without any real hope of getting rid of it.

The great school of historical research attached to the Sorbonne is known, significantly enough, as the ECOLE DES CHARTES, or School of Documents. The scent of sealing wax has for a FONCTIONNAIRE the same charm as the smell of tanbark for a show-horse. Each advance in science has broadened the field of PAPERASSERIE. Instead of bare forms in triplicate, on stamped paper, such as contented his predecessors, the modern FONCTIONNAIRE accepts no form unless it has six photographs attached, each clearly revealing the right ear. Fingerprinting has added a new delight to his work.

Once, in 1940, I rallied a French captain, a lawyer in civil life, on this national devotion to paperwork. I demonstrated that the equivalent of sixteen divisions of troops was pinned down by paper, far from the Maginot Line, filing idiotic documents in an hour when France needed every fighter. In time of war LA PAPER-ASSERIE CIVILE, intolerable, is paralleled by LA PAPERASSERIE MILI-TAIRE, insupportable. "Every French wit has railed at LA PAPER-ASSERIE," I reminded him. "Rabelais fired enough darts into it to reduce a whale to bloody froth. What good does it do?"

The captain smiled indulgently and said: "We French are an old people. We have the manias of old people. We cling to every scrap of paper. We laugh at our foible, but we recognize that it is our foible. Only the foibles of other people make us indignant. The English also breed satirists as manure breeds flies. Gilbert, Oscar Wilde, Shaw, so many. They too are an old people. They too love their foibles. They too love to laugh at them. If they ceased to be stuffy, they would cease to understand Gilbert. Then they would cease to love him. In the same way, if we abandoned LA PAPERASSERIE we might lose our love for Rabelais' account of GRIPEMINAUD and LES CHATS FOURRÉS. Surely you do not want us to abandon literature?"

It was a most lawyer-like argument, better than many I have heard in high courts in the United States, but I intimated that it did not satisfy me. The captain therefore resumed, "How can a man be sure who he is unless he has his CARTE D'IDENTITÉ in his pocket? He may be somebody else. But we are a nation of individualists. A Frenchman does not wish to be anybody else. His identity card is his guarantee of authenticity.

"Moreover we cherish clarity, precision. The written word is precise, it is explicit. It has only one correct meaning. The charm for us is in discovering that meaning. How can you have satisfactory litigation without a document to base it on? Abolish LA PAPER-ASSERIE and you reduce litigation to the status of a verbal squabble among savages. Also litigation is one of the favorite themes of French literature. My friend, I am afraid that you are anti-literary."

If a multitude of papers were essential to normal existence in

1939-40, one may easily imagine the situation after the Germans came. Now in addition to French civil and military papers, it was necessary to travel with the AUSWEISE of the German KOMMANDANTURS, to carry ration tickets for food, cigarettes, clothing and virtually anything else buyable. An individual without papers was helpless. So, as the illegal bodies of the Resistance grew, their need for false papers of all kinds increased until it took a real industry to supply its needs.

In France under the oppression an able-bodied man, particularly if he looked young, had to have papers to show to any policeman or German who challenged him. He had to show his papers every time he registered at a hotel or put up overnight at a lodging house. He had to have some special papers to pass from one region to another, to show that he had been exempted from forced labor, that he was not an escaped prisoner of war. Above all he had to have food tickets. FAUX PAPIERS tells the story of a specialist in "documentation," a forger of papers in industrial quantities. But if there was any hope that in PAPERASSERIE, as in finance, bad currency would drive out good, that hope was fated to be disappointed. According to Mr. Stern there is more PAPERASSERIE in France now than ever.

False Identity*

by LOUIS PARROT

"Police Discover Counterfeiters' Den."

How often in newspapers before the war we read these words followed by the description, always the same, of a little workshop established under the eaves, where an old man tried to change into vile gold the lead that the poor counterfeiters buy so dearly. One touch that the reporter never forgot to put in was the square of pale sky of the skylight. This touch gave the banal news item the romantic flavor of old Russian tales.

The fact is that this minor trade was much more akin to a folk

* From Les Lettres Françaises, October 15, 1944.

art than to the reprehensible industry which consists of making, very legitimately, thousands of banknotes. A man is a counterfeiter by avocation or by accident, just as one is a scissors grinder, and it required many sleepless nights on the part of a whole family to turn out one of these small, suspicious-looking bills that one had great difficulty in passing at the end of the week. It ranked with poetry as a badly paid trade, and its prestige dwindled under the constant harassing of the law.

But now this obscure trade has suddenly acquired unbelievable luster. The records of the Resistance have scarcely begun to unfold and already marvelous tales are coming to light. The counterfeiters of our childhood are mere tyros beside those whom the necessities of the Resistance brought into being. We used to talk of the worthless little five-franc coins that apprentice counterfeiters passed at the risk of hard labor. Tomorrow, history will tell of thousands of identity cards, true and false, that our friend Michel R.—aided by his admirable helpmate, Monique—turned out. And this counterfeiter, whose little shop provided all the Resistance centers with complete sets of personal documents—from the certificate of demobilization to the identity card, all in proper form and stamped with the most authentic seals—saved thousands of our compatriots and assured the safety of thousands of others.

It was in the heart of Paris itself, in one of those streets where the passer-by would never suspect that he was being watched from behind drawn curtains, that Michel R. worked. For thirty-four months he never stirred from his room. Outside the windows where he occasionally stood musing at the end of the day's work, the seasons went by, each in turn casting its hue of sun or snow over the wall opposite. Anxiety, fear and dread followed each other like the seasons. In the street below sometimes men dressed in green uniforms raised their eyes toward the window. But Michel R., whose trace they had sought everywhere, had no time to lose watching them move away into the crowd. He hurried back to his work. Orders were piling up; clandestine organizations everywhere were clamoring for their weekly deliveries.

The workbench on which this perfect counterfeiter worked consisted of the shelves of his linen closet. Pigeonholes filled with type, tweezers, and complicated tools were within reach of his hands. In front of him an electric bulb hung over a pile of handkerchiefs, casting a circle of light that could not be seen from the street. In a few seconds he could leave his shop, close the doors of the linen closet, and give the chance visitor an impression of perfect respectability. In the case of a more serious alarm, there was, under the boards of the floor, a safer hiding place where he could put the key pieces of his counterfeiting equipment, which had taken him long months of labor to procure.

When, on June 30, 1940, Michel R. returned to Paris after having escaped from a prison camp, he had in his pocket the first stamp that enabled him to make his first false identity cards; a magnificent rubber stamp of the "Colonel Commanding the Central Recording Office of the Seine," which he had burglarized from an office guarded by the Germans.

With the aid of this seal, Michel made out false certificates of ill health, by means of which some of his former comrades in prison were released. Nothing was simpler. All he had to do was to have police stations issue "true copies" of the documents stamped with the stolen seal. This seal passed easily for the stamp of the "Colonel Commanding the Nth Regiment"—and the competent authorities never detected the fraud.

A year passed and the first mass arrests began to take place. The Germans were tracking down patriots; denunciation began to be a well-organized service. To meet this threat, the Resistance had to perfect its own organization. The need for false papers became urgent, and Michel, who was then at Lyon, remembered the books of his childhood. In those days, at the time of life when children are crazy about maps and engravings, his hobby had been the Russian Revolution, famous prison breaks, and the stories of revolutionaries before the World War. He was convinced that no obstacle is unsurmountable and asked his friend Boris B., a former student at the Beaux Arts, to make him, in any substance, a die that could be used to print an identity card. They worked night and day, and finally succeeded in their aim. Using a drawing in hectographic ink on gelatin and a transfer onto an identity card, they produced a false card so absolutely "authentic" that it allowed them to cross the demarcation line into the occupied zone and return to Paris.

Now Monique and Michel were launched on the great adventure. They were to become the official purveyors of false papers for all the Resistance organizations. It was true that the method that they had worked out at Lyon was very rudimentary, but it could still be of great service.

By the beginning of 1943, Michel had read all the technical literature that he could find on printing, electrotyping, photo mechanical engraving, and rubber stamps. All that remained was to apply his knowledge. It was here that he ran into difficulties. There was a shortage of workers and raw materials. Michel's little shop could turn out exactly fifty false identity cards a week. It was then that he discovered a rotogravure man, and the activity of the false identity industry began to multiply.

E. C., the rotograver, agreed to work for Michel every Sunday, and from March, 1943, to June, 1944, his help was invaluable. Using a certificate of demobilization from Sathonay which a friend had loaned him, Michel had the stamp copied off by the designer. E. C. made films from it, and a friendly printer printed several thousand fairly passable certificates. Another printer, in Levallois, set up the text of the plates. Another false paper went into circulation—a magnificent paper certifying that the holder had been released from a prison camp for reasons of health.

Michel now had at his disposition a little vulcanizing press, a supply of rubber and enough powder for making molds. He went to work with them one Saturday evening and, after having labored until dawn, he brought out for the first time a set of practical rubber stamps. The success was complete. The papers, once stamped—and some of them bore as many as fourteen different stamps—could not be distinguished from authentic papers.

At a number of points throughout the land, the DÉFENSE DE LA FRANCE movement had set up centers for distributing false documents of all kinds. But models were scarce. They could not be invented, and any mistake might have serious consequences. It was therefore necessary to appeal for help in many quarters, to procure from MAIRIES old envelopes from the official mail to use as models for stamps that could not be otherwise obtained. When such correspondence also contained the signature of the mayor or his assistant, everything was perfect.

Recently I revisited Michel R. In a calm voice he told me stories whose faintest whisper in other times would have made the solidest pillars of the administration tremble. This little man with his modest air, whom nobody would notice in the street, accomplished without any ado a heroic task for which we shall never to be able to thank him enough. All of us knew messengers who were tortured for having been caught with a little package of false identity cards in their possession. We dare not think what tortures would have awaited Michel R. if he had been discovered. He, like all those who have risked their lives for the sake of a great cause, shrugs his shoulders when one reminds him of the risks he ran.

"It had to be done quickly," he told us. "We had to get Allied aviators and escaped prisoners back to England. As early as May, 1943, we began studying the problem of certificates of residence for the departments along the coast and frontiers, and we turned out BESCHEINIGUNGEN that allowed the holder to reside in the Departments of the Manche, the Côtes-du-Nord, the Finistère, and the Pyrénées by using stamps corresponding to these regions. At the end of the same month we could turn out the following papers: certificates of liberation from German camps, certificates of resettlement, census receipts, work certificates, deferment certificates for students, certificates of domicile in the forbidden zones, and about thirty stamps of different MAIRIES, as well as several German stamps, and about thirty stamps used for special occasions.

"The specialist who did our mimeograph work was obliged to compile a booklet, THE COUNTERFEITER'S MANUAL, 1943, to serve as directions for using all these papers properly.

"In July, 1943, we had to deliver two hundred and fifty stamps a week. In December our work had stepped up so that we could deliver five hundred."

From then on, Michel never left his room. He had barely escaped being arrested. Why should he go out since he could work so efficiently in his voluntary prison? With tranquil courage, Monique kept in contact with the centers of distribution. She carried the stamps in macaroni boxes and in a market basket with a false bottom. She acted as go-between for all the collaborators in the Central Office of False Papers—the printers, the designer, the engraver, and those who made the deliveries.

At the end of 1943, the Central Office had several stamps of the Republic in different sizes, a number of models of the Vichy seal, and German spread-eagles, which made it easy to imitate most of the official stamps. It could furnish everything: stamps of the general administrations, of police stations, ministries, hospitals, universities, schools, factories, industries and KOMMANDANTURS. It was in possession of the stamps of the German embassy, the Military Commander of Greater Paris, the Military Governor of France, and the Chief of the SS.

It was about this time that the Office of False Papers brought out civilian defense cards which permitted the holder to circulate at any time, driver's licenses, automobile licenses, departmental identity cards, draft cards for the class of '44, exemptions from forced labor, and finally—as a crowning achievement—the plates for false one-and-a-half franc stamps with a likeness of Pétain. These stamps amounted to an economy of 300,000 francs a month in sending out tracts and clandestine papers. "In this way," Michel told us with a smile, "our newspaper, DÉFENSE DE LA FRANCE, enjoyed free postal privileges during those last months."

And this tremendous activity went on right up until June 3, 1944. On that day the message, "My wife has sharp eyes," was sent out twice. The Allied landing was imminent. On June 5 Michel loaded a part of his equipment on a truck and set out to take his place in the MAQUIS. He joined his outfit on the 6th of June just as the message was sent: "He is severe but just." Direct action had begun.

An estimate of the work turned out by the Office of False Papers that Michel R. and his wife Monique directed with the help of several faithful and devoted comrades establishes the number of stamps furnished at about 12,000, representing about 2,000 different types of stamps. Most of them were struck off in four, six, eight and even twenty copies for various organizations. The breakdown goes something like this:

    1,000 stamps of municipal authorities
     250 police station stamps

    60 stamps of departmental authorities
    50 German stamps
    75 stamps of business establishments
   550 miscellaneous stamps

More than sixty square meters of rubber were used for this work.

As for the identity cards alone authenticated with the stamps furnished by the Center, it can be asserted that they amounted to more than a million.

But what even the most exact figures would not reveal is the courageous persistence and tireless tenacity that Michel and Monique R. put into their enterprise. Thousands of patriots who owed them their lives and who, thanks to them, were able to work, each in his place, to bring about the liberation, never knew that their fate was in the hands of the "counterfeiter" Michel R. For the thirty-four months that preceded his returning to the MAQUIS, this man who normally led as active an existence as most of us, had voluntarily walled himself in.

He went through those long periods of depression that prisoners know so well, but like them, he lived on hope. There were continual alarms. Often he heard the sound of boots on the stairs. Toward the end, when restrictions became more and more serious, the gas was shut off and he had to eat his food uncooked. The "customers" could not be kept waiting and the little stamp-making machine that Michel had installed in his kitchen had to work several hours a day. The room was filled with such a frightful smell of rubber that it was impossible to open the window for fear of rousing suspicions.

It was a dangerous life, full of a thousand daily difficulties in addition to the ever-present menace of a house search. Today, the Office of False Papers has gone out of business; and the stamps, the models, the photographs of stolen documents form a panoply on the wall, at the sight of which one cannot help feeling a grateful and respectful admiration.

HISTOIRE DE BRIGANDS ("*The Bandits*") *tells how the ration tickets were provided. The procedure in* HISTOIRE DE BRIGANDS *was followed* in hundreds of villages all over France, but the most fruitful source of tickets was Paris. The police stations, where the tickets were kept, were burglarized with astonishing regularity. It is not quite so astonishing, however, when one reflects that the Paris police were one of the nuclei of the Paris Resistance movement. Both pieces ran in the newly-legal LETTRES FRANÇAISES a couple of weeks after the liberation of Paris. Both authors had been active in the underground for years.

Edith Thomas, a novelist and newspaper correspondent before the war—her reports on the war in Spain were considered remarkable—is a young woman described by one Resistance colleague as "frail, timid, and audacious beyond belief." It was she who, meeting Claude Morgan, an old newspaper friend, in the spring of 1942, was his first collaborator on LES LETTRES FRANÇAISES after the arrest of Decour had isolated him. She restored the liaison between Morgan and the surviving members of the original National Writers' Committee. CONTES D'AUXOIS, a collection of her short stories, was first published by the EDITIONS DE MINUIT in December, 1943.

The Bandits*

by EDITH THOMAS

Mademoiselle was correcting copybooks. Five and six are eleven. Five and six are eleven. Eleven, eleven. Over and over again. Mademoiselle wrote in the margin in red ink a fine B for BIEN, neatly formed and underlined.

Outside the window she saw the meadows and kitchen gardens sloping down to the slow gray river, a little in flood. In the marshes, the frogs were singing.

From time to time planes went winging on to bomb some spot in Europe. That did not keep the frogs from singing, nor Mademoiselle from writing Bs in the copy books when five and six were eleven.

*From Les Lettres Françaises, September 23, 1944.

Mademoiselle's heart had also known its emptinesses. Now it was calm. Nothing ever happened in it. Absolutely nothing. The worst may happen; the thing that one would have thought unbearable, but one always manages to bear it. Or else you died of it, in which case the fall of empires is no more important than . . . than what? . . . and six are eleven.

A robin lit on the window sill and flew away again. Then someone knocked at the door.

They must have been strangers in the village because they knocked at the door of the MAIRIE. And everyone knows that there is never anybody in the MAIRIE and that you have to knock on the school door. Mademoiselle got up to see who it was. She put on her coat and looked at herself in the mirror. There she saw a face like a goat's, sticking out its tongue.

The knocking continued. Outside it was the gray hour that precedes the night, and it was beginning to be difficult to see things clearly. Mademoiselle saw two men standing in the twilight.

"What do you want?" she called to them.

"We want to get in," they said.

"What for?" she asked. "The Mayor has gone. There is nobody there."

The key of the MAIRIE felt cold in the pocket of her coat. "What do you want?" she repeated.

Mademoiselle was very small, but she was not afraid of anything. Not even of mice, not even of coming home alone at night over lonely roads, not even of these men who were there before her and whom she knew did not belong in the village.

"We want the food ration tickets," they said. She had opened the door of the MAIRIE and saw them now under the light of the lamp. They were boys about twenty years old. A little pale. They had drawn revolvers from their pockets and pointed them at her. Mademoiselle felt that something was happening in her life where nothing ever happened.

"Put out the light," they said. "We don't want to be seen from outside."

She put it out. It's like making love, she thought. Swift and tingling as love must be. "The tickets are not at the MAIRIE," she said, exactly in the same tone with which she said five and six are eleven. "The Mayor keeps them at home in his safe."

Then—they would be able to use them: "But I have got the clothing ration cards."

"Give them to us." She went to the cabinet at the end of the office and opened it.

"Here," she said. She noticed that her hands were trembling.

"Take us to the Mayor's house," they said.

She went out with them. There was nobody on the road in this twilight. "Keep me covered," she said (just in case somebody should see her). She was grateful to these boys for the quivering that she felt in her breast and in the pit of her stomach.

MADAME LA MAIRESSE was kitting socks for MONSIEUR LE MAIRE. It was a poor kind of wool, all stiff and tallowy. Even at that, she had only been able to get it in exchange for four dozen eggs. She was moved now by a profound regret for the eggs. She thought about all the things that she might have been able to get in exchange for them instead of this coarse, greasy wool. A frying pan, for instance, or even a pair of corduroy pants for her man when he worked in the fields.

From time to time, she looked at the road, and her hands kept on kitting all by themselves. There was nothing along the road except telegraph poles and banks of dry grass like at the end of winter.

"If I only lived in town," she said to herself, "with everything that goes on there. It is true that right now you are better off in the country than in town. Just the same, this wool isn't much good."

She noticed that the fire was dying down in the stove and that it was beginning to be cold. She got up to put in a log when she noticed Mademoiselle approaching. The Mayor's wife did not like Mademoiselle, whom she called "that brazen nanny goat" when she spoke of her alone with the Mayor. What was she up to now, the brazen nanny goat, when she must know that the Mayor had gone to town about this business of requisitioning the horses? But Mademoiselle was not alone. She was closely flanked by two men. And what could THEY be after? For, after all, whatever her other faults might be, Mademoiselle was not a man-chaser. The Mayor's wife let the window curtain fall back in place. After all, perhaps they were not coming here. It seemed to her that the curtain protected her from some vague danger. She thought of all the stories that were going around. On the table was a newspaper containing a long list of "terrorist crimes." The Mayor claimed that they filled the column up with all the crimes that had happened years ago and invented fresh ones. But still, when you were a woman, alone in the house . . .

She heard the doorbell ring and went to open the door.

"Madame," said Mademoiselle, "these two gentlemen want to speak to you."

She drew aside to let them pass. Then the Mayor's wife saw two revolvers and almost fell over backward.

"Wha-what do you want?" she stammered.

"The ration tickets," they said.

"The only thing is they're in the safe," she said.

"Open it."

"The trouble is I don't know the combination." Perhaps the Mayor would come back in time; he would know what to do.

"Try it," they said.

"I haven't got my glasses."

"Where are they?" they asked. "Don't move, we'll go get them."

Her eyes were fixed on a revolver and a heavy glove that held the revolver. She looked at Mademoiselle. Mademoiselle was as inscrutable and pale as ever. Beneath her blank expression, it still seemed that her long, yellow goat eyes saw everything. Could it be that she is in on this with them, this nanny goat? she said to herself.

"Here are your glasses," said one of the boys.

She felt a moment of daring. "Maybe those revolvers aren't even loaded."

One of the boys sniggered. (A couple of kids whose ears it would be a pleasure to box if they were mine!) He broke open the revolver.

"Take a look for yourself," he said.

The Mayor's wife began twiddling the knob of the combination.

✦

MONSIEUR LE MAIRE was coming back from town on his bicycle. He got off at every hill to catch his breath and give himself a chance to think. It was no fun being mayor in times like these. He would have done better to have resigned back in 1940. But his wife cared too much for the prestige of the position to hear of it; then, also, it would have been taken for an act of hostility toward the Germans. Undoubtedly the Mayor didn't like the Germans; but to go so far as to commit an act of hostility against them was something else. It was a thing that demanded reflection. So MONSIEUR LE MAIRE was reflecting.

There was this business about the new requisition for horses—the few remaining ones that the Germans had rejected last year. With what were the farmers supposed to plow their fields? And how were they going to take it? They would hold him responsible for it again. All the more so because of his father-in-law, an official of the new Vichy farm co-operative, who was suspected of favoring the big fellows. Yes, he would have done better to resign in 1940.

The Mayor had reached the top of the hill. From there he could see the whole countryside, with its villages and its hamlets and isolated farms, and the railroad and the river and the marsh on the other side. And the fields on this side cut up into small gardens, each with a few fruit trees. The whole landscape was gray with mist and twilight. The Mayor sighed and got on his bicycle to coast down the hill.

He had just learned also that the village was supposed to collect a levy of fifty tons of cherries for next summer. It was completely absurd. In the past years they harvested scarcely more than thirty to forty tons. And how could one tell how much there would be next summer even before the trees blossomed? Oh, they were clever, these people in the city who were supposed to look after the food supply. "And we don't even know where it goes," the Mayor thought.

"But we do know only too well where it goes," the Mayor answered himself. He was watching a train that rolled slowly along the railroad tracks, loaded and headed toward the East. Anyway, perhaps the war will be over next year, the Mayor said to himself, to bolster up his courage a little. He repeated this to himself every day, at least ten times a day when the weather was good.

One more curve and he was home. He put his bicycle into the shed, beside his wife's machine. There were voices in the house. "What's up this time?" the Mayor asked himself.

He wanted to rest, to tell his wife what he had learned in town, and to have a glass of wine to warm himself up. That was what he wanted to do instead of having to keep up a conversation with more people coming to complain. MONSIEUR LE MAIRE would have bet ten to one that was what it was.

"Put them up!" somebody said to him.

The Mayor lifted his hands over his head. In the meanwhile, one of the kids closed the door and leaned against it, his revolver in his fist.

The Mayor took it all in at a glance: Mademoiselle, stiff and straight and unperturbed, and his wife kneeling before the safe.

"Charles," she moaned, "Charles, you just got here in time. These gentlemen want the ration tickets, and I can't remember the combination. These gentlemen said they were going to blow my brains out."

The Mayor caught a quick smile on the faces of the boys. They looked like a couple of kids, he told himself. He thought of his own boy who had left for compulsory labor service in Germany. He would have done better to have done like these two. He had even told him as much. It was the boy's mother who was against it—because it was the law, she said.

The Mayor went to the safe and opened it. "Here are your tickets," he said. There was also some money in the safe.

"Is that yours?" they asked.

"No," the Mayor said. "It's for paying the guards—the men who are obliged to guard the railroad to prevent attacks against the Germans."

"If it was yours, we wouldn't take it. But since it belongs to the State, 'the State is us.'"

One of them put the money in his pocketbook. There were 2,353 francs and 70 centimes. They left the 70 centimes.

The Mayor wondered if he mightn't offer them a drink; he was thirsty. But he didn't dare because of what his wife and Mademoiselle might think. He had thought of every situation that might come up in the job of being a mayor, but this was a new one to him. After all, it was better for them to go.

"And don't go calling the gendarmes or you will wish you hadn't."

"But I'll have to put in my report though."

"As late as possible, then."

"Of course," said the Mayor.

Outside the boys saw the two bicycles under the shed.

"We'll send them back tomorrow to the station at X," they said as they got astride them. And the Mayor heard the tinkle of his bicycle bell fading away in the night.

In the house, Mademoiselle was slapping his wife's cheeks to revive her. The Mayor poured himself out a glass of wine. He wanted to tell about the requisitioning of the horses, but his wife, recovering from her swoon, sat up and screamed, "What a coward you are, a coward, a coward!"

"Would you have been pleased to have had me cause myself to be killed for a few miserable ration tickets?" said the Mayor who, having passed his diplomas, could turn as elegant a phrase as another when occasion warranted. "After all, those boys have to live."

A little later in the evening he mused, "I wonder if they will send back the bicycles."

Two days later, the Mayor was informed that two bicycles had arrived in his name at the station at X.

The Jews of France

The deportations, and the struggle against them, continued virtually until the Allied landings in 1944. The methods of the Germans and their traitor tools became continually more brutal, and the counter-measures of the patriots progressively more ingenious, as the following pieces indicate.

One form of deportation that had commenced earlier than the

others was that of Jews. The Germans had begun a systematic elimination of the Jews of the old Occupied Zone almost as soon as they entered France. In the southern zone and in North Africa, prior to November, 1942, there had been neither massacres nor mass deportations, but Jews had been degraded to a second-class citizenship. They had been barred from schools, professions and military service and their property had been sequestered. After November, 1942, the policy of ruthless liquidation of Jews was extended to the southern zone, and intensified in the North. The Jews of France were aided and protected by millions of their compatriots. The Church, spotty in its attitude toward the Resistance movement in general, was solidly against the persecution of the Jews. Nuns sheltered Jewish children and bishops helped Jews to escape the Gestapo. Prelates preached against the doctrine of race hate. Marshal Pétain, with his pietistic cant, was, naturally enough, well regarded by many of the high clergy, great believers themselves in discipline, and solid comfort, a doctrine they expressed as "respect for constituted authorities." The lower clergy was in general more favorable to the Resistance. On the Jewish question, however, the bishops were as intransigent as the CURÉS. The Archbishop of Rennes, now Cardinal Roques, told me a couple of days after the liberation of that city that he had intervened for Jews and helped them escape. He had also used his diocesan newspaper against the occupants, preached against deportation and protected priests implicated in Resistance cases.

The Church, in making cardinals of Monsignor Roques and of the then Bishop of Montauban, Louis Salieges, eminent as a patriot, tacitly recognized the error of the senior French cardinals, who followed the Vichy line so closely that they disqualified themselves as effective speakers for the Catholic point of view in postwar France. Cardinals Roques and Salieges can speak without danger that some godless editor will sneer at their war records. The Church sometimes reminds one of a racing stable with more than one entry in every stake.

FRATERNITÉ was a national publication—clandestine, of course—directed against the propaganda of race hate. The Resistants recognized this propaganda as the splitting wedge that Hitler used against nations.

Fraternité
September, 1943

Jews of France in Nazi Murder Camps

Let us send hundreds of thousands of letters to the authorities to protest against the massacre of French Jews.

ALL THE VICTIMS OF RACISM NEED YOUR HELP

At a time when mass arrests and deportations to the murder camps of the East are once more taking place, we are publishing a document which depicts the inhuman sufferings and the atrocious death of thousands of innocent people. This account, related by an eye-witness who made a miraculous escape from the unutterable hell of these camps, shows to what extremes of bestiality and sadism the Nazi beasts, who have already destroyed all moral and spiritual values in their own country, will go to achieve the same results in France and in all the other occupied countries of Europe.

Government and police officials who participate directly or indirectly in the arrest and deportation of the Jews should know that they are making themselves the accomplices of the Nazi executioners.

All of us, workers and intellectuals, believers and free thinkers, who have already helped to save thousands of families, should unite more closely than ever to combat racism. By so doing, we shall help to defend our own undernourished children and our own young men who are threatened with deportation, and at the same time do our share in the fight for the liberation of France.

ACCOUNT BY AN EYE-WITNESS

The true story of a deportee arrested by the Vichy police along with hundreds of other families in the region of Nice in August, 1942:

"Loaded into cattle-cars, we started out for an unknown destination. The train arrived at Marseille. Hearing the cries of the women and children, the populace gathered around the train. To calm the growing indignation, the Vichy police solemnly declared that the prisoners locked up in these cars would not be turned over to the Germans, but that the men would be sent to labor companies and the women and children to detention areas.

"The reality was quite different. The next day we arrived at Drancy. There we were stripped of everything we owned, money, linen, toilet articles, etc.

"Men, women and children were loaded once more into cattle-cars, seventy to each car. We traveled for three days without food of any kind or even a drop of water to drink. The cries of the children were frightful to hear.

"It was only at Koziel, in Upper Silesia, that the cars were unlocked and we were sent to a camp. Sixty-eight persons had died in the course of the trip.

"In this camp we were sorted into categories. The men from sixteen to fifty and the young women were kept as laborers. Their heads were shaved, and each person was given six yellow stars and ordered to sew them on to his clothing after cutting holes in the cloth at the spots where the stars were to be placed—one on each knee, two on the shoulders and two on the chest.

"The old men and the women and children unsuited for work were sent to Auschwitz.

"Auschwitz was a word to strike terror to the heart of any Jew. As the Nazis cynically told us, 'When you are sent there, it is to die.'

"What I saw with my own eyes while the departure for Auschwitz was being organized is indescribable. Ten-year-old children claimed to be seventeen, men of seventy claimed to be fifty, to escape being sent.

"In the labor camp itself, the beatings and the bestial tortures surpassed all imagination. Then too there was starvation. Even while we were eating our soup consisting of salted water, blows rained on our shaven heads.

"Detachments of six hundred persons were sent out every day to work on the roads and railroads.

"Every day from twelve to eighteen people died on the labor details. As a further humiliation to their victims, the Nazis gave the rations of the dead to any one who would carry the corpse back to the camp. Our hunger was such that there were always more volunteers than were needed.

"One day two Dutch Jews, feeling ill, did not dare mention their state (to be sick was the most heinous of crimes, for which the punishment was death). Arriving at the yard, they could no longer stand. The Nazis beat them until they were unconscious and then finished them off with their boot heels. Such scenes took place every day.

"In order to prevent escape, at the end of the day's work all the prisoners were stripped of their clothing and allowed to keep only their underwear.

"In the village of Schapiniec there is a hospital where women in childbirth are taken. As soon as they are born the babies are thrown into a bag and killed. As for the mothers, they are sent to Auschwitz, 'whence there is no return.'

"As fast as the high mortality and the fact that those who seem too tired to work are soon sent to Auschwitz, produce vacancies in the camp, fresh victims are shipped in from Western Europe to fill them."

Prisoners and Deportees

Résistance
January 25, 1944

IN THE PRISONS OF ANTI-FRANCE

A young RÉFRACTAIRE at present an inmate of the prison at Eysses (Lot-et-Garonne) sends us the following letter:

"I am going to give you a few facts. We were slated to be transferred to another prison. On December 8 at one p.m. we set out for the railroad station accompanied by a strong police guard. By way of making a demonstration, we sang as we were marched through town. We boarded a train.

"We waited until nine o'clock that evening. Then the order was countermanded and we returned to this prison. In the meanwhile we learned that we were to be sent to a camp near Paris. I need not tell you our eventual destination. It was only too clear.

"The following day we were again ordered to leave. We refused to obey and barricaded ourselves in the prison. After a discussion, an agreement was reached. The head warden gave us his word of honor that we should not be transferred. But for Vichyites, a word of honor is a scrap of paper. During the night we heard a loud noise. We barricaded the doors solidly. There was no more trouble until seven o'clock in the morning. This time it was the real thing. Five hundred troops of the GARDE MOBILE had come to take us by force. They tried to open the doors of the dormitories where we had locked ourselves in. Not succeeding in this, they broke the panes of the dormer windows with the butts of their rifles and threw tear-gas bombs into the room. The air was unbreathable; we were suffocating and our eyes smarted and ran. We held out and succeeded in getting word to the political prisoners locked up in the two other rooms of the prison. They broke down the doors of their cells and came running in a body to help us against the police. "The Marseillaise" rang out. We all sang in spite of the gas, and grappled with the police. At a distance of ten meters the police refused to fire. We had won; once more the police withdrew from the terrain.

"We are still at Eysses; but, as a result of the gas attack, twenty of our members are in the infirmary, suffering from serious injury to their eyes. Some of them even have lesions produced by the prolonged irritation. Not all of the victims are young men; among them there are also old men of sixty and wounded veterans of 1914-1918, some of whom have only one leg and were gassed in the last war."

Since receiving this letter, we are pleased to learn that about forty of the prisoners at Eysses have been able to escape and regain their liberty.

La Vie ouvrière
February 26, 1944

AGAINST THE DEPORTATION OF 273,000 NEW SLAVES

On January 18 Sauckel gave orders to Vichy to furnish the Reich with all the available manpower in France. On February 4, Pétain-Laval-Bichelonne punctually carried out these orders by decreeing obligatory labor for all men from sixteen to sixty years old and for women without children from eighteen to forty-five years old. Everything that the traitors may have to say about the aims of this requisition is only part of an obvious propaganda intended to cover up the mobilization of all the ablebodied men and women of France for the benefit of Hitler.

Secret documents that we have had at our disposition prove beyond any doubt that the occupying authorities have taken over the direction and control of all the organizations having to do with forced labor.

Basing their claim on the Vichy decrees, the BOCHES can, without further formality, lay hands on any Frenchman and assign him any kind of work they please. The traitors have "legalized," so to speak, these raids which the BOCHE does not hesitate to make.

Henceforth, with warrant in hand, the Nazi bandits are free to swoop down on any industry, any neighborhood, or any village, round up their quota of slaves, and deport them to anywhere they wish.

And this is not just something that MIGHT happen. We have learned that in many villages of Brittany the slave traders have already attempted to round up and deport all the male inhabitants. Our information adds that the Breton peasants put up an admirable resistance. Most of the men in question fled to the open country, and a number of skirmishes are reported to have taken place between them and the BOCHES.

Every industry should be a stronghold of resistance.

There is no question but what fresh attempts are to be made

to carry off the workers now engaged in the various French industries. Documents that we have received prove clearly that:

(1) Henceforth French industrialists are to be under a constant control and supervision.

(2) All rules concerning hiring and firing will be dictated by the Germans alone.

From this moment on, in every industry, the workers should therefore consider themselves alerted. Warned of the danger, they must make ready to defend themselves and prepare to fight off any attack aimed at seizing any of their number.

We repeat the directives which we have previously issued and which have already proved their efficacy on many occasions:

(1) Alert the entire personnel in every enterprise immediately.

(2) Make all preparations and take all necessary measures to assure:

(a) Immediate stoppage of work at the first warning;

(b) Seizure of the premises and the withdrawal of personnel to positions the most favorable for active resistance in case of an attempt to take the workers by force.

(3) Warn the other enterprises in the region and the population of the neighborhood in order that the workers may have their immediate support.

(4) In every enterprise not threatened, but in the same region as the one attacked, a general strike in support of the threatened industry should be put into effect.

(5) The workers involved should receive the immediate active support of all Resistance organizations, including that of armed units.

Resistance to deportation is an imperious necessity. The Provisional Government of General de Gaulle as well as all the organizations of the Resistance urge you to combat these deportations. But, like every other activity, it demands practical measures. Hence we are furnishing the above directives.

In order to insure an effective resistance in all industries, armed groups and reserves must immediately be organized, wherever they do not already exist.

To assert that resistance is necessary and then to take no steps to make that resistance count is idle and short-sighted. At a time like the present, we have no right to indulge in empty words.

Libération
March 14, 1944

A SUCCESSFUL OPERATION

Our comrades of the C.A.D.* with the help of armed groups of the Resistance, carried out a remarkable exploit. Breaking into the offices of the S.T.O.† located in the Place Fontenoy, at Paris, they succeeded in burning more than 180,000 census cards listing members of the class of 1944. The results of this census are thus made useless for at least six months to come. It should be added that the members of our task force were not obliged to use their weapons to execute their mission. Their only difficulty was to win over a young member of the CHANTIERS DE LA JEUNESSE ‡ who, taking his rôle as guardian of the premises too seriously, attempted to oppose them. Let us add that the young champion of deportation received, in the hospital where he is now resting comfortably, a gift package accompanied by a friendly note from his aggressors explaining that a national obligation more important than his personal orders had rendered his temporary immobilization necessary.

P.S.—After a check-up, here are the practical results of the operation.

All the census cards forwarded from the provinces were destroyed, except those from the immediate region of Lyon, the cards from the Departments of the Drôme and Saône-et-Loire having been either destroyed on the spot or stolen from the prefectures of these departments. The cards from the Rouen region (except those from the Department of Calvados, which were destroyed) are still in Rouen and consequently escaped burning.

* Commission d'Action contre la Déportation.
† Service de Travail Obligatoire.
‡ A Vichy youth organization.

PART FOUR

The Fight

The First F.F.I. Communiqué

The first communiqué of the General Staff of the Fighting French of the Interior issued on March 11, 1943, serves as a convenient though arbitrary marker for the transition from the period of scattered, uncoordinated violence to that of organized resistance. The headquarters of the Fighting French in March, 1943, was in liaison with the De Gaulle government at London, but it had no contact with large fractions of the Resistance movement in France. The tiny cells of the summer of 1940 had already grown into about a dozen large organizations, and those were beginning to coalesce and to exchange confidences. But the authors of the communiqué were being a trifle grandiloquent when they spoke of a national headquarters. The liaison between the De Gaulle government and the Forces of the Interior was never perfect, even at the very end. General Pierre Koenig, appointed by General de Gaulle just before the invasion to be commander-in-chief of the Forces of the Interior (while Koenig remained, perforce, on the exterior) remained ignorant of the identities of the regional chiefs technically under his command.

This communiqué must have been issued by Jean Moulin, known in the Resistance as Max or Rex, first official co-ordinator of the Resistance in France, and by General Delestraint (Vidal), his military adviser. Both were arrested by the GESTAPO in June, 1943. Max was tortured to death that month. Vidal survived until almost the end of the war. His German jailers murdered him to forestall his release.

Le Franc-tireur
March 20, 1943

The First Communiqué of the Fighting French of the Interior

March 11. A special communiqué was published this evening by the headquarters of the Fighting French of the Interior. Here is the text:

"The headquarters of the French partisans, situated somewhere in France, announce that the French patriots attacked a train loaded with German troops in the region of Châlon-sur-Saône. More than 150 German soldiers were killed. Hundreds of German soldiers were wounded. Two other trains were destroyed in the Department of the Côte-d'Or. The first of these trains was transporting enemy war material and was completely destroyed. The second was transporting coal destined for Italy. Twenty freight cars were destroyed. In all these operations, our partisans and our irregulars incurred no casualties.

At boxing shows many years ago it was customary to put on a divertissement known as a battle royal, wherein a number of colored men were equipped with boxing gloves and blindfolded and then encouraged to fight until only one remained standing. The various Resistance groups, until the end, were like blindfolded boxers, but boxers trying to co-ordinate their efforts against a common foe, rather than to hit one another. I have tried to arrange this group of news reports to indicate the slow growth in the size and importance of Resistance operations. The ambush at Guéret is the sort of thing that could have happened in the fall of 1942 as easily as in 1943. But in the Battle of La Truyère, treated in the last story of the group, the Resistance in one region of France is fighting a pitched battle against a German armored division!

Libération, Edition Zone Nord
October 19, 1943

The Massacre at Guéret

A group of fifteen to eighteen young RÉFRACTAIRES was living in hiding in the forest of Sardent, some fifteen kilometers from Guéret, in the Creuze.

In the early part of September, two young men who also claimed to be RÉFRACTAIRES came into the region. The inhabitants trustingly passed them on to the MAQUIS group, who admitted them to its number. Two days later the newcomers set out, as they claimed, to procure arms for their comrades.

A few days later, at seven o'clock in the morning, trucks carrying a hundred or more young SS men arrived from Limoges. A few peasants, who saw them unloading and sensed trouble, followed them at a distance. Eight of the RÉFRACTAIRES were making coffee in a clearing while the rest were still asleep. Without warning, the first volley mowed them down. The rest of the RÉFRACTAIRES were dragged out of their hiding place, beaten unconscious and thrown into trucks.

While the massacre was going on, other SS troopers laid hands on a sabot maker, who was suspected of having given food to the young patriots, beat him and threw him into a pond. When he was on the point of drowning, they fished him out and took him, still bleeding, to Limoges.

The victims of the first fusillade were still moaning in the clearing. The Germans finished them off with bayonets and tried to make their bodies unrecognizable by throwing incendiary bombs on the pile of corpses.

The whole population of Guéret and the surrounding country followed the funeral procession. Veritable mounds of wreaths covered the graves. Many of them bore the inscription: "To our comrades who died for France."

Such a crime must not go unpunished. We must learn the

names of the two stool pigeons and the German officer who ordered this slaughter.

MAQUIS is one of the words of this war that has passed into colloquial English (and probably will into dictionary English when the dictionary factories get into gear again). Quisling, used as a common noun, is another. They are about the only traces the German occupation of continental Europe will leave on our speech. The word itself was not new to the French language. It is the Corsican term for the high thick brush that covers the hills of that country (as it does those of northern Tunisia and Serbia) offering fine concealment for outlaws. Corsica used to be known as a country of bandits (after its annexation to France they migrated to the mainland and became policemen). When a man there found it convenient to light out from home people used to say that he had "taken to the MAQUIS." The word had literary currency in France largely because of Prosper Merimée's novel COLOMBA, which had popularized the banditti. It reappeared, with a new popularity, in 1942, when young men began to disappear to avoid labor service. "He has taken to the MAQUIS" meant "he has gone into hiding." But by extension the word began to mean first, the specific place where a group of young men hid out, and then the group itself with its organization. Thus people began to speak of "the MAQUIS" at such and such a place, when they perhaps meant a group of men living in a barn on a lonely farm. They spoke of "the leader of a MAQUIS" as one would of the Commander of a garrison. There were very small MAQUIS and very large ones that included thousands of men—male societies as complex as the monasteries of Mount Athos.

The word was still used in its old loose sense of going into hiding too. François Mauriac, referring to the period when he lived under an assumed identity in the flat of his friend Jean Blanzat, says, "When I was in the MAQUIS." But in a general way the word retained its connotation of wildness and savagery. "A region of MAQUIS" evoked the image of a region of mountain, moor and sparse population. I have noticed in English a tendency to use the word MAQUIS to denote a man who lived in a MAQUIS, a Resistant. But in French the word for a member of a MAQUIS is MAQUISARD.

The next story treats of a MAQUIS far larger than poor Guéret.

Le Patriote
December 1, 1943

The 11th of November: The Maquis of Saône-et-Loire Inflicts a Bloody Defeat on the German Troops

The prostitute press, bent on sullying French patriotism, slandering heroism and besmirching the most authentic values in the nation, has lavished its insults on the men of the MAQUIS. Sometimes it brands them as deserters selfishly shirking what it calls "a civic duty." Other times it portrays them as simple souls led astray by agitators in the pay of a foreign power. Or it tries to make them out to be mere gangsters robbing and terrorizing the civil population. Not a robbery, not a crime takes place that the agents of Hitler and Laval do not impute to the MAQUIS.

The young men of Saône-et-Loire have just refuted with their blood these iniquitous lies that are propagated in the interest of the enemy.

November 11, 1943! The French are preparing to celebrate the armistice of 1918, their hearts fixed on that other armistice to come that will mark the downfall of Hitler. Posters and leaflets have been distributed throughout the department by the Departmental Resistance Committee. A bleak and somber November dawn. Suddenly the streets of Mâcon echoed with the rumble of a long convoy of trucks. The inhabitants peeked from behind their curtains. The word went around, "The BOCHES are on the move!"

Yes, it is the BOCHES, who have chosen this day of national glory to attack a MAQUIS in the region of Baubery. The sinister gray column winds along our roads. They have decided to mop up this pocket of young Frenchmen who mock their power.

At Baubery the boys of the MAQUIS, all unconscious of the danger that threatens them, are laying a wreath on the war monument and singing "The Marseillaise," when messengers arrive with the news, "The BOCHES are coming!"

Shall they withdraw, scatter and refuse to fight?

Brief conferences of the leaders are held. Deliberately and courageously, these "slackers" decide to stand their ground. The enemy approaches and takes up his position. About five hundred Germans, seasoned soldiers equipped with automatic weapons and supported by mortars, are about to attack a hundred half-trained young men of whom hardly sixty are armed.

The enemy pounces on the farms that provided food for the MAQUIS and brutally seizes the farmers. Then repeating in Saône-et-Loire the tactics of total destruction that they employ in Russian villages, they vent their sadism by setting fire to five houses. This cowardly deed done, they come up against the men of the MAQUIS. The machine guns crackle. The Germans advance cautiously. Suddenly a hand grenade is tossed into a car full of German soldiers under the command of an officer. The car turns turtle. Some of its occupants are killed. The MAQUIS of Baubery has won its first victory.

There were to be other German casualties. At six o'clock, as night was falling, the soldiers of Hitler, beaten by a handful of young Frenchmen, withdrew to Mâcon. Their losses included nine dead and several wounded. Our own boys, alas, had had their losses too. But our list of dead and wounded was much less than that of the enemy.

From his bed in the hospital, where he is kept under guard, one of our wounded succeeded in getting this stirring message through to us: "Whatever they may do to me, now that I have killed some of them, I can die in peace!"

November 11, 1943! The day of the French victory at Baubery —a victory that will have its place in the warrior annals of Saône-et-Loire and in which our local boys proved that they are of the same stuff as the soldiers of Koenig, Larminat and De Gaulle. Lads who fell at Baubery, the French Resistance movement dips its banners to you in salute!

The F.T.P.

The next morsel, an excerpt from FRANCE D'ABORD, is an argument rather than a report. FRANCE D'ABORD was an organ of the F.T.P., a large Resistance organization to which I have already referred, which during nearly the whole length of the occupation ran its own war. It had liaison with other organizations but it did not merge its forces with theirs.

The first real joint operation of F.T.P. and F.F.I. forces (most of the other Resistance groups were eventually englobed in the F.F.I. or FORCES FRANÇAISES DE L'INTÉRIEUR) was the insurrection at Paris itself in the summer of 1944. In this the united forces worked under the command of an F.T.P. man, Colonel Rol. This was fitting since the F.T.P. had a larger enrollment than any other Resistance organization in the Parisian region. The F.T.P. drew its strength mostly from trade union members and Communists, and was consequently an urban organization. The tactics it advocated were based on surprise and dispersion, the only ones practicable in cities, where one had to operate under the noses of the Germans. F.T.P. tacticians often argued that MAQUIS of several hundred or thousand men, established in regions that could after all be encircled by a besieging force, offered too large a target for attack. The MAQUISARDS were by the nature of the war inferior to the Germans in artillery, tanks and aviation, they pointed out, and this disparity could not be overcome by parachute drops of supplies. Large concentrations therefore were an invitation to disaster. They suspected the former regular army officers who led the large MAQUIS of a blind fidelity to old "classic" concepts of warfare, and refused to put all their eggs in the F.F.I. basket. Besides, they argued, the very act of withdrawal from the

German-dominated districts made the MAQUIS impotent to harm the enemy by sabotage.

It was a debate that continued until the last German had been driven from French soil. The exponents of classic warfare argued that the mere existence of a quasi-regular, tangible army had a good effect on national morale and proved to the outside world that France had not given up the struggle. They also said that only such a force would be able to attack and pin down German units when the Allies made their landing. They were content to recruit and train their forces until that day came. They did not seek battle with the Germans until then, although they showed they knew how to resist heroically when attacked.

British officers parachuted into France to make contact with the Resistance were inclined to put more trust in the large organized MAQUIS than in the F.T.P. "army of shadows" whose existence they had to take on faith. So the "classic" MAQUIS got most of the arms that the R.A.F. planes brought from England and dropped by parachute. This caused jealousy among the F.T.P.

How They Fought

France d'Abord
January, 1944

OUR PLAN OF ACTION

Our losses are not to be compared with those of the BOCHES; and it is possible to reduce them still further by constantly improving our tactics, by making the fullest use of the element of surprise, by making judicious use of our protecting units, carefully planning our withdraws, using new tactics to mislead and confuse the enemy, and especially by always showing a spirit of decision and initiative. Whatever the situation may be, be it foreseen or unforeseen, every man must feel an unflagging determination to fight the BOCHE and his lackeys to the death.

The enemy will never be able to put his hands on us, if our

vigilance never wanes. Before, during, and between engagements, let us be on the alert. Respect security regulations, foil the police as well as the BOCHE. Fighting or waiting, let us always remember we are F.T.P. If we do this, our enemies will be powerless against us and the confusion in their ranks will spread. Let us not waste our strength.

Make the F.T.P. offensives even more efficient by appealing to all combatants to use the best tactics, to outguess the enemy, and to strike ever more staggering blows against the invader and his lackeys.

This is a slight indication of how they succeeded.

THE SCORE FOR THREE MONTHS

The list of the principal operations carried out by the F.T.P. in the course of the past three months shows a considerable progress in our armed fight against the invader.

The number of derailments has increased regularly in spite of the enemy's doubling the strength of the railroad guards. The great increase in the number of locomotives destroyed in railroad yards deals a serious blow to the enemy's transport without endangering the lives of railroad workers.

Finally the damage done to river-borne transportation, thanks to a well worked-out plan that has proved very effective, should not be underestimated, since two barges carry as much as a whole train.

By redoubling their effort against terrorist organizations and enemy production, by organizing multiple combat groups of F.T.P. in factories, railroad yards, mines, etc., to keep pace with the mass organization of the MAQUIS, the patriots will find a victorious reply to the tactics of the bandits of Pétain and Darnand and will build up, together, a united Resistance movement, an Army of the Liberation.

Le Franc-tireur
December 1, 1943

THE BATTLE OF GRENOBLE

IN THE CITY OF THE ALPS, BATTLE RAGES ON THE 11TH OF
NOVEMBER. . . .

For many months Grenoble, which already holds the place of
honor among the great cities of France, has carried on its daily
and heroic struggle in the national resistance.

On October 6, Monsieur Aubry, an engineer of this city, was
shot down by a German sentinel on guard in front of the Hotel
Royal, who fired at the same instant that he challenged him. Ten
thousand persons followed his coffin to the grave, singing "The
Marseillaise" and acclaiming General de Gaulle.

On October 17, five tons of explosives were carried in trucks
by sixty patriots at Pont-de-Claix. A few days later the burning
of the Soulage factories resulted in damages amounting to fifteen
million francs.

Finally on October 20, as an answer to acts of sabotage and
the execution of a few sub-human MILICIENS, Vichy sent thirty
members of a special anti-terrorist group to Grenoble. Surprised
at lunch by six armed and masked patriots belonging to the G.F.,*
they were disarmed and stripped of their pocketbooks and papers
by the "terrorists," who then withdrew without incident.

But the events of these last weeks have earned Grenoble a
special place of honor. The Vichy press, except for the local
papers, having passed them over in silence, they have not received
the publicity that they deserve. This then is what happened.

On November 11, in spite of the threats of the Germans and

---

* Groupe franc: specially trained armed bands of the Resistance formed to
operate in large towns and cities. They carried out many dangerous missions
such as executing spies, informers and traitors, armed robbery of vital documents, sabotage of arms depots, factories working for the Germans, etc.
Mortality was high among them, but their ranks were kept filled with volunteers. Students, professors, business men, etc., in the organization learned to be
an efficient combination of gangsters and G-men. (Translator's note.)

the injunctions of Vichy, patriots by the thousand put on a demonstration to affirm their faith in victory. Furious, the Germans retaliated. Four hundred and ninety-three persons (whom they labeled "Communists" for the occasion) were arrested, loaded into cattle-cars and deported to Germany.

Grenoble did not take long to reply to this measure. During the night between the 13th and 14th, the powder factory of Grenoble and two storage tanks of the gas plant were blown up. From 12:40 until 6 o'clock in the morning, the town was shaken by formidable explosions. Thinking it was a bombing raid, many inhabitants ran down into the streets. There they found German soldiers who, having completely lost their heads, immediately opened fire on everybody in sight. Nineteen people were killed, including an editor of the newspaper LE SUD-EST and a correspondent of LE NOUVELLISTE of Lyon. The next morning the town was a lamentable sight. Windows were broken, walls broken down or cracked, iron shutters from shop windows twisted or blown away, and sidewalks littered with débris. In the part of town where the explosion had taken place, the roofs were blown off several factories. Only the walls of the powder plant were left standing.

The next day the prefecture issued a notice that passes allowing circulation after the curfew remained valid but that, if any further attacks took place, all persons were cautioned to stay indoors even if they had passes. Which shows to what a state things had come!

The battle is still going on. On the night of the 15th, the HÔTEL MODERNE, the largest hotel in town, which the Germans occupied, was blown up. Latest information indicates that such attacks are still continuing.

Today Grenoble stands in first place on the honor roll of the Resistance.

Grenoble has other claims to glory. It has a university which has long been a favorite with American graduate students in France. And it was the birthplace of Henri Beyle, who signed the name De Stendhal to two great novels and who once wrote: "All my life I have wanted to be loved by a woman who was thin, melancholy and an actress. Now I have been and I am not happy."

Libération
January 1, 1944

THE SCORE BOARD OF THE M.U.R.*

During the month of December, 1943, the GROUPES FRANCS of the M.U.R. executed sixty-six traitors and informers in the South Zone alone.

Any more takers?

ATTACK ON THE "GARDE MOBILE" BARRACK AT BOURGOIN

During the night of November 19, a group of young men belonging to the Resistance attacked the barracks of the GARDE MOBILE at Bourgoin (Isère).

The operation began at three o'clock in the morning. The detachment divided into two groups. Climbing the outer wall, one of the groups took the guard post by surprise and neutralized the five men they found there. The second group entered the barracks and tackled the munition stores. The booty was loaded on a truck in the courtyard of the barracks. A very precious booty it proved to be, since it consisted of a ton-and-a-half of munitions, for the most part boxes of cartridges.

THE MAQUIS VINDICATES ITS HONOR

On several occasions during recent weeks, inhabitants of the region of Petit-Bornand in Savoie had been held up on the road by men from the MAQUIS.

The Resistance leaders in the region immediately opened an

* *Mouvements Unis de la Résistance.* Composed of three of the leading Resistance organizations, *Combat, Franc-tireur,* and *Libération.* (*Translator's note.*)

investigation and learned that the men guilty of these hold-ups had been expelled from the MAQUIS as followers of Doriot.

The two leaders of the band were condemned to death. One of them succeeded in escaping. The other was discovered and the GROUPE FRANC from Bonneville went to Petit-Bornand to keep an eye on him.

The bandit must have perceived that he was being trailed and tried to escape on a motorcycle. He was brought down by tommy-gun fire. In his pockets were found leaflets put out by the P.P.F.* and copies of L'EMANCIPATION NATIONALE.

The leader of the GROUPE FRANC assured the population of the region that they had no more to worry on this score and that the police of the MAQUIS would not allow acts of banditry to be committed and blamed on the MAQUIS.

THE DESTRUCTION OF THE ANCIZES
FACTORY AT CLERMONT

In the month of November, patriots carried out a thoroughly successful operation against the Ancizes steel alloy plant at Clermont-Ferrand.

This plant was closely guarded by a detachment of gendarmes. A group of patriots presented themselves at the main gate of the establishment one evening and passed themselves off as high police officials.

"You are not very well armed," the chief of the pseudo-official told the guards. "We are going to have tommy-guns issued to you immediately. Please load your weapons into this truck."

The gendarmes obeyed. In the meanwhile, other patriots, having climbed the walls, entered the factory and planted their bombs at their leisure. Under the very eyes of the disarmed and startled guards, the explosives accomplished their purpose.

In the meanwhile the patriots tranquilly made off with a respectable haul of antiquated rifles and revolvers.

* Parti Populaire Français: Doriot's fascist party, of which L'Emancipation Nationale was an organ.

Lorraine
February 15, 1944

DIRECT ACTION

In Lorraine during the month of January, acts of sabotage were carried out against the railroad lines. At Homécourt the line was blocked by a derailment. At Gérardmer, a locomotive was blown up.

In the Ardennes, a train was derailed between Sedan and Donchery.

The patriots of the Jura and Franche-Comté continue to distinguish themselves in their struggle against the invader and the traitors.

A hydraulic jack was blown up at Belfort. Coming after the sabotage of the cranes in the Valdoie-Ronchamps plant, this act proves the determination of the men of Belfort to do their part in crippling enemy transportation.

The three brothers Bastar, agents of the GESTAPO, have been executed. This follows on the heels of the execution of Basler and his friends. There are still traitors left, but already they are beginning to be alarmed and to take flight. But, wherever they go, the vengeance of the patriots will follow them. YOU, VILZER—YOU AND YOUR ACCOMPLICES, WILL BE SHOT DOWN LIKE DOGS!

At Vougeaucourt a train was derailed. Two injured. At Mouchard, seven locomotives were blown up. At Voirnans, a train loaded with tanks was derailed. Twenty killed.

At Montbéliard, the patriots attacked the prison in order to rescue one their comrades. They read off the list of all the political prisoners in the prison and liberated them also. As their automobiles were leaving the town they ran into a road-block. There was a short skirmish. Two Frenchmen were killed. Thirty Germans were killed or wounded.

All honor to the patriots of Belfort and Montbéliard; they are making their region the Grenoble of the North Zone.

Let the BOCHES not hope to weaken the resistance in Franche-Comté by terrorism. Hatred is growing. Soon a gigantic St. Bartholomew's Day will pay them for their crimes.

Against these sadists and savages, only one measure is possible: war to the death!

Libération
April 14, 1944

THE WAR IN THE CORREZE

A WHOLE SECTION OF FRANCE SUBJECTED TO THE MOST SAVAGE TERRORISM

"MAQUIS of the Limousin,* be on the alert!" LIBÉRATION warned, after having detected German preparations for an offensive against the MAQUIS along the western edge of the Massif Central.

The offensive lost no time in getting under way. With the active aid of the traitors who take their orders from Vichy, it is now in full swing, accompanied by the most savage excesses of an unbridled soldiery. Every day the list of BOCHE war crimes grows longer. The whole region is subjected to a reign of terror.

This offensive against the patriots of lower Limousin, which was launched on the edge of the Dordogne and has penetrated into the southern part of the Corrèze, is a purely German affair. Neither the gendarmes nor the GARDE MOBILE are taking any part in it. The enemy evidently has no confidence in these forces now under Darnand's command. Could there be any truth to the rumor that they refused to participate in the operations? Any blanket refusal is certainly improbable. But it does seem true that the enemy has met with some hostility among them. It is learned that some gendarmes and police officers (the chief of police at Brive, for example) have been arrested for showing not enough zeal in executing the orders of the BOCHES.

The MILICIENS are not taking any part in the actual military operations, either. But Darnand's thugs are still very much in

* The Limousin is the ancient province that includes, roughly, the Departments of the Corrèze and Haute-Vienne. (Translator's note.)

evidence. They are there—behind the lines—parading about with their tommy-guns. You see them accompanying BOCHE patrols and guarding railroad stations. Above all, it is their denunciations that provide victims for the reign of terror. They and their accomplices in collaborationism have already been responsible for the death of a goodly number of patriots. Without them, the BOCHE punitive measures would be blind and almost helpless.

As for the Germans, according to our last reliable reports at least, there seem to be no SS troops among them. This may have changed however, since convoys have been sighted headed for the region. The units engaged are those of the WEHRMACHT supplemented by Georgian detachments. These latter are at least as much to be dreaded as the Germans. Remnants of Vlassov's * army were reported to be operating in the Department of the Ain. They are playing an active part in the Limousin offensive, and their bestiality is added to the ferocity of their masters.

The Germans have thrown into the fight sizeable forces, certainly more than the equivalent of a division.

Their strategy consists of a drive from the southwest toward the northeast, using a widespread line of skirmishers, with the men in the front line close enough to one another to keep each other in sight in the open country or in the woods. But the MAQUISARDS are fighting back in spite of their inferiority in number and armament. If they fall back, it is under the protection of a rear-guard fighting every foot of the way. There are casualties, and not all of them among the patriots. Every day German wounded are evacuated to the field hospital that they have set up in a school in Brive.

It must be admitted the Germans have timed their offensive well. Winter is over. The ground is firm and dry. In spite of the

* General Vlassov, a White Russian general hostile to the U.S.S.R., commanded an army composed of renegade Russians (mostly Ukrainians and Georgians). As anti-Bolshevik propaganda, the Germans used these anti-Bolsheviks in some of their most frightful reprisals against French civilians. They encouraged Vlassov's men to commit the most hideous kinds of atrocities and generally used them to endeavor to convince the French that Russians were even less civilized than the Germans. Toward the end of the war, Vlassov turned against Germany, in a vain hope to save his skin, and aided the Czech resistance forces in Prague. (Translator's note.)

early spring in this region, the leaves have only just begun to show and do not yet provide the concealment that they would later in the year.

The enemy advance has nevertheless been slow, although the offensive began over relatively easy terrain and has not yet reached the rolling country of the true Limousin.

The attack on the RÉFRACTAIRES is, however, only one phase of the operation. The other and no less important objective is hunting down the patriots. The aim of the BOCHES and their auxiliaries is to terrorize the population and crush all resistance once for all.

Terror reigns. Arrests can be counted by the hundreds. Anyone suspected of patriotism is sure to be denounced and seized, unless he manages to slip away in time. It is a field-day for stool pigeons, and one can well imagine the part that personal grudges play.

Woe to anyone suspected of having aided the RÉFRACTAIRES or given them food or shelter. He is stood up against a wall without any pretense of trial.

As we have said, the operation began in the Dordogne. The valley of the Vézère has been devastated by the enemy. Peasants have been shot, women raped, and farms burned. The BOCHES have spread ruin through the once prosperous villages of La Bachellerie, Le Lardin, Terrasson, Mansac, Larche and Varetz, below Brive. The details are still incomplete, since the whole region is now cut off and can be penetrated only at great danger. And this is not the only region that the enemy has ravaged. All France has become the theater of his crimes.

The Jews who have taken refuge in this region are particularly singled out as victims. They are being hunted down and shot on sight. Three bodies were left lying in the ditch on the road from Bordeaux to Clermont: they were those of three Jews whom the Hitlerians had taken by surprise. All the houses where Jews had lodged were methodically burned, like the farms that had given shelter to the MAQUISARDS.

Looting is the rule. Houses are pillaged. Drunk or sober, the Germans destroy for the pleasure of it. Any furniture that is not destroyed is shipped home. For example, one sees freight-cars go by, labeled, "Gift of the inhabitants of Terrasson (France) to the bomb victims of Germany." The same procedures were used in the evacuated regions of the North. The BOCHE methods do not change!

To complete this brief and sinister picture, mention must be made of the deportations. The BOCHES are making large-scale round-ups with house-to-house searches. All the men from eighteen to forty are seized, in their homes or in the streets, herded into public squares and from there, under the threat of loaded rifles and machine guns, driven aboard trains to be carried off to Germany. Similar scenes have also taken place outside of the present zone of operations, at Cahors and Périgueux.

France d'Abord
February, 1944

SUPPLEMENTARY COMMUNIQUE NO. 63, OF THE F.T.P.

Major General Werner of the GESTAPO and his party were surrounded by one of our companies at a railroad crossing at Pontailler-sur-Saône (Côte d'Or).

Attacked by tommy-guns and hand grenades, all the officers accompanying him, except one, who succeeded in running away, were killed. The general was captured.

Documents establishing his responsibility for very numerous crimes committed by the GESTAPO against patriots having been found on his person, General Werner was immediately tried by a court-martial of the Resistance.

After having refused to give a written order for the release of all patriots now under arrest in the Department of the Côte d'Or, he was condemned to death. General Werner was executed in a military manner.

THE STAFF OF THE F.T.P.

Le Franc-tireur, Edition Sud
May 6, 1944

VICTORIES OF THE MAQUIS IN THE AIN AND THE JURA

Considering the plateau of the Jura as a citadel of the Resistance, the enemy is trying to clean it out by violent surprise attacks. Once more fierce fighting has just taken place in this region.

The operations began on Friday, April 7, at three o'clock in the morning and had as their principal objective the quadrangle formed by Morez, Bellegarde, Nantua, and Lons-le-Saunier. The German forces engaged amount to two divisions with all their motorized equipment, armored cars, light tanks, and 25- and 75-millimeter guns. The MILICE was also present but, with its usual well-known courage, confined its efforts mostly to mopping up and making arrests.

The battle, in which the Germans attacked with incredible violence, went clearly in favor of the MAQUIS. Our total losses did not exceed twenty dead, while the Germans lost at least three hundred men. Slight as they were, our losses would have been even smaller, had not Lieutenant Minet of the Ain MAQUIS and nine young men who were accompanying him been taken by surprise and killed at Montanges.

The principal clash occurred at Vulnoz, where a MAQUIS group had taken refuge in an almost inaccessible cave. More than a thousand Germans participated in the assault. A brisk fire of automatic rifles obliged them to withdraw, leaving almost two hundred dead behind them.

In the Jura, the MAQUIS mourns the loss of its commander, Major Vallin, who was shot at Viry after having been taken prisoner.

At Sièges, Lieutenant Nancourt and four other patriots were massacred after undergoing atrocious tortures.

In most cases the Germans have broken off contact with our forces and withdrawn. It can be stated that the operations represent a great success for the MAQUIS and show that much progress had been made since the battle of last February.

Unfortunately the Germans once more took revenge for their defeat on the civilian population. Five unidentified bodies were found at Cerdon and five others at Saint-Germain-de-Joux, where twenty-two farms were burned and the inhabitants deported. At Southounax-la-Montagne, a family of seven persons was massacred. The villages of Sougeat, Sièges, Le Grand-Coron and Southounax were destroyed. At Chavans-sur-Suran, the whole center of the village was burned. Monster round-ups were made at Claude, where 367 persons were deported and at Oyonnax, where 98 persons were carried off on Easter Sunday.

But it is in vain that the Germans, unable to subdue the troops of the Resistance, vent their spite on the defenseless civilians. The armed groups of the F.F.I. are relentlessly continuing their systematic destruction and disorganization of enemy installations.

AT LES GLIERES THEY FOUGHT TO THE DEATH

Our boys in the MAQUIS of Les Glières put up a heroic fight. Although Henriot * went to Thorens to pour insults on the patriots who were taken prisoner and Darnand crows over their defeat, it is nevertheless true—and all the inhabitants of the region know it—that the MILICIENS were helpless against the fierce resistance of the six hundred lads on the plateau. To wipe out this MAQUIS, it took a whole German division (the One Hundred and Fifty-first) with the support of artillery, mortars, mountain artillery and Stukas.

For three days the battle continued. Once again, Henriot lied when he affirmed that the RÉFRACTAIRES surrendered. On the contrary, they fought fiercely, as the figures prove:

Germans killed	350
Germans wounded	350
MILICIENS killed and wounded	150
MAQUIS casualties	150
Prisoners	160

* Pro-Nazi commentator on the Paris radio.

Henriot lied when he said that the young patriots had been deserted by their leaders. The truth is that their officers fought to the end in the midst of their troops. Captain X and three lieutenants were killed in the battle. A sergeant and a warrant officer also fell fighting heroically.

More than a hundred MAQUISARDS succeeded in escaping and have joined up with other MAQUIS groups in the region, which are still intact.

No, Monsieur Henriot, no, Monsieur Darnand, the MAQUIS is not beaten. The plateau of Les Glières is only one episode in the great battle that the patriots of France are fighting. This battle continues more fiercely than ever, as you must have discovered since your premature crowing over your victory.

La Marseillaise
June 15, 1944

THE WAR IN THE RHONE VALLEY AREA

DEPARTMENT OF THE RHONE: Destruction of the Oxhydrique Française plant, which was working for the Germans.

On May 26, the GROUPES FRANCS requisitioned the supply depot at Villeurbanne and distributed the supplies to the war victims who were most in need of them.

DEPARTMENT OF THE AIN: At Ambrieux, the MAQUIS turned in a false air raid alarm and, while the BOCHES were in their shelters, blew up forty-two locomotives in the railroad yards.

The towns of Oyonnax, Bellegarde and La Clusaz are in the hands of the Resistance.

PONT-DE-VAUX: June 8. Two MILICIEN detachments have been arrested and locked up in the cells of the GENDARMERIE. Stiff fighting between the look-out post of Marsonnas and the Germans, with a loss of thirty men for the latter.

DEPARTMENT OF THE JURA: The MAQUIS, attacked in May by a BOCHE Alpine division, succeeded in disengaging itself and inflicting heavy losses on the enemy.

DEPARTMENT OF THE SAÔNE-ET-LOIRE: Since June 7 Cluny has been in the hands of the Resistance. Weapons are being openly distributed in the streets. All the roads are cut by barricades and controlled by automatic weapons which have thus far succeeded in turning back German detachments. Salornay is also in the hands of the Resistance. Arms have been distributed to the population.

DEPARTMENT OF THE SAVOIE: At Les Chavannes, an engagement between a detachment of the F.F.I. and a German patrol.

At Freney, the roads have been blocked by dynamiting masses of rock.

DEPARTMENT OF THE LOIRE. At la Ricamarie, the Nadella factory, which had escaped damage in the bombardment, was not missed by our combat patrols.

At Rive-de-Gier, the Marel plant (armor plates for tanks) closed down after the destruction of the power station.

At Firminy, the Verdier factories are idle after the destruction of the high-tension lines.

"The late Philippe Henriot" referred to in the following account was the Vichy minister of propaganda, a prewar fascist deputy and, under the occupation, the most effective radio speaker of the collaborationists. Hatred of the "Anglo-Saxons" and the Russians, fake indignation at Allied bombings, and revilement of the patriots, whom he called "terrorists," were his favored themes on the air. He exulted over every massacre of "terrorists" by the Militia, and an orgiastic note came into his voice when he described the dead bodies of his "misguided" countrymen. On the night of June 28 fifteen members of the Resistance, disguised as militiamen, entered the Ministry of Information at Paris where Henriot was lodged. They forced their way into his bedroom and shot him to death.

Le Mur d'Auvergne
July 14, 1944

THE BATTLE OF LA TRUYERE

On June 20, a week after the glorious victory of Mont Mouchet, in which a German armored division lost 3,000 men, of whom 1400 were killed and the rest wounded, while a skillful defense kept our own losses down to fifty killed and sixty wounded—a week after this victory, the enemy once more made a furious attack against the troops of the Resistance in Auvergne.

This time the Germans sent into action almost two divisions. More than a thousand vehicles, among which were many tanks and armored cars, swept up the valley of the Truyère that morning.

A substantial artillery support, consisting of trench-mortars, 75s and 105s, backed up the infantry, while ten planes (what an honor!) strafed our machine-gun positions.

The Germans were prepared to make an all-out battle of it— which shows how little faith they had in the words of the late Philippe Henriot when he announced over the radio, after the battle of Mont Mouchet, that the Resistance in Auvergne had been completely wiped out. (Six thousand killed, he had announced, although our total force consisted of only twenty-five hundred men!)

In spite of all the resources that the German staff threw into the fight, our boys from the Puy-de-Dôme, the Haute-Loire, the Cantal, the Allier, the Aveyron, the Lozère, once more held their own magnificently.

All day long they defended their positions. Bridges and roads were cut. Machine guns and tommy-guns blazed. The Germans called for more reinforcements. But night was falling.

Our losses for the day were eighty dead and one hundred wounded. The BOCHE casualties in their frantic attempt to wipe us out were much higher than ours.

Once again Auvergnat shrewdness was to outwit them. During the night, our forces withdrew to a new position. The next morning the Teuton horde continued their attack on our now vacated positions. Still—so great is their fear of our troops—it took them all day to reach their objectives.

In short, here were 1,500 men hurling themselves against us, losing cannon and armored vehicles, consuming thousands of liters of gasoline, using up tons of ammunition, and all this to kill a hundred patriots and fail lamentably in their attempt to wipe out our forces.

Our thousands of patriots under the command of General Koenig, commander-in-chief of the F.F.I., will still lead you many a chase through the mountains of Auvergne. They will continue to cut roads and railroads, attack your convoys, and fight night and day for the liberation of their country. And you must know, O hated BOCHES, that soon it will no longer be possible for you to make your way back to your own country that you never should have left.

And How It Helped

The Battle of La Truyère against a German armored division—the Eleventh Panzer, I think—was fought two weeks after the Allied landings in Normandy, but nearly two months before those on the Mediterranean coast which finally brought relief to the South of France. During this period the F.F.I. in central and southern France took considerable pressure off the Anglo-American bridgehead in the North by engaging German units that might otherwise have reached Normandy. The Germans still had numerical superiority in Normandy then, because our men and matériel had to be fed in across beaches.

We had not taken even Cherbourg on the date of La Truyère. Moreover a great storm on about June 15 had so disrupted our ingenious landing arrangements on the east coast of the Cotentin peninsula that for a short while even the beaches were impassable. The Eleventh Division, which our intelligence officers expected almost hourly to arrive upon our front, got so thoroughly tangled up in operations against the F.F.I. that for a while our G-2 lost track of it. In July an American general told me, too optimistically, that it must have been destroyed. It wasn't that, but it never did reach Normandy. By the time it got the F.F.I. out of its hair the southern landing had taken place, and the rest of the Eleventh Panzer's war was fought against the Franco-American Sixth Army Group. If you ever meet a veteran of the Thirty-sixth Division ask him for further details.

Actions like La Truyère were the justification of the classic school of Resistant strategy. But the disaster of the plateau of Vercors, which came in July, 1944, within a few weeks of final deliverance, underscored in blood the arguments of the F.T.P. theorists. The Vercors is a high plateau just outside Grenoble. In its whole circumference it is accessible by just eight paths, all of them difficult except to experienced mountaineers. When the painter Jean Bruller took the NOM DE PLUME of Vercors in 1941, he did not know that the plateau was to become a French Thermopylae. The double association the name will have for historians of the Resistance is a pure coincidence. Bruller was demobilized in the shadow of the Vercors; it was in his mind when he adopted his writing name.

The geographical Vercors attracted the attention of other Resistance figures almost as soon as an Allied landing in France began to seem possible. They planned to take and hold it as a central bastion of military resistance as soon as they received the order from London. The order came by radio on June 9, 1944. The Resistance men seized the Vercors and it became a little republic of free men hundreds of miles behind the beachhead lines. There were about 3000 F.F.I.s there. The Germans made a raid in June and retired, not wishing to undertake a major operation then.

The flat top of the Vercors offered a good surface for a landing strip. The French smoothed it off so that Allied planes could land there. To the Germans, once they had failed definitely to throw the Allies out of Normandy, it seemed obvious that there would be another landing in the South and that the F.F.I. were preparing the Vercors to receive airborne Allied troops. So on July 19 they attacked the Vercors with between one and two full divisions. The paucity of footpaths by which the Vercors was accessible made it easy to defend; it also made the redoubt hard to get out of. The defenders held and appealed for Allied air aid. On the morning of the 21st, twenty planes towing as many gliders appeared above the landing strip. The gliders came in among cheering patriots—and disgorged German paratroopers who massacred everybody within gunshot and then dug in.

The patriots had neither mortars nor artillery to use against the paratroopers, who soon received reinforcements. Attacked front and rear the defenders were slaughtered. Few indeed made their way out. There were neither prisoners, nor wounded; only dead. And among these dead was Jean Prevost, a leader among young French writers. He had come to Grenoble soon after the armistice, to take refuge from the depressing present in a long excursion into the past—a study of De Stendhal's writing methods. Alpinist friends of his had brought him into the ranks of the militant Resistance. He had become an adept of the paths leading to the Vercors, which he could see from his library window as he wrote. He became a captain in the F.F.I. The Stendhal study was published and was something of a triumph. "Mobilized" in June, 1944, Prevost went up to the Vercors. On the morning of August 1 he was shot to death while trying to escape by one of the paths he had helped reconnoiter. On his body were notes for a study of Baudelaire, upon which he had been working during interludes in the battle. He chose to be a company officer, because, he told a friend, "in the ranks you find the profound honesty of the race."

Notes on the Vercors

by THE TRANSLATOR, WHO VISITED IT IN THE SPRING OF 1945

After the battle was over, the Germans cold-bloodedly launched a campaign intended to make the name of the Vercors as much of a symbol of horror as it had been of hope. Town after town was destroyed. At La Chapelle-en-Vercors, where there never was any fighting, the Germans assembled the entire population in the village square, locked the women and children in the schoolhouse, methodically looted the village—destroying everything that they did not think worth loading on their trucks; burned down every house but one, and killed every male inhabitant between the ages of fourteen and sixty. The operation took nearly twenty-four hours.

The officer commanding the operation was very polite. It was the old CURÉ of La Chapelle who gave me this gem of wisdom: "Sometimes I think that the good Germans are worse than the bad ones."

There are no witnesses to tell exactly what happened at the hamlet of La Mure. Several days after the battle, a girl walking along the road below the village and seeing no sign of life went to investigate. At the entrance to the village she found two men hanged from an ingenious scaffold so improvised that each man had one foot on the ground and the first one to collapse would cause the rope to strangle both of them. Before hanging them, the Germans had gouged out their eyes and torn out their tongues. The women and children had been walled up in one small building and roasted to death. Not a living thing was left in the village. They had shot even the cats and dogs.

One heroine of the Vercors is the schoolteacher at Beaufort, a woman of about seventy. When the Germans had already destroyed most of the village and were about to blow up the school, she met them in the doorway and did such a professional and authoritative job of telling them that they ought to be ashamed of themselves, that finally they WERE ashamed of themselves and left the school and what remained of the village untouched. What they did not know was that the schoolteacher was the secretary of the local Resistance organization and that the basement of the school was a regular arsenal crammed with ammunition and supplies for the MAQUIS.

Army of Shadows

There were men in the underground army capable of writing about that curious warfare as Pozner had written about the fighting in 1940, but they lacked the opportunity to do so. Joseph Kessel, a popular novelist before the war and an officer of the ARMÉE DE L'AIR in 1939-40, took part in the first struggles of the Resistance. He came out of France by airplane late in 1942, charged with a mission of liaison between the Forces of the Interior and General de Gaulle. While in Britain he wrote ARMY OF SHADOWS (L'ARMÉE DES OMBRES), a panorama-novel of the Resistance movement. Like DEUIL EN 24 HEURES, ARMY OF SHADOWS falls neatly into detached segments.

The two chapters that follow, "The Execution" and "The Rifle Range," are self-explanatory as short stories. In the first, I would like to call your attention to two peculiarly modern themes, as up-to-the-minute as DDT or an interest in Henry James.* One is the reality of torture as an important factor in contemporary life, another is the necessity, sometimes, for a civilized man to kill another. Until the advent of Hitler in 1933 torture had been for modern man only something related in old books; even to read about it was considered a bit morbid. Under Hitler it became a part of daily life in Europe, like bread tickets and the official radio. Because torture is real Gerbier in the story finds it necessary to kill a man who has proved unable to resist it. In the same way a farmer might have to kill a cow that had been exposed to foot-and-mouth disease, in order to protect his herd. One evil entails another. It would have seemed fantastic to a man of 1880 or 1925 that he should ever have to kill another man, personally. If it became necessary for reasons of state that a man should be killed in those days a jury would tell somebody else to kill him. But the

---

* Since writing this I have seen two unfavorable allusions to James in book magazines; it is possible he is no longer any more up-to-date than he was in 1925.

characters in "The Execution" are not gangsters in a James M.
Cain thriller. They are decent men forced to exist under fascism.

The Execution *

by JOSEPH KESSEL

A note from the organization to which he belonged had instructed Paul Dounat (whose name was now Vincent Henry) to
be in Marseille toward the middle of the afternoon and wait in
front of the Reformed Church for a comrade whom he knew
well. Dounat had been at the appointed spot for a few minutes
when a gasogene car drove past him and stopped some thirty
meters beyond. A man of short stature stepped out. He wore a
derby, a dark maroon overcoat, and his shoulders lunged heavily
as he walked. This man whom Dounat had never met went
straight up to him and said as he showed a sûreté card, "Police—
your papers."

Dounat did not move a muscle. His false identification papers
were perfect. The man with the derby said with more amenity,
"I see that everything is in order, monsieur. I shall beg you
nevertheless to accompany me to our offices. A simple verification."

Dounat bowed. He had no fear of the verification either.

The driver was standing beside the running board of the car.
He was thickset and had a boxer's crushed nose. He opened the
door and pushed Dounat inside with a single movement. The
man with the derby got in right behind him. The car started off
very fast up the slope. Then Dounat saw, ensconced in the corner
of the seat, with his head held back so as not to be seen from the
outside, André Roussel, who also bore the name of Philippe Gerbier and who had let his mustache grow. Paul Dounat felt all his
blood suddenly rush to his heart and he collapsed on the folding
seat like a man disjointed.

* The Execution and The Rifle Range, reprinted from Army of Shadows,
copyright 1944, by permission of the publishers, Alfred A. Knopf, Inc.

The make-believe police official mopped his tonsure-shaped bald spot, considered his hat with disgust and growled, "Dirty kind of job!"

"Felix, no matter how much you hate derbies you'll have to put it back on again just the same," said Gerbier absently.

"I know it," Felix growled, "but only when we stop."

Paul Dounat thought to himself, "That's when they'll kill me."

He formulated this thought with indifference. He was no longer afraid. The first shock had drained him of all living emotion. As always, the moment he no longer had any choice he resigned himself to the worst with a strange docility and ease. Only he would have liked to drink something strong. His veins seemed to him quite hollow.

"Look at him," said Felix to Gerbier. "He's the one who sold you out, all right, you and Zéphyr and the radio man."

Gerbier agreed with a slight movement of his eyelids. He didn't feel like talking. He didn't feel like thinking. Everything was made obvious by Paul Dounat's very attitude: treason, and the inner mechanism of this treason. Dounat had been brought into the Resistance by his mistress. As long as she had been able to animate him Dounat had shown himself useful, intelligent and courageous. When Françoise was arrested, he had continued to act out of inertia. Caught in turn, but quickly released, he had become the instrument of the police.

"We should have stopped using him when Françoise disappeared," said Gerbier. "That was a mistake. But we have so few people and so much to do."

Gerbier lit a cigarette. Through the smoke Dounat appeared to him even vaguer and more insubstantial than usual. Good family, good manners. . . . Pleasant features. . . . A small mole in the middle of his upper lip attracted attention to his mouth, which was well-shaped and soft. His face was smooth, without sharp ridges and ended in an indeterminate, rather full chin.

"Obviously defective will-power," thought Gerbier absently. "He needs someone to make up his mind for him. Françoise, the police, and now us . . . for underground activity, the rôle of informer, death."

Aloud he said, "I think, Paul, that it's useless to give you our proofs and to ask you questions."

Dounat did not even raise his head. Gerbier continued to smoke. He experienced the kind of boredom which a tedious and necessary formality inspires. He began to think of everything he had to do afterwards. His report . . . send out two instructors . . . draw up messages in code for London . . . the meeting with the big boss who was coming from Paris . . . choose the command post for the following day.

"Couldn't we hurry?" Gerbier asked Felix.

"I don't think so," said Felix. "The Bison knows his job as nobody does. He is driving as fast as anyone can without attracting attention."

Dounat, with his chin resting in one hand, was looking toward the sea.

"I'm in a hurry, too," Felix continued. "There's that old post I have to look over again. I have to change the handlebar on that young liaison agent's bicycle. And then there are the parachutists coming tonight who have to be met."

"What about the chief's new false papers?" asked Gerbier.

"I have them on me," said Felix. "Do you want them now?"

Gerbier nodded.

Paul Dounat understood perfectly that if the two men spoke so freely in his presence it was because they felt assured of his silence, of his eternal silence. They were already concerned with the moment—and this moment was near at hand—when he would be effaced from the human order. But this condemnation left Dounat without anxiety or inner turmoil. For him, likewise, his death was an accepted fact. It belonged in a sense to the past. The present alone had a value and a meaning. And now that the car had passed the point of the Old Port, the present was composed entirely, and with a prodigious intensity, of that expanse of blue water, of those islets, indented like antique galleys, those pure and arid hills, the color of light sand which seemed to hold up the sky on the other side of the gulf.

Suddenly, because the car was passing before a hotel on La Corniche which Dounat recognized, Françoise's face assembled, absorbed all the scattered features of this magnificence. Françoise was standing on the edge of the terrace that jutted over the sea.

She was wearing a summer dress that left her neck and her arms bare. She held the light and the warmth of day in the generous substance of her face. With a light and familiar movement Dounat was caressing the nape of Françoise's neck. She was leaning her head back a little and Dounat could see her throat, her shoulders, her bosom swelling, expanding, like a plant that ripens all at once. And Françoise kissed him on the mole in the middle of his upper lip.

Unconsciously Dounat touched this little brown spot. Unconsciously, too, Gerbier touched the mustache, still bristly, that he had worn since his escape from the Camp of L. Felix was eyeing his derby with disgust.

A turn of the road snatched the hotel from Paul Dounat's sight. The image of Françoise with her head thrown back disappeared. This caused Dounat no astonishment. These games belonged to another age of the world. The underground life, then, had not begun.

Felix knocked with the brim of his derby against the glass that separated him from the driver. Then he crammed the hat on his bald-crowned head. The car stopped. Paul Dounat ceased to gaze at the sea and turned toward the other side of the boulevard. There stood a hill with a cluster of peaceful, humble and wretched little houses and villas clinging to its steep slope. The car had stopped before a lane without asphalt or pavement, that climbed straight up between those low houses and melancholy little gardens like a mountain path.

The driver lowered the glass pane behind him and said to Gerbier, "The car'll have a hard time of it on that grade."

"And it'll make a lot of noise. . . . Everybody will come to the windows," said Felix.

Gerbier looked narrowly at Paul Dounat's profile. The latter, expressionless, was again turned to the sea.

"We'll walk it," said Gerbier.

"I'll go with you, then," said the driver.

He had the hoarse voice of men who have smoked too much, drunk too much, and who have had to shout orders for a long time. His massive, tanned face, with deep-sunk gray eyes, almost filled the window frame.

Gerbier looked at Dounat once more and said, "It's not necessary, Guillaume."

"Really not," said Felix.

The driver in turn looked at Paul Dounat and grunted, "I agree with you."

Gerbier waited for a creaking streetcar with passengers overflowing on the steps to pass. Then he opened the door, Felix got out and Dounat, on a gesture from Gerbier, did likewise. Felix took one of Dounat's arms and Gerbier the other.

"I'll go and fetch the cases and I'll be back for the body after dark," said the driver, putting in his clutch.

Dounat climbed the abrupt slope, crowded between Felix and Gerbier as between two friends, and he thought about the way in which the Communists sometimes got rid of their traitors. They would get the man at night to the seashore, dispatch him, undress him, roll him up in wire netting and throw him into the sea. The crabs, through the meshes, would entirely devour the body. Françoise had been with Dounat the night he had heard this story. A pitiless burst of passion had inflamed her face, ordinarily so sweet and gay. "I'd like to take part in such an operation," she had said. "There is no death vile enough for people who sell out their comrades." Paul Dounat remembered that outburst, and also his mistress's neck, which had flushed a deep pink, and he was docile as he climbed the steep lane between Gerbier and Felix.

Now and again they saw on the doorsteps a woman in a black skirt, with disheveled hair, lazily shaking a carpet. Children played in the sordid little gardens. A man leaning against a fence was scratching his bare ankles above his felt slippers as he looked at the three passers-by. At each of these encounters, Felix would press the revolver which he held firmly grasped in his pocket and whisper in Paul Dounat's ear, "A single word and I'll let you have it right away."

But in the arm that he was holding Gerbier felt only limpness and obedience. Again he experienced a sense of deep boredom.

They finally turned into a narrow blind alley flanked by windowless walls and blocked at the end by two identical cottages built flush against each other. The shutters were raised in the one to the left.

"NOM DE DIEU!" said Felix, stopping savagely. His frank, round face expressed utter bewilderment.

"Ours," he said to Gerbier, "is the cottage on the right with the closed shutters."

Felix swore again.

"The other day when we rented it the shack next door was empty," he added.

"It's too bad, of course, but all the more reason for not attracting attention," said Gerbier. "Come on."

The three men quickly reached the end of the blind alley. Then the door of the right-hand cottage seemed to open of its own accord, and they went inside. The boy who stood behind the door immediately pushed it shut again, slid back the panel of the spy-hole and turned the key. All his movements were executed without noise. But in their haste and their cadence there was an ill-concealed nervous tension. And Gerbier had further evidence of this when he heard a jerky whisper, "The room in back. . . . Do go in the room in back. . . ."

Felix pushed Dounat by the back of the neck and followed him.

"It's him . . . the traitor . . . who's got to be . . . ?" the boy who had admitted the group asked in a barely audible voice.

"He's the one," said Gerbier.

"And you're the leader?"

"I'm in charge of this job," said Gerbier.

They in turn entered the back room. The shades were drawn, and after the glare of daylight the darkness seemed at first intense. But enough light came in through the ill-fitting slats to enable them to see clearly after a few moments. Gerbier could make out the plaster peelings that quivered on the ceiling, the moisture stains on the walls, the two unmatched chairs, the mattress placed directly on the floor and covered with a quilt. And he could examine the comrade chosen by Felix to assist in Dounat's execution. He was a tall, straight young man, lean, modestly dressed, with a sharp-featured and sensitive face. He had rather prominent, fiery eyes.

Felix pointed his derby in the direction of the young man and said to Gerbier, "That's Claude Lemasque."

Gerbier gave a half-smile. He knew that an assumed name often revealed an element of character when the person chose it himself. This one had come into the Resistance movement bringing with him the religion of secret societies.

"He's been crying for a long time after a tough assignment," Felix added.

Lemasque turned to Gerbier.

"I came more than an hour ago," he said, speaking very rapidly, "to put everything in order. That's when I saw the awful business next door. They got here this morning, or during the night at the earliest. I passed by here in the evening and there wasn't anybody. When I saw the open shutters I ran out to call Felix on the phone, but he was already on his way. There was nothing to be done, was there?"

"Absolutely nothing, I assure you, absolutely nothing," said Gerbier, with all the deliberation and all the evenness of tone that he could put into a few words.

This lad spoke too much, spoke too low, spoke too fast.

"It's a good spot," Gerbier went on, "we'll manage."

"We can go on to the questioning, if you wish," said Lemasque. "Everything is ready up there in the attic. It's a little like a court. I've put armchairs, a table, some paper."

Gerbier half smiled and said, "We're not here to hold a trial."

"We're here for this," said Felix impatiently.

He had pulled from his pocket the butt of his revolver that he had been continually fingering. The metal shone in the half-light. Lemasque glanced for the first time toward Dounat. The latter was leaning against a wall and was looking at no one.

The men who surrounded him continued to lack volume and reality. But things were armed with a power he had never known them to have. The crumbling ceiling, the moldy walls and the furniture seemed to wait, observe and understand. The objects had the relief, the substance and the density that Dounat no longer had. Yet his eyes eventually had fastened on the drab, reddish-brown quilt. Dounat recognized it. In the dubious hotels, in the poor transient houses where, between missions, he had been lucky enough to meet Françoise, Dounat had always seen this quilt. This also belonged to another age of the world. Refinements no longer had a place in it. Hazards, the dangers of secret activity, gave their form and their color to love. Françoise would sit down on the red quilt, touch up her hair and in a choked, happy voice would relate the events of her days and nights. She loved this work, she loved the leaders, she loved the comrades, she loved France. And Dounat felt that she carried over this passion physically to him. Then he too loved the Resistance. He was no longer harassed, he no longer felt any anxiety about living without a home and without a name. He was no longer lawless, hunted, lost. Under the red quilt he would press against Françoise's shoulders and breasts. That warm, exalted, brave body became a kind of wonderful lair, a place of asylum. An extraordinary starry security enveloped pleasure.

"Well?" asked Felix, pulling out his revolver completely.

"It's impossible . . . it's impossible . . ." said Lemasque. "I was here before you were. You can hear everything. . . . Listen. . . ."

In the adjoining cottage a little girl began to sing a thin, monotonous melody. The song seemed to rise from the very room.

"They're not walls, but cigarette paper," said Lemasque with fury.

Felix put his revolver back in his pocket and swore.

"Aren't those damned Englishmen ever going to send us the noiseless guns we keep asking them for?"

"Come with me," said Gerbier. "We'll see if there isn't a better spot."

Gerbier and Felix left the room. Lemasque hurriedly placed himself in front of the door as though Dounat had wanted to escape. But Dounat made no movement.

Nothing was happening as Lemasque had anticipated. He had prepared himself, with deep exaltation, for an act that would be dreadful but full of solemnity. Three men would sit: a leader of the organization, Felix, himself. Before them the traitor would defend his life with lies, with desperate cries. They would get him tangled in contradictions. And Lemasque would kill him, proud to pierce a criminal heart. Instead of this grim justice—a little girl's song, the steps of his accomplices that resounded in the floor above, and in front of him this man with light auburn hair, young, with a sad, docile face, with his mole in the center of his lip, who kept looking obstinately at a red quilt.

As a matter of fact, Dounat no longer saw the quilt. What he now saw was Françoise, naked, in the midst of the police who were tormenting her. Dounat was leaning more and more heavily against the wall. He felt himself on the point of fainting. But there was not only terror in the depth of his weakness.

The little girl continued to sing. Her quavering, fragile voice communicated an unbearable anxiety to Lemasque's nerves.

"How could you do it?" he suddenly asked Paul Dounat.

Mechanically the latter looked up. Lemasque could not guess the nature of the images that gave Dounat's eyes their humble, shameful and troubled expression. But he saw in them such deep human misery that he felt like screaming.

Gerbier and Felix reappeared.

"No use," said the latter. "The cellar connects with the cellar next door and the attic carries the sound even more than here."

"But we've got to do something, we've got to," murmured Lemasque, whose thin hands were beginning to flutter with impatience.

"We ought to have a heavy knife. The Bison always has one on him."

"A knife?" murmured Lemasque. "A knife. . . . You're not seriously considering it?"

Felix's frank, round face became very red.

"Do you think we're doing this for fun, imbecile?" Felix said in an almost threatening tone.

"If you try it I'm going to stop you," Lemasque whispered.

"And I'll smash your teeth for you," said Felix.

Gerbier smiled his half-smile.

"Look in the dining room and in the kitchen to see if you find something we can use," he said to Felix.

Lemasque feverishly approached Gerbier and said in his ear, "It's impossible—just consider it, I beg you. It's murder."

"In any case, we're here to kill," said Gerbier. "Do you agree?"

"I . . . I agree . . ." Lemasque stammered. "But not that way. . . . We must . . ."

"The way it's done, I know, I know," said Gerbier.

Lemasque was not used to that half-smile.

"I'm not afraid, I swear to you," he said.

"I know, I know. . . . It's something quite different," said Gerbier.

"It's the first time I've done this kind of thing, you understand," Lemasque went on.

"It's the first time for us, too," said Gerbier. "I guess it shows."

He looked at Paul Dounat, who had pulled himself together a little. His weakness had vanished, and so had the image of Françoise. The last age of the world had come.

The door opened.

"God-damned house," said Felix, his hands empty.

He looked very tired, and his eyes traveled all around the room, but avoiding the spot where Dounat stood.

"It occurred to me," Felix went on huskily, "it occurred to me that perhaps we'd do better to leave him here till tonight, till the Bison comes."

"No," said Gerbier. "We're all very busy, and besides I want to report to the chief that the matter has been closed."

"NOM DE DIEU DE NOM DE DIEU, we can't smash in his skull with the revolver butt, after all," said Felix.

Paul Dounat at this moment made his first spontaneous movement. He beat his arms feebly and placed his open palms before his face. Gerbier realized to what extent Dounat feared physical suffering.

"Much more than death," thought Gerbier. "That's the way the police were able to force him to betray."

Gerbier said to Felix, "Put a gag on him."

When Felix had stuffed his thick checked handkerchief into Dounat's mouth and Dounat had fallen on the mattress, Gerbier said distinctly, "Strangle him."

"With . . . our hands? . . ." Felix asked.

"No," said Gerbier, "there is a dish towel in the kitchen, which will do very well."

Lemasque began to pace the room. He did not notice that he

was pulling so hard on his fingers that the joints cracked. Suddenly he stopped his ears. The little girl in the next-door house was beginning to sing again. His facial expression was such that Gerbier was afraid he was going to give way to a nervous fit. He went up to Lemasque and brutally knocked his hands down.

"No fuss, now," said Gerbier. "Dounat's got to die. That's what you came for and you're going to help us. One of our radio men was shot because of him. A comrade is croaking in Germany —isn't that enough for you?"

The young man wanted to speak. Gerbier didn't give him a chance.

"You're an employee at the town hall, I know, and also a reserve officer. And it isn't your job to choke a defenseless man. But Felix is a garage mechanic, and I'm an engineer. Only the truth of it is that you and Felix and I are no longer anything but members of the Resistance movement. And that changes everything. Would you have thought before this that you were going to get a kick out of manufacturing false seals, false stamps, false documents, that you would be proud of being a forger? You asked for something harder to do. You've got it. Don't complain."

Felix had returned noiselessly and he was listening.

"We have a specialist for executions," Gerbier went on. "But he isn't free today. And so much the better. Everyone needs to have his share of the hardest work. We've got to learn. It's not vengeance. It's not even justice. It's a necessity. We have no prison to protect us from dangerous people."

"That's right," said Felix. "I'm glad I heard you."

His frank, round face had reassumed a kind of implacable serenity. He carefully stretched out the long, stiff dishcloth he had brought back. Lemasque still trembled. But his trembling was weakening, as at the end of an attack of fever.

"Carry Dounat to that chair," said Gerbier. "Felix will get in front of him. I'll hold his arms, and Lemasque will hold his knees."

Dounat did not resist.

And vaguely astonished to see that everything was transpiring with such ease—with so few inner obstacles, especially—Gerbier took his place behind the back of the chair, above which Paul

Dounat's head protruded. But at the moment of seizing Dounat by the shoulders Gerbier hesitated. He had just noticed, on Dounat's neck, a little below the ear, a mole similar to the one on his upper lip. Because of this little spot the flesh that surrounded it seemed more living, more tender, more vulnerable, like a bit of childhood. And Gerbier felt that this flesh was not capable of enduring one ounce of suffering. By this flesh Dounat's treason became innocent. The Bison could face torture. And Felix. And Gerbier himself. But not Dounat, nor, for that matter, the young man who, clinging to the knees of the condemned, was breathing like a man in his last agony.

Opposite Gerbier Felix was waiting for the leader to give him a signal. But Gerbier's arms were so heavy that he could not lift them to Dounat's shoulders.

Without a doubt Felix, at this moment, has a more frightful look on his face than this wretch, thought Gerbier.

Then he thought of Felix's goodheartedness, of his faithfulness and his courage, of his wife, his ailing and undernourished little boy, of everything that Felix had done for the Resistance movement. Not to kill Dounat was to kill Felix. Dounat alive would betray Felix. That also was inscribed in the little brown spot and the too tender flesh of the neck. Gerbier suddenly had the strength to raise his arms. It was not Paul Dounat's fault if he was going to die and it was not the fault of those who were killing him. The only, the eternally guilty one, was the enemy that imposed the fatality of horror upon the French.

Gerbier's hands fell on Dounat's shoulders, but at the same time Gerbier said in his ear, "I swear to you, old man, you won't feel any pain."

The rolled dishcloth swung down over the feeble neck. Felix pulled savagely at both ends. Gerbier felt the life ebbing very fast from the arms he was holding. It seemed to him that their convulsions passed into his own body. Each of them accumulated in Gerbier a new force of hatred against the German and against his tools.

Gerbier had Dounat's body carried to the mattress and covered it with the red quilt.

He went over to the window. Through the slits in the blinds an empty lot could be seen. The spot was well chosen.

Felix was putting on his derby. Those short, sturdy legs were rather unsteady.

"Do we go?" he asked in a hoarse voice.

"Just a moment," said Gerbier.

Lemasque went over to Gerbier. His sharp, nervous face was covered with sweat.

"I didn't think," he said, "that one could do so much for the Resistance movement."

He began to weep silently.

"Neither did I," said Gerbier.

He cast a quick glance at the red quilt and said to Lemasque in a kindly tone, "You must always carry cyanide pills on you. And if you're caught you must use them, old man."

The Rifle Range

by JOSEPH KESSEL

The central part of the old barracks communicated with the rifle range by means of a very long vaulted corridor. The seven condemned men entered it one by one, flanked by soldiers of an SS unit. Gerbier found himself approximately in the middle of the line. The student was in the lead and the peasant came last. The condemned men advanced slowly. They still carried the shackles on their feet. The corridor had no outside openings. Electric globes at regular intervals filled it with a confused light. The shadows of the condemned men and those of their armed guards formed a gigantic and vacillating escort on the walls. In the resounding silence of the hallway the booted tread of the soldiers made a deep, heavy sound, to which was added the clanking of the chains of the condemned men and the scraping of their shackles.

"It composes a kind of symphony," said Gerbier to himself. "I wish the chief could hear it."

Gerbier remembered the expression that had come over Luc Jardie's face when he spoke about music. And Gerbier was almost dazzled to come upon this face in the vaulted corridor. The chains clanked. The irons scraped.

"It's really curious," said Gerbier to himself. "Our shackles make me think of the chief. But for them . . . perhaps . . ."

And suddenly Gerbier thought, "I'm an idiot."

He had just realized that any image and any sensation at that moment would have brought him back to Luc Jardie by an unforeseen and inevitable detour.

"The word 'love' has meaning for me only when it applies to the chief. He means more to me than anything," said Gerbier to himself. But it was then that an answer came to him from his viscera, "More than anything and less than life."

The shadows danced, the shackles groaned.

"Saint Luc is what I love most in life, but Saint Luc could disappear and I should still want to live.

"And I am going to die . . . and I am not afraid. It's impossible not to be afraid when one is going to die. . . . It is because I am too limited, too much of an animal to believe it. But if I don't believe it till the last moment, till the ultimate limit, I shall never die. . . . What a discovery! And how it would appeal to the chief. I must go into this more deeply. . . . I must . . ."

At this point Gerbier's flashing meditation was broken off abruptly. At the first moment he did not understand the cause of this cessation. Then he heard a song that filled the whole sound-volume of the corridor. Then he recognized this song. "The Marseillaise." The student had begun it. The others had immediately taken it up. The student, the rabbi, and the worker had fine voices, full and impassioned. It was they that Gerbier heard best. But he did not want to listen to them. He wanted to think. These voices hindered him. And above all, he did not want to sing.

"'The Marseillaise.' . . . It's always done in situations like this," said Gerbier to himself. For a moment he rediscovered his half-smile.

The line of the condemned men advanced slowly. The song passed over Gerbier without touching him.

"They don't want to think, and I do . . ." he said to himself.

And with savage impatience he waited for the familiar stanzas to spend themselves. The corridor was long.

"I shall still have some time to myself," Gerbier decided. "The Marseillaise" came to an end.

"Quick, quick, I must explore my discovery," thought Gerbier. But the student's strong, pure voice rose again. And this time Gerbier felt himself caught and tightly held within as by a magic hand. The CHANT DU DÉPART had always had this effect on him. Gerbier was responsive to its accents, to its words. He stiffened. He did not want to do like the others. He had an essential problem to solve. Yet he felt the melody surge within his chest. He clenched his teeth. His companions were singing . . .

> "UN FRANÇAIS DOIT VIVRE POUR ELLE. . . .
> POUR ELLE UN FRANÇAIS DOIT MOURIR . . ."

Gerbier clenched his teeth harder because these verses were already singing in his throat. Was he going to let himself be carried away?

"I won't yield. . . . I won't yield. . . ." Gerbier said to himself. "It's the mob instinct. I don't want to sing, just as I don't want to run before the machine guns."

This association helped Gerbier to hold back the song that was ready to burst from him. He had the feeling of having surmounted an inner danger.

The shackled line at last reached a little door contrived in the thickness of the wall on the left. The shadows stopped dancing. The scraping of the chains ceased. And also the song. A sentry opened the door. A natural light spread across a section of the corridor. The student again took up the strains of "The Marseillaise" and the condemned men, one after another, entered the enclosure of their death.

It was a stereotyped military rifle range. A bare rectangle enclosed by rather high walls. Against the back wall and separated from it by a narrow space, one saw the stop-butt for the targets. A few old shreds of cloth and of paper quivered on its slopes in the sharp morning breeze. The light was sharp and melancholy. One by one the condemned men stopped singing. They had just perceived a few paces away six campaign machine guns. An SS lieutenant, very lean, with a metallic face, who was in command of the firing squad, looked at his watch.

"BOCHE punctuality," growled the Communist worker.

The student took a deep breath of fresh air and tugged at his little mustache.

"I won't run. . . . I won't . . ." Gerbier kept saying to himself.

The others, as if fascinated, did not avert their eyes from the lieutenant. He shouted an order. Some soldiers advanced with keys and undid the locks that held the prisoners' shackles. The irons fell to the ground with a muffled sound. Gerbier thrilled to feel himself suddenly so light. He had the impression that his legs were all new and young, that he must try them out without delay, that they demanded space, that they were going to carry him away at a winged pace. Gerbier looked at his companions. Their muscles were agitated by the same impatience. The student especially could barely control himself. Gerbier looked at the SS officer, who was tapping a cigarette on his right thumb. He had green, expressionless eyes.

"He knows very well what my legs want," Gerbier suddenly reflected. "He's getting ready for the show."

And Gerbier felt himself more securely chained by the assurance of this man than he had been by his irons. The officer looked at his watch and addressed the condemned men in a very distinct French.

"In one minute you will go and stand with your backs to the machine guns and facing the stop-butt," he said. "You will run as fast as you can. We shall not fire immediately. We shall give you a chance. Those who get behind the butt will be executed later, with the next batch."

The officer had spoken with a strong, mechanical voice, as if announcing the routine of a maneuver. Having finished, he lit his cigarette.

"We can always try. . . . We've got nothing to lose," said the peasant to the rabbi.

The latter did not answer, but his eyes avidly gauged the distance that separated him from the stop-butt. With the same

unawareness the student and the young Breton were doing likewise.

The soldiers aligned the seven men as the officer had ordered.
And no longer seeing the machine guns, feeling their muzzles at
his back, Gerbier was seized with a strange contraction. A spring
within him seemed to be impelling him forward.

"Go . . ." said the SS lieutenant.

The student, the rabbi, the young Breton, the peasant set off
immediately. The Communist, Gerbier and the land-owner did
not stir. But they had the impression of balancing back and forth,
as if they were struggling to maintain their equilibrium between
two opposing forces.

"I won't . . . I won't run . . ." Gerbier repeated to himself.

The lieutenant with his revolver fired three bullets that sped
past Gerbier's and his companions' cheeks. And the equilibrium
was broken. . . . The three condemned men followed their comrades.

Gerbier had no sense of advancing of his own accord. The
spring he had felt being wound inside him had been released and
was hurtling him straight forward. He could still reflect. And he
knew that this race that was bringing him toward the stop-butt
served no purpose. No one had ever come back alive from the
rifle range. There were not even wounded. The machine-gunners
knew their job.

Bullets hummed above his head, against his flanks.

"Idle bullets," said Gerbier to himself. "Crack shots. . . . To
make us run faster. . . . Waiting for a more meritorious distance.
. . . Grotesque to wear ourselves out." And yet at each whistling
that passed close to him Gerbier lengthened his stride. His mind
became muddled. His body was getting the better of his mind.
Soon he would be only a hare maddened by fear. He would not
allow himself to look at the butt. He wanted none of that hope.
To look at the butt was to look at death, and he did not feel
himself in a state of death. . . . As long as one thinks one cannot
die. But the body was winning . . . still winning over thought.
Gerbier remembered how this body, in spite of himself, had
relaxed in London, at the Hotel Ritz. . . . Bright points of candlelight flickered before his eyes. . . . The dinner at the home of

the old lady with the chief. The points of candlelight burned, burned, like sharp suns.

Then there was darkness. A wave of thick, black smoke swept from one end of the rifle range to the other across its whole width. A dark curtain had fallen. Gerbier's arms hummed so violently that he did not hear the explosions of the smoke-shells. But because his mind had not quite reached the breaking point he understood that this deep fog was intended for him. And as he was the only one who had never accepted the state of death he was the only one to utilize the screen of fog.

The other condemned men stopped short. They had abandoned themselves to their muscles for a last game. The moment the game ceased, their muscles no longer carried them. Gerbier summoned all his reserves of wind and muscle. Now he no longer thought at all. The bursts of machine-gun bullets followed him, the bursts surrounded him, but the gunners now could fire only at random. A bullet tore a shred of flesh from his arm. Another burned his thigh. He ran faster. He passed beyond the butt. Behind was the wall. And on that wall, Gerbier saw . . . yes, there was no doubt of it . . . a rope. . . .

Without using his feet, without feeling that he was pulling himself up with the strength of his wrists like a gymnast, Gerbier reached the crest of the wall. A few hundred meters away he saw . . . yes, there was no doubt of it . . . a car. He jumped . . . he flew. . . . The Bison was waiting for him, the motor was running, the car started off. Inside were Mathilde and Jean-François.

The Bison drove very well, very fast. Gerbier was talking, and so were Jean-François and Mathilde. Jean-François was saying that it wasn't difficult. He had always been a good grenade thrower in the reconnaissance corps. The important thing was to time the action accurately as Mathilde had done. And Mathilde was saying that it was easy with the instructions they had received.

Gerbier listened, answered. But all this was only superficial. Without value. One single question, a capital question obsessed his mind.

"And what if I hadn't run? . . ."

Jean-François asked him, "Something wrong? The comrades who were left behind?"

"No," said Gerbier.

He was not thinking of his companions. He was thinking of the lieutenant's metallic face and of his expressionless eyes when he was tapping his cigarette on his thumbnail, and of the fact that he was so sure he would make Gerbier run like the rest—like a frantic rabbit.

"I'm disgusted with living," Gerbier suddenly said.

The car crossed a bridge, then a wood. But Gerbier still saw the face of the SS officer, the cigarette, the thumbnail. He felt like groaning.

Until then Gerbier had been convinced that he detested the Germans with a fullness so perfect that it could not be increased by anything that might be added to it; convinced, likewise, of having exhausted all the sources of a hatred which he cherished. Now he suddenly felt himself devoured by a fury that he had not yet known and that exceeded and renewed all the others. But sticky and unhealthy and ashamed of itself. The fury of humiliation. . . .

"He has befouled my hatred . . ." thought Gerbier despairingly.

His torment must have encroached upon his face, for Mathilde made a movement of which she appeared incapable. She took one of Gerbier's hands and held it in hers for a moment. Gerbier seemed not to notice this gesture. But he was more grateful to Mathilde for this than for having saved his life.

PART FIVE

The War Behind the War

Louis Aragon

QUESTION: How do you tell a democracy from a totalitarian régime?

ANSWER: In a democracy, if your doorbell rings at seven o'clock in the morning, it's the milkman.—LE GAULLOIS, November, 1943.

There was a humorous clandestine paper, LE GAULLOIS—the name itself a play on De Gaulle and L'ESPRIT GAULOIS. But the humor was often acrid. Jokes, like the sample above, were too near to reality.

A man in a bar in Paris in August, 1944, said to me, "What really brought the liberation home to me was when I went back to my apartment in the evening after seeing the first American troops in Paris. I closed the door, and suddenly I thought, 'I can lock it tonight and be sure that no one will break it in.'" He had been in the Resistance, and he wasn't joking.

LES BONS VOISINS is a story of a visit from the GESTAPO, a PERQUISITION À DOMICILE. It is not as grim as some, but neither is it as funny as it sounds. Its author, Louis Aragon, is certainly one of the half-dozen best known writers in France today. His personality, his politics, and the volume of his production contribute to his renown, but tend to obscure the question of just how good he is. A combative exponent of pure literature in the twenties, when method, style, and a sort of undirected revolt for its own sake were his chief preoccupations, he became an equally combative plumper for the World Revolution in the thirties.

In both phases he wrote well, but in the second he was more intelligible. This was held as a fault against him by many of his old admirers. After the Moscow pact of 1939 between Hitler and Stalin, Aragon, like other French Communists, was in an awkward position and showed no particular ardor for the war, although he was called up and served. But after the occupation he began to write again, both publicly and in clandestinity. Like Vercors he had many sobriquets. He wrote both prose and verse; the verses are easy to remember and to quote. Some he signed Jacques Destaing and others, François La Colère.

He has a Shavian habit of writing prefaces that are apparently designed to antagonize potential readers. During the first three phases of his career he made three complete sets of enemies, and now that the struggle for national survival is over, he seems to be rapidly acquiring a fourth lot. But "The Good Neighbors" is a very funny story.

The Good Neighbors *

by LOUIS ARAGON

It was just like in the movies. They all came pushing in together. Except that there's no revolving door in our house and eight guys crammed in our third floor walk-up makes it pretty close. Especially in the summertime.

We were just about to sit down to eat. We eat supper early to save electricity. Pauline called out from the kitchen for me to put them out. She said everything would get cold. They got a big laugh out of that. Pauline came in with the soup and she was so surprised, she nearly dropped it. Our place isn't very big or fancy but it's ours. You get attached to things you've had for a long time. We have more memories than furniture, if you know what I mean.

Eight of them. The fat one was the boss. He tipped his big hat backwards and scratched his head. There was a very skinny

* Reprinted from *Aragon: Poet of the French Resistance*, edited by Hannah Josephson and Malcolm Cowley, copyright 1945, by permission of the publishers Duell, Sloan & Pearce, Inc. (Translation by Eugene J. Sheffer.)

one with big hands, like lobster claws stretching out to grab anything in sight. The others . . . well, they were like the pictures in the paper.

In two shakes, everything was topsy-turvy. I tried to reason with the fat guy. I kicked because I remembered they were supposed to have an order, a paper of some kind. That tickled them, too. It seems that nowadays it's not done that way.

The first thing Pauline got excited about was her bedspread. They tore it off the bed in one swipe, and twisted the sheets up like a dirty handkerchief.

One guy was rummaging in the cupboard, another in the linen closet. Papers were flying around. A box full of pins was upset on the floor. They looked under the chairs and stuck long needles into the upholstery. Two or three of them just stood there, cluttering up the place.

And the language they used! When the skinny one called Pauline "Old woman," I let go. "Look here, you," I said to him. That started them off again. Everything struck them as hilarious.

The man who was searching me shook out my wallet. A lot of useless little pieces of paper I'd been too lazy to throw away fell out. My soap ration card too. He asked me all kinds of questions and insisted that my key ring was used for goodness knows what. The fat one had got hold of the letter-holder trimmed with seashells we brought back from Tréport, and he was going over the gas bills as well as Alfred's letters. Then he wanted to know all about the people in the photos.

In the picture we took at Meudon three years before the war, I couldn't remember the guy standing behind cousin Maurice. A big fellow with a birthmark on his cheek. A friend of the Picherelles, I think. But that's all I knew. The fat guy thought that was suspicious and he started plaguing Pauline about it, so we'd trip each other up. As usual, Pauline contradicted me: "A friend of the Picherelles? Where on earth did you get such an idea? He's Madame Janneau's boy friend. You know Madame Janneau, the CORSETIÈRE."

Then I was foolish enough to say that Madame Janneau's friend was a blond and that this one was dark. And when you start arguing about the color of a person's hair. . . . The fat guy was very interested.

"There, now," he said, "why don't you two get together on these things?"

That really got my goat. What business was it of his whether the man was Madame Janneau's friend or not?

"Don't you worry," he said. "It's my business all right." And he kept fiddling with his hat.

The men who were cluttering up the room doing nothing stood there like ninepins. And was it hot!

Finally, I said to him, "When a person goes into a home he usually takes his hat off. Isn't it enough for you to tear the place apart?"

Pauline set up a howl. They were pulling her clean pillow cases out. They'd have to be washed, what with their dirty paws . . .

The skinny one had a nasty look in his eye. "Watch out, you fat tub," he jeered at her.

"None of that stuff!" I was hopping mad but he paid no attention to me.

One of them, a short stocky man with a red mustache, looked like a plug-ugly. He was giving the sewing machine a going-over, not missing a thing. He opened the drawer, spread the contents on the floor, emptied the shuttles, unwound the thread and all the spools of silk. With a kind of feverish curiosity, he examined every piece of metal, the thingamajig for making pleats, all the gadgets Pauline considers her prize possessions. Then he'd fling them all over his shoulder. The stuff landed anywhere and an argument started when one of his pals got hit in the neck.

I said, "Gentlemen, please . . ."

This time, they didn't laugh. They both turned on me and started asking me questions about the government.

I couldn't answer them because Pauline was yelling so loud. She was struggling with a big guy and trying to snatch our wedding picture away from him. The one in the silver frame. And then when the little spoons crashed out of the cupboard drawer, I couldn't get a word in edgewise.

Finally, I showed them Marshal Pétain's picture in the place of honor on the mantelpiece. It's the one where he's stroking a dog (the family portrait, Alfred used to say). But that didn't impress them a bit.

The fat one sneered and said gruffly, "Oh, sure, that's easy, my fine friend. All you customers have a picture hung up."

The others nodded. You could see they'd been through this before.

"But what are we accused of?" asked Pauline, sniffling.

The fat one gave her a look to send shivers down your spine.

"You're not being accused of anything, madame," he said. "You're under suspicion and that's much worse."

It's worse, all right. The skinny guy was feeling the embroidered cushion my sister-in-law Michaud made when she became blind. Suddenly he let out a whoop.

"What did I tell you?" he said. I don't know what he told anybody, but I do know that he started pulling off the petitpoint embroidery and tearing the feathers out of the pillow. Afterwards, he claimed he'd felt something hard inside. Maybe he felt it, but he didn't find it.

Pauline was screaming her head off. The skinny guy had the nerve to put his lobster claw over her mouth. And did I catch it when I tried to interfere! After all, I'm sixty-two years old. I know how to behave and I respect the laws of my country. But when they start getting rough with the ladies . . .

"Don't get yourself into a sweat," the redhead said. Actually, the place was stifling.

Two of the cops had sat down at the table and were lapping up the soup. They poured themselves some wine and clinked their glasses. When I said something about it to the fat guy, he said, "Don't try to change the subject."

I couldn't have if I'd tried. I didn't know what the subject was. I kept trying to figure out why they had come. It was probably an anonymous letter . . . people are so mean nowadays. . . . But what could the letter possibly have said?

Pauline started to sit down on the hassock. That made the skinny one suspicious. He pushed her off, tore off the fringe, and poked his hand in. She tried to open a window but they wouldn't let her, in spite of the heat. I guess they thought she might try to rouse the neighbors.

"Now, gentlemen," I said, "will you kindly tell me to what we owe the pleasure . . ."

"The pleasure! Did you say the pleasure? Are you trying to make monkeys out of us?"

I must admit I was putting it on a bit thick. The visit of these gentlemen was not exactly what you'd call a pleasure. But . . .

"But what?" asked the fat guy, sitting down in my favorite red and brown armchair, as though the whole business had worn him out. "You're beginning to get on my nerves with your phoney remarks, your 'ifs' and 'buts.' Are you trying to question ME? You've got things topsy-turvy! Hey, Pfeffer!"

The skinny guy turned around. He was busy taking the clock apart. My beautiful clock, with the works showing behind the glass, a clock that goes for three months without winding. It will need a complete repair job now.

"What is it, Boss?" he asked.

The other one sighed. "Pfeffer, am I questioning the gentleman or is the gentleman questioning me? What do you think, Pfeffer?"

Pfeffer raised his eyebrows as though he were thinking it over. "I wonder . . ." he said.

"Well, this has gone far enough," the boss said. Then to me: "Where are you hiding the stuff? Tell us where it is, and make it snappy!"

"What stuff?" I said.

I swear I didn't have the faintest notion what stuff he was talking about. But he thought I was holding out on him and said so. Then he changed his tack and asked suddenly, "What do you think of Premier Laval's politics?"

What did I think of politics? It seems I should have answered straight off; stopping to think about it proved my ideas were not so good.

"I beg your pardon," I said. "You're the one who says that . . ."

He shrugged his shoulders. "He doesn't even have the courage of his convictions. . . ."

I tried to explain that the question had caught me unawares. No one had ever asked me such a thing before.

"That shows the kind of people you travel with," the fat guy said, very pleased with himself.

The skinny guy grunted to show he thought so too.

It was no use trying to justify myself. I wanted to say that I didn't think anything about Premier Laval's politics, any more than I thought about any other premier's politics. Some people make it their business to worry about politics. Not me. If a man is put at the head of a government, there must be reasons for it. As I don't know what the reasons are, how should I have any ideas about his politics? Whatever his politics are, he was put there to see that they're carried out . . . so . . . Of course, I couldn't explain that to the fat guy. He wouldn't listen. It looked as if he were asking me questions just for the pleasure of hearing his own voice.

By now all Pauline's clothes and mine were lying on the floor. The short guy with the red mustache got on a chair and rummaged in the boxes on the closet shelf. He dragged out some old artificial flowers, a black apron Alfred used to wear when he went to kindergarten, all kinds of odds and ends. The room looked a sight. The two men at the table finished the soup and said, "Well, how about the next course?"

At this they all held their sides. When they finally stopped laughing, the fat guy pulled his hat down over his eyebrows.

"So it seems you listen to foreign broadcasts?" he said.

There, what did I tell you? An anonymous letter. That's what it was.

"But I don't even listen to the domestic ones," I said, poor innocent that I was.

"Aha! So you don't listen to the domestic broadcasts? Did you hear that, Pfeffer? Our friend here has the gall to boast that he doesn't listen to our domestic broadcasts."

"But . . ."

"No buts. Why is it you don't listen to our domestic broadcasts and you do listen to the foreign ones? Do you find them more interesting? Better informed, perhaps? More entertaining? Some crust!"

"What do you expect me to listen with?" I finally got in.

"With what? Stop the clowning! With what, he asks! With my hindside, maybe . . . with your radio set, you fool!"

"But I have no hindside."

The words just came out like that. I was trying to say I have no radio set. They hit the roof.

"Look here, you old goat, are you trying to be funny? How would you like it if I took you up on it and made sure you had no hindside?"

I got red as a beet and apologized as best I could. But they got me so muddled, I didn't know what I was saying. I meant that I didn't have any radio so I couldn't listen to our domestic broadcasts.

"Sure, if you have no radio. . . . That's to be seen. But if you have no radio, how do you manage to listen to foreign broadcasts?"

"Exactly. I ask you how."

"You ask me! Pfeffer, he asks me! Everything's topsy-turvy again. Who's asking who? Try to keep your place, now. I asked you how you listen to foreign broadcasts."

"But I don't!"

The fat guy let out a long whistle. "Can you beat that? It took you plenty of time to figure that one out. You don't, eh? They all say the same thing. You might use a little imagination."

"But I don't need any imagination."

"You always need it. Especially in the spot you've gotten yourself into."

"But what spot?"

"Will you get it into your head that I'm the one who asks the questions? Come here, madame."

Pfeffer pushed Pauline beside me. Several of them still stood around, like candlesticks, not saying a word. I wanted to tell her not to worry, that everything would come out all right, that it was an anonymous letter. But Pfeffer clapped his hand over my mouth and snarled, "None of that, you! No coaching!"

At that point the redhead, who had been messing around with the curtains, let one fall down. It was pitiful.

The fat guy started pestering Pauline about domestic broadcasts, foreign broadcasts.

When she swore we had no radio, he yelled, "You say that because you heard your husband say it!"

I tried to explain that it would have been the first time any such thing had happened in thirty-five years but no one paid any attention to me.

"You can see for yourself that we have no radio," Pauline said.

His hat slid backwards on his red neck, uncovering a bald spot. He lifted his right forefinger and shook it at her.

"A little logic, madame, if you please. How do you expect me to SEE something that's not here? That's a woman for you. Pfeffer, there are two things you must never ask of a woman: logic or the time."

"Especially when you wreck the clock!"

It was true, but Pauline's nerve gave me gooseflesh. I admired her. I've been admiring her and she's been irritating me for thirty-five years.

"Madame, mind what you say. Wrecked the clock, indeed. It's easy to say . . ."

"And easy to do."

". . . but it would have to be proved. How do I know the clock worked? Why, you may even have hidden leaflets in it."

"How could I hide anything in it when you can see all the works through the glass?"

"Very clever, madame. Very. We didn't expect such pertinent remarks from you."

Pauline flew off the handle because she thought he had said "impertinent." I had to stop her and tell her she was putting herself in the wrong, although we'd done nothing bad. Then Pauline switched her anger to me. It didn't help a bit.

"Well, how about coming back to those foreign broadcasts?" said the fat guy. "You claim you don't listen to them because you have no radio."

That seemed perfectly clear to me. But it didn't to him.

"You say 'I have no radio' and you think that's all there is to it. But . . ."

He pulled up the armchair and leaned forward with both hands on his thighs. I noticed he was wearing a gold chain on his left wrist. "But . . . can you prove to me you have no radio?"

"You can see for yourself."

"It's not up to me to prove it," he said solemnly. "It's up to you." He pointed his finger at me and then at Pauline. "A fine thing it would be if I was the one who had to prove that you have no radio! How should I know whether you have one or not? You'll say I don't see one. Is that a reason? First of all, I didn't look. . . ."

He let his eyes wander over the mess in the room.

"My men have only searched the place superficially," he added, with a smile. "Anything in the kitchen, Petitpoint?"

Petitpoint and the other guy who had got away with the soup were going through the kitchen drawers. They both answered together, "Nothing, Boss," with their mouths full. I can't imagine what they dug up, things being as they are. But Pauline is always hiding away provisions that she somehow manages to scrape up.

"So what does that prove?" the fat guy went on. "Your radio may be somewhere else, being repaired. You were forewarned, so you sneaked it out. Besides, you didn't seem very surprised when we came in. You had your answers all ready."

"I swear we . . ."

"Don't swear. It's not nice. You always regret it later. Come now, admit you listen to foreign broadcasts, that we haven't been wasting our time, or yours."

Suddenly, he was friendly and good-natured.

"Now confidentially, it's no great crime to listen to foreign broadcasts. Everybody does it. We know it very well. And it's very understandable. They're more interesting than our own broadcasts, better informed, more entertaining."

But I was stubborn. "I don't know anything about it, since I don't listen to our broadcasts."

He lifted his arms with a shrug: "What's the use of putting on an act AMONG OURSELVES? The war has lasted too long. You get bored. I know how it is. So one day, just by chance, while you're sitting by the radio . . ."

"But I have no radio!"

"Don't keep interrupting me all the time. It's not polite. So, as I was saying, one day, just by chance, while you're sitting by the radio, you turn the dial, you run into some static, you try to get rid of it. You can't hear very well and you want to hear better. You don't mean any harm. It's a kind of a game. A man isn't a conspirator just because he listens to foreign broadcasts. On that basis, you'd have to suppose that the whole country is full of them. That, by the way, is not far from the truth. But, anyway, it's not so very serious. No harm intended. Well, do you confess?"

I shook my head. Then his voice changed, became threatening. "You refuse to admit the facts? Very well. You've not seen the last of us. After the suspicious way you talked about Premier Laval . . ."

"Now, look . . ."

"I won't look. This has gone far enough. That's why the country's in such a state. So many people talk against Premier Laval. That's a TEST. You probably don't even know what a TEST is. Pfeffer, he doesn't know what a TEST is."

He shrugged with a tired, discouraged air. Had I known what a TEST was, I still wouldn't have had a chance to tell him. He was talking for Pfeffer's benefit now. "You see, Pfeffer, when you've been in this game as long as I have you'll sometimes lose patience with the kind of people we run into in the line of duty. Intellectually speaking, tch . . . tch . . . tch . . . They're all mixed up. You constantly have to lower yourself to their level, choose words they can understand. The poverty of their vocabulary, Pfeffer, is beyond belief. How can you expect to get anywhere with them? And the French language is such a model of clarity and simplicity. Just think of the German language! An officer of the FELDGENDARMERIE was telling me the other day that in German they have words of seventy letters. Can you imagine? And look at these idiots with a plain little French four-letter word."

He stopped, as though struck by a sudden doubt.

"Four letters, Pfeffer. . . . But I expected you to make some comment. A little French four-letter word. How about it?"

Pfeffer looked very worried. What was the boss driving at? A four-letter word? He didn't know whether he was supposed to laugh. He glanced towards the other men, the ninepins. They didn't help him.

"A little FRENCH word, Pfeffer. How ignorant you are! It's not French, it's English! Come now, don't look so shocked. You can still use English words without being an Anglophile. For instance, the word TRUST. . . . Well, that's an English word. Yet it's a word that belongs in the vocabulary of our National Movement. They must be identified to be fought properly. TRUSTS, not TESTS, of course. You're a nitwit, Pfeffer."

Pauline made the mistake of interrupting him. It's what she always does, I tell her, but she won't listen to me.

"Talking of TRUSTS," she said. "Are you going to beat it?"

I must admit it was very rude and didn't make any sense. The fat guy and Pfeffer started to bluster. I tried to say something. "Pauline's like that, Inspector. For thirty-five years . . ."

"Maybe you've stood it for thirty-five years," he yelled, "but I won't take it for thirty-five seconds!"

Just then, the two in the kitchen came out with a bottle of oil. Petitpoint was in seventh heaven.

"You see, Boss, black market. There's nearly a quart of oil here."

"It's only a small bottle," Pauline said, "and it's my July ration."

The fat guy wouldn't listen. "Black market," he said, "black market. They listen to foreign broadcasts and they buy oil on the black market!"

At that point, I got into the argument. It was too silly. I didn't put it that way, you understand, because I began to realize it wouldn't do any good. The fat guy was waving his arms around. "I'll confiscate it! Yes, I will! When the whole country is short of fats. . . . That cooks your goose!"

Pauline was heartbroken. Her oil . . .

"This is the limit!" shouted the fat guy. "Plot all you like, but don't starve the poor. France will never recover as long as there are people like you!"

Again his voice changed in that strange way he had.

"Come, now, tell me who sold you this oil."

"Surely," said Pauline. "Madame Delavignette."

"Did you hear that, Pfeffer? Delavignette. Dela . . ."

"Yes, Madame Delavignette, our grocer," said Pauline.

"The one on this street?"

"Sure. Next door. Naturally, since she's our grocer."

"And how much did you pay for it?"

"I don't recall now. Let's see . . ."

"Eight hundred francs a quart, huh?"

"Are you crazy? Oh! . . . I'm sorry, Inspector."

That started them off again. They piled a lot of stuff on the writing table: my old notebook, the gas bills, the bottle of oil, a detective story that they thought was suspicious because it was called THE VICHY MURDER, and some odds and ends. One of the silent ones was sweating over a statement for me to sign. I wanted to read it before signing. That's not done either, I found. Finally, I signed to get rid of them. The fat guy took the paper and blew on the signature. Then he held it away from his face to read it. He frowned. He looked at it again. And then he let loose: "What's this tomfoolery? What did you sign there?"

I bent over. "My name," I said. "Unfortunately, that's my name."

"What do you mean, unfortunately? Do you claim your name is . . ."

"Pétain. Robert Pétain. Yes, it's been a nuisance in the neighborhood. But I can't help it. It's my name. Oh, we're not related."

The Inspector was in a stew. Did he give it to me! At last I took my identification papers out, to show him I wasn't fooling, that it really was my name and my father's before me, poor man. If he'd known, he would have changed it. But when my father was young, it was just a name like any other.

"That's enough from you," he said, shoving his hat over his eyes. "Your cracks aren't funny. But if your name is what you say it is, then who is Sellières, Simon Sellières? You claim it's not you? How annoying! Are you sure? We were supposed to search the apartment of a certain Sellières, Simon. Let's see now, what number is this?"

"Number?"

"I mean the house number."

"Eighteen."

"Damn! This Sellières lives at sixteen."

Then Pauline, as usual, thought she could get the upper hand. She started shouting, "So you can't even count up to eighteen and you come around breaking into people's homes . . ."

Again, she didn't make sense, because house numbers don't

go consecutively from one to eighteen, but by odd or even numbers. And suppose they could count to eighteen, it still wouldn't
give them the right to go breaking into houses. The fat one told
her off.

"Besides, you signed the statement," he added, "and the investigation will be continued."

It did no good to protest and to say that if I'd known, I
wouldn't have signed. I'd signed and that's all there was to it.

"You're sunk," said Pauline. "It's just like you."

In half a shake, Big Hat had his ninepins assembled. They
were gone as fast as they'd come. But with them went the oil,
the gas bills, and some cookies they found at the last minute.
The skinny guy went out last. Holding the doorknob in his claw,
he turned around towards us and said, "Hr-rumph!" That was
their last word.

The house was in a fine state. An unholy mess! What made it
look so dreadful was the curtain and the pillow feathers. I looked
sadly at the empty bottle (no more wine until Tuesday) and the
empty soup plates.

Pauline was furious. Everything was my fault. The names she
didn't call me! She griped most about the business of Madame
Janneau's boy friend. "Sure," she said, "he was a friend of the
Picherelles. But why did you have to get the Picherelles mixed
up in it? Why did you have to mention them in front of the
police?"

I couldn't see why I shouldn't mention them.

"You know very well," she said. "Don't make yourself out a
greater fool than you are. Their son is with De Gaulle."

"Well, they couldn't tell that from an old photo. Besides, the
man in the snapshot was only a friend of theirs. He got run over
or caught pneumonia or something."

Suddenly Pauline lost all interest in the Picherelles. I was about
to open a window to let some fresh air in, but she stopped me.

"Leave the window alone," she said and rushed into the kitchen
towards the back wall. I looked at the time. Good heavens, of
course! Then we sat down next to the gas stove, our ears glued
to the wall. From the apartment next door came a booming
voice:

"Today, the 753rd day of the str-r-ruggle of the French people for their liberation . . ."

Pauline shook her fist in anger. "The scum!" she said. "They almost made us miss the news!"

The Universities Resist

The day-to-day life of 40,000,000 people did not change immediately when open war began in the MAQUIS. Students for example continued to attend the universities. When the Vichy police, acting as agents for their German masters, ran a dragnet through the student quarters to pick up men for forced labor, eligible students disappeared. But they returned to their studies when the alarm had passed. Only when repeated narrow escapes from the police made it apparent that a student's number was up would he definitely take to the MAQUIS.

The library and the classroom, the student felt, were the primary positions he had to hold. This was because every student knew that Hitler had set out to destroy France as an intellectual power. By limiting the number of educated French men and women in the New Europe, Hitler planned to perpetuate the reduction of France to impotence. It was to be a pantry and vacation land for the master race, populated by second-class Europeans with just enough instruction to make them good servants. Exception would be made for a small élite of Germanophile "leaders," who would be permitted enough education to give them an advantage over their compatriots.

It was the task of the French universities to prevent this wrecking job. There is an integrated national university system in France. The University of Paris and the seventeen provincial universities are closely co-ordinated, and teachers move from one to another until they settle into their ultimate earthly chairs. There is therefore a great deal closer intellectual rapport between the universities at Caen and Montpellier, for example, at opposite ends of France, than between Providence College and Brown, which are at opposite ends of Providence, Rhode Island. The connection of universities with secondary schools and of these latter with the lower schools is also much closer than in this country.

The French public educational system thus offered a natural framework for a national resistance movement. It could fight as a unit, and it did. It was easy for Vichy to find a few traitors for the big jobs in the educational system. Abel Bonnard was a member of the ACADÉMIE FRANÇAISE so old and obscure that his existence had been almost forgotten, except when colleagues made jokes about his ladylike ways. These earned him, early in the occupation, the nickname of GESTAPETTE, a telescope-word from GESTAPO and TAPETTE, which is the French slang for a fairy. This creature was made minister of public instruction. He installed a few friends of his own sort as rectors of universities, but there was no trained teaching personnel with which to replace the incumbents.

The only way to eradicate patriotism from the schools would have been to abolish them. Not even the Germans were ready to do that—yet. They even continued to make sporadic gestures of conciliation to the French intellectual élites. The Germans were unable to the end to believe that educated men could be sincerely democratic. In Nazidom a university degree had become not an evidence of scholarship but a grade in the social hierarchy. German nationality was a license to kick other Europeans in the face and each successive diploma entitled the German receiving it to kick a greater number of his own countrymen. Theirs was the army in which privates snapped to rigid attention to salute corporals.

They had some vague idea until the end that they would make France a corporal among nations, if the French would only behave. Some of the German leaders' complaints about French "ingratitude" were sincere. They had expected France to jump at the offer.

L'UNIVERSITÉ LIBRE, the organ of the Resistance movement in the universities, was one of the oldest Resistance publications. The following comments on a rise in matriculation fees and a change in the curricula for secondary schools are examples of the constant fight on the educational front.

L'Université Libre
May 15, 1943

THE POOR WILL PAY

A governmental decree has just ruled that the registration fee for the baccalaureate and the tuition fees in the universities are to be doubled.

This appreciable increase in the cost of education will prevent still more students of moderate means from completing their educations. Another triumph for the supporters of the doctrine of the "élite"!

This measure is intended to compensate the universities for the fact that the new budget has slashed their appropriations as much as 75 per cent. Thus out of tens of thousands of young people will be squeezed a sum sufficient to pay for three hours of "occupation costs."

Professors, do not allow the universities to be emptied and your students to be victimized. As guardians of our culture, insist that it be kept accessible to all. Raise your voices once more in solemn protest. Insist, until your demands are granted, on an increase of the number of scholarships and free tuitions and the annulment of this decree.

L'Université Libre
February 14, 1944

THE NEW PROGRAM IN HISTORY AND GEOGRAPHY

In the first place it is an absurdity to change the scholastic programs at a time when there is a shortage of books, notebooks, and paper and when, according to Bonnard's * own office, we

---

* Abel Bonnard, notorious collaborator, Member of the *Académie Française*, Minister of Education from 1942 to the liberation. Nicknamed *La Gestapette* (*tapette:* "fairy"). In general, gentlemen of his type got along very well with the Nazis and vice versa. At the present writing, Monsieur Bonnard is a refugee in Franco's Spain. (*Translator's note.*)

must get along with textbooks that no longer are adequate for the existing program. At present, pupils in the second year of the LYCÉE need two history books (those formerly used by the first and second years) and two geographies (formerly used by the first and fourth years). Pupils in the last year cannot procure the books that the new program, formulated by the ministry, demands. Some books are out of print; others are forbidden by the Germans. The paper shortage prevents publishers making reprints. In this matter, as in everything else, scarcity and incoherence are the marks of the present régime.

To these conditions we must add a deliberate obscurantism and a systematic negation of our national traditions. The history program of both Bonnard and his predecessor are characterized at every point by a fanatic and reactionary view of history. The great movements for the liberation of mankind are either deliberately travestied or omitted altogether. The Reformation, for instance, is explained as "a weakening of the Christian idea." Calvin and Cromwell are suppressed. The history of the Low Countries in the seventeenth century is skipped over. A nation that freed itself from Spanish oppression, became a great maritime and cultural power, gave shelter to Descartes, and produced a Rembrandt and a Spinoza, does not even merit mentioning!

The geography program has also been remodeled to fit the German demands. Instead of the Eurasia of the geographers we find Eurafrica, the dream of the Nazi geopoliticians. Almost as much time is consecrated to the study of Africa as to the U.S.S.R. and the rest of Asia and Oceania. 150,000,000 against approximately 1,500,000,000 inhabitants. This predilection for Africa is counterbalanced by a disdain for the Americas, which fare hardly better than Asia.

As for the study of Europe, it has been revised and simplified. Although Europe is still considered as extending as far as the Ural Mountains, in any detailed study of its regions, no mention is made of the European part of the U.S.S.R. Belgium, the Netherlands, Denmark, Yugoslavia and Greece are also omitted as being hostile to Germanization, but it is "recommended that special attention be paid to Germany, Hungary, and Rumania."

Even more significant are certain omissions concerning France.

The second-year program lists the regions of France that are to be studied: Alsace is not included. The whole northeast of France is forgotten: the iron of Lorraine, the products of Alsace, the forests of the Vosges, Metz, Strasbourg, Mulhouse, and Nancy. Auvergne is cited as "the typical historical region that has played a rôle in French unity." The North of France is no longer considered as having a part in our national economy, and Flanders is not even mentioned among the ancient provinces of France. The program for the last year is similar. It is permissible for a young Frenchman of seventeen to present himself for the baccalaureate examination without ever having heard of Alsace, Lorraine or Flanders. But Bonnard will be struck from our history much sooner than these provinces that he and his accomplices would like to remove even from our memory.

At a dinner a few months ago Bonnard was going into ecstasies over the youth of Germany and Italy. "Ah," he sighed, "how long France takes to die!"

But France will learn to live again; and whatever you may say or do, she will live anew! This is her true program. As for those that you decreed, neither parents nor professors nor pupils have consented to follow them; and nothing will remain of your work of ignorance and servility except the evidence of your ignominy.

The struggle on the university front was sometimes violent. The students of the University of Paris demonstrated at the tomb of the unknown soldier at the ARC DE TRIOMPHE on November 11, 1940. Several of them were shot by German military police. This was the first large public manifestation of the Resistance. We have already seen how the students of the University of Lyon greeted the Berlin Philharmonic in the spring of 1942. In the universities as everywhere the fight grew bloodier and grimmer as the day of liberation approached. This is the story of the murder of the University of Strasbourg—which has since risen from its grave.

The students and masters of the University of Strasbourg had been evacuated to Clermont-Ferrand, in Auvergne, at the beginning of the war. There they doubled up with the students and masters of the University of Clermont-Ferrand in the latter's buildings. This worked out well enough because both student bodies had been much diminished by the call-up of male students to the army.

Strasbourg is near the Rhine, and was directly under the enemy guns across the river. It was entirely evacuated in September, 1939. When I visited it on Christmas of that year the only inhabitants were pigeons and a few soldiers guarding the French end of the Kehl bridge. This had not been destroyed, and the sentries in the blockhouse at the French end could look over at their German opposite numbers. All the inhabitants had been moved to the south and southwest of France.

After the Pétain armistice the Germans invited the Alsatians to come home. Many did. Then in November, 1940, Hitler incorporated Alsace and Lorraine into the Reich. The inhabitants were offered a choice between German citizenship and emigration. But if they emigrated they could take only personal belongings with them. Thousands chose French citizenship, poverty and exile. Thousands of others had remained in southern France.

The presence of the Strasbourg student body at Clermont-Ferrand was always particularly offensive to the Germans. But they tolerated it until November, 1942, when they crossed the line of demarcation. They then began a systematic persecution of these young people who refused to be Germans. They had ruled that Alsatians of military age were liable to conscription into the German Army. The students obtained false identity cards which indicated they had been born in other provinces of France. Even so they were of course liable to labor service.

The Resistance in Alsace was particularly heroic, and much of it was directed from Clermont-Ferrand. Smuggling of Alsatians across the border into "free" France was a perilous business. But it was carried on constantly. The Resistance felt Alsace must not be allowed to be detached from France: the liaison must be maintained. The University of Clermont-Ferrand was a symbol of solidarity. The Germans decided it must be destroyed. This is what happened there in November, 1943:

Libération
January 1, 1944

THE GESTAPO DESTROYS THE UNIVERSITY
OF STRASBOURG

Every Frenchman should know how on November 25, 1943, the GESTAPO destroyed the University of Strasbourg, evacuated to Clermont-Ferrand.

This incident, which the French press in both zones obediently failed to mention, not only dishonors Himmler's GESTAPO, but redounds to the disgrace of Pétain and his followers.

Once more we ask the question: What is the meaning of the Vichy travesty? Would anyone dare to maintain that the old scoundrel who rules over the banks of the Allier River—and nowhere else—still represents anything of France?

In a French university, situated in a city theoretically in the zone where French sovereignty still exists, the Germans make a gangster raid, kidnap hundreds of Alsatians who had preferred to share the sufferings of their country rather than to accept the gilded slavery that Hitler offered them, manhandle and kill professors and students—AND VICHY SAYS NOTHING! And Pétain goes on presiding over the capers of his puppets! His silence is as much of a crime as consent.

Truly we have never felt so envious of the lot of the Belgians, Dutch and Poles. They, at least, are alone against the enemy. They do not have to blush at being led by traitors.

REPORT BY AN EYE-WITNESS

At ten o'clock on the morning of November 25, 1943, all was calm in the new university buildings where the University of Clermont-Ferrand and the University of Strasbourg have been in session simultaneously since 1939.

At 10:35 professors in the amphitheater on the ground floor

looked out the windows and saw armed German soldiers approach and take up positions in front of the building. For the moment nothing further happened. The professors went on with their courses. Perhaps it was only a maneuver. At the end of the hour, the professors informed the students what they had seen from their rostrums. The building seemed surrounded. The classes were dismissed.

Suddenly a great commotion broke out. There were shots and cries. German soldiers swarmed into the building shouting an order in German for everyone to go to the central courtyard. They accompanied the order with kicks, blows and shoving. By 11:15 five hundred people were penned into the courtyard, which is a sort of areaway surrounded by the buildings on every side. From time to time some late comer would be pushed in to join them. Shots were heard. A sergeant climbed upon a bench and ordered the prisoners to raise their arms above their heads and keep them there. It was cold. None of the prisoners had had time to get a coat. They were kept standing there for three-quarters of an hour.

At noon the teaching staff was ordered to step forward. Their arms still above their heads, they were marched to the stairway leading into the main lobby. There a detachment of GESTAPO agents in civilian clothes, with tommy-guns on their shoulders, were standing about. Perfect brutes, to judge by their faces. A few officers in uniform seemed embarrassed and stared at the ceiling.

At this point a certain Mathieu, supposedly a student in history, registered in the University of Strasbourg, took over. He wore a Basque béret. His assistant was a young German girl in a fur coat, who had been sitting in some of the public courses of the university. They called for identity cards. The staff of the University of Strasbourg, with the exception of four professors, among whom were Professors Bounhours, Olivier and Forestier, who was suffering from bruises from a kick he had received, were ordered to line up on the right. The professors of the University of Clermont-Ferrand and the four other professors were placed on the left. Next the students were brought into the lobby and sorted out in the same manner.

One young man attempted to explain that he was not a student but an engineer who merely happened to be on the premises. He was felled by a shower of blows and kicks. Another man was dragged in by two German soldiers. Having ordered the soldiers to hold his arms, one of the GESTAPO men proceeded to slap him with all his might.

The dean of the Strasbourg faculty, Monsieur Dangeon, vice-rector of the academy, was in his office at 10:30. The Germans burst into the building, shrieking and with drawn revolvers. They kicked down the door and began demolishing the instruments in the physics laboratory. Hearing the disturbance, the dean went into the corridor. There he met Monsieur Collomb, professor of Greek epigraphy. Hardly had he had time to ask him what was going on when a GESTAPO man rushed into the corridor, screaming at him to put up his hands. The professor turned around. The German gave him a hard kick in the back and, since the amazed professor had not yet put up his hands above his head, pressed his revolver against his chest and fired. The professor dropped to the floor. The dean went down the stairway. On the way, he met Mademoiselle Colas, secretary of the university, who had just been thoroughly beaten up by the Germans. As she passed near Professor Collomb, Mademoiselle Colas had heard him groan. A quarter of an hour later the laboratory assistant Benoit, on his way down to the lobby, saw the professor's dead body still lying where he had fallen.

Meanwhile everybody in the lobby was searched. Trucks arrived. Professors and students were loaded into them and sent to the military barracks.

The prisoners were herded into a space between the military prison and another large building. They were ordered to line up in ranks of four, all facing in the same direction. It was growing colder.

They were ordered to do a right-face. This was in order to keep them from seeing the fresh contingents of prisoners who were being brought into the courtyard. For raids were still going on and new prisoners constantly being brought in. The laboratory superintendant Weill, of the University of Strasbourg, came in dragged by two soldiers. He had a bullet in the thigh. Later it was learned that a boy of thirteen who was going by the university on his way to school had been shot because he "looked as if" he were making fun of the soldier who ordered him off the sidewalk. Six bullets were found in his body. The body of another young man was found on a bench near the law school. As he was running down the avenue about noon, he had been struck by a bullet and had lain on the bench. It is believed that the Germans finished him off.

It was getting colder and colder in the courtyard. Some of the older professors seemed about to faint. Finally at seven o'clock a gate was opened and the men prisoners were admitted to a large mess hall. The women were taken elsewhere.

The Germans seemed to be in a less brutal mood now. The GESTAPO men had left. One of the guards disliked the whole business and said so openly. A German non-commissioned officer who spoke French was very friendly and did his best to console the prisoners. It was announced that food would be served. And eventually each of the prisoners did receive a cup of so-called coffee.

About nine o'clock the doors of the large audience hall were opened. A GESTAPO board in civilian clothes was in session.

"Where are the women?" one of the men asked.

The doors closed again. An hour later they opened, and the men prisoners were admitted in groups of ten. They were lined up before a large table behind which sat the supposed student, Mathieu, and the German girl. On the table was a folder, labeled in large letter: "Dossier of the University of Strabourg," and in the upper right hand corner, "Georges M." To the left of the door were the French police.

Each prisoner as he came into the room presented his identity card to the French police, who copied down the data. Next Mathieu and his assistant passed judgment on the suspects, motioning some to the left and others to the right—on the left, those who were to be detained; on the right, those who were to be released. The screening was not done on any particular system, it seemed.

It was four o'clock in the morning. Those who were to be

released were allowed to leave. In all, four or five hundred persons had been arrested, of whom thirty were held.

As one of the GESTAPO men said, rubbing his hands together in satisfaction, "This time, I think, the University of Strasbourg is done for."

L'Université Libre
January 15, 1944

AFTER THE TRAGEDY AT CLERMONT-FERRAND

THE VICTIMS: On November 25, Monsieur Collomb, professor of Greek and papyrology of the Faculty of Letters of Strasbourg, was assassinated by a German police officer in plain clothes, at eleven o'clock in the morning in the corridor of the registrar's office.

It was in his own home that Monsieur Eppel, professor of Protestant theology, was mowed down by a volley of bullets fired by the police who had come to arrest him. He sustained serious abdominal wounds and four perforations of the intestines. R. Weill, formerly a laboratory assistant, who was found in the cellar of the building, was wounded in the thigh. A sixteen-year-old boy was killed on the Avenue Vercingetorix the same afternoon.

THE PRISONERS

At the end of December eighty-five persons were still being detained in prison, among whom were thirty-eight inhabitants of Alsace and Lorraine (twenty-three men and fifteen women). Among the prisoners are Professors Kirrman, Sadron, Yvon, Unbegaun, the laboratory assistants Hering and Weill, Mademoiselle Will, professor at the LYCÉE of Clermont, Mademoiselles Kuder and Colas, secretaries of the faculty, the librarians, etc.

THE TRAITOR

The fifteen hundred persons arrested on the morning of November 25 were screened rapidly. About three hundred and fifty of them were held and brought up before a special board during the night between the 25th and 26th. This board was composed of German police agents, four French police inspectors and the traitor Georges Mathieu. Mathieu was born at Clermont-Ferrand on April 23, 1923. He is the son of a colonel and was a student of law in 1940-41 and a student of history since October, 1941. Mathieu had participated in the Resistance movement in the Puy-de-Dôme. Arrested and imprisoned by the Germans for six weeks, he was released after having gone over to the service of the GESTAPO. His schoolmates were so ill-advised as to keep their confidence in him. For months Mathieu supplied them with false identity cards; on November 25 he handed them over to the BOCHES. A terrible warning to trustful patriots.

Marc Bloch, professor of economic history at the Sorbonne, was the true pattern of a French scholar. His father had been professor of ancient history at the University of Lyon. Bloch, after graduate studies at Leipzig and Berlin as well as in France, had begun his teaching career in the LYCÉE at Amiens, then served as professor of medieval history at the same Strasbourg University that has had such strange adventures since. He had published in 1924, when he was thirty-eight years old, a monograph upon the medieval practice of touching for the King's evil, "with a luxury of details and precisions," according to a learned colleague.

Later he had produced books upon the invention of the watermill and its generalization in medieval Europe, upon the medieval wine trade, upon the concept of liberty in feudal Europe, and finally his principal work LA SOCIETÉ FÉODALE. This progress from meticulously objective studies of detail to one of ensemble typifies the French method in history. "Historians" like Spengler or Belloc prefer to start with a big theory and then twist details to fit, omitting those that cannot be twisted.

Each of Bloch's monographs had traced an important thread in the medieval fabric: the divine character of the king; the rise in the value of human labor (in the old slave days of the Roman Empire, the watermill had not been worth inventing); the commerce that linked the medieval world together, the complex relations between masters and men (nobody, however, was his own master). He concurred in a colleague's dictum: "The historian is not one who knows. He is one who seeks, in order to try to understand." Not an exciting type. In the Resistance he was known as Narbonne. This is his story.

Our Narbonne of the Resistance

by GEORGES ALTMAN (CHABOT)

For a long time we refused to believe that the brutes had really dared to quench so bright a light.

It was already too much to know that they had beaten him and tortured him—that this frail human body with its natural elegance, that this intellectual, so endowed with moderation and rare discrimination, had been cuffed about, plunged in a bathtub full of ice water to the verge of drowning, flogged with riding whips—yet without breaking down his grim silence.

No, nor could we bear this thought either: Marc Bloch, our Narbonne of the Resistance, delivered over to the Nazi beasts. We shrank from the thought of this man so perfectly typical of French dignity and of deep and exquisite humanism—of this MIND becoming the fleshly prey of the vilest hands.

A number of his friends and comrades in the underground Resistance were gathered there at Lyon, when the news came to us that he had been arrested.

"They have tortured him," we were told. A prisoner had seen him at the headquarters of the GESTAPO with blood flowing from his mouth. (A bloody wound in place of the quizzical smile that he had given me at our last parting, at the corner of the street, before he was snatched into the realm of horror!) At these words,

"He was bleeding," I remember that tears of rage came to everyone's eyes. Even the most hardened of us bent his head, as if
overwhelmed by an injustice too cruel to bear.

For months we still hoped. He was deported perhaps, or still
in prison, or transferred to some other town. We were without
news of him until one day recently the message came: "There is
no more hope. He was executed at Trévoux on June 16, 1944. His
clothes and papers have been identified." They killed him along
with several others, whom his courage sustained to the end.

We know now how he died. A boy of sixteen stood trembling
beside him. "It's going to hurt," he whimpered. Marc Bloch
gripped his arm affectionately and said, "No, young one, it doesn't
hurt at all." Then he fell, the first of the victims, shouting, "VIVE
LA FRANCE!"

In the classic simplicity of his last words, at once so sublime
and so unpretentious, I see an admirable symbol of the serene
integrity of a life in which a new and vital discovery of the past
served only to strengthen a faith in the eternal values of man—a
living faith for which he could die.

Before the Resistance, I had known Marc Bloch only through
his books and through his world-wide reputation as a great historian. I knew from other scholars in his field what a contribution
the vision, originality and discoveries of Marc Bloch had made
to economic history, this new branch of learning in which he was
so shining a light.

One of our dearest comrades, a young student of philosophy,
who for a long time, and in the very thick of the fight, was the
mainspring of our movement and of our clandestine newspaper,
FRANC-TIREUR, in the Lyon region, spoke to me one day of Marc
Bloch.

"He insists on joining up with the Resistance," he told me.
"Wait till you see what a swell guy he is!"

I still recall the day when Maurice, his face glowing with boyish
pleasure, brought me his new "recruit." It was a gentleman in his
fifties, the ribbon of the Legion of Honor in his buttonhole, gray-
headed, with an intelligent face and eyes that twinkled behind
his glasses. In one hand he carried a briefcase, in the other a cane.
Rather formal at first, after an instant he smiled, held out his

hand and said simply, "Yes, I am the PROTÉGÉ that Maurice told you about."

Thus it was that Professor Marc Bloch joined the Resistance—with a smile, the same smile that was on his lips when we parted for the last time.

From the first I was impressed by the passion for doing things in an orderly and methodical way that our CHER MAÎTRE brought into our lawless, and necessarily bohemian, life. (CHER MAÎTRE—this term of academic respect struck him as well as us as comic: it seemed a vestige of the past, real but already so remote, so incongruous with our occupations, that it was like a top hat among tommy-guns.) For the time being the CHER MAÎTRE was enthusiastically learning the rudiments of the techniques of conspiracy and insurrection. Shortly we found the Sorbonne professor sharing, with astonishing unconcern, in the pariah existence that the Resistance groups in our cities led.

I know that he would forgive me if I say that he loved danger and that he had, as Bossuet says, "a warrior soul dominating the body it inspires." He had rejected the armistice and Pétain. He continued the war in the post where fate had placed him. But into our clandestine work, into our contacts and meetings, our missions, our recklessness and our dangers, he brought a taste for precision and accuracy and logic which gave his tranquil courage a sort of preposterous charm, which for my part, I found fascinating.

"Come now, let's not go plunging ahead. We must study the problem from every angle. . . ."

The problem in question might be to pass on an order to the regional leaders of the United Resistance Movements, to organize the transportation of weapons, to print an underground pamphlet, to arrange for Resistance authorities to take over the power on D-day. . . .

When, in our secret rendezvous, I saw Marc Bloch standing on some street corner, his coat collar turned up against the evening chill, his cane in his hand, exchanging mysterious and compromising slips of paper with our young lads in sweaters, with as placid an air as if he were passing out examination papers to his students, I said to myself—as I still say to myself—that no one, except those who lived through it, can imagine the exaltation that reigned in the civilian underground Resistance in France.

Soon he was known throughout the Resistance. Too well known. For he insisted on being accessible to everybody who wished to see him. He had carried over from his academic life the idea that a task is never as well done as when you do it yourself. No load was too heavy for him to want to take it on his own shoulders. An enthusiast for organization, he was obsessed, and rightfully so, with the necessity of perfecting every cog in the intricate machine of the vast underground administration through which the United Resistance Movements controlled the MAQUIS, GROUPES FRANCS, the propaganda service, the clandestine press, saboteurs, demolition squads, and the fight against deportation. His was a warrior soul but not a military one in the professional sense of the term; he often said jokingly, "In the other war, I could never win a promotion.* You know, I am the oldest captain in the French Army."

Like all of us, he was obliged to abandon his true identity and adopt a double, triple or quadruple alias: one for his false identity card, one for his comrades in the organization, and one for his correspondence. How did he come to choose at first the incredible name of Arpajon? † It tickled his fancy to bear the name of this little town in the southern suburbs of Paris. When the name Arpajon became "too hot to handle," as our phrase went, he decided to "stick to the same line" and called himself Chevreuse after the town a few stations further along on the same suburban railroad. When Chevreuse in turn got "hot," we decided that it was more prudent to make him leave the Ile-de-France altogether. It was then that he became Narbonne.

It was as Narbonne that he became the delegate of FRANC-TIREUR in the regional directorate of the Resistance at Lyon and remained one of the principal directors of the Resistance movement in the Lyon region until the tragic raid that led to his execution.

* This was not the strict truth. Marc Bloch went to war a sergeant and came back a captain. He had the croix de guerre with four citations and the Legion of Honor, à titre militaire, for bravery. (Translator's note.)

† For a Frenchman to take the name Arpajon is about like a New Yorker choosing Mr. Rahway or Mr. Weehawken as an alias.

He was Narbonne for the Resistance and Monsieur Blanchard for his landlord. It was under this latter name that he traveled about the country, to attend for example the meetings of the National Writers' Committee at Paris. He had entered into this life of danger and lawlessness with as much zest as if it were a sport and he brought to it a youthfulness and a physical stamina that I used to admire as I watched him run to catch the streetcar that went by his makeshift lodgings—whose most important article of furniture was a kitchen stove in which he periodically burned his secret papers.

I often stopped by these lodgings to pick him up. It was arranged between us that instead of climbing the stairs, I was to whistle from the street below a few notes from Beethoven or Wagner. Usually it was the first notes of "The Ride of the Valkyries." He came down with a smile on his lips and never failed to say, "Not bad, Chabot, but still a little off key, you know."

Narbonne always carried a book along on his secret errands, not only to read but to use for jotting down appointments in a mysterious code of which he was proud. But in order not to waste his time, he chose his authors carefully. The last book that I saw in his hands was Ronsard.

Imagine then this man made for creative contemplation and quiet concentration in a study full of books, running from street to street, decoding along with us in some attic of Lyon the secret correspondence of the Resistance. . . .

Then the disaster happened. After a year of constant tracking, the GESTAPO succeeded in running down a part of the directorate of the United Resistance Movements. Marc Bloch was arrested, tortured and imprisoned and died a noble death.

The other day in the great amphitheater of the Sorbonne, the universities of France tendered a solemn reception to General de Gaulle. "The Marseillaise" was sung. Professors and students fervently acclaimed the symbols of our reconquered liberty. Marc Bloch had often talked to me of this day that he had hoped to live to see. For he loved his profession, just as he loved his family, just as he loved France.

"When all this is over," he would murmur, "I shall go back to my classes."

His place is empty in these halls where a whole generation listened to him with respect. May the name of Marc Bloch, the great teacher, and of Narbonne, the martyr of the Resistance, live forever in the halls of the university that he loved so well.

The Lawyers Resist

The lawyers too had their front, and their organ, LE PALAIS LIBRE, PALAIS meaning PALAIS DE JUSTICE. Vichy made constant efforts to infiltrate collaborationists into judicial posts, and to force the courts to yield to a German conception of law. The bar resisted this pressure by the threat of a general strike of magistrates and lawyers, which would have thrown the country into literal anarchy. Most magistrates took the oath of allegiance to Marshal Pétain, to avoid being replaced by collaborationists who would have railroaded patriots to execution.

They could not, of course, prevent the Germans from executing patriots, but they could refuse the executions French legal sanction. The murderers would not be able to say, after the war, "These were no war crimes. Frenchmen sentenced Frenchmen." They could also, especially in the first two years of occupation, set up protecting delays and thwart the will of the occupying power in many ways in civil cases. Vichy eventually had to set up a special tribunal, a court outside the court system, to convict "offenders against the State," which meant resistants. The members of this unconstitutional court delivered the goods—to the executioners.

The editorial on Nazi law from the PALAIS LIBRE sets forth the divergence in viewpoints. The news items that follow indicate that in the legal profession dissidence was not without risks.

Le Palais Libre
May, 1943

NAZI JUSTICE

The whole evolution of Roman law and French law has tended to define right and wrong according to an objective and increasingly humane standard. The evolution of Hitlerian law tends to deprive the human individual of all protection and to make a barbarian chief the only arbiter of good and evil.

Professor Karl Schmitt, legal expert for the Nazi régime, furnishes this double definition: "Right is whatever is useful to the German people. The law is whatever the Führer says."

Speaking before a congress of jurists assembled at Düsseldorf on May 14, 1942, the under secretary of state in the Ministry of Justice, Freisler, goes still further: "Right is whatever corresponds to the needs of the Nationalist Socialist commonwealth. Everything else is reprehensible and consequently punishable."

This is the basic concept of the "European idea" expressed in legal, or rather, penitentiary language. The master race controls not only the work and blood, but also the private life, the thought, and the supposed intentions of each individual. Every act, every abstention, every intention that is not agreeable to the masters is subject to penal repression.

And what masters! Freisler, the chief of the Hitlerian judiciary administration, is a former lawyer from Cassel, disbarred for malpractice. He is one of those whose duty it is to decide what is suitable and corresponds to "the needs of the life of the National Socialist commonwealth."

Our education as jurists, our heritage of principles elaborated by clear minds and answering to the demands of our reason, everything which, in spite of the diversity of our concepts, makes us the men and women of a single discipline, revolts against such a return to the formlessness, arbitrariness and chaos of a society without laws.

For us legality is not defined by the interest of any single community, be it National Socialist, master race, or group of bandit chiefs. It aims at the protection of man as a social and individual being. We are the guardians of a conquest not yet completed, but infinitely precious to civilization.

French jurists, proud of the part that our ancestors played in this conquest, we shall endeavor to preserve it against the assaults of the Nazi barbarians.

WOMEN LAWYERS ARRESTED

After the arrest by the GESTAPO of Maître Python, member of the Bar Association, who has since been released, and Maîtres Georges, Izard and Govare, lawyers at the COUR DE PARIS, the French police have arrested Mademoiselle Odette Moreau and Madame Mirande Thomas.

The authorities actually succeeded in finding an examining magistrate, Monsieur Grenier, who was willing to sign a warrant against these noble-hearted patriots, against these lawyers, against these women. Then he turned them over to the BOCHES.

Madame Mirande Thomas is the mother of two children, four and ten years old. Her husband is a prisoner of war in Germany. The Paris Bar Association wishes to express to these courageous young women its sympathy and admiration.

OUR MARTYRS

René Parodi, assistant prosecuting attorney, grandson of the playwright Alexandre Parodi, son of Dominique Parodi, honorary inspector of national education.* René Parodi was fifty-seven years old.

This courageous and incorruptible magistrate, a man of generous heart, scrupulous conscience and sincere convictions, was arrested by the Germans in 1942. When the GESTAPO went to look for him at his home they did not find him. Warned of their intentions, Parodi had gone to give himself up. Following the advice that the prosecuting attorney had given him, he believed, in his

---

* And brother of Alexandre Parodi, French delegate to the United Nations.

innocence as an honest man, that he had nothing to fear. For two months he was kept in solitary confinement at Fresnes, without any interrogation. Finally one morning his family was informed that it might claim his body since, according to the Germans, he had hanged himself in his cell.

René Parodi was in perfect health. He had not left any farewell message for his family to which he was deeply attached. His character and his past life show him to have been incapable of suicide unless forced to it by the most abominable tortures. René Parodi died assassinated by the BOCHES.

"Another innocent victim of Hitlerian barbarism," one high magistrate writes us. René Parodi is a martyr in the cause of patriotic resistance to oppression, a loyal Frenchman slain in the service of France, he will one day be avenged.

And the Peasants

On all the silent fronts the war went on without benefit of firearms. Vichy had substituted tame unions for those it had suppressed. The laborers, to Vichy's gratification at first, joined these unions in mass. They retained their membership in the old illegal unions at the same time. Soon the men voted themselves into control of the new unions and began using them to formulate embarrassing wage demands. They constantly called public attention to the rising cost of living, a consequence of German exactions, and to the unsafe material conditions in mines and factories, the consequence of the stripping of French industry. They demanded protection against Allied bombing, since men at work constructing shelters could produce no war goods for the enemy. Also, it embarrassed the Germans to be reminded of their impotence against the Allied air offensive. While they were making these public moves the sabotage and the evasion of labor service went on.

The peasants obstructed the delivery of foodstuffs to the Reich by methods which they developed progressively. They constantly exchanged ideas on how NOT to have products available for requisition. It was considered patriotic to withhold stocks from the Germans and sell them to other Frenchmen, even at high prices. This was, unfortunately, a habit-forming kind of patriotism, and after liberation the peasants in many cases continued to think it their right to hold out for high prices. They could not understand that the black market had lost its moral sanction. This has been the source of some ill will between country and city. Throughout the occupation the farmers lived better than other Frenchmen. Many of them fought with great valor in the Resistance, but a peasant capable of risking his life or resisting torture is not always capable of selling eggs at a reasonable price or of resisting a chance to make a double profit on a pig. Connoisseurs of slyness will appreciate the directions to the winegrowers for concealing the true extent of their production. In France wine and wheat rank as almost equal necessities. Much of the wine requisitioned by the Germans was destined to be turned into industrial alcohol. A great deal of the rest of the requisitioned wine was to be resold to Frenchmen in the cities at super-black market prices, for the German officials were venal to an extent unparalleled in any American political machine. From the private soldier to the GAULEITER, every German in France was a dealer in goods and privileges. Graft was Hitler's payoff to the German people—everybody from Goering down had the right to lick his fingers. But if a little Nazi reached too far he got his fingers stepped on. Great quantities of the butter requisitioned in Normandy was used as a lubricant for machines in war factories—at a time when millions of French children were developing rickets because of inadequate diet.

It would have been impossible for a French agriculturist, under occupation, to make a living if he had sold all his produce at the official level set by the Vichy Government at the behest of the Germans. The black market permitted the farmer to exist and also permitted millions of other people to escape the slow starvation which would have been their lot if they had tried to live on the official ration.

In Soviet Russia today agriculturists must cede their produce at official prices until they attain the quota of production which has been set for them. They are allowed to sell the surplus at any price they can obtain, which generally means from five to ten times as much. This legalized black market furnishes them with an incentive to fill the official quota as rapidly as possible. It also induces industrial workers to step up their own production so they can earn extra money with which to buy extra food. The quota food, marketed through governmental agencies, assures everybody of just adequate nutrition at official prices. The surplus food keeps everybody working.

But in France under the oppression the peasant, if he had not concealed his production, would have been forced to cede ALL at the Germans' own prices. The expectation that French peasants would let themselves be had in such fashion was fantastically out of line with their character. It was, in short, just German.

In June and July of 1944 I lived in a war correspondents' camp near the hamlet of Vouilly in Normandy. The camp was on the property of Madame Hamel, a rich proprietress who knew every one of her fifty dairy cows by name, who looked like a marquise in a portrait by Madame Vigée-Lebrun, and who supervised the job when a cow had to be coupled to a bull. Her sole assistant in this chore was the dairymaid.

The camp included, besides fifty war correspondents, a dozen public relations officers and about a hundred enlisted men who served as drivers and cooks. It was fixed at Vouilly for so long a time because the American First Army was temporarily stalled, first by lack of means for a major offensive, then by rain and mud and finally by a desperate German resistance on the approches to Saint-Lô. The camp was about fifteen miles from Saint-Lô. We used to drive out to the battle every day, getting a little closer to the city each time, and then return to camp to write our stories.

I became well acquainted with Madame Hamel. In the evening, when I had finished my work, I used to visit with the family in the kitchen of the farmhouse, which was so big it was locally called a château. Madame Hamel was an open-handed woman: every evening she would send her son out to the correspondents with as many pitchers of milk as they could drink. Cider was piped from the cellar directly into her kitchen, and any soldier who wanted some could turn the spigot. But she was a good manager.

Americans have never been taught by dire necessity to eat all the food on their mess tins, and the swill from our chow tent was of a bulk and quality unprecedented in Normandy. So Madame Hamel asked if she could have it for her pigs. There was so much that all her neighbors too had enough for their pigs and some even bought young pigs to fatten upon our swill. Vouilly became a little Secaucus.

Madame Hamel had a radio set which she had concealed all through the occupation, although she had had German soldiers billeted in her house. While the Germans played cards among themselves on the other side of the kitchen wall, Madame and her family would be listening to the B.B.C. broadcasts from London. The German soldiers had never had a standing invitation to enter the kitchen at will and help themselves to cider. After the liberation of Vouilly Madame's neighbors used to gather openly in the kitchen to listen to this now licit radio.

On July 18 the Twenty-ninth Division took Saint-Lô and I got frightened nearly to death watching them. I came into the kitchen that evening to tell Madame Hamel and her neighbors about it.

"Now we should be able to advance rapidly," I said. "We won't be with you long. On to Paris!"

"That's fine," one man said, "but what about our pigs?"

"My Dear Little Louise" *

The rural French are, of all breeds in the world, the least conceivably destructible. During our breaking-out offensive in Normandy, First Division artillery headquarters, which I was with, occupied four command posts in five days. A French family was living in one wing of the first house we used, although most of the roof was gone and a couple of the bedrooms had only three

* Permission *The New Yorker*, copyright 1944. The F-R. Publishing Corporation.

walls, but the farmhouses in which we had our second and third command posts were deserted. The Germans had forced all the inhabitants to leave. In our fourth one, we found civilians again. The Germans, not expecting so quick an advance, had not evacuated people from what they still considered the rear area. In the barnyard of that place, we found a dead PANZER grenadier of a SCHUTZSTAFFEL division. His paybook said that he had been born in Essen, and on his body there was a typewritten form which he had filled out but obviously had not had time to hand in to his company commander, asking for what we would call an emergency leave to go home. His reason was "Bombing deaths in family—urgent telegram from wife." He had been hit by a fragment of shell, but it had not torn him up much. A detail of our fellows buried him in back of the barn.

The dead cows were more of a problem. One of the things about the breakthrough that made us happy was that we got out of dead-cattle country. The war moved more swiftly and it was no longer necessary to drop artillery shells on every field and crossroad. Besides, the cattle in Brittany were fewer and more scattered than in Normandy, where every pasture was full of them. You needed a bulldozer to bury cows properly, unless you were going to take all day about it, and nobody had men to spare for a large-scale interment detail. They lay in the fields with their four legs pointing stiffly in the air, like wooden cows discarded from a child's Noah's Ark, and their smell hung over the land as the dust hung over the roads. Men are smaller than cattle and they are always buried first; we lived in the stench of innocent death.

At our fourth command post, there were more dead cows than usual, because, the people on the farm told us, eighteen extra cows had arrived with the Germans a couple of weeks before. There had been two sets of Germans in the farm buildings—ten paratroopers who had showed up driving eight cows, and forty SS men who had appeared driving ten cows. The paratroopers, one of whom was a captain, had got there first and taken up quarters in the farmhouse. The SS men, arriving later, had billeted themselves in the outbuildings, but only after a noisy argument, in which they had failed to get the paratroopers out of the big house. The captain had too much rank for them. The paratroopers had been fighting a long time and were very down in the mouth, the people of the house said. A soldier who served as interpreter had told the French family that the war was over, that Germany was beaten. But the SS fellows, who had come from soft berths in Warsaw and Brno, were still GONFLÉS À BLOC (blown up hard) and talked as if they owned the earth. The SS soldiers had brought a refugee family with them, to milk the cows, the people on the farm said. Every day the paratroopers drank the cream from their eight cows and threw the milk away. Both sets of Germans had departed abruptly, but the SS had left one man to guard the cows, presumably in case the reports of the Allied attack proved exaggerated. A shell had killed the cowtender.

I am sure that I will remember our two deserted command posts longer and more vividly than the two that were inhabited. Perhaps that is because you think more about people when they aren't there, and because you can be your own Sherlock Holmes and reconstruct them in accordance with your own hypothesis.

The first deserted farm was a solid rectangle of stone and stucco buildings with walls nearly a foot thick. The farmyard, on which all the buildings fronted, could be reached only by narrow lanes that pierced the solid row of buildings at the front and at the back. It would have been a tough defensive position to crack if there had been any tactical reason to defend it. The farmhouse was very old and must have belonged to an aged, rich, crippled, bigoted woman or to a crippled man who had a fat old woman for a housekeeper. There was a crutch in the farmyard, lying as if it had fallen off a departing wagon, and in one of the bedrooms there was a pair of old, mended crutches that must have been discarded for newer ones. In the kitchen, by the great open hearth, there was a reclining chair with an extension on which to rest your legs, and in one bedroom there were several old and dirty corsets, whose whalebones, despite the garments' immense girth, had all sprung because of the continual effort to encompass a bulging body.

There was a tall Norman clock in every room. Clocks of this sort are made in little towns, like Périers and Colombières and Marigny, which nobody outside Normandy ever heard of before that summer. Every crossroads seems to have had at one time its clockmaker as well as its baker and harness maker. The wooden cases of these timepieces are generally rather austere, but the dials are framed by hammered gilt sculpture; sheaves, golden apples, plows, and peasants in donkey carts are favorite motifs. The pendulums are vast, and they too are encrusted with ornament. A bride, I imagine, although no one has told me so, brings a clock as part of her dowry, and a house where there are many clocks has been ruled in turn by many women. This house was full of hideous modern religious images and of wax fruits and flowers under glass bells. There were no books except devotional ones and those that gave quick ways of making the computations a farmer must make in doing business with wholesalers. There were many of each kind.

The farmsteaders had left the place in a great hurry, and some soldiers, either German or American, had been there afterward and rummaged through the house, littering the floors with things, useless to them, that they had pulled from the cupboards— women's high-collared blouses, skirt hoops, dingy photographs of family outings and one of a man in a cuirassier's uniform, with breastplate and horsetail helmet, and three or four parchment manuscripts. One, dated 1779, was the deed of sale of a farm, another was a marriage contract dated the Year 3 of the First Republic. The contract enumerated the items the bride was to bring in her dowry, which included six pillowcases, one canopy for a bed, and ten handkerchiefs; the whole thing was to come to a thousand and fifty-seven francs. If the husband died before the wife, she was to be allowed to withdraw that much from the estate in consideration of her dowry. If the wife died first, the widower was to keep the pillowcases, handkerchiefs, and all the rest, probably to bestow on his next choice. I wondered, naturally, which of them had survived the other. There were canopies over the beds in all the bedrooms; one must have been the canopy listed in the contract. The house had stone floors that did not shake even when some heavy guns just across the road were being fired, which happened for one entire night we spent there.

The guns were only three thousand yards behind the front line, but they were firing at a target—a railroad station or road junction

—eleven miles away. They belonged not to division artillery but to a remote, unfamiliar entity called Corps. The battery commander, a harassed-looking little captain, called on our artillery general as soon as we moved in and said he hoped the general did not mind guns; there were a lot of generals who couldn't sleep on account of the noise and he had had to move twice already. He was like a man apologizing to his new neighbors for having noisy children; he was sensitive. Our general said that the guns were music to his ears, and we all smiled mechanically and obediently. The captain said, "I'm sure glad to hear that, because I feel I have an ideal setup here."

Across the yard from the house, in a small storeroom, lived a donkey so old that he had a gray beard. His hoofs were long and misshapen, like the nails of an old dog who gets no exercise, and he stayed in his gloomy cell, blinking out at the world, without enough energy to walk into the adjoining barn and eat the hay, although he would accept cabbages if they were brought to him.

From the crippled woman's, or man's, house we moved into a region that had been heavily bombed on the first day of the offensive and was completely deserted except for the surviving animals. An officer who had done some reconnoitering had found a hamlet, Chapelle-en-Litige (Chapel in Litigation), which was intact. Bombs had fallen into all the adjoining fields and bomb craters had made the roads into it almost impassable, but its half-dozen houses and the dependent barns stood untouched. One officer, who considered the Air Forces a form of artillery totally lacking in professional direction, said, "If they had dropped hundred-pound bombs instead of five-hundred, they'd have killed just as many cows without spoiling the roads."

The façade of the granite house in which we set up shop was hidden by pear trees EN ESPALIER, laden with fruit and lush with leaves. An old hen had made a nest in a branch under the hayloft window and was rearing her chicks there; they were hard to find, buried among the pears, and produced a noise that was inexplicable to us until we discovered them. Some of the soldiers with us took up quarters in smaller houses, and once they had found niches for themselves, we all strolled about the village looking over the interiors of the houses. The owners had evacuated them in an

orderly fashion, taking most of their belongings with them. There
was not much left except furniture.

I found a pile of letters, most of them old, a few recent, lying
on a dressing table in one of the houses. In a near-by cupboard
was a long row of schoolboys' notebooks filled with exercises in
drawing, arithmetic, and composition. All the books bore the
inscription, written in a hand which became progressively less
slack, "CAHIER D'ALBERT HÉDOUIN." A couple of recent business
letters were addressed to VEUVE HÉDOUIN, and I assumed that
Albert was the widow's son. There were also in the cupboard a
number of the usual breviaries and cheap books of devotion, including a pamphlet of prayers for prisoners of war. Idly, because
as a camp follower I had nothing else at the moment to do, I
took some of the letters and, sitting down on the threshold of
the plain little house I was in, started to read them.

One was dated September 25, 1914. It began, "My dear little
Louise: I utilize a little moment to send you news of me. I am
in good health and hope my letter finds you the same. I'd rather
be at Chapelle-en-Litige than where I am, for it isn't nice to sleep
outdoors. If this thing ends soon, I won't be sorry. I am with
Anatole and Désiré, and they are in good health, too. Probably
the buckwheat has been harvested, if the weather is as good there
as it is here. I'd like to help thresh it and drink a big bowl of
cider instead of being here, but it's useless to think about it. When
you wean the little colt, leave him in the barn for two days, then
turn him into the fields of broom, where the donkey is. Put
some branches on top of the gate, so he won't try to jump over
it. When you get this letter, send me some news of what goes
on at home. Have you made a barrel of cider for Pannel yet and
have the cows turned out well? Excuse me for being brief, my
dear little Louise and cherished babies. I write this letter in the
open air, sitting on my knapsack, and now I must go. Your husband, who loves you and kisses you again and again, Louis
Hédouin, Three Hundred and Thirty-sixth Infantry. P.S.—Put
the donkey in Fernand's field."

The next letter was dated in November, 1914, and began, "My
dear little Louise: It is with great pleasure I learn that you are in
good health. I too am in good health. Dear little Louise, I think

you should make at least three barrels of cider, although I know it will give you a lot of trouble. Considering the price of apples and the price of cider, it pays better to make cider than to sell apples. And make a good barrel for us, so that we can have the pleasure of drinking it together when I come home." ("Come home," I thought. "That war had four years to go then.") "My dear little Louise, you tell me that you have planted some wheat. Good. Prices are going up. I hope you have sowed oats, dear one. Dear little Louise, I hope you are well. Also the cows and the calves. Butter is selling at a pretty good price, if it can only continue. I was glad to hear you had someone help you thresh the buckwheat. Dear little Louise, I wish I could have been there, but it's useless to think about it. Here one is and here one stays—until when, nobody knows. Your husband, who loves and will never cease to love you and the dear little children, Louis."

Looking up, I saw that four or five cows, probably wanting to be milked, were staring hopefully at me, and I wondered how Louis Hédouin would have felt if he had known that in thirty years not even a woman would be left to care for the cattle in Chapelle-en-Litige. There was another letter, also written in 1914, in which he said he had been to mass and then eaten some ham dear little Louise had sent him; he would rather have attended mass at home, but it was "useless to think of it."

"Dear little Louise," he went on, "you say you have had a card from Aimable and he is in good health. So much the better, for you can't imagine how unhealthy it is where he finds himself. I couldn't either, unless I had been there, but don't worry, I'm all right. Dear little Louise, you say that Marie has had a letter from Pierre and he is a prisoner. So much the better. That way he is sure to survive. I know that threshing must be a lot of trouble to you. I am sorry you are alone and have so much work to do. Do you remember, on that evening before I went away, Enée said that this business wouldn't be over before Easter? I am afraid he was right. It is sad when I think of it. Days are indeed long. Louis."

And on March 15, 1915, he wrote that he was sorry to hear that Louise was suffering but hoped she would soon be delivered—the first indication I had had that he knew she was pregnant.

"My dear little Louise," he continued, "I had a letter from Papa the same time as yours. He says he has sold the old cow for three hundred and forty-five francs. It's not bad, when you think she only had four teeth left. What about the black cow you thought was going to calve March 8 and what are you doing with the Jersey? Tell me in your next letter. Dear little Louise, you say you have threshed the oats. Good. There must have been some loss, but you did the best you could. The worst of it is we probably won't be home in time for the haying this season. Excuse me for not having written. We were taking ammunition up to the front lines. Lately things go badly. The regiment has refused to march to an attack. Everybody is sick of this business, and we lose courage and ask for an end of this terrible war. A sweet kiss from your husband, Louis."

Then, on the 22nd of March, the latest date I found on any of his letters, Hédouin wrote, "My dear little Louise: I have received with great pleasure your letter of the eighteenth. Your mother writes to me that you have had a nine-pound boy and are doing well, and the boy, too. My dear little Louise, you did well to have a midwife from Remilly, and she didn't charge much, either—eight francs. My dear little Louise, I'd like to be with you, but it's useless to think of it. Distance keeps us apart. I hope God will help you in your troubles. My parents write me that at home people are saying this will end soon. So much the better. Dear little Louise, the boy will be called Albert. Before telling you, I waited to see whether you would have a boy or a girl. Your husband, who loves you,

Louis.

"P.S.—What about the black cow?"

Nineteen-fifteen. I did a bit of subtraction. Albert would have been twenty-four in 1939—just the right age. I thought of the graded notebooks and the pamphlet of prayers for prisoners of war.

Plain People

La Vie ouvrière
March 6, 1944

THE WORKERS' FIGHT

A ONE HOUR STRIKE BY THE METAL WORKERS OF THE NORTH. The Trade Union Committees and Steering Committees of the Metal Workers of the North had asked the metal workers to stop work for one hour on January 17. The purpose of this demonstration was to demand higher wages and better food. Fifteen thousand workers took part in this strike and sent delegations to the administrations of the industry.

A NEW AND IMPORTANT DEMONSTRATION BY THE MINERS OF SAINT-ETIENNE. LA VIE OUVRIÈRE tells of a successful eight-day strike by the 11,000 miners of Saint-Etienne which took place in November, 1943. These same miners have just given a new example of their fighting spirit. The underground steering committee of the local union, in accord with the underground organization of the trade unions, had decided to call out the miners of Saint-Etienne in order to commemorate the mine catastrophe in the Chana pits. It will be recalled that a number of miners were killed in this catastrophe because of the absence of safety measures. A great campaign of agitation was undertaken and the following directives passed out:

(1) To the miners of the Chana pits, a twenty-four-hour strike and a procession to the cemetery.

(2) To the miners of other pits, a slow-down in the course of the day.

Finally, a delegation was appointed to submit a list of demands. Among these demands were: Respect for safety regulations, the immediate payment to the families of the victims of the sums that are due them and which the companies are wrongfully withholding, free coal for the widows and orphans. There were also other demands concerning salaries, pensions, fines, etc.

The directives issued by the underground steering committees were obeyed to the letter. On January 21 not a single miner went down into the Chana pits; and in all the other pits work ceased an hour earlier—all this in spite of menacing notices stating that no stoppage of work would be tolerated.

At Gardane the company had decided to make up for the Christmas holiday by working Sunday, December 19. In response to an appeal by the workers' committee, not a single miner went down on that day.

In The Seine-Inferieure: At Rouen, in the Lozon plant, as a result of a move to obtain a wage increase, the workers have been granted a raise of 20 per cent. At Le Havre in the CEM plant, the workers unanimously refused to work Sundays. In the Mazeline plant, a bonus which has heretofore been paid was suppressed. The workers insisted on and obtained the payment of this bonus. . . . At Sotteville the general assembly of the railroad workers demanded a raise of 1,000 francs per month. The list of demands drawn up by the underground committee is having no difficulty in obtaining signatures.

Combat du Languedoc et du Roussillon
October 15, 1943

ADVICE TO WINEGROWERS

Vichy has just set forward the deadline for declaring the amount of the wine harvest in order to know in advance the amounts that will be available for turning over to the Germans. Because of the lack of sulphur and cupricides as well as the dearth of manpower caused by deportations to Germany, winegrowers have had a hard year. But Frenchmen know that, if they have been reduced to a ration of one liter of wine a week, in a country where even in the time of the great phylloxera blight there was never any shortage of wine before, it is because of the enormous quantities of wine that are being sent to Germany.

Winegrowers have found themselves subjected to a control by revenue agents that is to become even more strict this year. We therefore remind them of some of the means that may be effective in tempering the zeal of some of these agents, whose names will shortly be published.

(1) Winegrowers, you cannot resist inspections, but it is your right to leave it up to the revenue agents to ascertain the content of your vats, in case they dispute your declarations.*

(2) Do not allow the agents to touch your barrels without making a protest and pointing out that their handling of the wine may cause it to spoil.

(3) If it is discovered that you have less wine on hand than you stated in your declaration, do not say that you have used it for your own household needs, as such an admission will be held against you. Attribute the shortage to a material accident, for you are not bound to declare to the revenue office any accidental leakages that may take place in your own cellars.

(4) If on the contrary (as it more frequently happens), it is discovered that you have not declared the total amount of your production, contest the findings and blame everything on the manipulations of the revenue agents.

(5) Finally, if a police report is drawn up against you, gain time by refusing to pay the fine, allow your case to be taken into court and judged in absentia. Then demand a revision of the sentence and, when it is sustained, appeal to the Court of Appeals and, if necessary, to the Supreme Court, to set the judgment aside. By that time the Allied armies will have come to deliver you.

Les Lettres Françaises
September, 1943

THE THRESHING MACHINE

It was a fine August day. A faint breeze stirred in the scent-laden air. The slow rhythmic throb of the threshing machine

---

* This is quite a chore. The great vats contain varying quantities of wine in different states of fermentation. Measuring the level of wine in each vat is a messy job and the measuring must be followed by complicated calculations in volume. Also there is a risk of spoiling wine if you mess with it at the wrong time.—L.

rose like a long melancholy song. How remote the war seemed!

A cloud of golden dust hung in the air about the threshing machine in the barnyard. Legs planted apart, hands behind his back, the farmer Chapuis superintended the work. A frown wrinkled his forehead as he debated whether he should obey the order that had secretly been passed on to him.

"What right have they to tell me what to do? I can do what I want with my own crops, can't I?"

Like all the other farmers in the village, Chapuis had received a mysterious warning not to use the thresher for more than half a day altogether. "The Germans are demanding that the wheat be delivered within the next fortnight. We must have nothing for them to requisition. Each family will thresh just enough for its own needs."

When he received the order, Chapuis had flown into a rage. "I'll do what I want and nothing else!" he had said. But now the threshing machine was working on his farm. The half-day was almost up. Should he dismiss the workers? His first obstinacy had given way to a laborious inner debate.

"I am within my rights," he repeated to himself.

He was by no means a collaborationist, but he could not bring himself to admit that simply by going about his business as a farmer he would be playing the enemy's game. No matter what anyone said, no one was going to stop him from harvesting the crops that he had sowed and getting a fair return on his labor, just as his father and his father's father had done before him!

But another train of thought crept into his mind and gave him pause.

"If it were a lot of good-for-nothings or people of just one party, I wouldn't give it a second thought. But their committee includes members of all parties, it represents the whole village."

And Chapuis understood that it was the village itself that was urging him not to let his crops be requisitioned. It was true that Ardouin and Blondel and August Jouare had kept the threshing machine working only half a day. He thought also of Emile Villebois who had ignored the order and seen the machine burned up in his own back yard. Slowly he made up his mind. He would go along with the others. He called the workers and paid them off.

It was a clear August day. The air was laden with the smell of new-mown fields. How remote the war seemed! And yet, it is here, in everything about us. Sometimes it manifests itself in the bloody clash of mighty armies; sometimes in the silent struggle in the conscience of a man standing beside a threshing machine.

Le Franc-tireur
August 25, 1943

THE BOOTY

In 1942 France paid out to the German occupational authorities 156 billions of francs.* At the present rate of increase, the payments for 1943 will amount to 264 billions.

The schedule of food supplies for the month of August provides that the Department of the Cantal shall supply 700 steers for the French population; 200 steers, 200 calves, 280 sheep and 70 hogs for the occupation troops, and 900 steers to be sent to Germany.

In all the cattle-raising departments the situation is similar. In the month of August alone, 31 trains, of 450 head of cattle each, will be sent to Germany from the Southern zone.

2,000 TONS OF BUTTER A MONTH

The German authorities have just made known their new demands for food. Among other products, they are to requisition 2,000 tons of butter a month. Hitherto all the butter turned over to the Germans by the French government was intended to supply the occupational forces. The new demands constitute a serious problem for the feeding of the French population. If 2,000 tons

---

* At the rate of exchange of 1945, $3,120,000,000. To get a better idea of the amount paid, we should bear in mind both the exchange value of the French franc and its actual purchasing power in France. At the outbreak of World War II, the dollar was worth about 38 francs. However, the purchasing value of 38 francs was far above that of a dollar in America. For instance, one could get board and lodging in a fairly good hotel on the Riviera for 40 francs a day.—L.

of butter are to be delivered every month, it will not leave enough butter to make it possible for the French population to buy seven the limited amounts provided for by our present food cards.

Hope and Despair

At times during the last two years of war great waves of hope surged over the country. Sometimes leaders had hard work to restrain their men, sure for subjective reasons that deliverance was at hand. At others the chiefs had to remind their men sharply that the war wasn't won yet, the hardest pull still lay ahead. Sometimes these waves had their origin in events outside France, the surrender of the Germans at Stalingrad, for example, or the landings in Sicily. Often they were followed by disillusion.

Here are two expressions of this intoxicating joy that came to Frenchmen even while they lived under the menace of the GESTAPO. They triumphed over their conquerors; sometimes, in anticipation, they almost pitied them. The "PAUVRES ALLEMANDS" of LE RIRE D'EUROPE is not entirely ironic. If you watch even a rat long enough you will begin to identify with him.

La Voix du Nord et du Pas-de-Calais
February 3, 1943

THE GREAT DAY!

This is it! The day is at hand! Not the day of agony as in 1940, but of joy, strong and austere, born out of suffering. For some weeks now France has been in the throes of the ecstasy of a rebirth. Our ears are cocked to hear the news. Optimism is in the air. We can feel the great day approaching and are silently making ready for it. Assurance gives us courage. Over all France there is something of the spirit of the eve of a holiday, that great holiday that will be the liberation. Oh, ours is not a vulgar, noisy joy.

It is not the heavy, brutal, sadistic joy of the Germans in 1940, nor the smug smirking joy of the Italians after their stab in the back. No! France knows only too well what sacrifices have been and must yet be made to bring about the results that permit her even now to contemplate the future with confidence. Her joy is stern and unostentatious, deep and without pomp; for it is made up of pride in her historic mission, the memory of sacrifices, remorse at the impotence to which she was doomed by the fault of the partisans of capitulation. It is a virile joy built on the satisfaction of having kept up the struggle and the desire to fight on to the end.

It is the kind of joy that sweeps over a soul that has suffered, when it feels itself reborn and moved by a generous eagerness to give itself unstintedly to the common cause. It is the sure joy that one modestly feels when there is a useful task ahead to do.

A sure joy! Yes! for henceforth there is nothing that can shake it. Victory is at hand, it draws near, bringing the day of liberation with it. Throughout the world the tide has set in. Events themselves have communicated even to the most lukewarm and the most skeptical among us something of the sacred flame that has never ceased to inspire patriots since 1940. Frenchmen are now convinced of the imminence of the upheaval that they have so long awaited. The facts are there: the victories in Russia and Africa, the decisions of Casablanca, the defeat of enemy propaganda. These facts themselves justify our certitude and constitute irrefutable reasons for our faith.

Radio Paris and the ECHO DU NORD may continue to propagate their lies. For all their sniggers and sneers, the announcers and journalists know that they are preaching in the desert. The failure of the cause to which they have attached themselves brings out their bitterness and spite. Their inanities of late have taken on a vicious cynicism of the lowest brand in an effort to keep from losing face and from becoming the laughing-stock of their auditors.

Forces Unies de la Jeunesse
August, 1943

THE LAUGHTER OF EUROPE

Poor Germans! . . . They destroyed Warsaw with incendiary bombs, massacred 20,000 people at Rotterdam, burned out whole quarters of London, wiped out Coventry—and now Goering is searching the scorched earth for the ruins of a town that once was Hamburg.

There is laughter in London and Warsaw and Rotterdam and Tours and Abbeville. There is laughter—and there will be yet more—in the prisons and factories of Germany. Men are laughing because they are being avenged.

Poor Germans! . . . The Dutch, the Belgians, the French had to flee before them in woeful disarray, floundering toward the South—and now, on the roads out of Hamburg and Berlin, they are in flight—they, the overlords of Europe! And Europe laughs in joy!

Poor Hitler! . . . He had promised a hundred times that he would respect Austria, Poland—and of course, the neutrality of the Belgians and the Dutch. He had lied a hundred times.

Poor Hitler! . . . He had laughed a hundred times, at Benes, at the Poles. He had laughed at us, he had laughed at Churchill, branding him as a madman because he dared to fight back; and the laughter of Hitler shook Germany with a great wave of laughter.

Poor Germans! . . . Poor Hitler! . . . The Germans no longer laugh. Hitler no longer laughs. Germany weeps tears of blood and gall, but Europe feels laughter swelling in its breast, and soon the laughter of Europe will burst forth in a mighty blare.

After the elation of the two previous pieces, the gloom of this portrait of Paris under the Nazis in 1943 recalls the paintings of Maurice Utrillo, those rows of meaningless houses giving on empty streets, that somehow make us cry. Many months after the liberation I managed to find out the name of the man who wrote it. He was Georges Altman, who was also the author of "Our Marbonne." The illegal journalist's mood suddenly changes to one of rage—against the fat cats of treason, the "legitimate" press. In the last of these three selections, the writer, Claude Morgan, is savagely elated. He has his fun with Monsieur Cousteau, a proto-Nazi tough guy who is beginning to welch. On November 23, 1946, Cousteau was sentenced to death for treason.

Le Père Duchesne
September, 1943

The Swine Have Sullied Paris!

by GEORGES ALTMAN

What a funereal splendor drenches Paris, peopled by Germans— and empty! The great monumental spaces, the impressive vistas, the long pale avenues reaching silent and empty under the last rays of this fourth autumn of our woe.

A city decanted, specter of a city. Some Sunday take the streets that lead into the Champs Elysées. Drooping against the green of our trees, strange flags with black swastikas on white disks hang heavily from the balconies of the luxuriant buildings. Nobody . . . Germans. More Germans . . . Nobody. Nobody except some German brass in white summer blouses, strolling as if on the parade ground of a super-smart barracks. A horse-drawn vehicle, a turnout, passes: a pair of JUNKERS, beaming, with binoculars slung over their shoulders. Not a distinguishable sound anywhere except the sounds that THEY make: their boots or motors and, toward evening, their fifes and drums in the distance. Paris sleeps, dreams, crushed beneath their weight, beside them, pushed aside, still heart-breaking with grace in the golden halo of her sunsets.

Anyone who has never heard, in the afternoon, along some Parisian avenue a hurdy-gurdy, dug up from the days before the war, tinkling its quaint complaint before the HÔTEL PLAZA-ATHÉNÉE crowded with laughing German sailors, does not know the frightful sadness that rises from the banks of the Seine. Anyone who has not—on some wide boulevard shaded by its great trees, that once was filled with all the city sounds that mark the day's work done —been stifled by the total silence, so complete that he could hear even the faint rustle of the leaves, has not yet grasped the sense of Paris occupied, Paris mute, Paris blighted.

But it was not enough to turn over to the Nazis, the SS, the firing squads, the capital of the world. It was not enough to see the announcements of the executions of hostages posted on the walls.

It was not enough to see the VÉLODROME D'HIVER jammed for three nights with Jewish women and children.

There had to be men, Frenchmen, who would consent, with zeal, with joy, with delight, to execute every day—yes, and to go beyond—the shameless orders they received, to fawn upon the executioners, to thank the assassins. By publishing, signing and proclaiming their infamy, so sure were they that it would last as long as they!

These organs of imported hate, this written pestilence that decks the Paris newsstands and which each day offers—let it be said, in vain—its dreary frenzy, can never be acclimated to the air of Paris where wit, Voltairean merriment, the serene delight of thought, the passion for justice, integrity and liberty, have flourished. Just as the tramp and chants of the German columns clash outrageously with the setting of Paris, so the prostitute press clashes with the soul of Paris.

LE MATIN, L'OEUVRE, PARIS-SOIR, LES NOUVEAUX TEMPS, L'APPEL, AUJOURD'HUI, LA FRANCE SOCIALISTE, and the weeklies, LA GERBE, JE SUIS PARTOUT, RÉVOLUTION NATIONALE, AU PILORI, that clutter the newsstands—who reads them, who believes them? Nobody There they are. They bear witness to the contemptible attempts to poison the soul of a nation for the benefit of an enemy who is bent on our extermination. Bugle calls to servitude, trumpet calls to summon us to submit to every form of tyranny, tallyhos against the victims. A scramble to see who can be cruelest and vilest to please our tyrants.

Oh, it is true that there was nothing very wholesome about the pre-war press in France! We know its vices—its congenital vice that made it the henchman of money and power. But who ever would have thought that the greatest newspapers of yesterday blended with some few newcomers in the field would make such an abject harmony? And that they would openly go over from the "secret funds" * to the open funds of the enemy. But this is what has happened.

Paroles Françaises
November, 1943

The Other Danger: The Saboteurs of French Thought

The retreat of the WEHRMACHT on all fronts constitutes, as we know, a brilliant victory. At least, so the press—or, if you prefer, the sheets that obey the orders of Vichy—gravely explain to us.

For it would seem, except for the Resistance newspapers, there no longer is any French press. It is dead, killed by public indignation; and if tomorrow the single column concerning the value of ration points from day to day were suppressed, it would not have a single reader left.

Nevertheless, all these publications that have fattened on our defeat are making millions, thanks to government subsidies.

This is an extremely immoral state of things. Which is why we call upon all the Frenchmen who hold their noses when they read these papers to do their bit to put a crimp in the spreaders of false news that all the newspapers now permitted to appear have become.

Here are a few practical means of sabotage:

(1) Get together with your neighbors and buy only one newspaper and pass it around among you.

(2) Since all the newspapers are under the control of Vichy and will say the same thing, buy a different newspaper every day, which

* The "secret funds" were unaccounted funds at the disposition of the government. The reactionary governments of Laval, Flandin, and Tardieu used these funds not only to subsidize newspapers but to back pro-fascist organizations. (Translator's note.)

will confuse the circulation managers and upset estimates of the number of copies to be printed.

(3) Return the paper to the newsvender after having read the official announcements. He will return it as unsold and keep the profit instead of turning it over to the traitor press.

(4) Do not hesitate to write letters to the editor expressing your disgust.

Finally—and this is very important—boycott the merchants who advertise in the prostitute press and inform these merchants of your resolve.

Be assured that if everybody follows these directives in making things as difficult as possible for the collaborationist press, it will help to hasten the liberation.

The owners of the newspapers that are being published at present have shown themselves to be nothing but dealers in paper. Strike at them in the only place where they will feel it—in the pocketbook!

Remember that if, following the example of the heroic sailors of Toulon, the newspapers of France had scuttled themselves (as some few of them did have the courage to do), the slave dealers of Vichy would have found it impossible to continue their evil enterprise.

Soon the prostitute press will have to answer for its treason. Do not fatten it up before its execution.

Claude Morgan is a merry little man with an ingratiating Celtic face that matches his name. Physiognomy however is as usual misleading because Morgan is a NOM DE PLUME *and his real name is triple-distilled French. It is a* NOM DE PLUME *that dates from before the war. He was educated as a civil engineer but turned to journalism and in 1939 was on the staff of the leftist evening newspaper* CE SOIR. *He served at the front, was taken prisoner, escaped and returned to Paris.*

There he was employed, under his real name, in the LOUVRE *as some vague kind of assistant curator—"an intellectual loafer," according to him. The services of the* LOUVRE *were full of such vague employees during the German occupation. Monsieur Jaujard, the director of national museums, and Monsieur Billiet, the direc-*

tor of the LOUVRE, retained their posts even under Vichy since museums were non-political. But Jaujard and Billiet were anything but non-political, and the museums were regular forcing beds of resistance movements. They were particularly valuable for meetings of intellectuals, since the comings and goings of painters, sculptors and writers in such cultural purlieus could hardly be considered subversive or worthy of special notice. Among its other activities, the Louvre group kept the R.A.F. and later the A.A.F. informed of all movements of art treasures to provincial châteaux for safekeeping, so the flyers might avoid bombing the châteaux.

Morgan, before and during the war, was a hard-hitting controversialist, and as editor-in-chief of the liberated LETTRES FRANÇAISES, he still is.

Les Lettres Françaises
March, 1944

Monsieur Cousteau Is Sore

by CLAUDE MORGAN

Monsieur Cousteau has taken exception to a remark that appeared in LES LETTRES FRANÇAISES. He himself tells about it in an article in JE SUIS PARTOUT for February 18, entirely consecrated to defending himself.

The traitor had had the impudence to declare: "The ideal thing would be for the DURS * of the Resistance and the DURS of the collaborationist movement to remake France between themselves." To which we replied, "No community of action between the assassins and their victims." And we added, "Fear of punishment has caused a serious awakening of sentimentality in Cousteau. When is he going to resign from JE SUIS PARTOUT?" This put him into such a rage that he called us Jews, which is, of course, the final word in any argument. He is a DUR, a real DUR. At least, he

---

* The word dur as it is used in this article cannot be translated by any single English word. It means "tough-minded," "regular guys," "old-timers," "practical men," etc. (Translator's note.)

says so. We shall find out later whether it is true or not. For how could we know it now? Thus far the intellectuals of the collaborationist movement have had it very easy indeed. Not a hair of their heads has been touched. A man is not a DUR simply because he dares to say so in public—under the protection of mighty police forces.

It is easy to write articles for JE SUIS PARTOUT: you can work at home like a respectable person. No need to abandon your work every time the doorbell rings. As for the DURS among the collaborationists, if there are any, we shall see them at work, later.

If Cousteau did not pay tribute to the DURS of the Resistance out of sentimentality, what WAS his real motive? Because he wished to remain a gentleman, he explains. A most unusual gentleman who applauds the murder and torture of his fellow countrymen! An astounding gentleman who never missed a chance to denounce French writers to the enemies of France, in the columns of his paper. Unless this word also, like so many others, has changed its meaning since June, 1940!

We may be sure that this was not his real reason. He gives his real reason at the end of his article. "We are well aware," he states, "that there are many putrid opportunists in the collaborationist movement."

If Monsieur Cousteau gave credit to the courage of the DURS in the Resistance, it was simply to shame his little playmates.

Resistance Humor

The humor of the Resistance is a little painful. It would be instructive to compare the files of LE GAULLOIS with those of PUNCH, or of the Topics of the Times column in THE NEW YORK TIMES during the same period. The twenty-odd miles of Channel that separated France from England made more difference in the point of view than the thirty-odd hundred miles of ocean that separated England from the United States. Even PUNCH was only on the edge. As for the Topics of the Times, although the dates correspond, it seems to have been written in some different period of history from LE GAULLOIS.

The proper attitute toward German soldiers one meets in the streets is hardly a hilarious topic. The cowardice of collaborationists, the spectacle of the satellite rats quitting the sinking ship of German state are subjects for laughter, but the laughter is savage. Finally, the jokesmith always haa to fall back on Laval.

Le Gaullois
October, 1943

ADVICE TO THE OCCUPIED

(1) They are there, placid and good-natured. Don't kid yourself however. They are not tourists.

(2) They are the victors. Be "correct" with them. But don't think to curry favor by anticipating their desires. Don't be too zealous. What is more, they won't think any the better of you for it.

(3) You do not speak their language or you have forgotten it. If one of them speaks to you in German, shrug your shoulders and, without any remorse, go about your business.

(4) If he asks you a direction in French, do not think that you are obliged to go along with him to point out the way for him. You are not on a walking tour together.

(5) In a café or restaurant, if he tries to engage you in a conversation, give him politely to understand that what he has to say does not interest you in the slightest.

(6) If he asks you for a light, pass him your cigarette. Never, since the beginning of time, has man refused a light even to his mortal enemy.

(7) If he thinks it is clever to inculcate defeatism into the hearts of citizens by giving band concerts in our public places, you are not obliged to be present. Stay home or go to the country and listen to the birds.

(8) Ever since the occupation began, he has been holding parades in your dishonor. Will you stand there and watch them?

Turn around and look at the shop windows instead. It is much more fascinating; for at the rate at which he is loading up his trucks, soon there will be nothing left for you to buy.

Libération
February 29, 1944

COLD FEET AND YELLOW STREAKS

A short time ago, a daily paper on the look-out for human interest stories asked one of its staff to do a feature article on the measures that the city schools of Paris had taken to protect the pupils in case of air raids. The author of the article gave special mention to the school in Rue des Feuillantines to which the LYCÉE BUFFON has been evacuated. The air-raid shelter set aside for the pupils within the school grounds was found to be the best shelter in all Paris—since it leads into the Catacombs. A shelter capable of resisting a five-ton bomb!

The day after the article appeared, an official car stopped before the school. Two gentlemen got out and asked if they might inspect the cellars of the school, by order of the Prime Minister's office, which is installed in the HÔTEL MATIGNON.

Satisfied with their inspection, the two gentlemen withdrew after having announced that the ministry would probably be moved to Rue des Feuillantines. The very next day the City of Paris received orders to vacate the school without delay.

These gentlemen, who so dread getting messed up themselves, were naturally not in the least concerned with the safety of the children.

They have no more hearts than they have guts.

Libération, Edition Zone Nord
November 16, 1943

THOSE TERRORISTS!

Two automobiles set out from Vichy to Paris together. In the first was the minister of finance, Monsieur Cathala. In the other was His Excellency Monsieur de Brinon, Vichy ambassador to Germany. Monsieur Cathala's car was in the lead by a few minutes, when two of his tires went flat at the same time. Since the car carried only one spare, it was impossible to go on. It was therefore decided to ask the ambassador's car for help. Monsieur Cathala and his chauffeur stood in the middle of the road to wait for it to come along. As soon as it appeared, they began waving their arms to stop it. But the minister of finance and his chauffeur had barely time to fling themselves face down in the ditch. The ambassador's armored car bore down on them with all its machine guns blazing and soon disappeared into the distance, triumphant at having fought its way out of the terrorist ambush laid by the minister of finance.

Le Populaire
September, 1943

THE SINKING SHIP

After Italy, now it is Finland that has come to the end of her rope and is trying to get out of the war. She has discontinued her foreign propaganda broadcasts and is trying to renew her friendship with America. As in Italy, the people are demanding peace.

Hungary is refusing to send any more troops to the Eastern front.

Rumania is casting about for a way of getting out of the hornets' nest into which her perfidious leaders have pushed her. She has asked Turkey to open negotiations with the Allies on her behalf.

In Bulgaria, resentment against the Axis—or what remains of it—prevails.

In short, Hitler's fortress is crumbling on every side.

Soon we shall see the final assault.

THE ENSLAVED NATIONS IN REVOLT

Serious disturbances have broken out in Norway where a number of policemen have been arrested and deported. Martial law has been proclaimed and former army officers are being sought by the GESTAPO.

In Denmark, there have been numerous acts of sabotage directed especially against the railroads.

In Greece, there was a general strike at Salonika.

In Belgium, there is a mounting wave of attacks on Germans and collaborators.

THE NEUTRALS SEE THE SIGNS OF THE TIMES

We are informed that:

For the first time in three years, Spanish movie theaters have begun showing English newsreels.

For the first time since the defeat of France, Sweden has withdrawn permission for German troops to cross her territory in transit.

Le Gaullois
November, 1943

PIERRE AND ADOLF

Rightfully concerned about his future, Hitler asked Laval to have him naturalized as a French citizen. Laval took Adolf to Pétain's office, gave him a letter of recommendation and waited outside the door to learn the outcome of the interview.

An hour later Hitler came out.

"What did the old man say?" Laval asked.

Adolf looked him up and down contemptuously and did not answer. Laval repeated his question. Then Adolf turned on him and snapped, "I have nothing to say to you! I do not speak to BOCHES!"

The Collaborationist

Much of Resistance writing echoes Père Duchesne's theme, "It wasn't enough to see the Germans in Paris—there had to be Frenchmen to thank them." Here the editor of COMBAT DU LANGUEDOC takes it up with southern passion. This thought that there were Frenchmen to sell their brothers' flesh, even though they were a small minority (perhaps a quarter of one per cent) is the wound that remains in the French mind. Every Frenchman feels in some degree guilty for the débâcle of 1940—if only because he let himself be bamboozled into a sense of security before it happened.

But the traitors personify the guilt of all, which makes the honest men all the more bitter against them. In punishing the traitors, Frenchmen were punishing a part of themselves.

Only he who feels himself without guilt is reluctant to cast a stone; he lacks the requisite imagination. General de Gaulle, the most self-righteous of Frenchmen, was one of the least vindictive against the erring brothers.

During the occupation there was not a hamlet that did not have its traitor. Traitors are curious animals. Some are willing to die if only one will admit that they did not profit by their treason: take the thirty pieces of silver out of the story, they seem to think, and Judas would be a decent fellow. The pathology of treason would be a curious study.

I once met an avowed collaborationist in Antrain-sur-Couesnon, a small town in Brittany. It was early in August of 1944, just after the American breakthrough. Often, in the confused fighting that followed that event, the F.F.I. of a locality captured their own town, and the Germans near it, before the American soldiers got there. That had happened at Antrain.

The collaborationist was locked in a cell of the GENDARMERIE, which would correspond to an American State Police barracks, except that the GENDARMERIE are national police. He was a pot-bellied little man of fifty-six, with a face puffed from a beating some women had given him. "They were widows of men he betrayed to the militia," a Resistance man who had brought me to see him said. The collaborationist lay on a concrete dais, which was the nearest thing to a bed the cell contained, his grotesque, nearly feminine figure covered by blood-stained pajamas and a dressing gown.

Some Resistance men had gone to his house and dragged him from his bed at night. His head was swathed in a turban of bandages. "No, no, I didn't betray them!" he cried to me. "I never betrayed them. It's a lie!" He added, "I'm willing to be shot as a collaborator, but not for having betrayed those men. Somebody told the women I had betrayed their husbands, but it isn't so."

In the cell besides me, the collaborator and my guide, were a young gendarme in a tan uniform and black leather leggings, and a great, heavy-set farmer armed with a captured German rifle, who was serving as the prisoner's special guard. All three Frenchmen began to argue with the prisoner at once. My guide was a small, nervous fellow in civilian clothes, but with three slanting gold chevrons on the lapel of his jacket to show he was a sergeant.

"You know that you talked to the militia the day before they jumped those fellows!" cried the sergeant. "And then, animal, the night after they murdered our men, you had the officers of the militia to dinner at your house."

"Shut up, thing of filth!" the gendarme shouted at the prisoner, from professional habit, although the prisoner was not speaking.

"It wasn't you who always had a good word to say for the BOCHE, hein?" the farmer rumbled.

"Yes," the man on the concrete dais said, "I was pro-German. I acknowledge it. I worked for them. I took money from them. But my prices weren't exorbitant. It is finished for me. I want to be shot."

"Let me get this straight," I said. "You want to be shot?"

"Yes," he said.

"He is not hard to please, you see," the gendarme said to me. "A curious mentality."

The sergeant said, "He's an architect. He built barracks and blockhouses for the Germans. Aren't you ashamed of yourself, miserable object—you, an educated man?" he howled at the prisoner.

The potbellied man looked fixedly at the wall without replying.

"Why did you work for the Germans?" I asked. "Did you think they could win?"

"Not after the Allied landing," he said, "but then it would have been disgusting to change. I could have run away, but I stayed. I am willing to be shot."

"We had a MAQUIS of about eighty men near here," the sergeant told me. "Here in northern Brittany, there isn't cover for large groups of resistants, as there is in the wilder regions. But these were men of quality, most of them noncommissioned officers in the old army. On the night of June 7, one day after the first American landing, the men of the MAQUIS were going to attack a German road convoy moving north toward Normandy. The man you have just seen betrayed them. He knew that everybody in the countryside hated him. Children made fun of him. Women spat at him. People called him 'Auntie.' He hated us all. That evening two hundred militiamen and Gestapo Germans attacked our fellows. They had machine guns, mortars and grenades. We had a German machine pistol, perhaps twenty rifles and one revolver. We had founded our group with only the revolver and we had captured the other weapons one by one.

"We killed twenty-one of them. They took eight prisoners, put them in a truck, and drove to a quarry near here. Seven of the prisoners were French and one was American. The American was a parachutist who had landed here on June 6. The MAQUIS had fitted him out in civilian clothes so he would not be spotted. The militia refused to admit that he was a soldier, although he had his identity disks. They were found on his body later. They stripped him and the other fellows and tortured them—tore out their fingernails, crushed their most sensitive parts, that sort of thing, so that they would give information about the MAQUIS. Then they took them to the edge of the quarry and shot them, so that their bodies fell over the cliff. Then some of the militiamen climbed down and finished off one or two survivors with pistols.

"They told nobody. A farmer who saw the shootings informed the gendarmes, and they climbed down next day and got the bodies. Now you understand why this man will not admit he gave them the information and why he wants to be shot. He does not want to be released from jail. It would be the worst thing that could happen to him."

Traitors and Their Fate

Combat du Languedoc
July, 1943

FOR OUR COUNTRY—AGAINST TRAITORS

For eight months the BOCHES have occupied the former Free Zone, and for eight months the Gestapo has raided, searched, arrested, tortured and killed hundreds of patriots in our region.

Behind the reinforced walls of the military prison of Toulouse, and later in the jails of Paris and Compiègne, men and women of every social class, of every political party, of every religion, are suffering and dying for our country. More than two thousand persons have passed through this processing prison and in it have undergone the worst kinds of torture, from clubbing to lashing, including jabbing with needles, ingenious injections and quartering.

TO THE STOOL PIGEONS

But what sickens us most is not that the BOCHES should practice these massacres and acts of barbarism. As BOCHES, that is their business. A tiger is a tiger till his last day. It is his calling, his natural taste and his pleasure. If there are any among them who recoil from these cruelties, they carry them out nonetheless by the FÜHRER's orders. A German is not a man; he is a tool in his leaders' hands.

There are men still more loathsome than the actual executioners: they are the purveyors for the executioners, those Frenchmen who deliver other Frenchmen into the hands of the torturers.

The most outstanding informers have been warned and publicly denounced by the London radio. But the list of these vermin is too long to be read over the air. So we have decided to make a public listing, in this modest clandestine newspaper, of those who are collaborating with the Gestapo.

Our action has a dual purpose:

First, to inform patriots of the danger they run in associating with these stool pigeons. Certain of these sorry individuals mask their true character, get you to talk . . . and then report you. So, look out!

Our second purpose is to warn the guilty that they will not be forgotten on the day of reckoning. When the German machine guns are no longer there to protect them, the republican justice of the people will be unleashed against them. All known crimes will be punished. Some think all will be forgiven and forgotten, as it was after the victory of 1918. They are mistaken. In the joy of victory one may forget. After a defeat it will be necessary to seek out and punish those without whose help the enemy could never have conquered our nation or persecuted our patriots.

In 1918 our country alone had been betrayed. In 1943, besides our country, individual persons have been handed over to the BOCHES. These victims, knowing the names of those who handed them over, will demand justice and retribution.

The fact is that this retribution has already begun. It is naturally not possible for us to cite names and to reveal facts. But the important thing is that the informers should know that already some of them have paid the penalty.

TO PATRIOTS

Patriots too, in their prisons, are wiping out with their blood the crimes of the cowards and the traitors.

Thanks to her soldiers and to her resisters, France will come out alive from the ordeal and will be able to say to the world, "Thus have my true sons atoned for faults of which they are guiltless." And the astonished world will learn, once again, that nothing can ever crush France, immortal France.

When a BOCHE tortures and massacres, that is his business as a BOCHE and a Nazi.

But when a Frenchman sells other Frenchmen to the enemy, that is the depth of abjection.

On the day of liberation, the patriots and the whole French people—which still knows what honor is—will wipe out this foul scum of informers for the GESTAPO. In the free and renewed France of the future, there must not remain even the memory of such crimes.

[A list of traitors followed the above text.]

Le Franc-tireur
June 1, 1943

TREASON DOES NOT PAY

Notice to traitors. Doctor Michel Guérin, secretary general of the P.P.F. for the Department of Vienne, was stabbed to death at Poitiers on May 13, by four persons who succeeded in escaping. Doctor Guérin was an editorial writer for the AVENIR DE LA VIENNE. He signed his articles Pierre Chavagny.

On the morning of May 14, Monsieur Din, mayor of Pierre-fitte, formerly a member of the Communist Party, was shot down in the street by two young men who made good their escape. Monsieur Din succumbed to his wounds.

Two French judges, including the president judge of a court in Seine-et-Marne, have been assassinated for having condemned Frenchmen to death for sabotage. A third judge was wounded. They had all received letters informing them that they had been condemned to death by a patriotic organization.

WELCOME PHILIPPE HENRIOT

The lecture given by Philippe Henriot before several thousand listeners at the Imperial Cinema at Tarbes was interrupted by three bomb explosions.

La Voix du Nord
April 8, 1943

SWEET LITTLE BUTTERCUP

The gendarme sergeant at Honschoote, Victor Millescamps, is abusing his power and showing too much zeal in carrying out the orders of the German authorities. He is turning in reports on persons carrying more than four or five kilograms of wheat, potatoes or beans. We should consider this merely a deplorable pettiness and absence of conscience on the part of this flunky of the new order, if we were not aware that Victor Millescamps is not neglecting to look after his own personal interests and is requiring a certain farmer's wife to bring him a pound of butter every week.

Underground fighters of our region, keep a close watch on Victor Millescamps. If you continue to report scandals such as this, you will enable us to complete our list of the profiteers of the occupation period.

L'Espoir
September, 1943

LEGION FIASCO

Times have certainly changed since 1941, the date of the first public demonstration of the Legion.

The people of Marseille still recall the monument erected in the Old Port, facing the Cannebière. For several days all officialdom had come there to deliver orations before the crowd of legionaries and the bishop had given his blessing to this fine assemblage.

The Germanic hordes, everywhere victorious, had just conquered the Balkans. The Russian steppes were the scene of impressive victories. . . .

But since then, what changes!

After the tide had turned before Moscow, came America's entry into the war, the landing in North Africa and the entry into the war of the whole French Empire; then the victories of Stalingrad, Tunisia and Sicily, the flight of Mussolini and the eclipse of Fascism. Even the blindest saw then that Germany had lost the war, that the Allies, continuing their triumphal march, would soon be coming to free us, and that there would be a few accounts to settle.

That is why on August 29, 1943, the anniversary of the Legion, there was a public demonstration . . . without legionaries.

In the Aix Square and at the LYCÉE PÉRIER, a few officials, very uncomfortable, looked at one another in silence.

The ceremony, lasting only a few minutes, finally ended to the relief of all concerned, for everyone was obviously anxious to leave.

No parade through town.

Nothing, less than nothing. . . .

Times have changed!

Libération, Edition Zone Nord
November 16, 1943

BRUTES

Some time ago a police squad, led by Commissioner Dumonet of the special police force of Laval, arrested in the Department of Nièvre a score of patriots and locked them up in the Girls' Normal School, Boulevard Victor Hugo, at Nevers, which had been turned into a prison for the occasion.

There the patriots underwent special interrogations which are the modern form of the ancient judicial torture. One of them was bound to a table, completely naked, for twenty-six hours, while the police inspectors took turns beating him with horsewhips and bludgeons made of electric wires. Six others were taken away unconscious to the hospital, some with their bladders pierced, others with their noses crushed by kicks. At the hospital, in spite of their condition, they were subjected to special restraints and chained by their feet.

Our friends in the region decided to put an end to this torture, and on November 5, at 7:45 p.m., a rescue squad entered the hospital buildings. After chloroforming the police guards, they carried away the six prisoners.

This operation lasted only thirteen minutes.

Les Forces Unies de la Jeunesse
July 1, 1943

GOOD WORK, GENDARMES!

Our region has just witnessed two deeds which deserve to be reported and held up as examples.

The gendarmes of X., having been ordered to seize certain RÉFRACTAIRES, went before dawn to a place where they knew they could be found and warned them. A few hours later they presented themselves most officially to arrest them. Needless to say, there was no longer anyone to be found.

In another place the gendarmes were ordered to arrest a RÉ-FRACTAIRE who was still living at home. Instead of going straight to his house, they spent a good two hours making the rounds of the neighboring houses (to collect information, so they said), just time enough for the young man to slip away.

Such deeds must increase in number. When the French Government orders the French gendarmes to do nasty jobs which are a disgrace to the traditions of the service, it is hoped that they will bungle their orders as often as possible.

We will remember.

L'Humanité
February 1, 1944

WARNING TO JUDGES

Magistrates who accept the wretched task of sitting on those assassins' tribunals which are known as Military Courts should know that, not only will they be answerable tomorrow to the justice of the people, but that patriots will strike down as many of them as they can without waiting for the hour of liberation of our land.

THE DUTY OF PATRIOTIC POLICEMEN

Policemen who are at present placed under the orders of the assassins' chief, Darnand, must understand that the situation requires that they make clear-cut decisions.

The time has come for patriotic policemen to go over from passive resistance to the active struggle against Darnand, whom they themselves should kill like a mad dog. The time has come for patriotic policemen to use their weapons against the Darnand-Pétain-Laval-Henriot terrorists, and to join, with their weapons, the RÉFRACTAIRES of the MAQUIS to intensify the struggle against the enemies of our country.

Le Franc-tireur
December 1, 1943

WARNING OF THE NATIONAL COUNCIL OF RESISTANCE TO MEMBERS OF PARLIAMENT WHO MAY NOT HAVE UNDERSTOOD

The National Council of Resistance, being informed that Philippe Pétain and the Government of Vichy, acting on the suggestion of certain writers in the pay of the enemy, are considering calling together the National Assembly which disbanded more than three years ago after abdicating its powers, addresses to all members of Parliament who may be invited either to sign petitions in favor of such convocation, or to attend the convocation, a solemn warning.

Whereas the convening of a National Assembly by the usurping power whose seat is at Vichy can only be illegal,

Whereas no sovereign assembly can be held in France under the foreign master,

Whereas, therefore, a National Assembly, summoned by Vichy and under the German heel, can only be a new occasion to furnish the enemies of the nation, within and without, further means to render yet more harsh the yoke which weighs on France and on the liberty of her citizens,

Acting as the only genuinely French authority constituted on the home soil, as the only voice of the national will, validly expressed under the terror by the Resistance movements and by the accredited representatives of the political parties and tendencies which have remained faithful to the nation,

Serves notice on all members of Parliament that their duty is to refuse to sign any petition in favor of such convocation, if any be presented, whatever may be the penalties or threats they may have to bear on this account,

Warns any members of Parliament who may disregard this notice that they will be fully answerable to the nation on its liberation.

WARNING TO THE ASSASSINS IN THE "MILICE" AND THE P.P.F., MERCENARIES OF THE ENEMY

Numbers, strength, the future are all on our side. There is not a reasonable Frenchman who does not know this. In every aspect of its struggle, the Resistance has the complicity of the entire nation.

As for you, mercenaries of the enemy, MILICIENS, P.P.F. and others, you are not even an ordinary minority, but a gang without influence, though not without resources. You represent nothing, but you are sometimes in a position to do harm to your fellow Frenchmen—not to us who are members of secret organizations which you can never touch, but to innocent and unarmed people on whom you safely vent your impotent rage. In a number of towns the MILICIENS and the P.P.F. have struck down men who were not active in our ranks, but who, known simply as republicans and patriots, offered an easy mark.

But enough is enough. When a traitor falls, when a French purveyor of the GESTAPO is executed, France applauds. We shall not let the traitors retaliate by killing decent people who cannot defend themselves. For each new murder they commit, the MILICIENS and the P.P.F. can expect immediate and merciless reprisals. The MILICIENS and the P.P.F. are powerless to impede our victorious struggle. Yes, we know how to deal with them. They will not come out on top. And the Resistance has already shown how well it can avenge its fallen comrades.

To this whole miserable gang the French Resistance sends a warning which, from this instant, means business: "For an eye, both your eyes, and for a tooth, your whole mouthful!"

PART SIX

Martyrs . . . Assorted

"It Is Hard to Die"

The annals of the Resistance carry so many stories about decent people of so many sorts who were done to death that I have dug into the heap and grabbed up a few samples haphazard. Besides the Georges Mandels, the Decours, the Péris, the Blochs and their like, the famous ones, France had thousands of men and women who paid exactly the same price for the right not to blush.

In the autumn of 1944 the president of the National Association of Manufacturers came to Paris. On his return home he told the press that the rigors of the German occupation had been exaggerated—he had found the HÔTEL CRILLON very comfortable; the Germans had disturbed nothing there. The reader will note that Gloriod, the broadcaster from an illegal radio station mentioned in the text, was condemned to death by a council of war in the HÔTEL CRILLON. The Germans had not stripped the CRILLON —they had used it. This Mr. Babbitt evidently found magnanimous.

Henri Fertet, the sixteen-year-old boy who wrote his last letter at Besançon, had never learned the art of crisp understatement À LA NOEL COWARD. But then Coward was never in any danger of being shot. So we may forgive Henri for being a bit prolix. And if his handwriting did tremble, we may accept his excuse that he had only a stub of a pencil. He wrote one line worth remembering, anyway: "C'EST DUR QUAND MÊME DE MOURIR." Fertet belonged to an F.F.I. detachment named for Guy Moquet, a seventeen-year-old boy shot by the Germans at Nantes in October, 1941. Max Jacob was a strange little man whom some critics held *to be a great poet and others a great painter. The Germans killed him because, although a Catholic mystic, he had been born a Jew.*

Executions and Hangings

Défense de la France
July 5, 1943

A MARTYR FOR FRANCE

Gloriod, a volunteer in the Air Force at the beginning of the war, was arrested March 23, 1942, in the suburbs of Paris for having participated in secret radio broadcasts.

He was kept in solitary confinement for nine months; underwent privations that reduced him to a frightful physical condition. Condemned to death by the court martial, at the HÔTEL CRILLON on April 6, 1942.

He was executed at the age of twenty-three on May 13, 1943, at 3 o'clock in the afternoon, along with eleven other patriots.

Frenchmen! That is what is going on in France and you do not know it.

Libération, Edition Zone Nord
October 19, 1943

THE EXECUTION AT BESANÇON

On the 18th of September the military court of the FELDKOM-MANDANTUR, No. 560, of Besançon, condemned to death fourteen young Frenchmen and two Spaniards, accused of "terrorist activities."

On the morning of September 26, these sixteen victims of Nazi fury were executed at Besançon.

The following letter was written by the youngest of these heroes, Henri Fertet, age sixteen. Henri was born at Senoncourt, Doubs, baptized August 15, 1927, in the Church of Saint-Victor, arrested July 7, 1943, at Besançon-Velotte, condemned to death the 18th of September, shot the 26th of September, along with fifteen of his comrades, and buried the same day (eight to a grave) in the cemetery of Saint-Ferjoux:

"My dear Parents:

"This letter is going to cause you a great deal of pain, but you have been so brave that I am sure that you will try to keep up your courage, if only for my sake.

"I cannot tell you what moral suffering it has been for me not to be able to see you, not to feel your tenderness about me, if only from a distance. During these eighty-seven days in prison, I have missed your love more than your packages and often I have asked you to pardon me for all the grief that I have caused you. You cannot have any idea how much I love you today. For before this, I used to love you as a matter of course. But now I understand all that you have done for me. I think that I have come to feel a true, a sincere filial love. Perhaps after the war one of my comrades will talk to you about me and will tell you how much I spoke of my love for you. I hope that he will not fail to carry out this sacred trust.

"Thank all the people who have taken an interest in me and particularly our near relatives and friends. Tell them of my faith in eternal France. Give my very best love to my grandparents, my uncles, aunts and cousins.

"I thank Monseigneur for the great honor that he has done me, an honor of which I hope that I have shown myself worthy. With these last words, I also send my greetings to my schoolmates at the LYCÉE. Which reminds me, A. owes me a package of cigarettes and J. has my book on the prehistoric man. Give the COUNT OF MONTE CRISTO back to E., and give Maurice A. forty grams of tobacco that I owe him.

"I die for my country. I want France to be free and Frenchmen to be happy. Not a proud France, the first nation of the world, but an earnest, hardworking and honest France. That the French be happy, this is what counts. In this world one must take one's happiness where one can.

"As for me, you need have no worry. I shall keep up my courage and good spirits to the end, and I shall sing the 'SAMBRE ET MEUSE,' because it is you, my dear mama, who taught it to me.

The soldiers are coming to get me. I must hurry. My writing may be shaky, but it is because I have only a little stub of a pencil. I am not afraid of death. My conscience is so clear.

"Papa, I beg you, remember that if I die, it is all for the best. What more honorable death could I have? I am dying voluntarily for my country. We shall meet soon, all four of us, in heaven.

"Good-bye, death calls me. I shall ask to be neither blindfolded nor tied to the stake. I embrace you all. Just the same it is hard to die. All my kisses.

"VIVE LA FRANCE!

> Henri Fertet
> Condemned to death at sixteen!"

> Libération
> April 7, 1944

THE DEATH OF MAX JACOB

We announced the arrest of Max Jacob by the GESTAPO some time ago.

Although of Jewish origin, Max (as all his friends, young and old, called him) was rather sensationally converted many years ago to militant Catholicism. So much so that the founder of the "Order of the Pink Jersey Penitents" had practically withdrawn from the world to make a prolonged retreat at the ancient monastery of Saint-Benoît-sur-Loire. His friends had found it difficult to take seriously the conversion of this past master of burlesque caricature, lover of mystification, professional cabalist and inventor of cubism in literature. Max let them have their fun, but so ordered his life as to accord his duty toward God with an unquenchable sense of humor. Old and sick, he had given up writing.

Learning that he had been arrested and sent to Drancy, his friends took alarm. Jean Cocteau and André Salmon, who are on good terms with the gentlemen in green helmets, tried to use their influence. It is even rumored that the elegant Monsieur Cocteau, athirst for martyrdom, went so far as to offer up his tender person as a substitute for the prisoner. Having failed to move the occupational authorities, the two poets went to Drancy and attempted to see Max.

They were brutally informed that "the Jew Jacob" had been dead for a week.

L'Humanité
March 1, 1944

HEROES' DEATHS

On October 15, 1943, Comrade Pierre Moulié, age fifty-two, died heroically, murdered by the Germans. This comrade, one of the earliest members of the Communist Party, was municipal councilor of Ivry and secretary of the Republican Veterans' Association.

Obliged to flee to the Corrèze to avoid arrest, he consecrated himself to the common cause by training young men for the difficult task that lies ahead and giving them the benefit of the advice and friendship of a veteran of the first World War, in which he had won the MÉDAILLE MILITAIRE and the CROIX DE GUERRE with fourteen citations. He was their leader and almost a father to them. With him in the MAQUIS were seventy young men who had refused to work for Hitler. They lived in two isolated abandoned farms.

Our comrades were denounced. On November 14 the village was surrounded. The following morning at five o'clock the attack took place. Our comrades were armed and barricaded themselves in one of the houses. The battle raged for an hour. Finally the Germans set fire to the house, and our comrades, having exhausted their ammunition, took flight.

Comrade Moulié, wounded in the shoulder, tried to escape. One of the Germans pursued him and killed him with a bullet in the head and a bayonet wound in the abdomen.

Seventeen of our comrades went down fighting at his side. The wounded were shamelessly finished off with bayonets, boots and rifle butts.

The town of Donzenac gave a public funeral to our eighteen comrades who died like heroes for having refused to accept Hitlerian barbarism for their country. The population gathered to pay its solemn last tribute to these patriots. Two thousand persons followed their bodies to the cemetery of Donzenac, where lies our comrade Moulié, mourned by all who knew him.

Eighty out of two hundred Germans were killed in this one-sided battle by our comrades, who deserve our gratitude and admiration.

It is our duty to avenge them!

Such are the pure and noble heroes that the traitors of Vichy are trying to besmirch, but the people of France are with those who fight for the liberation of France against those who have sold out to the BOCHES.

Les Lettres Françaises

HANGINGS AT NÎMES

by Jean Paulhan

Fifty boys of the MAQUIS in the Cévennes went by truck to Aigoual, where they hoped to establish a camp. They spent the morning looking over the location and making their plans. About two o'clock in the afternoon they were ready to leave. But fifteen of them, who lived at Saint-Hippolyte-du-Fort, decided to stop off on the way to see their families. They telephoned to the post office of Saint-Hippolyte. "Are there any Germans in the neighborhood?"

"Not a one," the postal employee replied. But another employee, who had overheard the conversation, alerted the German garrison of Sauve. When the trucks arrived, an hour and a half later, they fell into an ambush. The MAQUIS put up a fight, killing two Germans and losing five of their own men. Then they scattered out among the houses of the lower town. It was then that the man-hunt began. More than two hundred Germans, who had arrived in the meanwhile, searched Saint-Hippolyte house by house. Twenty-one boys of the MAQUIS were captured. All of them were to be hanged at Nîmes three days later.

A friend of LES LETTRES FRANÇAISES was an eyewitness to the execution. The men were hanged from the bridge on the Lassalle road. One of them was so badly wounded that he had to be given two shots of morphine to enable him to walk. One of the ropes broke and the victim was shattered on the rocks in the dry river bed below. A sergeant finished him with a bullet in the nape of the neck. Then the body was hauled up to the bridge and hanged again.

The prefecture at Nîmes announced two days later that the German commander responsible for the execution had been degraded and executed. Nobody believed a word of it.

Increased resistance provoked a reaction in accord with the brutality of the Nazis and the panic of the collaborationists. The Germans abandoned the last pretense of conciliation or legality. Vichy, which at its best had been a subsidiary of the German Foreign Office, now became simply an adjunct to the GESTAPO. The old Marshal had long since been relegated to the background; now Laval himself lost the favor of the occupant. The Germans even suspected him, quite correctly, of planning to turn his coat and make a deal with the Allies. Neither he nor they could understand that this was now impossible.

After all Sir Samuel Hoare, who had compacted with him in 1935 to abandon Ethiopia to Fascist Italy, was still a great man in the Foreign Office. And the American publishers and bankers who got their views of France through René de Chambrun, Laval's son-in-law, were still influential in Washington. But these erstwhile friends were having none of him. The time was not auspicious. The dirty-looking little man must have felt like a sporting girl whose Saturday night customers cut her in church Sunday morning.

The power, which was simply Hitler's commission to kill and torture, had fallen into the hands of Joseph Darnand, Jacques Doriot and the sinister mouthpiece Henriot, pathological traitors all. Darnand, chief of the militia, was a pre-war CAGOULARD, a member of a fascist conspiracy to seize power by violence. Doriot, who had begun as a Communist, like some of our own red-baiters, had swung half-circle and founded a party of repression, the PARTI POPULAIRE FRANÇAIS or P.P.F. Like the National Socialist Party in Germany, the P.P.F. maintained a kind of double-talk MYS-TIQUE, professing to be the friend of the workers at the same time as the paid tool of the industrialists. There were even P.P.F. "labor unions."

In 1936 Miss Janet Flanner, then (and now) European cor-respondent of THE NEW YORKER, had predicted that Doriot would be dictator of France in the fall. But the voters, less gullible than she believed, elected the Popular Front Government of Léon Blum. The rest of Doriot's life was to be devoted to revenge on the masses who had rejected him.

The pieces that follow can be grouped under the heading of "Repression" or more exactly "Attempted Repression." The first is my one and only attempt to report on a massacre. It was retro-spective reporting, but it made the repression slightly more real to me. The gap between our common experience and the sordid savagery of Ascq is too great to cross at a bound. Comblanchien, read first, may help to make Ascq credible.

The Comblanchien Massacres *

The helpless are killed by frightened men. The Militia and the Germans, in the summer of 1944, knew that retribution clutched at their shoulder. So they struck sometimes reflexively, as Bill Sykes, haunted by his crime, struck out at shadows. The one massacre I had a chance to investigate in the fall of that year turned out to have been of that sort, rather than a systematic slaughter like the one at Ascq.

In order to get to Comblanchien in the Department of the Côte d'Or, where it happened, I had to go through ten days of

* Permission The New Yorker, copyright 1945. The F-R. Publishing Corporation.

conspiracy, frustration and bedchamber intrigue at Paris. The last because the offices of the Army Public Relations Officers were in converted bedchambers of the HÔTEL SCRIBE.

It was a question of getting transportation to Comblanchien, a couple of hundred miles distant. The French War Crimes Commission, set up in a magnificent but unheated apartment on the Place Vendôme, was eager to assist me but had neither vehicles nor gasoline. The French Ministry of Information proffered an automobile and a driver, but had no gasoline either. Only the United States Army had gasoline.

SHAEF, Supreme Headquarters Allied Expeditionary Force, had only recently removed from London to Paris, and the officers attached to it considered themselves in the front lines. Gruffness and the military affectation are always encountered in direct proportion to the distance from the battlefield. The officers who lack combativity stay back willingly; the incompetents are sent back to join them. The military affectation is a defensive screen, a product of the fake officer's knowledge of his own insufficiency. The corridors of the SCRIBE harbored the most extraordinary collection of leadswingers and poodlefakers ever gathered outside of Hollywood. Their most conspicuous common trait was hostility toward the correspondents, whom they had been appointed to assist. Our existence was a humiliating reminder to them that they had a job; they preferred to think of themselves as delegates to an international convention of Rotary Clubs. A minority of well-meaning old-timers like Colonel Ernest Dupuy and the British Brigadier Turner seemed to be out-voted consistently.

PRO informed me that the Army was not interested in assisting an objective report on atrocities. At home the soft peace people were attacking the French reports of such butcheries as "more atrocity bunk, like in 1917." As far as the PRO was concerned, the pro-Nazis could continue these lies unchallenged.

I wanted thirty gallons of gasoline, and that conflicted with their need of all the gasoline in Paris to propel their automobiles up the hill of Montmartre. Their way of expressing this thought was "every drop of gasoline is needed for the combat forces." At the same time, as a later court-martial would prove, other behind-the-lines officers were peddling millions of gallons of gas to the black market.

For ten days, while the SHAEF heroes fought the battle of Montmartre, I remained immobilized like Patton at the gates of Metz. He had no gasoline either. I heard afterward that several of the officers concerned received Bronze Stars for fouling things up more than usual. I can think of no other reason they should have got them. Finally I chanced to meet Lieutenant Colonel Max Boyd, whom I had known in North Africa. He was press agent for the Eighth Air Force, with which I had no connection (the SHAEF dodoes were supposed to service me) but he gave me the gas as soon as I told him what I wanted. And so the expedition to Comblanchien and the following stories became possible.

The automobile provided by the Ministry of Information was a Delage, a big car that ate gasoline twice as fast as a jeep. It was the only one the ministry possessed that had four viable tires. The driver, a naturalized Belgian with a prognathous face, lived near the Place de la République in Paris. He had a habit of recounting the fighting in the Place de la République every time we stopped for a glass of wine, which was often, since we soon got into a wine country. "ÇA RATATINAIT!" he said each time. He wore a beret, carried a revolver and thought of himself as a romantic character.

The War Crimes Commission had sent along a photographer, a man with a withered arm and an ascetic face. He told me that he was used to driving his own car and was always nervous when anybody else was driving. During most of the trip he sat tense on the edge of the back seat. He considered the driver vulgar. The driver thought him pretentious. They argued continually. Both came equipped with empty bags and baskets, and at each stop they went foraging among peasants or village storekeepers, returning with cheese, wine, sausages, or in default of anything else, hazelnuts. I could not blame them. Both had children, and in Paris nourishment was scarce. But we got to where we were going.

The commune of Comblanchien, in the Department of the Côte d'Or, lies on the stretch of the national highway that runs between Lyon, to the south, and Dijon, to the north. Comblanchien is six miles north of Beaune and three miles south of Nuits-Saint-Georges, in the Burgundy wine country. The commune has an area of a thousand acres; most of them are on the eastern side of the highway, falling away gently toward the railway that parallels the road at a distance of half a mile and forms Comblanchien's eastern boundary. A narrower strip of the village lies west of the highway, and in this direction the ground slopes up and more abruptly. A hundred feet above the road on this side there is a big, box-like, gray-and-white building which the people of the countryside call a château but which looks more like an old-fashioned American summer-resort hotel. From a small cupola on the roof of this building there is an excellent view of the surrounding country. The thousand acres are, except for a few fields of cabbages and sugar beets and the open mouths of four or five granite quarries, fairly well covered with grapevines, as one might expect in this region. The Comblanchien granite has more than a local reputation and when transportation was available it was sent as far away as Paris. The wines of Comblanchien are classed mong the Côte de Nuits, but they are a secondary CRU and have no such fame as those of Vosne-Romanée and Vougeot, both near-by communes. The wines bring good prices but not the extravagant sums that make the heir to a few acres in one of those more favored communities a rich man by birth.

The village had five hundred and twenty inhabitants according to the last pre-war census, but it has rather fewer now. None of them are what the French call "rich rich," but a few are comfortably off. The proprietors of the Comblanchien vineyards work with their hands, like their hired help. The stone quarries are owned by outside companies and worked by employees who get modest wages. What distinguishes Comblanchien from other communities in the region is the burned-out shells of its houses.

There are perhaps a hundred houses in Comblanchien. About fifty of them are strung out along the highway; the rest are either scattered or grouped in clumps of two or three among the vineyards and fields that extend from the highway down to the railroad. Forty of the fifty on the highway are now in ruins. One of the town's three cafés and one of its three general stores have survived. Its one church is burned out, and so is the post office.

The part of the community back among the vines and fields has suffered less; there are about a dozen charred ruins here and there. At one side of the road, as you come into town from the north, you see a rude sign that says, "Honor to all our liberators, who will avenge the martyrs of our dear village. Long live Comblanchien! Long live France! Long live De Gaulle!"

"The events at Comblanchien" or the "things that happened at Comblanchien," as they are usually called by the people of the countryside, have some of the elements of a mystery story. Around nine-thirty on the night of August 21, 1944, about two weeks before the liberation of the region, some German soldiers disembarked from a troop train that had halted in the village and, together with the Germans from other detachments in the vicinity, set fire to many of the houses, after killing all the miserable people they caught in them. Most of the other inhabitants of Comblanchien had hidden in the vineyards, and toward morning the Germans went away. The German authorities never offered any explanation of the attack, and the mayor of Comblanchien, a timid man, never asked for any.

There was nothing to stop the Germans from coming back and completing the massacre by daylight, but they didn't. The people of Comblanchien continued to work in the vinyards by day and sleep there at night until the region was liberated. Then Monsieur Jordan, a sergeant of the gendarmes in Corgoloin, a village near Comblanchien, started an investigation to establish what had happened. Comblanchien has no GENDARMERIE of its own, because it is not large enough; it has only a GARDE-CHAMPÊTRE, or constable. Jordan, who was in the MAQUIS, had been hiding in the vineyards on the night of the attack. He came out of his hiding place when he saw the fires and, slipping around among the Germans, he heard them crying, "HUNDE! SCHWEINE! TERRORISTEN! HUNDE!" "I think it was because they were so frightened," he said afterward. "It is unimaginable how frightened they were." He has not been able to discover any other motive for the massacre.

Comblanchien, for four years after the Germans marched into Burgundy, in June, 1940, was without a history, but it was not happy. Like thousands of other communities in France, it had an unending premonition of outrage. All through the land, fear was the most nearly intolerable feature of the occupation. France was a kidnapped country; the kidnapper might let her live in a locked room, but when rescue seemed at hand the kidnapper might try to kill her. Everyone had the feeling that the Germans might arrest or kill anybody, at any time, for no reason that would make sense to a civilized man. Materially, life was difficult. In Comblanchien there was more food than in a big city, but only the farmers really had enough. The quarry workers earned seven francs an hour, but the purchasing power of the franc had almost vanished, so textiles and matches and tools and clothing and tea and coffee, which came from outside Comblanchien, cost incredible amounts. These workers, who had only little patches of ground in which to grow things, could raise just a few vegetables and rabbits and chickens. They ate the vegetables and bartered their chickens and eggs and rabbits for such treasures as spools of thread to repair their clothes, or bits of leather with which the Comblanchien cobbler could patch their shoes. They seldom got meat and, though they lived in a wine-growing district, they rarely could afford to drink wine. The vineyard workers were in much the same predicament.

Many couples in Comblanchien serve both the regional industries; the husband works in a quarry and the wife works in the vineyards. The commune owns some woods, and on Sunday the laborers of Comblanchien would cut enough firewood to last them the week. The buses which ran along the highway were infrequent and overcrowded; the men and women who were employed in other villages of the region couldn't be sure that they could ride to work. Only the relatively well-off owned bicycles, so people often walked five or six miles to work every day and back again at night, hurrying to get home before the nine-thirty curfew the Germans had imposed. There was not much chance for the people of Comblanchien to do any poaching; the Germans had attempted to confiscate all the sporting guns in the region, and the peasants who had defied the order to disarm and had retained their weapons kept them carefully hidden against the day they would have something more important than partridges to shoot. Besides, the German soldiers, who were always underfed, killed most of the game in the country. They shot at anything edible and even dynamited streams and fish ponds.

There were, it is true, some residents of Comblanchien upon whom the German occupation imposed no material privations. These were the dozen or so well-to-do farmers who were getting such high prices in Dijon that they were accumulating great wads of banknotes, although in a currency that shrank in value every day. But even they felt the oppression of something worse than want. The mere presence of Germans made everyone feel subhuman. The sound of German voices filled the farmers with a MALAISE, like the sound of rats scurrying within the walls of a house. The Mayor, Monsieur Moron, was the wealthiest man of the commune. He owned a large pink building on the west side of the road, where he made and stored wine, and a good solid stone house on the east side of the road, where he lived. He was a tall, rather good-looking man, but no hero. "PAS D'HISTOIRES" was his motto, which might be freely interpreted to mean "For God's sake, no trouble." Moron is a common surname in Burgundy and has no pejorative connotation.

The next wealthiest citizen was the deputy mayor and president of the communal council, Monsieur Chopin. Chopin is also a Burgundian name. Chopin is a good solid chunk of a man with a bull neck and a strong, big-barreled body like that of one of his prize plow horses. Both men regarded the Germans with a mixture of apprehension and dislike, the first sentiment dominating in Monsieur Moron and the second in the more choleric Chopin.

One person in Comblanchien who did not seem to mind the presence of the Germans overmuch was Robert Ravigneaux, a café proprietor, whose bar was often filled with German soldiers who traveled the national highway in convoys by night and stopped at Comblanchien to drink. Ravigneaux overcharged them for their drinks, and he told the townspeople that this was his form of resistance. The convoys didn't travel by day, because they were afraid of an Allied air attack. But even with their limited hours, they always seemed to have time to stop for refreshments, and there were no German equivalents of the "Off Limits" sign posted on the roadside cafés. Ravigneaux was a noisy, quarrelsome fellow who was not a native of the region—he had come to Comblanchien from the northeast of France five years before the war. He had an artificial left leg which was painted a pale flesh pink and on which he wore a sock and garter, just as he did on his other leg. When he got drunk, he would pull up the trouser of his amputated leg, slap the painted wood, and tell people that he had lost his leg in the last war, although everybody in Comblanchien knew that in 1944 he was only thirty-nine. Ravigneaux was drunk much of the time; it was his handsome, full-bosomed wife who watched the cash.

From time to time after the surrender of France, German soldiers were stationed in Comblanchien, in the Occupied Zone, and then withdrawn. In May, 1944, a new detachment arrived and moved into the château. This unit was known in Comblanchien as the Schoning Company, because it was commanded by OBER-LEUTNANT Schoning, a naval reservist who in civil life had been an architect in Kiel. The men under him were Marines. The Germans had found little for their Marine Corps to do aboard a portbound navy, so they had assigned detachments from it to various duties all over Europe. Schoning had about fifty men. Their job was to patrol the area, and chiefly the railroad, between Beaune and Nuits-Saint-Georges, to guard against sabotage.

The OBERLEUTNANT was not much of a warrior. He was forty— just too young to have fought in the other war and just too old to have received any concentrated military training in the Nazi ré-gime. He lived in fear that "terrorists" would attack the château, although the region is not really adapted to serious guerrilla war-fare; it is too well cultivated and thickly inhabited. The vineyards would make excellent cover for a few snipers, but men cannot lie flat on their bellies forever. Schoning had been taken in by the Reich's propaganda. He saw terrorists everywhere. Soon after he arrived, he issued an order that every one of his men must learn to operate a field telephone so he could call the FELDGENDARMERIE at Beaune immediately if the château were attacked. "The lives of each and all of us may depend on his comrades' presence of mind," Schoning's order read.

What he lacked as a fighting man he made up for by abnormal arrogance. This sort of over-compensation, as I have explained, is not confined to the German Army. He snarled and shouted constantly. Also, he never appeared outside the château without a machine pistol under his arm. As a joke, he invariably poked this weapon in Madame Ravigneaux's face when he visited the café. He was there often; he was an alcoholic, like Ravigneaux, himself a snarling man. There was something congenial to Schoning in the other disagreeable presence, although Schoning spoke no French and neither Ravigneaux nor his wife knew any German. The OBERLEUTNANT's ignorance of French increased his suspicion of the citizenry. If anybody in Comblanchien laughed within his hearing, he was sure a joke had been made about him, and he would order the interpreter in his company, an Alsatian named Paul Zenses, to translate what had been said. Zenses had been drafted into the German Marines after the Nazis had "incorporated" Alsace and Lorraine into the Reich, in November, 1940. When Schoning was not with him, the Alsatian was on friendly terms with some of the local people. However, Schoning communicated his edginess to the rest of his men, and the groups that patrolled the railroad frequently fired at animals or shadows, thinking they were MAQUISARDS. People got used to hearing bursts of fire at night and thought nothing of them.

There had never been any special reason Schoning should fear an attack or the people of Comblanchien should have been subjected to any unusual repressive measures. There had been no acts of resistance in Comblanchien since the beginning of the occupation, although a number of the men there belonged to MAQUIS groups that operated elsewhere in the region. Some of these men had joined a group that had been establishd in a near-by district immediately after D-day, when General Koenig, in London, had called all the French Forces of the Interior to rise in active resistance. But after these orders had been countermanded, the Comblanchien men had returned to their homes, with the exception of two who had got themselves shot.

Now the local MAQUIS affair had apparently blown over, and anyhow everybody was too busy in the vineyards and fields to worry about it. Protracted panic is a luxury beyond the means of working people. If the local Germans had wanted to make trouble, however, an opportunity lay at hand. All the men who had been in the MAQUIS could be distinguished by the new shoes that the Resistance organization had distributed to them. The shoes were of army issue and had been hidden from the Germans when the French military were officially disbanded, in 1942. The shoes were too good to give up, even if they did identify the wearers as men subject to the death penalty. Jordan used to go about telling the youths to stain their shoes and scuff them. But the Germans in the château were too stupid to notice such things, the men figured.

By late August the inhabitants of Comblanchien had almost forgotten the affair of the MAQUISARDS, except for the young blowhards, who sometimes drank and boasted about the feats they claimed they had brought off. The GARDE-CHAMPÊTRE of Comblanchien, who is not precisely Hercule Poirot, had been in the MAQUIS too, and he was soon going about telling people he had killed five Germans, which was, to put it mildly, inexact.

Even Monsieur Moron breathed easy. He had been summoned to the château to talk to Schoning three times, and each time he had gone in the fear that he would be held as a hostage. On the first occasion, Schoning had merely wanted to tell him that the water supply at the château was inadequate and that he would have to send a hogshead of water up the hill to him every day. The second time Schoning wanted to complain that the water had not been delivered promptly one morning. Schoning had been exceedingly nasty about it and had shouted even louder than usual. The third time Schoning was furious because a woman who had been doing housework for the Germans refused to come any more. She said she was sick, but the mayor suspected that her husband, who worked in a quarry, had told her to give up her job at the château. The other workmen had probably threatened him. Schoning had ordered the mayor to find a substitute, but he had been unable to find one. However, Monsieur Moron had not been bothered again.

There was a great deal of work to do late in August. Most families, taking advantage of the double daylight-saving time, worked in their gardens right up to the nine-thirty curfew before going indoors to begin their suppers. A minute or two after curfew on the evening of Monday, August 21, an hour easy to fix in the memory because the soup had just been put on everyone's table, a bell rang in the cottage of the watchman at the more southerly of the two grade crossings in the commune to warn of the approach of an unexpected train from the south. This crossing, No. 191 on the railway maps, is something less than a mile from the other, No. 190, and between them the rails run through a shallow cut. The passing of an unscheduled train was not unusual. The Germans had been using the railroad to move troops and matériel up toward Normandy. This sort of activity had increased since the Allied landings in the Midi on August 15, because the Germans were systematically withdrawing from the South of France, evacuating base units as well as fighting troops.

The watchman at No. 191 was, and is, Louis Maublanc, a youth of nineteen, who lives in the cottage with his widowed mother and a swarm of small brothers and sisters. A moment after the bell rang, Maublanc went out to close the swing gates of the crossing. He went over the track to close the farther gate and had just got back on his own side of the track when the train came along. It was a long train, he remembers—perhaps fifty cattle-cars, filled with troops. French railroad cars are small, but even figuring only forty men in each, there were two thousand soldiers. They were carrying rifles, tommy-guns, and machine guns. The engine stopped on the crossing. Some officers got out of the cars, walked up to the locomotive, and spoke to the engineer. Maublanc says that he heard the man shout something about Comblanchien, so the officers had probably asked where they were.

There is a story in the countryside that the train was deliberately stopped at Comblanchien, but that is not true. The train stopped at Comblanchien because there was another train on the track at Nuits-Saint-Georges, three miles north. Many of the men in the cars were drunk and were singing and howling at each other. It is hard to tell when German soldiers are angry, the French say, because they are always howling anyway. The cars must have been well stocked with wine—the right of way where the train had stopped was littered with empty bottles next day—and the non-commissioned officers aboard were taking no notice of all the drunkenness. This did not seem unusual to Maublanc. German soldiers heading north were never happy; they undoubtedly knew that things were going badly up there and that they might be killed. So they were generally drunk.

Dusk was coming on, but there was still enough light, Maublanc noted regretfully, to work by in the gardens, if he hadn't had to go indoors because of the curfew. He was looking toward the west, where the sunset colors were fading in the sky. Suddenly he saw a burst of tracer bullets flying from the western slope. At once the Germans in the train started shouting much more loudly than they had done before. Some of them began firing machine guns in the general direction the bullets had come from. Others piled out of the cars and flung themselves flat along the tracks. Twenty of them poured into the Maublancs' cottage and pointed machine pistols at the widow Maublanc and her little children. Other soldiers grabbed Maublanc by his arms and throat. In all the things being shouted at him, he could distinguish one word again and again—"TERRORISTEN!"—a word that even Frenchmen who speak no German understand.

Meanwhile, somebody gave an order and the train moved past the crossing and into the cut, whose embankment offered some protection from the fire from the slope. The train was so long that when it stopped the locomotive was almost at grade crossing No. 190. From the new position the machine gunners on the train laid down a real barrage. There was a volley of answering machine-gun fire from the west. Many villagers believe that the Germans attacked Comblanchien with malice aforethought and that they invented the story of the shots directed at the train. It has been established, however, that there actually was firing from the west. A few hundred yards west of the railroad line there is a poplar tree. When Jordan went over the ground, weeks later, he found bullets in both the east and west sides of the trunk and that many branches had been cut away from it. Lambert, the crossing watchman at No. 190, says that he saw five German soldiers on the train hit, but this testimony was impossible to check, because the train, when it did leave, carried away all the soldiers it had arrived with. Young Maublanc, who, like every other inhabitant of the region, knew that there was not a force of resistants within a hundred miles capable of attacking two thousand soldiers, was as puzzled as the Germans. The soldiers who had seized him finally flung him to the ground and left him there. Why they didn't kill him he doesn't know. As for his mother, she was so confused that she can recall almost nothing of what happened.

Nobody knows, and possibly nobody ever will know, who fired those first shots. Most probably, Jordan thinks, one of OBER-LEUTNANT Schoning's timorous, trigger-happy patrols let off a few rounds at a shadow in the vineyards, as the patrols often had before. It is known that two patrols were out when the shooting began. There is nothing to indicate that the first shots were aimed at the train or even came near it. The source of the heavier west-to-east fire which, a few minutes later, answered the barrage from the train is not mysterious. But what seems clearly to have been a coincidence, a German motor convoy had stopped on the national highway in Comblanchien at the same time the train halted at the first grade crossing. It consisted of a dozen vehicles, each manned by a driver and a helper. There may have been in the group a couple of VOLKSWAGEN carrying officers, and perhaps some trucks had aboard a few hitch-hiking soldiers, but in all there could not have been more than fifty men. However, some of the trucks had machine guns mounted for use against strafing airplanes. The men in the convoy were scattered among the cafés of Comblanchien when the soldiers on the train began firing toward the highway. The convoy men, in their turn, shouted "TERRORISTEN!" and ran to their machine guns. The fire was by now coming from two directions, most of it far overhead. Some of the convoy soldiers, therefore, fired to the east, toward the gunflashes they could see below them from the railroad; others fired west toward some flashes they saw.

OBERLEUTNANT Schoning, who was finishing his dinner in the château when the firing from the train started, was immediately frightened. "Terrorists have begun their attack on the château!" he shouted to Zenses, who has since told Jordan what happened in the château that night. No one else had heard, or at any rate paid attention to, the first few shots from the slope. It was the shooting from the east that made the first impression. The machine guns at the château immediately began firing in the direction of the supposed attack. It is not known whether the fire from the château or from the trucks was responsible for the casualties—

assuming there were any—on the train. The château was hit, but not many times. Jordan found a couple of bullet holes in it later, but it is not certain that OBERLEUTNANT Schoning even knew the house had been struck. Zenses, who was sure that an attack on the château was beyond the means of the local resistance, felt that there was a horrible misunderstanding of some sort. The fire from the château, he feared, might hit the innocent people of Comblanchien, and he thought that perhaps Schoning could avert a massacre. After a couple of minutes of the firing, which did not seem to be directed at the château, Zenses suggested to the OBER-LEUTNANT that he be sent with a patrol down to the village to see what was happening. "I will take a patrol down there myself," Schoning said. "You will come with us." It was a heroic decision for the ex-architect; his pride had prevailed. The OBERLEUTNANT and ten or fifteen of his men put on helmets, filled their belts with incendiary grenades, slung machine pistols over their shoulders, and went down to their usual destination, Ravigneaux's café.

Ravigneaux and his wife were in the café when the firing began. They heard the first burst and then the sustained fire. Some truck drivers from the convoy had been drinking there and they had run out without paying. That was all the Ravigneaux could tell Zenses. Schoning saw the convoy people firing from the trucks. There was still fire from the east, but it was going over their heads. Schoning said to Zenses, "There is some mistake, but I cannot do anything to stop it. You go back to the château. I have no more need for you." Zenses, before he went back to the château, paused in the village street and looked down toward the railroad, from which, he could readily see, many of the bullets were coming. It was now completely dark. As he looked across the vineyards, he saw a pillar of flame rise, halfway between the railroad and the highway, about where a peasant named Sergent lived. He realized even then that the Germans had begun to burn the village.

Max Henry was one of the most respected citizens of the Burgundian commune of Comblanchien. However, he had a hard time bringing up his family after the German occupation began. He was not a farmer but a salaried man, one of the few white-collar workers in the village, and he owned only the bit of ground surrounding his house. A man on a fixed salary was in a bad position, especially if he had to maintain appearances. Monsieur Henry had two grown children to educate—a twenty-year-old son, Claude, and a sixteen-year-old daughter, Denise. Both went to the college in Beaune, six miles south of Comblanchien, and they continued to go despite the occupation. By August, 1944, Claude had finished a course preparing him to be an officer in the merchant marine. He must have been an optimist to choose that career, as he did, shortly after the armistice with Germany, when the French merchant marine had almost ceased to exist. He was to go to Paris on September 20 to take his final examinations for a commission.

Monsieur Henry was a bookkeeper at the Comblanchien quarry of Civet, Pommier & Company of Paris, dealers in cut stone. He had worked for the company for twenty-five years, the last thirteen of them in Comblanchien. He was in his early forties. During the first year of the war he had been acting superintendent of the quarry, for a brief period, after the superintendent had been mobilized, in September, 1939. Then, in the spring of 1940, Monsieur Henry himself was mobilized and a rigger in the quarry was made temporary superintendent. After the demobilization, the company took Monsieur Henry back, but only as a bookkeeper, and kept the rigger on as nominal superintendent. The original superintendent, who had got a higher salary than Monsieur Henry had, was not rehired. Monsieur Henry had to take over all the correspondence, because the ex-rigger was uneducated. So Monsieur Henry was something more than bookkeeper, and his chief was something less than superintendent, and neither of them got a full superintendent's salary, which was probably the company's idea in the first place. Monsieur Henry was paid twenty-eight hundred francs a month. This would not have been lavish for a man with two children in school even if the franc had had its prewar value, but the franc had lost almost all its purchasing power. Fortunately, the Henrys had their house and chicken yard and vegetable garden and enough vines to provide them with family table wine, and Madame Henry was an excellent manager. She was a thin, worn-looking woman with high color in her cheeks and black hair drawn tight in a bun behind her head. She came from the Department of the Meuse, and her husband from Reims.

Madame was decidedly better educated than the farm women of the community, but she worked as hard as any of them, and Claude and Denise worked too, when they were home. Monsieur Henry was very tall and thin, so thin in proportion to his height that when he was a young man he had been excused from military service; in 1940 the army was less particular and he was mobilized as a private.

Monday, August 21, 1944, was a hot day, and Claude and Denise, who were home from college, went swimming in a stream with friends. One of the friends took a picture of Claude posed on a diving board. Madame Henry still has it. It shows a tall, long-legged boy with heavy eyebrows, a straight nose, and the French variant of the crew haircut. On the evening of August 21, until nine-thirty, when the curfew imposed by the Germans compelled everybody in Comblanchien to go indoors, the whole Henry family picked string beans in the garden. Because of double daylight-saving time, it was still light at curfew, but they had to go into the house just the same. They washed up (there was a bathroom in the Henry house, which was one of the most modern in the village) and sat down to supper. Like many of the buildings in the commune, the house fronted on the national highway, which ran through the village; it was on the east side of the thoroughfare. Monsieur Henry had built it himself in 1931. The exterior was of simulated graystone, an unconvincing concretish substance, and the house had six rooms, four on the ground floor and two in a kind of turret above. The front door was in the middle of the house and opened into a hall. Monsieur and Madame Henry's bedroom was at the right on the ground floor as you went in. Denise's bedroom was behind theirs. The dining room was on the left side as you entered, and the kitchen and bathroom were behind that. The staircase leading to the turret was in the hall, and a shorter flight of stairs in the back led down to the basement. Claude's bedroom was on the second floor, in back; at the front of the turret was a spare bedroom.

The family had begun supper in the dining room when, Madame Henry told me while I was in Comblanchien, they heard two shots which, she said, sounded "like a signal." The sounds did not alarm them, because the patrols frequently fired shots for trivial reasons; the idea that these shots were a signal was purely retro-spective. Then there was a real outbreak of shooting. It seemed to come from the southeast and it was so loud that all the Henrys dropped to the floor. This firing—though the Henrys did not know it—came from along the railroad line. Madame Henry remembers that as the family lay on the floor her husband pulled her away from the window. After a while there was a pause in the firing. Monsieur Henry, perhaps to reassure the others, said that there was no accounting for Germans; he was going to bed. He went into his bedroom and began to undress. Madame Henry followed him and sat down on the bed, but she was afraid to take her clothes off.

It happened that Claude Henry was a member of the FORCES FRANÇAISES DE L'INTÉRIEUR, and an effective one, but he had kept his activities so secret that not even his parents knew of them. He lived at home only during the college vacations and on week ends. He had helped in COUPS DE MAIN and acts of sabotage in parts of central France less accessible to the Germans than the Côte d'Or, in which Comblanchien is situated, and had organized Resistance groups in several villages. He had also tended a para-chute strip on which Allied planes dropped arms for the MAQUI-SARDS. Claude, driving an old truck, would pick up the weapons and distribute them to comrades.

When, on the night of August 21, his parents went to their bedroom, Claude went upstairs to his room, which faced east and south. Denise followed him after a couple of minutes. Look-ing out a window, they saw, through the gathering darkness, gun flashes down along the railroad, which was half a mile away, and then Claude pointed out to her what he said were groups of Germans moving up along the two roads that wound through the Comblanchien vineyards toward the village. Some of the men had flashlights, which they swung about as if they were looking for something. They stuck pretty well to the roads; the Germans were always timid about going into the vineyards, where, they fancied, the broad leaves might conceal snipers. Then Claude and Denise saw a house, midway between the railroad and the high-way, begin to burn. The flames rose very high in an instant; the Germans were using incendiary grenades, which are usually effective immediately. "They are coming this way!" Claude said, and he hurried Denise down into the basement, shouting to his parents to join them. Madame Henry hastened downstairs, but Monsieur Henry, the methodical, bookkeeping kind of man, stayed in his room to dress.

A moment later there was a great crash on the ground floor. Some of the Germans had hurled grenades through the window of the dining room, setting fire to the house, and others had fired machine pistols and automatic rifles through the front door, their favorite way of breaking a lock. The three in the cellar heard boots and gunstocks on the floor over their heads, and then they heard the soldiers shouting at Monseiur Henry. Claude, who had had six years of German at school and college, knew that the intruders were questioning his father. Claude also knew that his father did not understand a word of the language, so he ran up from the basement. His sister went up the basement steps behind him, but ran out the back door into the garden, where she threw herself down among the vines. Madame Henry remained in the basement, too frightened to move.

Before his son had appeared, Max Henry had come out into the hall from his bedroom, although he had not finished dressing. The Germans presumably pushed him back against the wall and poked the muzzles of their atuomatic weapons against his body. He must have waved his hands in protest; he must have heard again and again, without understanding, the German words for "concealed arms."

Denise, lying in the garden, saw the window of her brother's room, on the second floor, light up and Claude appear, followed by three or four Germans. He was gesticulating, evidently trying to convince them that there were no weapons concealed there, and he was talking fast. "He was talking the entire time I could see him," Denise told me when I was in Comblanchien. "Then they all went out of the room."

The house was already burning, and a minute later the flames mounted high in the sky. A dozen Germans ran out the front door, shouting and laughing. The night should have been growing darker rapidly, now, but there was still light in the village, because the Germans had set fire to a score of houses, and the highway was illuminated by the fires in the houses lining it. Neither Max nor Claude Henry came out of the house. Denise, cowering among the vines, heard her mother call her name. She called back, and Madame Henry crawled through the garden to her daughter's side. She had come up from the basement and out the back door the moment the Germans left the house. Flames were roaring in both the dining room and the bedroom at the front of the house, but they had not got into the hall between them, Denise said.

Madame Henry, who earlier in the evening had been the most timid member of the family, now found a courage that still astonishes her. "Claude and Papa must be in there," she said to her daughter. "Let us go in and find them." The two women went into the house through the back door. Max Henry lay in front of the door to his bedroom. His head had been severed from his body, apparently by a burst of machine-gun bullets. His blood puddled the floor of the little house he had built for his family. Claude Henry was lying at the foot of the staircase, his feet resting on one of the lower steps. He lay with his once handsome face among his brains. The Germans had probably killed Monsieur Henry while Claude was still frantically talking upstairs; Claude must still have hoped to save the elder Henry when Denise saw him in his room with the Germans. When Claude had reached a point on the stairs from which he could see his father's body, a German behind him had presumably shot him in the back of the neck with his revolver. Then another German, apparently, fired a redundant shot into the boy's head as he lay dead.

"We must put the bodies in the basement, where they will be preserved from fire," the mother said. The slight woman and the strong girl picked up the butchered bodies of their men—first the father and then the son—and carried them down into the basement. One of them must have made a third trip for Max Henry's head. The bodies were not touched by the fire and later received a proper burial. The women went outside again, but Madame Henry, acting as incomprehensibly as people often do in crises, said, "The fire hasn't caught upstairs yet; maybe we can save some bed coverings and a mattress. They will be almost impossible to replace." So they went in and got some blankets. The flames reached upstairs before they could make another trip for a mattress.

Madame Henry and her daughter lay in the garden all night. Houses were burning everywhere and there were intermittent bursts of gunfire. German soldiers passed back and forth on the highway a few yards from the two women, carrying things they had stolen from wrecked houses—quilts and chandeliers and chamber pots. They loaded them onto the dozen or so trucks of the convoy that had halted in the village that night. The magpie compulsion of a German soldier is hard to believe unless one has seen German trucks, overflowing with a ragman's treasure of miserable household wares, wrecked along a roadside after a strafing. .

The Henry house was one of a row of four on the highway that stood a little apart from the rest of the village. A woman named Gabut was in the house next to the Henrys', with her four children, when the enemy came. The Henry women heard her shrieking to the Germans not to kill her after her house had been set afire. She said afterward that she thought she had been spared because she had a crippled, subnormal child that could not stand up. A German pulled the child from its crib, and when the child fell to the floor he became interested in it. The crisis of blood lust past, he ran out of the house without killing the woman.

On the other side of Madame Gabut's house was the house of a man named Salomon, a Communist who had led the abortive MAQUISARD uprising near Comblanchien in June. Salomon had left the village some time ago, but his wife and her sister had lived in the house during most of the summer. This night, however, they, too, were away. It is logical that if this had been a premeditated punitive expedition against Comblanchien the Germans would have gone immediately to Salomon's house, since he was a known "terrorist." But they did not. The fourth house in the row was inhabited by a sixty-three-year-old man named Joseph Blanc, a retired postal employee living on a pension, and his wife and daughter. The Blancs, like their neighbors, must have trembled when they saw the Gabut and Henry dwellings burning. They ran to the basement of their house, but the Germans left them alone, at least for the moment.

Two widows, mother and daughter, who lived not far from the Henrys, but on the other side of the highway, were less fortunate. One of these women, Madame Chapuzot, the mother, was sixty-

eight. She worked in the vineyards when there was work for
her and made mattresses at home when there was none. Her
daughter, Madame Voye, was forty-six, a cheerful, hard-working
woman who hoed in the vineyards, did housework, and washed
bottles for the wine merchants whenever she had a chance. The
Henry women heard these two widows shrieking and begging the
Germans to spare them, but the soldiers killed them both. It is
hard to imagine that the Germans thought the two women dangerous. They were killing now simply because they had had a taste
of blood, like weasels loose in a chicken yard.

At a farm in the commune they killed a young farm laborer
named Marcel Julien. He was a pleasant, uneducated boy of
eighteen who, unlike many Frenchmen of his age, had never been
in the MAQUIS or done anything untoward. The Germans spared
the other men on the farm, however. Their choice of victims that
night was entirely capricious. The men who saw Julien killed say
the German who shot him was wearing shorts and an undershirt,
carried a carbine, and was "slobbering" with fury. This led the
people who later tried to reconstruct the massacre to think that
this particular murderer must have come from the German truck
convoy and not the troop train. German Army truck drivers were
known to discard their outer clothes in hot weather. After some
of the soldiers from the train had reached the national highway
and encountered the men from the truck convoy, who numbered
about fifty, both parties must have realized that they had been
firing at each other and not at an attack by what they called
TERRORISTEN. At any rate, the exchange of shots between the two
groups ceased. The killing and burning, however, went on un-
interrupted. In fact, it was now on a partnership basis. Some of
the inhabitants of Comblanchien say that they recognized, among
the soldiers attacking the houses, several of the Marines in OBER-
LEUTNANT Schoning's detachment, but identifications in such circumstances are undependable. It is certain, however, that at
eleven-thirty, an hour and a half after the murder of the two
Henrys and the two widows, a band of Germans went to the Salomon house and began shouting for the "terrorist women" to come
out. They must have meant Salomon's wife and sister-in-law, and
this indicates to Monsieur Jordan, the gendarme, that officers

from the troop train must have made contact with Schoning sometime between ten and eleven-thirty and asked him to point out the houses of people he suspected of "terrorism." In the absence of the Salomon women, the Germans set fire to the house and then went on to Blanc's, next door. They demanded that Blanc hand over the women, whom they said he was sheltering. The old man shook his head helplessly, and they shot him to death. They also fired at and wounded his wife and daughter, but the women escaped and managed to hide in the vineyards.

Monsieur and Madame Blaise Lieutard were a couple of retired railroad employees who had built themselves a house not far from the Henrys', fifty yards back from the road. They had lived in Comblanchien nine years. They had both worked in the GARE DE LYON, in Paris, for thirty years, he as an electrician and she as a messenger in the railway offices, and they had a joint pension of a thousand francs a month. The Lieutards had come to Comblanchien after their retirement because Madame Lieutard's sister, Madame Gauthron, lived there and Madame Lieutard wanted to be near her. Madame Gauthron was the village dressmaker and was married to a stonecutter in one of the quarries. Monsieur Lieutard was a wiry little southern Frenchman of sixty, but, as his wife says when recounting her story of the dreadful night, "he looked older because he had had so much trouble." In Comblanchien the Lieutards had practiced severe economies, like all French couples of their type, who save throughout their working lives for the house they will build when they reach the pension age. Their pink stucco house—four rooms and a kitchen—might have seemed exiguous and jerry-built even to a promoter of Long Island building developments, but to Madame Lieutard it was the fulfillment of a lifetime's hopes. She is a short woman with a broad, flat face and straggly, faded blond hair. Her eyes are blue-white and she has stubby little hands and feet; she could not have been pretty even when she was young, but her face, when she talked of the past glories of the little house, was radiant. On the ground floor there were two rooms and a storage "cellar." There was no inside staircase; to get to the second floor you walked up stone stairs on the outside of the house. The Lieutards had what Madame Lieutard called a LOUIS QUINZE bedroom, on which they had spent twenty thousand francs. In a corner of this room, and in a corner of the living room, which adjoined it, there were green-enameled fireplaces. In the kitchen was a magnificent green metal salamander for heating water and a sink into which water ran from a long, convoluted pipe about as thick as a strand of macaroni. They had fine curtains on all the windows, and two overstuffed chairs which would have attracted attention in the window of any furniture store on the outer boulevards of Paris. Madame was in despair when she thought of it. They were very comfortably off before the war, when the franc still had some value. Besides their pension, they had the usual chicken yard and garden and cages of fat rabbits, which were a joy as well as an auxiliary source of nourishment. Like all rustic French workers who have had to live in the city for a long time, they took immense pleasure in their return to the country. They had but one cause for anxiety: their only daughter, a Madame Pascal, was a widow, her husband having died shortly after the Lieutards retired. She had two children, a boy and a girl. Her husband had left her no money and she had had to go back to her old job in the material office in the GARE DE LYON. Her parents, however, were able to help her out now and then with a few hundred francs or a fine hamper of country CHARCUTERIE.

Living conditions did not become difficult for the Lieutards until after the armistice. Under the Germans, it was impossible for them to live on their pension and send anything to their daughter and her children, so Monsieur Lieutard went back to work, as chief electrician at the railroad station in Beaune. His salary was seventeen hundred francs a month, but his pension stopped, since he was now working again, so his income was only seven hundred francs a month more than it had been. Monsieur Lieutard had no bicycle and could not afford to buy one, so he walked the six miles to Beaune and back every day. "And he had slightly flat feet," Madame Lieutard recalls. Walking made him very hungry, but food was even more expensive in Beaune than in Comblanchien, so he had to eat in the workmen's restaurant there. It served nothing but vegetables and noodles, and all the cooking was à L'EAU, which is repugnant to most Frenchmen, who believe that boiling takes all the nourishment out of food. When he got home at night, he was sometimes so hungry that there were tears in his eyes. He often ate bread with mustard on it, for lack meat. When the chickens laid, the Lieutards had to barter the eggs for thread or salt or other necessities they could not afford to buy, and when they killed a chicken it went into the package they sent to Paris every week for their grandchildren. Sometimes Monsieur Lieutard did not dare look at the rabbits, for fear he would be impelled to kill one and stew it, and thus enrage his wife. Cigarettes were of course beyond his means, so he planted a little tobacco in the garden. He had heard that it should be dried in the sun, but he never had the patience to wait; he would put the green leaves on the stove and try to toast them dry, so that he could smoke them immediately. Early in 1944, the Lieutards' daughter, who had saved up some money, decided that it would be easier to feed and lodge the children in the country than in Paris, even without her job, so she came to join her parents and brought the children with her. The girl was fifteen, the boy thirteen. She confided her savings—twenty-five thousand francs— to her mother for safekeeping. Madame Lieutard hid the money in one of her overstuffed chairs, one that had cost three thousand francs. The Lieutards were happy to have their daughter and her children with them. Madame Pascal helped her aunt, Madame Gauthron, with the dressmaking, and the children went to school. It was no longer necessary to send packages to Paris, so Monsieur Lieutard got a taste of meat once in a while now. During the summer the old electrician watched the German troop trains that passed through the station in Beaune and drew his own conclusions about how the war was going for "CES MESSIEURS." He talked to the train crews, who told him about air bombardments and sabotage along the line. He became optimistic, and used to say to his wife, "When this is over, we will offer ourselves a nice faceful of food and then we will repaint the house."

When Lieutard heard the firing begin on the night of August 21, he summoned his family into the storage "cellar," a windowless part of the ground floor. The women were in their slips—they slept together upstairs, while Lieutard, exiled from his LOUIS QUINZE room, shared a room on the ground floor with his grandson. "It was a genteel little room with green walls and folding beds," Madame Lieutard says with infinite regret. The Germans ran up to the house and entered it. The Lieutards and Pascals slipped unnoticed out the back door of the "cellar" and into the garden, but there they were trapped, for they were fenced in by chicken wire except at the front of the house, and if they went out that way, they would run into the Germans. Monsieur Lieutard tried to tear his way through the wire at the side of the house. A German soldier, coming from Madame Lieutard does not know where, turned a flashlight on him. Madame Lieutard, Madame Pascal, and the two children took refuge behind a hen coop and lay flat on their bellies. Madame Pascal's legs are long and her feet extended beyond the shelter. It was mere chance that the German didn't see them. Monsieur Lieutard turned toward the light and said, in a faint voice, "QU'EST CE QUE C'EST?" "He sounded as if his throat was stopped up, my little man," Madame Lieutard says. The German fired—an explosive bullet that went in at Lieutard's right collarbone and came out the middle of his back, leaving an opening as big as a saucer. The inoffensive little man crumpled on the bit of garden earth he had spaded up so many times in the past nine years. "He bled! he bled!" Madame Lieutard says. "He had planted celery on that spot, but he bled so much the celery never came up. They killed him like a wild boar." Madame Lieutard's comparison seemed to accentuate the difference rather than the similarity between poor Blaise Lieutard and a savage beast. The German leaned over the stricken man and put his weapon to the victim's head and blew it to bits. Then he went away, shouting for his companions, probably to show them what he had done.

The women, clawing at the fence behind the chicken coop with a strength they had never suspected they had, were able to make a small opening between the wire and a fence post, and through this the children and then the mother and grandmother succeeded in wriggling. They crawled on all fours through a field of wheat stubble, lacerating their hands and knees and tearing their light garments to shreds, before they reached the nearest vineyard, where they hid under the leaves like vermin. And from between the vines Madame Lieutard saw her small house, her treasure, burn. The overstuffed chair with Madame Pascal's twenty-five thousand francs in it burned, too. Some of the chickens and rabbits survived, and Madame Lieutard, who now lives with her sister, visits the ruined house morning and evening to feed them. I discovered her there when I visited Comblanchien. "I found a fork among the ashes today," she said, "but it was all black and twisted. We had such pretty tableware! Oh, monsieur, if they had not burned the house, I would have had a roof to shelter my head and I would have had all our things to remind me of my poor husband! Or if they had not killed him, we could have got along without the house; we would have had each other! But this way they have left me nothing."

The Germans also killed a seventy-two-year-old man named Simonot, a stonecutter, but no witness to the crime remains in Comblanchien. Simonot lived with a spinster sister even older than himself, and she has moved away from Comblanchien.

Not even the bar of the irascible Robert Ravigneaux, where OBERLEUTNANT Schoning and his men had done a great deal of boozing while they were stationed in the village, escaped. When Schoning and Zenses, his interpreter, visited the café early that evening, as the trouble was just beginning, Schoning advised Ravigneaux and his wife to close their shutters and stay indoors. But at midnight the couple, in their bedroom, heard someone shouting, "Robert! Robert!" Whoever was calling sounded the final "t," which is silent in French but is pronounced in German. With that they heard a crashing in of shutters and windows, as if gun butts were being used on them, and then grenades exploded on the first floor. The house caught fire immediately, and Ravigneaux and his wife barely had time to save themselves. "It must have been the SALAUDS from the château," the surly innkeeper says, "because the others wouldn't have known my name. That's what you get for treating the Germans decently. Not that I was ever friendly with them!" he adds hastily when other villagers are listening. He is not a popular man.

The mayor of Comblanchien, Monsieur Moron, was more fortunate. The Germans came to his house, said they were going to burn it, and ordered him and his wife to get out. Madame Moron told them that her little girl was ill and had a high fever, and Moron's son, a classmate of the unfortunate Claude Henry at the college in Beaune, talked to them in German. They finally left the house without setting fire to it, but they carried away a small barrel of wine. The survival of the mayor's residence and his wine warehouse, across the road, did nothing to increase his popularity with his less fortunate fellow-citizens, but it seems to have been sheer chance. Of a hundred-odd buildings in the village, the Germans burned fifty-two, and their decision to spare some was apparently as haphazard as their decision to destroy the others. In addition to killing eight people, the Germans arrested twenty-four men and boys. They put these prisoners aboard the troop train, announcing that they would carry them away as hostages. The selection of the hostages was as inexplicable as everything else about the affair. One of them was a boy of fourteen, and none of them were important citizens—not, for example, the mayor, the deputy mayor, or the town clerk. Next day, at Dijon, the Germans released twelve of the hostages. All had expected to be shot. The Germans put the twelve others aboard a train for Germany, but when the train was bombed by American planes, two more of the prisoners escaped. They eventually made their way back to Comblanchien.

The shooting, burning, and looting continued until dawn. In the middle of the night, a truck rolled up from the FELDGEN-DARMERIE at Beaune, hauling a field gun. By that time it must have been obvious to all the Germans that they had not been attacked, as they may have thought at first, by the Resistance forces, but the gunners fired a dozen rounds at the town hall and church. They hit the belfry of the town hall, knocking off a piece of stone bearing the letters "R.F." (RÉPUBLIQUE FRANÇAISE), but did no other damage. Shell cases found on the highway show that the gun was a 37-millimeter piece. This shelling was probably done for "moral effect." At dawn the truck convoy went on its way, the soldiers in it singing happily. The Germans from the troop train marched back to their cars in cadenced step, singing manly songs about morning in the forest and village maidens with dewy eyes. OBERLEUTNANT Schoning had already gone to the château. In the vineyards, haggard women peered through the leaves at the smoking sockets of their houses.

Toward eight in the morning, it was discovered that the church was burning. The iron grille at the entrance had been locked, and the Germans, after firing a few ineffective shots at the lock in an attempt to break it, had gone off on some other drunken inspiration. But probably an incendiary bullet or grenade, going through a window, had started a smoldering fire that burst into flames hours later. Monsieur Gilles, chief of the commune's volunteer fire company, and Monsieur Chopin, the deputy mayor, went to the mayor and asked for the key to the engine house, so that they could get out the fire engine. The mayor said that the Germans had started the fire and might renew the massacre if an attempt were made to save the church. He refused permission to take out the engine, and the church burned to the ground.

Later in the day some of the Germans from the château appeared on the highway. They pointed to the ruins of the town and shouted, "BOOM BOOM KAPUT! TERRORISTEN KAPUT!" They seemed to find the scene amusing and laughed a great deal, but they made no move to attack any of the people they saw rummaging in the ruins of their houses. Schoning communicated with nobody in the village from then on. During the first week in September he and his Marine detachment evacuated the château and left town. French and American troops arrived in Comblanchien on September 7.

While the fires were still at their height on the night of the massacre, Monsieur Jordan, the gendarme from Corgoloin, came secretly to Comblanchien to see what was happening there. Monsieur Jordan is a sallow, long-faced man with a hawk nose and a grizzled mustache. He is intelligent and logical and has a professional fondness for phrases like "reconstitution of the crime," since for the past sixteen years he has been a police officer. Until he fled to join the MAQUIS a couple of weeks before the massacre, Monsieur Jordan had been a MARÉCHAL DES LOGIS, or sergeant, of the national GENDARMERIE. For the sixteen years of his service he had been stationed at the GENDARMERIE nearest Comblanchien, in the neighboring commune of Corgoloin, so he was intimately acquainted with the district and all its people. During the occupation he had pretended to help the Germans, but he had consistently forewarned everybody he was instructed to arrest. He had salvaged a few weapons so damaged that the Germans had thrown them away, and he had painfully and ingeniously repaired them, so he and the three gendarmes under him were armed with carbines and a sub-machine gun in addition to the gimcrack revolver and nine rounds per man the Germans allowed French gendarmes to retain. The four gendarmes had gone into the MAQUIS after they had been warned of an impending raid upon their cache of arms. On the night of the massacre, Monsieur Jordan remained in Comblanchien for an hour watching the Germans. He realized by then that he could do nothing to amend matters, so he crawled off through the vineyards until he got well away, because, even though there was no moon, the flames cast a brilliant light. After the liberation, he returned to the GENDARMERIE at Corgoloin. As soon as he had cleared up a few routine matters, like the arrest of a couple of Germans in civilian clothes who remained in the region, he began a careful investigation of the slaughter of his fellow-citizens at Comblanchien. His findings have not pleased all his neighbors, for people everywhere like to believe in diabolical plots, and Monsieur Jordan has not been able to establish that there was one.

When he began his inquiry, there was already a story in the countryside that the arrival of the train and of the truck convoy at Comblanchien had been co-ordinated that night for the purpose of making an attack on the village. It had become an article of faith that the few shots before the massacre were a prearranged signal. "The few shots, of course, might have been a signal," Jordan says, "but there had been shots like them in the night on dozens of previous occasions, always proceeding from those nervous Marine patrols. As to the thesis that there really was an attack on the train by men of the Resistance and that the Germans fired in defense, I am in a position to say that it cannot be sustained. There were no F.F.I. patrols in Comblanchien that night. Moreover, if the handful of men of Comblanchien had meditated anything so mad as an attack on a two-thousand-man troop train, would Claude Henry, an F.F.I. officer, have been picking string beans in the garden when the train arrived?"

Monsieur Jordan also heard in the countryside a story that people had seen rockets fired from the château before the attack began, but he could never actually find these people. There was

also a story that Schoning's Marines had appeared, completely
equipped for battle, at the Ravigneaux café an hour before the
first shots, but Monsieur and Madame Ravigneaux and Paul
Zenses, the Alsatian interpreter, who subsequently deserted from
the German Army and joined up with the French, agreed that
Schoning had appeared in the café AFTER the firing started. There
was also a very persistent report that the German commander of
the troop train had insisted, at Corgoloin, the station below Comblanchien, that "the train must go through because we have to
get to Comblanchien this evening." The Corgoloin stationmaster
told Jordan that the officer had wanted to get as far as Dijon, not
Comblanchien, and that the train had stopped there only because
another one was ahead of it. "The strongest argument against the
thesis of a deliberate punitive attack on Comblanchien," Jordan
says, "is the fact that if they had wanted to kill all the people, the
Germans could have remained on the scene the next day and
killed them at their leisure. But they didn't. Well, then, there
was no premeditation. Well, then, what happened?

"This is what happened. Two detachments of Germans, arriving
here simultaneously from two directions, with their customary
brutality exacerbated by fear and chagrin, frightened each other
into an exchange of shots. The precipitating influence was probably one of the patrols from the château, which were always
frightened. The patrol fired two or three shots and soldiers on the
train replied with a massive fusillade. Those of the truck convoy
replied to this fusillade with a nourished fire. The château joined
in. Train and convoy fired on the château. This I know because
I have found imbedded in the château two machine-gun bullets
that came into it through open windows. No glass is broken, but
remember that it was a hot night. One bullet had entered at such
an acute upward angle that it was lodged in a ceiling. It must
therefore have been fired from the road directly below the château.
The other had lodged in a wall almost on a level with the window-
sill and therefore must have been fired on an only slightly rising
trajectory—from the train on the other side of the village. The
evidence of the scarred poplar tree, standing between train and
convoy, proves that the Germans fired on each other.

"Now, however, please remark that I do not exonerate these

brutes for what they did. Mistakes sometimes occur, even in armies which, like the German, propagate a legend of their own perfect discipline and skill at warfare. If some innocent inhabitants of the village had been caught in the crossfire and wounded, that would have been regrettable but not a crime of war. But notice—the Germans descended from the train and killed eight persons in their houses, firing point blank. These persons were not only unarmed; of the eight, three were men more than sixty years old and two were women, persons unlikely to be dangerous. They did not kill only in the first access of fury, because it was an hour and a half after the first attack that they killed old man Blanc. Long after they discovered their mistake, they continued to burn houses. What was their crime? In my opinion, any court would convict them of murder."

The Repression

Les Etoiles
February, 1944

PASS THIS NEWS ALONG

Nantua-Oyonnax. On December 6, 1943, two patent collaborationists, a hotel keeper and his wife, were covered with swastikas and paraded through the streets of Nantua and Oyonnax by the boys of the MAQUIS. In reprisal, on the 13th, SS detachments, sent from Paris, surrounded Nantua and arrested one hundred and sixty men from eighteen to sixty years old, among whom were three professors at the LYCÉE, two instructors, two monitors, and ten seniors in the same school. The latter were sent directly to an internment camp. Dr. Mercier, father of four children, was shot beside the road. At Oyonnax, Nicod, a former deputy and mayor, the president of the Veterans' Legion, and an industrialist of the town were shot also.

St. Etienne. The five LYCÉE students, arrested and abominably tortured by the GESTAPO in November, have been tried by the

German court. One of them was sentenced to three years of hard labor, two to two years, and the others to one year in prison. They have been transferred to Germany. They are in great danger. The LYCÉE principal who received the visit of the GESTAPO agents and did not see fit to warn the boys' families, will be held responsible for anything that may happen to them.

Clermont-Ferrand. On January 9, one hundred and thirty Alsatian students who were imprisoned in the military barracks were transferred to Germany.

It will be recalled that it has been established that the person at the root of the Nazi raid on the University of Strasbourg at Clermont-Ferrand was an AGENT-PROVOCATEUR, the student Mathieu. This person, after having furnished false identity cards to his classmates, designated the victims to the GESTAPO. When the Germans made their descent on the university, Mathieu accompanied the GESTAPO men and furnished them with information concerning the students and professors. Mathieu no longer circulates in the streets of Clermont except under military escort.

Nice. In December three patriots were executed after having been forced to dig their own graves. Six others were found in the quarries with their eyes gouged out.

In December the patriots Stuerga and Grandperret, an optician of this city, were given a funeral worthy of their heroism. The entire population of Vence followed their coffins to the cemetery.

During this same period, Courbet, printer and bookseller; Joseph Ross, aged forty, lawyer; Spolianski, professor of literature; and Fresco, aged nineteen, a student in the trade school, were either shot by the GESTAPO or died as a result of torture.

The magistrate Leprost, an enemy of patriots, who showed great zeal in prosecuting these men, has been seriously wounded.

Aix. The well-known Hitlerian, Verdun, presiding judge of the Special Court at Aix, who has shown particular ferocity in prosecuting patriots, has met the fate that he deserved.

Toulouse. In the early part of January, the professor of physical education, Nakache,* world swimming champion, was arrested by

* Nakache's special offense was that he was not only a Jew but a consistent winner over "Aryan" swimmers, and he refused to retire from competition.

the GESTAPO, at the same time as the internationally known phthisiologist, Professor Kindberg. There is no further news of them.

Les Etoiles
February, 1944

THE MASSACRE AT GRENOBLE

Doctors Valois, Sauvage, Buttorlin, Audinois, and Girard, of Grenoble and its environs, have been assassinated by groups of MILICIENS. Doctor Valois was killed in his bed, before the eyes of his wife and child, by fifty-two sub-machine-gun bullets. Doctor Sauvage was taken into a woods and tortured. His body was then tied in a bag and thrown into the courtyard of the PALAIS DE JUSTICE.

One or two of these doctors were leaders in the Resistance movement. The others, like millions of other Frenchmen, were only sympathizers who had made no secret of their faith in the victory of the Allies. Some of them, such as Doctor Girard, professor emeritus of surgery, were old men.

At Lyon, the MILICIENS held a press conference to boast of their crimes and proclaim their intention to commit others. The Laval press announced these murders but, in obedience to orders and as a part of their "anti-terrorist" campaign, attributed them to the Communists.

These are the facts. Our comrades will be avenged.

In the meanwhile, the doctors in the Resistance should bear in mind that clandestine warfare has certain strict rules:

(1) They should take care to hide their activities from the thugs of the MILICE.

(2) If they are found out, they should not wait for the murderers to kill them in their own homes. They should arm themselves and take to the MAQUIS.

(3) They should demand that the Resistance organizations distribute existing stocks of arms as soon as possible.

We have mentioned in these same pages the assassination by the MILICE of the journalist Pain and of Dean Gosse and his son, a lawyer of this city. To this list, we must add the murder of Professor Bistely, professor of chemistry at the Medical School, shot down while lecturing to his classes, and those of two school-teachers and three other persons mowed down by machine-gun fire in the streets of the city, late in December.

The Grenoble massacre is an indication of what awaits the intellectual élite all over France now that Darnand, the chief of the murderers, is a minister in the Vichy government. At his direction, lists of intellectuals have been drawn up. As a sop to uneasy consciences, the monstrous institution of "special tribunals," composed of three members and authorized to hand down sentences on the spot for immediate execution, gives these murders an appearance of legality. It was thus that Darnand inaugurated his reign of terror at Paris by having the CAGOULARD Deloncle,* his ex-accomplice, executed—presumably because he knew too much.

The killing of Deloncle may be dismissed as a settling of accounts among gangsters. But almost at the same time, by the murder of the philosopher Victor Basch, president of International League of the Rights of Man, Darnand's henchmen committed a crime against French culture that the world will not soon forgive.

Libération
March 14, 1944

EVERYBODY IN PRISON

On January 31 twelve hundred women interned in the camp of Royallieu, near Compiègne, were deported to Germany. As they were marched across the city, they sang "The Marseillaise," "L'ALSACE ET LA LORRAINE," and "LA MADELON," and shouted, "VIVE LA FRANCE! Down with the BOCHES! VIVE DE GAULLE!" Loaded into trucks, they managed to make a French flag out of three

* Deloncle was one of the organizers of the *Cagoulard* movement, which flourished particularly in industrial and career-army circles before the outbreak of the war. This movement in which many of the leading figures of France, including Pétain and Darlan, were more or less involved, was a secret fascist organization which plotted to overthrow the government with the assistance of German and Italian arms. (*Translator's note.*)

scarves and flew it from the last truck in the convoy. At the railroad station they even tussled with the German soldiers. Among these women of all classes, workers, BOURGEOISES, and intellectuals, there were also women of the nobility, such as the Comtesse de Monlaud and the Duchesse de Tels. They were sent to the camp of Ravensbruck in South Germany.

The latest convoys of men, among whom were André Marie, the deputy from Rouen, General Challes and Mancel and other superior officers, as well as most of the dignitaries of the Orthodox Church of France, have been sent to Buchenwald near Weimar.

The American prisoners in the camp of Royallieu have been transferred to Clermont-sur-Oise. Royallieu will be used as a "staging" camp. Internees will be held there a few days before being sent on to Germany or elsewhere. The English will be sent to Saint-Denis.

The tempo of arrests is increasing everywhere, and the close collaboration between Darnand and the GESTAPO is becoming more and more obvious. It is learned that the VÉLODROME D'HIVER has been requisitioned in preparation for raids to round up pedestrians in the streets. Already certain MÉTRO trains, movie theaters and cafés have been the object of wholesale raids on the pretext of examining identity cards. These brutal raids are carried out sometimes by the French police and sometimes by the GESTAPO. Hardly are the prisons, like Fresnes, emptied by transferring the prisoners to Compiègne, than they are filled immediately. Frenchmen are being arrested in mass. Soon there will not be a family in France that does not have some of its members in a prison or a concentration camp.

Libération
April 7, 1944

WHOLESALE MASSACRES

Last month the SS detachment at Angoulême decided to undertake "punitive action" against the MAQUIS, which on more than one occasion had carried on fruitful operations against the occupying forces, in the course of which they had seized tanks and taken prisoners. In their rage, the Nazis surrounded the woods, bombarded the villages with cannon, and set fire to the forest in the hope of wiping out the Resistance forces. Warned in time, fortunately most of our friends were able to withdraw to another location. Nevertheless, about a hundred men fell into the hands of the Germans, and more than fifty of them were shot.

A farmer who had given employment to a RÉFRACTAIRE for a few months was arrested and summoned to give the name of the man from whom he rented the farm. His landlord was arrested in Ribérac and brought to the farm. The Germans locked both the landlord and his tenant in the house, drove the women and children off the farm, and set fire to the house. The two men, already riddled with bullets, were burned alive. Another inhabitant of Ribérac was shot and his head cut off. His family was forbidden to bury the corpse for several days.

Combat
May, 1944

FOR THREE HOURS THEY MASSACRED FRENCHMEN

We must face the fact: we have been vaccinated against horror. All these faces disfigured by bullet wounds or boot heels, these mangled men, these women and children assassinated, inspired us in the beginning with the revolt and loathing necessary to justify our taking up the fight. Now this fight is so accepted a pattern of our daily lives that, though we never forget the reasons for it, they may not always be uppermost in our thoughts. But the enemy is there; and, as if it were his resolve never to allow anyone to put them out of mind, he increases his efforts, he surpasses himself, he achieves each day new extremes of brutality and cowardice.

Today, in any case, he has surpassed anything that we could ever have imagined; and the tragedy of Ascq * serves to remind all Frenchmen that they are engaged in total and implacable warfare against an enemy devoid of honor.

* A village in northern France between Lille and Tournai.

What are the facts?

The 1st of April, 1944, during the night two explosions took place, tearing up a rail and derailing two cars of a German troop train. The track was blocked. There were no casualties.

About eleven o'clock, while Monsieur Carré, the station master at Ascq, who had been summoned from his bed by the employees on the night shift at the station, was telephoning to make arrangements for repairing the line, a German officer belonging to the transport service followed by several soldiers rushed into the office in a fury, struck down with their rifle butts the station master and two other employees, Peloquin and Derache, who happened to be there. Withdrawing to the doorway of the office they poured a volley of tommy-gun bullets into the unconscious bodies. Carré and Peloquin were severely wounded in the belly and thighs. Then the officer led a sizable detachment of troops into the village, searched the houses after breaking down the doors and rounded up about sixty men, who were taken to a pasture opposite the station. There they were shot. Twenty-six other men were also shot down near their own homes. In addition to the eighty-six men killed, there were a number of wounded.

The employee Derache succeeded in putting in an alarm to the prefecture of the department, which in turn appealed to the German General Headquarters to intervene.

It was only on the arrival of the officers from General Headquarters that the massacre came to an end. It had gone on for three hours.

I do not know whether we visualize clearly enough all the implications of this blunt report. But is it possible to read, without indignation and loathing filling one's whole being, these simple figures: eighty-six men in three hours?

Eighty-six men like you who are reading this paper fell before the German rifles, eighty-six men who could fill three or four rooms the size of the one where you are sitting, eighty-six faces haggard or grim, contorted with horror or hatred.

And the slaughter lasted for three hours, a little more than two minutes for each victim. Three hours, the time that some of us this very day may have lingered over dinner, conversing peacefully with friends. The duration of an evening at the movies, where people were at that very moment being amused by a spectacle of imaginary adventures. During those three hours, minute after minute, without interruption, in a single village of France shots rang out one after another and bodies writhed on the ground.

This is the image that we must keep before our eyes to make sure that nothing will be forgotten, a sight to hold up before those Frenchmen who still stand aloof from the fight. For out of these eighty-six innocent victims were many who thought that, having done nothing against the German might, they need fear no harm from it. But France is indivisible. There is but a single wrath, a single martyrdom. And when Monsieur de Brinon writes to the German authorities, not to protest because they massacred so many Frenchmen but to complain that, in so doing, they intruded on his own functions as a society sleuth, he renders himself guilty of that martyrdom and responsible before that wrath. For it is not a question of deciding whether these crimes shall be forgiven, but only of knowing whether they shall be punished. And if we had any tendency to doubt that they shall be, the vision of this village, splashed with blood and now peopled only by widows and orphans, would suffice to assure us that the crime SHALL be expiated, since henceforth it is the concern of ALL Frenchmen and since, faced with this new massacre, we find ourselves united in martyrdom and strong with the strength of vengeance.

The effort of France must rise to a maximum. Later we shall make the reckoning of our dead. Until the day when we shall have conquered, to conquer is our only aim. All else is vanity and a waste of our strength.

THE LATEST INFAMY OF THE "MILICE"

Servile imitators of their Nazi masters, the MILICIENS of Darnand's SS, have been turned loose against France by the Vichy Government.

These men, whom the lure of money and power has drawn into the service of the enemy, have by their treason burned their bridges behind them.

Nothing is too cruel or too base for them. In all domains, they rack their brains to equal or surpass the worst excesses of the Nazis. All France holds them in execration and contempt. The Germans themselves feel nothing but disgust for them. But even this is not enough.

There still remained a step to take to make their ignominy complete. Hitler had invented the shameful and atrocious institution of hostages. The MILICE owed it to itself to go even further.

Early in April we learned that the MILICE had arrested Monsieur Jacob, chairman of the Stockbrokers' Association of Paris; Monsieur de Menthon, eighty years old; Monsieur d'Aligny, Monsieur Touchard and several others. Who were these men and what was their crime?

Were they patriots suspected of "anti-nationalist agitation"? No, they were merely the brother-in-law of General Catroux,* the father and cousin of Monsieur de Menthon, the son of the Communist deputy Touchard, and members of the families of Le Trocquer, Larminat, etc. In short, what the MILICE undoubtedly would call "good hostages."

For the more respectable a man is, the more innocent he is of any political activity, the more ideal a hostage he makes.

In the territories liberated from enemy oppression, justice has begun to function once more, and traitors have been summoned before the newly restored tribunals to answer for their crimes. Their accomplices are beginning to worry. To meet the threat of such a dread precedent being established, they would like to resort to a kind of gangster solidarity: for every one of their ilk condemned to death, they threaten to execute one, or ten, or a hundred innocent persons chosen among the friends and relatives of the men to whose leadership the liberation of France is entrusted.

Will these men have the terrible courage to execute the sentences, knowing that for every criminal punished, ten or more

---

* Catroux and Larminat were generals who served with De Gaulle. Le Trocquer and De Menthon were ministers in the Gaullist government. (*Translator's note.*)

innocent people will be assassinated? This is the reasoning of the MILICE.

Since they could not reveal their scheme to the public in all its cold horror, they needed help to camouflage it. And who could better help them than the sinister old man whose livery is the uniform of marshal of France? And Pétain, ever ready to be of service, has dared to proclaim that it is "contrary to honor" for a soldier to be judged by others than those from whom he received his orders.

What Old Man Defeat means by "honor" France has learned only too well during the past four years. But this time he has gone too far. It is not the soldiers of the armistice army * who were on trial at Algiers. These soldiers may honestly have believed that they were called upon to serve France. When Vichy sent them to throw away their lives to prevent the Allied landing in order to permit the Pétain clique to remain in power, they obeyed the orders of their superiors.

But the MILICIENS did not enlist on the German side until after the enemy had violated the last clauses of the armistice, invaded the part of France where, until then, the government had kept up an appearance of sovereignty, and demobilized the armistice army by a kick of the German boot. They were the volunteers of treason. Today they are answering for their crime and must receive their just punishment.

The message of approbation that they received from Pétain in no way diminishes their guilt. Nobody can accept as head of a legitimate government a man who consented without a murmur to be nothing but a prisoner without the slightest power and who lent his name as cover for all the oppressive measures that Hitler decreed.

The orders of Pétain and his anti-French government merely render their authors the principal accomplices in the betrayal of France. Of this the MILICIENS are fully aware. The wheel is turning, the moment of liberation is drawing near. Their only hope

---

* Certain officers of the armistice army were sent to North Africa to insure continued loyalty of the native troops. After the Allied invasion of North Africa, some of these officers were tried for their cruelty in the administration of concentration camps.

lies in desperate measures. The seizure of hostages is undoubtedly the most ignoble trick that they were able to think up. In choosing to use it, they showed Frenchmen how deep in infamy they could plunge. They have placed themselves outside of any law and of any justice. They have put themselves on a level with mad dogs to be shot down on sight.

For them, and them alone, there is now no further need for courts and judges. They have signed their own death warrants. All that remains for patriots is to carry them out.

After the foregoing pieces the one that follows needs no explanation.

Défense de la France
February 25, 1944

The Duty to Kill

Thus conscience does make cowards of us all.
—HAMLET

Frenchmen!

Some of you may have believed up to the present that they could, in defiance of all sense of honor, elude the dreadful duty of war. Believing themselves protected by the "finesse" of a Pétain or the "shrewdness" of a Laval, they virtuously called everything that resembled war "terrorism."

Now the veils are falling away. You have no choice: either you will come back into the war or you will perish. You will fight or you will be carried off into slavery. To remain free, to save your lives, to protect your children, your wives, your parents, your soil, henceforth you must resort to arms. And if you refuse, if you wait for time or the course of events to deliver you, you are less than the she-wolf who will fight for her young, you are more contemptible than the humblest animals of creation who will fight to the death to defend their offspring.

And it is not even as if cowardice would save you. You try to shrink back still further, but now cowardice no longer pays. Even by wallowing in treason, you could no longer keep the illusion of liberty. The veils have fallen. The truth that Pétain had hoped to conceal stands out: to fight means freedom, to cringe means slavery.

Do not try to reason! There are certain problems that one has not even the right to consider! It is by trying to understand everything that one slips into surrender. Inner convictions, virile resolutions, sense of duty, truth itself melt away under excessive analysis. Weigh the question once for all, and then, decide: Do you want to live or to die?

What the German demands of France is total slavery. To lessen the threat to the rear of his armies, he is carrying off the cream of France as hostages. Prisons have become nothing but way-stations on the road to massacre or deportation. Constantly they are emptied only to be refilled again immediately. To carry out his plans, the enemy has appealed to the dregs of our population, the black sheep, sadists, pimps, and irresponsibles. They allow this gang to embellish itself with the name Militia. And Laval, hypocritical father-confessor of evil consciences, represents it as the mainstay of law and order. In reality it is the mainstay of ill-gotten fortunes, the bodyguard of traitors, the rampart of a bourgeoisie a-tremble at the righteous indignation of the masses. Its commander is Darnand, the ex-hero, the soldier turned policeman, the climber whose ambition is to equal Himmler.

What is the answer to these demands and to these methods? Only one decision is possible: KILL.

We have no special yearning to murder. Rather do we yearn for a serene and happy life in which we could create, build and love. But death to those who would prevent us from living! Do we not kill the venomous snake or the wild beast when they attack us? In that case, the only defense is to kill.

Let no one protest that this is against all morality, that we should rather turn the left cheek when someone has slapped our right cheek. To accept in silence the wrong that had been done you may be a sign of greatness of soul or of saintliness. But to allow evil to be done without protest, to fail to defend one's country, in the name of Christian charity or humaneness, is vile and hypocritical weakness.

Our duty is clear: we must kill.

Kill the German to cleanse our land, kill him because he has killed our loved ones, kill him to be free.

Kill the traitor, kill the man who has denounced his neighbors, the man who has aided the enemy.

Kill the MILICIENS, exterminate them because they have deliberately chosen to betray Frenchmen, because they leapt at the chance to betray. Shoot them down like mad dogs at the corner of a street. Hang them to lamp-posts, as the people of Dauphiné have done at Grenoble. Destroy them as you would destroy vermin.

Kill without passion, without hatred. Never stoop to torture or to cause deliberate suffering. We are not executioners; we are soldiers.

Kill without pity or remorse because killing is your duty, a painful duty: THE DUTY OF JUSTICE.

Frenchmen, the time has come. This is the great fight. It is too late even to think of flight: the boat has sailed, AND YOU ARE ABOARD.

Rejoin your units. Make the total gift of yourselves. Bring us your help, your money, your house, your life. We are in this fight to a man. Desertion is impossible.

Frenchmen, the fight to the death has come. It is useless to seek for any other means of defending your existence than force and bravery. IF YOU DO NOT DARE TO RISK IT, YOUR LIFE LOSES ALL VALUE and is not worth our trying to defend it. But if you fulfill your duty as a warrior, then we shall be brothers-in-arms.

Frenchmen, weigh this carefully in your hearts!

WHICH DO YOU CHOOSE, LIFE OR DEATH? *

---

* Vercors, considering this same problem, wrote in an essay not included in this book: "By his abominable acts, the enemy has made hatred almost a duty"—and then addressing himself to the enemy, "Of all the reasons for hating you, O you that I cannot call my fellow men, this single one would suffice: I hate you because of what you have made of me. Because you sowed and cultivated in me, with the diabolical persistence that is yours, sentiments for which I can feel only disgust and scorn." Reluctantly, Vercors had come a long way since the "good German" of Le Silence de la Mer.—L.

PART SEVEN

Victory!

Liberation Begins

In the fairly early days of the moving pictures, when I used to like them—I was about seven years old then—there was a formula for a successful two-reeler that never failed to thrill us. The Indians, sometimes in league with a villainous white man (a kind of Laval) would get the hero and heroine into a cabin and set fire to it and ride around it shooting from the backs of their ponies. The films were silent then but I could hear those Indian yells much more distinctly than I have ever heard anything on a sound track. Just when it seemed that the Indians were going to inflict great pain and anguish upon the hero and heroine, there would be a flash to a plain with the United States cavalry riding across it. The first trooper carried a big American flag like the one in the assembly hall of P.S. 9, Manhattan, and it billowed in the wind. The soldiers wore floppy black hats and the colonel rode a white horse and waved a sword. I had never been told then that a man on a white horse was a symbol of militarism, so it was all right with me.

The picture would flash back to the Indians, and by this time the hero had a bandage on his head and a particularly villainous Indian was sneaking up behind the heroine with intentions I was not qualified to surmise. It went back and forth that way for what seemed a long while, and then the cavalry arrived and everything was all right. At the end of the picture, after the fadeout kiss, the flag filled the whole screen. It is probable that after such a traumatic experience the hero and heroine were left with a severe neurosis, but I never worried about it.

Now we are coming to the happy part of our story of France,

435

the arrival of the Allies, the insurrection of Paris and the discomfiture of the Germans. But since we are more than seven years old we must remember that the liberation was not a completely happy ending, or for that matter an ending at all. It left the French with their dead to bury, their wounds to heal, their burned cabins to rebuild and a lot of phobias about Indians (read foreigners). The first reaction of a rescued man is gratitude. The second is "What the hell kept you so long?" The third, quite possibly, is "Why didn't you prevent this?" But on June 6, 1944, at any rate, when the BBC made the first announcement that the Allies had landed in Normandy, all France was full of joy.

French Forces in Action

L'Homme Libre
Friday, June 9, 1944

THE FRENCH FORCES * SHARE IN
ALL THE FIGHTING

At 7.30 a.m. on June 6 the first landing barges beached on the coast of Normandy.

The moment which 40,000,000 Frenchmen had been awaiting for four years had arrived. The hour of liberation had sounded.

The sea was stormy, rougher than could have been wished. Because of the bad weather the landing had been delayed for twenty-four hours. The operation, planned with extraordinary precision, was carried out with such a use of strength and such perfection of organization as are difficult to imagine.

Four thousand vessels of all kinds had crossed the Channel during the night.

Every ten minutes the heavy guns of the Navy pounded the German fortifications with broadsides of 4000 tons of shells.

* There is no further mention of them in this newspaper.

The naval bombardment had been preceded by an aerial bombardment of unprecedented intensity.

Between midnight and seven in the morning the heavy bombers poured 8000 tons of bombs on military targets.

FIRST RESULTS, FIGHTING NEAR CAEN

The landing took place on a coastal area extending 80 kilometers south from Le Havre, the center of which is Caen. At the end of the first day several bridgeheads were firmly held on French soil. The Allied spearheads were fighting on the outskirts of Caen.

Combined with the landing operation, an aerial avalanche struck at the areas immediately behind the enemy lines.

Airborne forces had been landed behind the coast at designated points between Bayeux and Avranches. It is now known that these pockets of parachutists have effected a junction with the forces striking against the coastline.

The air strength involved consists of over 11,000 first-line aircraft. The parachutists were carried by a fleet of transport planes which, flying at an altitude of 300 meters, stretched out over a distance of 400 kilometers.

11,000 FIRST-LINE AIRCRAFT LEAD THE ATTACK

To cover the landing of the parachutists, a smoke screen was laid down at a height of 1700 meters.

The initial attack encountered an astonishingly weak defense.*

Churchill has declared to the House of Commons that the German underwater defenses were much weaker than expected.

A fleet of countless mine sweepers, whose crews could be reckoned at several tens of thousands of men, had cleared the approaches to the coast. This particularly dangerous work was carried out with remarkable zest and almost without any German opposition. The German Navy's speedboats of the E-boat type which tried to intervene were beaten off with such losses that for the next twenty-four hours they did not repeat their attempts.

* The editor obviously was not on Easy Red Beach. Neither was the BBC announcer from whom he got his information.

Only on the third day did Admiral Doenitz, driven by desperate necessity, again launch his flotillas against the Allied naval units. They were again driven off.

A naval expert of the BBC was able to say that the operation, on a scale unprecedented in the history of warfare, had been successfully carried out only because of the Allies' complete command of the seas.

Remarkably enough, not a single German submarine made any attempt to intervene.

UNINTERRUPTED LANDING OF TROOPS AND EQUIPMENT

Ever since Tuesday the landing of troops and equipment on the French beaches has continued at a quickened pace.

The first wounded have arrived in England. Considering the size of the forces involved, the losses are amazingly light.

Along with the wounded, the first German prisoners were landed in British ports.

The Allied aerial superiority is overwhelming. The LUFTWAFFE, at first caught completely off guard, did not intervene the first day. The few Nazi planes that did show themselves were shot down.

The second day some air fights took place. But the losses announced in the Allied communiqués prove that the engagements were still comparatively insignificant. Goering's air force has not only lost air supremacy, but is outclassed by the numbers and quality of the planes and fliers of the Allies.

THIRD DAY OF THE LANDINGS

The first communiqués from General Eisenhower's headquarters express obvious satisfaction. Operations are stated to be proceeding according to plan. German resistance is stiffening. We must certainly not indulge in premature optimism. The fighting will be hard, but France will triumph with the aid of her Allies.

On the coast the German batteries are still in action. They are being shelled by the Navy and bombed by the air forces.

The task of the air forces is to cut off all movement behind the enemy lines. They are bombing intensively all key communications points and rail junctions so as to shut off German reinforcements. Limited at first to the immediate rear area, these bombings are now spreading toward the interior. Thus, in the Paris area, the stations of Achères, Versailles and Massy-Palaiseau have been destroyed by tons of explosives.

Another tactical bombing operation, about which it is still impossible to say whether it is aimed at preparing a new landing or at isolating the German troops in the southwest, is concentrating on cutting all the communication lines in a vast zone extending from Lorient to the Gulf of Gascony.

GENERAL EISENHOWER'S INSPECTION TOUR

On Thursday morning the commander-in-chief of the Allied troops, General Eisenhower, inspected the principal Allied bridgeheads. He met General Montgomery, the most popular British general, familiarly called "Monty," who is in command of the main spearhead of the landing.

At present all the beaches in the landing zone have been occupied. The road from Bayeux to Caen has been cut. Bayeux has fallen. On all sides reinforcements are pouring in by gliders and boats. Before Caen the Allies have thrown back German counterattacks. With three 380-mm shells, the WARSPITE has wiped out a park of fifty tanks. Large numbers of transport planes and gliders are landing on the Cotentin Peninsula.

COMAC

The COMAC, or COMITÉ D'ACTION MILITAIRE, which makes its first appearance in the next exhibit, was a triumvirate. Each of three large resistance organizations, FRONT NATIONAL, MOUVEMENT DE LIBÉRATION NATIONALE, and CEUX DE LA LIBÉRATION, was represented by one member. Members of smaller movements were under their command, for it had been decided that it was impractical to have a high command comprising some dozens of equal members. The trend toward larger Resistance groups had progressed steadily. In December, 1943, M.U.R., itself an amalgam of three large movements, had been expanded and re-christened M.L.N.—MOUVEMENT DE LIBÉRATION NATIONALE. FRONT NATIONAL included the FRANC-TIREURS ET PARTISANS FRANÇAIS along with many middle-class and conservative elements. F.T.P. was its fighting branch. CEUX DE LA LIBÉRATION was a predominantly northern movement that included all shades of pre-war political opinion. Only in February, 1944, were the three great organisms brought together and plans for COMAC first set up. The three members were known as the three V's—from their names in the Resistance —Valrimont, who represented M.L.N., Villon, of FRONT NATIONAL, and Vaillant of C.D.L.N. All three were resistance names. Vaillant was Jean de Vogüé, the former naval officer who had refused to stay in England after Mers-el-Kebir and had returned to France almost an Anglophobe. Jointly they commanded the F.F.I., FORCES FRANÇAISES DE L'INTÉRIEUR, subject to the orders of General de Gaulle who was outside France. The intermediary between De Gaulle and COMAC was General Pierre Koenig, also outside France, but nevertheless titular commander of the forces of the interior. The intermediary between Koenig and the COMAC was an intelligence system under an officer known as Colonel Passy whom the COMAC cordially distrusted. The setup was complex and the liaison imperfect, and the divergencies of Fighting French of the exterior and interior have been carried over into peacetime and still affect French politics. In 1944, however, they had to present a united front against: (1) The Germans, whom they all detested, and (2) The State Department and the Foreign Office, whom they all distrusted. All factions of the Resistance suspected Anglo-American diplomacy. The British had turned against France after the last war and helped to build a strong Germany, the patriots remembered. The Americans wanted a conservative, capitalist setup in France and would try to make a deal with "moderate" elements—which meant collaborationists. That at least was the French conviction. It was, of course, as baseless as a rabbit's prejudice against hound-dogs. Every time General de Gaulle spoke up sharply to remind Mr. Roosevelt or Mr.

Churchill that France was no poor relation he entrenched himself deeper in the hearts of Frenchmen.

The jubilation grew with each Allied victory. The Germans had blustered, on the day of the landing, that they would throw the Allies back into the Channel. Then they had said they were trying to draw more Allied soldiers into Normandy so they could bag them all at once. But the successive excuses irresistibly reminded the French of the 1940 alibis for not taking England, and the 1941-2 "explanations" of why Moscow and Stalingrad had not fallen. When the Americans punched through at Saint-Lô and then cut south through Avranches and into Brittany, the rapture could not be stilled. Even the "white but stiff" mustache of Monsieur Henry Stimson became of news interest to Frenchmen. Everything American was glorious. André Rabache, the French correspondent mentioned in the story, lived in such a roseate dream that he inadvertently got ahead of the army and was captured. But he escaped again. "C'ÉTAIT DU SPORT." Rennes was wonderful. So were the omelettes.

New Orders for Patriots

Libération, Edition Zone Sud
July 14, 1944

To all officers, noncommissioned officers and soldiers of the French Forces of the Interior, members of irregular combatant groups and irregular corps of the liberation, men of the MAQUIS and of the patriotic militia:

The COMITÉ D'ACTION MILITAIRE (COMAC) of the National Resistance Council, the high command of the F.F.I., congratulates you on your achievements since the landing of the Allied armies.

You have impeded the enemy's transportation by cutting his communication lines.

You have cut his power lines.

You have harassed the enemy in the rear of the combat zone.

In a communiqué from the Supreme Allied Headquarters the effectiveness of your action has been highly praised.

COMAC orders you:

—to carry out any military action that is asked of you by the Interallied General Staff acting through General Koenig;

—to keep the lines of communication that you have cut from being re-established;

—to help the Allied troops wherever you can;

—to sabotage more than ever all production in the enemy's service.

The action of the F.F.I. has, even now, liberated some portions of the national territory. Soldiers of the Resistance have attained their assigned objective: the liberation of our territory. Gendarmes and National Guardsmen and soldiers of the First Regiment of France have joined your units. Many Frenchmen have joined your ranks in order to fight. The eyes of the nation are upon you.

The enemy will endeavor to crush our victorious forces and the assassins of the SS have already carried out bloody reprisals on the unarmed civilian population.

In order to support the forces engaged in the battle of liberation, in order to drive out the invader, in order to prevent bloody reprisals, COMAC orders you:

(1) to intensify partisan warfare at every point;

(2) to seize the enemy's weapons depots, to attack and disarm his isolated units, to take prisoners, who will receive the same treatment as soldiers of the F.F.I. who fall into the hands of the enemy;

(3) to support our units which are threatened by the BOCHES and in danger of attack, by cutting communications and placing ambushes on the lines of approach;

(4) in case of attack by superior enemy forces, not to hesitate to give ground;

(5) wherever you are sufficiently well armed, to accomplish immediately the liberation of sections of our territory, in accord with the COMITÉ DE LIBÉRATION, with the support of the local population, and taking into account the enemy's capabilities for counterattack and your capabilities for defense. You will mobilize in the liberated territory all able-bodied men and economic re-

sources with a view to the liberation of neighboring areas and the victory of France and her Allies.

Death to the invader!

VIVE LA FRANCE!

STRIVE NOW FOR VICTORY

The Allied armies have landed on French soil. The "Atlantic wall" has collapsed.

In the battle now engaged, the French Forces of the Interior, which group all the armed units of the Resistance, have supported the Allied armies in a manner that has been highly praised in a communiqué of the Interallied General Staff.

The Resistance forces have in other parts of our territory liberated entire regions.

The Vichy news broadcasts do not tell you that already at this moment the French forces are in control of numerous regions in the center and the southwest.

The enemy has lost control of territories whose area is greater than that occupied by the Allied armies. The bloody reprisals which he is carrying out against the unarmed civilian population cannot alter the fact of his impotence to defeat the French Forces of the Interior. His attempts to attack the points already liberated are destined to be countered by the action of all the neighboring regions, and of all Frenchmen.

The battle of France has begun and must be won.

The Provisional Government of the French Republic calls upon France to fight. Our only regret is that the Allies have not given the French Resistance more effective assistance which would allow it to take immediately a sizable share in the war. We hope that everywhere our forces will be supported by immediate shipments of arms, equipment and food supplies.

In a very recent appeal General de Gaulle said to the French people that "in no case must they allow themselves to be put out of combat without having fought." . . .

Wherever possible we must liberate territory and prepare for the uprising.

We must drive out the men of Vichy and punish the traitors. In a word, our effort now must be to fight to win with the French people for the greatness of France.

Rennes Liberated

L'Homme Libre
Saturday, August 5, 1944

THE AMERICAN TANKS ADVANCE 100 KILOMETERS IN TWENTY-FOUR HOURS. Rennes was liberated Thursday afternoon, but it was Thursday morning that the American press broke the news to its readers. This was not due to a miracle of journalism, but to the difference between European and American time.

MORE IMPORTANT THAN CHERBOURG. After Avranches the Americans encountered practically no organized resistance. While one column drove south toward Rennes, another advanced toward the west in the direction of Saint-Malo.

The fall of Saint-Malo is imminent. The port has been by-passed by a considerable distance, since after having taken Dol the armored divisions of General Bradley have reached Dinan.

"The garrisons of Brest and Saint-Nazaire are threatened," states the expert Daniel Moore in THE NEW YORK TIMES.

An armored column has pushed far beyond Rennes. It has advanced 100 kilometers in twenty-four hours, which is a record, and on Friday morning was only 100 kilometers from Nantes.

"The capture of Rennes is more important than the capture of Cherbourg," Stimson states.

Rennes is the largest rail center of Brittany. Five national roads cross there. It is also a great air base.

A CAVALRYMAN'S DREAM. An Allied correspondent describes the battle as the realization of a cavalryman's dream. The armored columns spread out in all directions and dashed forward without worrying about their communications with the rear.

The Germans had only four remaining divisions to oppose the American advance. They are overwhelmed.

"I am reliving hours like those of the Battle of France, but this time, instead of the pursued, I am the pursuer," André Rabache said.

Rabache belongs to the AGENCE FRANÇAISE INDÉPENDENTE. The dispatches that he reads into the microphone of the BBC somewhere in Normandy or in Brittany and which are immediately rebroadcast by radiophone, giving a living picture of the battle and permit us to follow the advance from hour to hour. Everywhere they go, the radio trucks are surrounded by an enthusiastic throng.

MONT-SAINT-MICHEL SPARED. These last few days, Rabache has found it difficult to keep in contact with the advance elements. Because of the rapidity of the advance, the liberated cities are less damaged by the fighting. If Avranches was seriously damaged by bombing, Granville is intact:

"All the houses still have their roofs," Rabache says. "The inhabitants are in the streets with their arms full of red and white flowers. The girls wear tricolor ribbons in their hair. Men armed with pitchforks drive flocks of prisoners before them."

The celebrated Abbey of Mont-Saint-Michel is unharmed. Once more we shall be able to eat the famous omelets of LA MÈRE POULARD. Hundreds of American drivers could not help pulling up beside the road to take an admiring look at the most beautiful of the bays of Brittany.

AND THE ENGLISH TOO! Southwest of Avranches the Americans have liberated Mortain. In this sector, they are on the point of effecting a junction with the British troops who have surrounded Vire. The capture of Vire had been announced, and it appeared that the two German armored divisions that were making a stand in the region of Villedieu, Percy and Tessy were cut off. They have succeeded in withdrawing. The fall of Vire is nonetheless imminent.

Montgomery is also exerting considerable pressure in the Villers-Bocage-Avnay sector, where the Germans are counterattacking furiously.

A third operation, concerning which we have no precise details, is going on south of Caen. The Anglo-Canadian efforts will soon bear fruit and it is to be expected that in that sector also the action will become a war of movement.

The Liberation of Paris

The crowning demonstration of France's will and power to live was the insurrection at Paris. The insurrection permitted the French to say that Paris had liberated itself. This was a part-truth which was and will be of incalculable advantage in the psychological recovery of France.

We prefer to remember the American Revolution as an American victory. We do not like to estimate in cold percentages or historical probabilities how much of that victory was due to the French army and fleet. Between 1783 and 1939 we were content to be vaguely grateful once in a while, as long as the French did not annoy us by reminding us too sharply of what they had done. The French attitude toward World War II, in the future, will increasingly resemble this post-Revolutionary American state of mind. People tend to appropriate the credit for their own good fortune. The insurrection gave France a point of historical splendor on which to focus these emotions. In a military way, the insurrection had not the slightest effect on the outcome of the campaign or the war. Spiritually it was the most important event of the summer of 1944.

On the evening of Monday, August 21, 1944, all the war correspondents attached to the Twelfth Army Group, which comprised the American First and Third Armies, were summoned to a press conference at the headquarters of General Omar Bradley, the group commander. General Bradley, the honestest, least pretentious soldier who ever lived, and one of the best, had a custom of telling the press exactly what he was going to do. He had begun this practice in northern Tunisia, and he may have thought it brought him luck, because that campaign worked out exactly as he had said it would; the Allies entered Bizerte in eleven days from the time the General unrolled the maps. Afterward, in France, he had made a couple of wrong predictions on time. At the conference following such an error, he would not try to hedge, but would say, "I guess my face should be red, but I'll stick out my neck again." Then he would diagram the next play. On this particular evening he knew the correspondents were all wondering about when they would get into Paris. Group headquarters were then at Laval, in Mayenne, a department sandwiched in between Normandy and Brittany. We wouldn't have to think about Paris for eight or ten days, General Bradley said, because the Americans would by-pass it on the south and come around behind it, in an effort to trap as many Germans as possible of the great army that was in full flight across France. The German garrison left in Paris, mostly base troops and headquarters types, would pull out and join the general retreat, it was hoped.

On the very next night there was a change in plans. A messenger from the Resistance forces in Paris reached the American lines with the news that a general insurrection had been proclaimed there on August 19, and that the F.F.I. were disputing possession of the city with the Germans. The leaders of the insurrection asked immediate aid.

So Bradley diverted the Fifth Corps from the looping movement and pushed it straight toward Paris. The American Army, with one of its occasional exhibitions of tact, wanted French troops to be the first into Paris. The only French division with the Allies in the North, General Leclerc's Second French Armored, was therefore placed at the tip of the corps. Getting in was not a complicated operation, although for various reasons Leclerc's people did not penetrate the city until Thursday evening, August 24. Friday, the 25th, was clean-up day, the happy DÉNOUEMENT when all the villains got theirs. Only this time the "United States cavalry" were Frenchmen in American tanks. By that time, as in the old movies, the tense part was over. That had been going on during the glorious week of insurrection, when the F.F.I. went out into the streets and fought German tanks with champagne bottles filled with incendiary fluid. The F.F.I. could have remained safe by waiting a few more days. The Germans, if undisturbed, might have wrecked the city before they pulled out. They were caught sitting on their own mines.

But the F.F.I. saved something even more important than a

thousand years in stone. They saved the self-respect of a nation. This is the story of their battle, as it appeared in LES LETTRES FRANÇAISES, no longer clandestine, in the weeks immediately following the liberation. Claude Roy, the author, is a young reporter with a very pretty wife.

Roy's prose may sound implausibly ecstatic, but it conveys the crazy euphoria of the days that produced it. There never was such a mad, happy city as Paris when the army that was to have liberated it arrived, and joined with a populace that had already freed the city, except for a few thousand Germans blockaded in a dozen scattered strong points.

Riding through the PORTE D'ORLÉANS on August 25, in a Belgian-built Chevrolet captured from the Germans, I cried like hell myself and shouted "VIVE LA POLICE!" at the first cop I saw. Then fifty women jumped on the car and kissed me and a second lieutenant named Jack Roach who was driving, and a reporter named Alan Morison from THE STARS AND STRIPES, who was riding along. So you can see that the atmosphere was abnormal.

Mine Eyes Have Seen *

by CLAUDE ROY

Later, much later, when the memory of the hurricane of wrath and joy that has just swept over us has faded on the horizon, some writer will be able to do justice to the days we have just lived through. Right now it is hard to write otherwise than under the breathless dictation of history still in the making. Let us try to set down as exactly, as faithfully as possible, what it has been our privilege to see, hear and live, in the past week. Even that will be something. Today the writer can only be the stenographer of destiny.

✦

* From *Les Lettres Françaises*, September 9, 1944.

SATURDAY. Last night Paris slept a hectic, tossing and interrupted sleep. The night fell on a city without a police force. Crowds collected at the closed doors of the police stations to read the proclamation of the COMITÉ DE LIBÉRATION DE LA POLICE.* In the Rue des Saussaies, the Rue Laurent-Pichat and in the Bois de Boulogne, a fine black snowstorm of burnt paper fell. The BOCHES were burning their records. The trucks of the WEHRMACHT scuttled through the streets of Paris. The ant hill had been kicked over. In the Place de la Concorde a truck went by loaded with washstands. Another was piled high with boxes; a soldier sat on top of the load holding a sewing machine in his arms.

Where were the Allies? At Versailles, at Rambouillet, at Marly? Nobody knew exactly. Bits of burnt paper fluttered in the sunlight. A little black flake settled in the blond hair of my wife. Last evening, as we emerged from the Rue de Buci into the Rue de Seine, headed in the direction of the Senate, she exclaimed, "Fireworks!" but as the red and blue squibs swished by our ears with a DZING, BZZ, we perceived that they were tracer bullets fired from a tommy-gun. For shelter, we ducked into a BISTRO where the proprietor was waiting for the electricity to be turned on. The word was that the Allies were at Versailles. On the Boulevard Saint-Michel the Germans opened fire on the crowd that was jeeringly watching them finish their packing. The gentle-

* The police of Paris had gone on strike August 15. The metamorphosis of the Paris police, from the hated symbol of authority to the beloved champion of the populace, was one of the bizarre aspects of the insurrection. When I lived in the Rue de l'Ecole de Médecine in the Latin Quarter in 1926-7, "A bas les flics!" was the traditional street cry. It means "Down with the cops!" When I came into Paris on August 25, 1944, I saw a bus filled with policemen armed with rifles on the Rue Denfert-Rochereau, and the crowds were shouting, "La police à l'honneur!" A week later I was in an all-night bar on the Rue Pigalle with Peter Lawless, a good fellow now dead, and two French couples who had adopted us, when an old derelict staggered in, very dirty and very drunk, and began a long rambling speech to the company at large. There was a stern-looking policeman at the bar, in uniform. In 1926, or even in 1939, I should have expected him to throw the old bum out on the sidewalk. But instead, the policeman said, almost affectionately, "Silence, pépère"—"Be quiet, pop." Then turning to us, the policeman made a speech. "You see this unfortunate," he said. "He is a stowaway of social life" (un resquilleur de la vie sociale). "It is not his fault." And then he discoursed for twenty minutes on Marxian economics. The trend has not yet affected the New York City police force.—L.

men of the MILICE had already cleared out. They had such nice uniforms and pretty little tommy-guns. Just "to keep order," they explained. BON VOYAGE. The Germans are shooting, and there are casualties. The swine are getting mean.

THE FLAG! People were shouting in the street. I opened the window. In front of the little café, from every window, they were pointing to something that I could not see. My CONCIERGE screamed up to me, "The flag is raised over the PRÉFECTURE!" I went down into the street. It was true. On the roof of the PRÉFECTURE, a small black dot was moving, a fellow who had just hoisted the flag. The flag floated in the wind. One flag, two flags. The flag on the towers of Notre-Dame. The flag on a balcony.

The square in front of Notre-Dame was black with people. Everywhere there were red-white-and-blue arm bands. The leaders of the COMITÉ DE LIBÉRATION DE LA POLICE were addressing their men dressed in civilian clothes. The great main door opened. In a few minutes the police had moved in to occupy their PRÉFECTURE. The telephone girls were up to their ears in work. Thousands of policemen in civilian clothes set out to reoccupy the police stations abandoned during the strike.

Opposite the HÔTEL DE VILLE, where the flag was already floating, the colors were hoisted over the offices of the ASSISTANCE PUBLIQUE.

The first "Marseillaise"! "The Marseillaise" of insurrection. A "Marseillaise" hoarse, straggling and frightfully off pitch. A man showed me his identification papers: he was a prisoner liberated that very morning by the F.F.I. He seemed haggard and bewildered. Liberty had cut his breath short like the first dive of a swimmer into cold water. I went into the courtyard of the PRÉFECTURE—COUR JEAN CHIAPPE.* A strange name. The prefect of police appointed by the provisional government was being inaugurated. A flag was run up on the big flagpole. A second "Marseillaise," a thousand male voices, a thunder that echoed in the square courtyard as if in a well.

---

* Chiappe, préfect de police before the war, was a notorious fascist and conspired to overthrow the Republic. When the Germans occupied France he became an enthusiastic collaborationist. He was killed while on his way to Syria in an airplane. Vichy claimed that the plane was shot down by the R.A.F. (Translator's note.)

A chauffeur of the police force, Titin, had his picture taken with one of his pals, posing in front of three cars, a black Hotchkiss, a Delahaye, and a little eleven horsepower Citroën. Tricolor cockades. They were the three cars belonging to Abel Bonnard, which along with his valises and documents had been "liberated" by patriotic police when he was attempting to flee to Germany. Everybody laughed.

A few traitors had been arrested. They were brought in, pale, their hands above their heads, amid a chorus of boos.

A large automobile went by. It was filled with armed men wearing tricolored armbands carrying pennants of the F.F.I. I recognized two friends of mine, movie operators. I had seen them every day. I had known nothing of their activities in the Resistance, nor they of mine. They had come from the HÔTEL DE VILLE, which their men had occupied along with the COMITÉ PARISIEN DE LIBÉRATION.

Julien and Allard told me the story of the arrest of Laval's prefect of the Seine, Bouffet. Tommy-guns in their hands, they had barged into his office. Bouffet, still arrogant, received them.

"I protest," he said. "I demand to know by what authority you are here."

"By the authority of General de Gaulle and the Provisional Government of the Republic."

"What do you want?"

"To strip you of your office, arrest you, and replace you."

"Have you anything to prove your authority?"

The patriots patted their tommy-guns. "You have five minutes to get your personal belongings together and follow us."

His bravado wilted immediately. The ex-prefect of the Seine was locked in the disciplinary barracks of the PRÉFECTURE DE POLICE, where Monsieur Paul Taittinger * later joined him.

POWDER TRAIL. The French flag flies over the SORBONNE, now freed of the traitors of the mind and Nazi intellectuals. A student kisses his girl. The most beautiful day of our lives. An old professor puts on his pince-nez to see better. The crowd sings "The Marseil-

* A pre-war French fascist politician.

laise." The most beautiful day of our lives. A girl flings her arms up, laughs and dances. The most beautiful day of our lives.

German trucks roll along the streets shooting at random. But over the Hospital of Saint Vincent-de-Paul, over the School of Mines, over all the police stations our flag is flying. Throngs gather in the street to read the white posters of the CONSEIL NATIONAL DE LA RÉSISTANCE and the Communist deputies. Summons to nation-wide insurrection. In the streets, on the way to take up their posts at strategic positions, pass boys with tricolor armbands already sticking out of their coat pockets. Their weapons are concealed in violin cases, slip covers and paper packages.

A large black automobile filled with arms goes by; it belongs to General Bridoux, the Vichy minister, and has been "liberated" by the insurgents. Another car goes by, that of the Cardinal Archbishop of Paris, Monsignor Suhard.* Merely "borrowed," this one.

"Of course, we did have to break the glass to be able to fire from the doors, but the cardinal will get his car back shinier than ever."

Nazis go by in stampedes. Stunned and with haunted faces. They fire at random. Passers-by are killed. Little by little, the streets are emptied of everybody except the F.F.I. wearing their armbands, messengers keeping up liaison between the various patriotic groups, and others on official business. The leaders are organizing the defense, plotting arcs of fire, making preparations to defend the public buildings that our side has captured. The chairs and tables on the TERRASSES of the cafés are piled out of the way. The iron shutters are pulled down in front of shops. The rumor is that the Germans are going to make a desperate attempt to enforce a curfew at two o'clock in the afternoon. The whole staff of LES LETTRES FRANÇAISES assembles at the PARIS-SOIR † building. F.F.I. members, tommy-guns under their arms, guard the entrance. They have been occupying this immense building since last night. Papers are lying in a corner—cables and headlines from yesterday's papers: ATTEMPTING TO BREAK THROUGH IN A NEW

* Cardinal Suhard's cordial relations and suspected sympathies with the Nazis made him unpopular with French patriots. (*Translator's note.*)

† *Paris-Soir:* leading afternoon newspaper before the war, taken over and published by collaborators during the occupation.

SECTOR, SOVIET FORCES RECEIVE A SEVERE SETBACK NEAR TCHERNIGOV! The F.F.I. trample on the crumpled paper. "I AM LEAVING GERMANY WITH AN IMPRESSION OF REASSURANCE," DECLARES MONSIEUR BRUNETON AT BERLIN. . . . TERRORIST CRIMES. On the bulletin board an announcement reads: ADVERTISEMENTS RECEIVED TODAY WILL BE INSERTED FROM AUGUST 18 ON. JEWISH BUSINESS FIRM FOR SALE: SMALL TOOLS AND STEEL, BALES, 32, RUE DE LANCRY. . . . YOUNG FRENCHMEN, ENLIST IN THE GERMAN NAVY!

Instructed by the FÉDÉRATION DU LIVRE to report for work, linotypists, rotary pressmen and workers are at their machines.* Munitions are piled up in the temporary guard room.

1.30 p.m.

THE SIEGE OF THE PRÉFECTURE DE POLICE

A phone call from the PRÉFECTURE DE POLICE. The Germans are beginning to attack.

Rue du Louvre, Rue de Rivoli. A Red Cross flag: the F.F.I. first-aid stations are already set up. Stray bullets whistle across the Place du Châtelet. Not a soul in the streets. A volley sweeps the Boulevard du Palais. The defenders open up on a German truck. The firing dies down. The truck seems to be abandoned, its passengers put out of action. I start out, and the firing begins again. I run toward the PRÉFECTURE, where the door opens to receive me, and make it in a sprinting finish.

Armed men come and go in the courtyard. Already there are a number of trucks and weapons-carriers and light trucks, captured from the enemy. The supply service is having difficulty finding

---

* The staffs of the clandestine newspapers had arranged to seize the plants of the collaborationist journals as soon as the insurrection broke out. The printers were already enlisted in the Resistance. The seizure took place on schedule, and while bullets made unpleasant noises around them the ex-clandestine staffs got out regular editions with news of the street fighting. Boys were peddling them in the streets when we got in, just as if there had never been an occupation. But the German soldiers trapped in several strong points were still shooting. The headlines and notices quoted by Roy were of course in the last collaborationist edition of *Paris-Soir*, printed before the insurgents seized the plant.—L.

enough ammunition for the combatants. One man is armed with a French tommy-gun, another with an English gun, another with a French automatic rifle and still others with German weapons. The crackle of the volleys reverberates noisily in the courtyards, corridors and stairways. During the occasional lulls, the great main doors open to let in or out ambulances or stretcher-bearers waving white flags with red crosses.

The steady fire of the defenders, policemen and F.F.I. from the Latin Quarter, who had rushed to the defense of the PRÉFECTURE, swept the square in front of Notre Dame, the Boulevard du Palais, the QUAIS and bridges. As soon as the SS began their attack, the police stations had been alerted by telephone. The police reinforcements, coming down the Rue Saint-Jacques and the Boulevard Saint-Michel in an audacious maneuver, took the attackers in the rear. The defenders made counterattacks and sorties that brought back prisoners and booty. One F.F.I. attempted single-handed a surprise sortie into the square. He attacked an automobile, a Peugeot 401 camouflaged by the WEHRMACHT, killed its occupants and, under heavy fire from the German infantry, started the engine and came roaring into the courtyard.

In the prefect's office, where I went to telephone, one of the three secretaries who had come back to the citadel that morning was still smiling. Her little rayon dress was spotlessly white, and a bouquet of roses, somewhat wilted, stood beside the telephone. Liaison men in khaki shirts, their tommy-guns under their arms, came and went. She smiled. Captured boxes of explosives, magazines and detonators that the Germans intended to use to blow up the bridges of Paris were brought in. She smiled. The cannon made the windows shake. She smiled.

"I shan't get my swim at the DELIGNY * today," she said pleasantly between two telephone calls.

She was to pass the night at the switchboard. The next morning, the little rayon dress was still astonishingly, marvelously, and gloriously white.

* Les Bains Deligny are floating baths moored in the Seine, just about opposite the Louvre. The water isn't too clean, but the girls get a wonderful tan sunning on the planks, and when you walk over the bridges you can look down at them.—L.

Men came in to telephone to their homes.

"Don't worry about me, Nini. I have already got five square-heads to my credit. ON LES AURA! They're on the run."

"Above all stay indoors. . . . Mind the kid. . . . MAIS NON, I'm not in any danger at all. . . . Have you got bread and something to eat? Above all, don't go out."

A hairy-armed husky took down the receiver and put in a call to his buddies on the outside. "Remember to give the prisoners their chow. Got to show them that we aren't bastards like they are."

"The prisoners" were the collaborationist mayor of Clamart and his staff. The husky and his combat group had captured them that morning.

"Pinching them was a pipe. . . . They came along like lambs! We did have one real job though. The BOCHES had mined the whole quarter of Clamart ready to blow it up. We had to take the detonators out of their whole gallery of mines, crawling around in the dark, with armored cars on our tails. What the hell, it had to be done."

THE TANK ATTACK—At four o'clock the German tanks went into action. Their cannon smashed down the main door leading into the cathedral square and caused damage and casualties. A barricade of sandbags and trucks was erected immediately. A couple of young men calmly set about filling bottles with gasoline in case the tanks succeeded in breaking through. But the fire of the defenders kept the infantry from following up this partial success of the tanks. They fell back.

A couple of dead Germans were carried in on a stretcher, head to feet. Covered with blood, all faces look alike. We took their arms and ammunition. Some photos fell out of the pockets of one of them and were walked on by the combatants. One of the F.F.I. offered a cigarette to a prisoner. He began to tremble, convinced that it meant he was about to be shot. Another of our lads, still black with sweat and dust, gave a swallow of mint cordial to a young SS man who was lying there, his face drawn with exhaustion. I couldn't help thinking of the thousands of

F.F.I. taken prisoner and shot on the spot, of the twenty-year-old kids and the MAQUISARDS assassinated by the enemy. I thought of the captured combatants of the F.F.I. in east and central France, whom, at that very moment perhaps, the Nazis were standing up against walls and mowing down with tommy-guns. One could still read on walls throughout Paris the red posters in two languages announcing that the Nazis would treat all fighters in the F.F.I. as FRANCS-TIREURS. "Poor devils!" one of the defenders said to me. He meant the prisoners. But the little phrase that appeared daily in the German communiqués stuck in my mind, "IN FRANCE, FIFTY TERRORISTS HAVE BEEN EXECUTED."

5:30 p.m.: The Germans' trench-mortars tried to blanket the courtyard with shells. They were quickly silenced however. Next they tried crawling over the roofs to get into the PRÉFECTURE. They came through the café on the corner of the Place du Palais and the Boulevard Saint-Michel. Our men, who were holding the street, and the defenders of the inner courtyard sprayed the roof with bullets. I saw a figure in a FELDGRAU uniform flap its arms, drop a gun, and topple into space.

At six o'clock I found myself firing, with a group of policemen, from an office window on the Quai du Marché Neuf looking across the Quai Saint-Michel. The windowpanes were shattered to bits. Powdered glass, magazines, cartridges, and weapons littered the nondescript desk and covered the blotter, the inkwell and the artificial leather armchair. The stutter of machine guns re-echoing through the offices and halls made a deafening racket. Five enemy trucks were knocked out on the Quai Saint-Michel. A truck loaded with gasoline was blazing beside the NOTRE-DAME HÔTEL at the corner of the Rue Saint-Jacques. The office from which we were firing was that of the Divisional Commissioner David, chief of the Political Brigade. In this room, only a few days earlier, David —David Bloody-Hands, as they called him here—was torturing patriots.

The truck was still ablaze. The flames had spread to the awning of the café and were licking the walls of the NOTRE-DAME HÔTEL. From all the windows of the PRÉFECTURE, the shooting ceased while, at the risk of their lives, the F.F.I. and the insurgent policemen, who by this time had captured the Quai Saint-Michel, tried to move the flaming truck and save the building already blackened by the flames. The firemen arrived.

During the evening there was a rumor that the Germans were asking for a truce. The order to cease fire was given. An extraordinary and bewildering silence settled over the immense building where all day long the inner courts, the long corridors and metal stairways had re-echoed with the rumble of cannon, the steady crackle of automatic rifles and the sharp reports of rockets and carbines.

Field kitchens went into operation in the courtyard. A meal of sorts, a cup of hot coffee, and two packs of cigarettes were passed out to each of the weary fighters.

Dressed in the most heterogeneous uniforms, weighed down with magazines, German hand grenades, and weapons of varied origins, these men were able for a moment to enjoy the feeling of a precarious but already reassuring victory. One of them had tied his arm band around his felt hat. He had a tommy-gun, two potato-masher grenades stuck in his belt, the bottom of his pants legs tucked into heavy red woolen socks, heavy shoes, and a checkered shirt with rolled-up sleeves. He seemed to have stepped out of an American film—the hero of VIVA VILLA himself.

The truce turned out to be a myth. All night long and for several days after, the fighting around the PRÉFECTURE, the Parisian stronghold of the national insurrection, was to continue.

SUNDAY—THE BARRICADES—MONDAY. I succeeded in getting out of the PRÉFECTURE about noon Sunday. On orders from the general staff of the F.F.I., Paris was bristling with barricades, and the fighting went on. The fiercest battles took place at the HÔTEL DE VILLE, in the Latin Quarter, and around the MAIRIE of the Batignolles. The German flag still flew over the Senate, the Ministry of the Marine, and the HOTEL MEURICE. The Germans were digging in strongly in certain parts of the city. From doorsteps and windows, housewives followed the news of the battle. But soon they too were mobilized. The rear must hold; the rear must do its part. "The rear" was, for example, the little square of

the Montagne Sainte-Geneviève where the entire population between the ages of three and twelve and from seventy to ninety
was sawing wood for the bakeries, collecting food for the F.F.I.,
cleaning weapons, or ripping up paving blocks to build barricades.

A word about the geography of these barricades. At first people
brought down from their apartments the sandbags of the Civilian
Defense. Then they tore up paving blocks of stone or wood,
requisitioned materials from lumber yards, pried up the heavy iron
gratings around trees, and felled the trees themselves. A charred
German tank, toppled on its side, was piled high with mattress
springs and a cretonne-covered armchair. At LES HALLES, vegetable
wagons and pushcarts were piled together. Rue Mazarine was
completely blocked by a huge municipal garbage truck. Cabbage
stalks lay rotting in the August sun. In the Rue de Rivoli, the
gilded letters of a tailor's sign topped off a formidable barricade
with the word "Fashion." Urchins trundled heavy building stones
on a wheelbarrow. At Saint-Germain-des-Prés and at the corner
of the Rue Saint-Jacques, portraits of Hitler and other Nazi leaders
decorated the crest of the improvised ramparts. Cardboard signs,
set askew on sandbags and mattresses, read: "ACHTUNG, MINEN," or
"National lotttery drawing Tonight."

A parish priest, who was also an officer in the engineers, made
a scale drawing of the barricades in his quarter. Blue pencil in
hand, his cassock tucked up, he surveyed the disposition of his
forces. When everything was finished and the automatic rifles
and machine guns in place, the whole quarter turned out to
admire his barricade. It was the handsomest, the solidest and
the most formidable of all the barricades.

From hour to hour the barricades closed in tighter on the
Germans, a methodical trap, the spider web of the patience,
ingenuity, and the great victorious wrath of an embattled Paris.

TUESDAY. The battle is raging all over Paris. To circulate in the
streets, all one has to do is to pause at street corners, avoid German
tanks, have an F.F.I. pass, keep down behind the parapet while
crossing bridges, not mind flying glass, stray bullets, isolated
snipers, Germans or MILICIENS, de-paved streets, and still-smolder-

ing fires. These perils passed, one can reach, for instance, the MAIRIE of the Batignolles, in the heart of insurgent Paris.

THE MAIRIE OF THE BATIGNOLLES.—A citizen is insisting on his right to pass through the barricades. He is the happy father of a little daughter born three days ago. He has finally decided to go out to declare her birth to the Bureau of Vital Statistics at the MAIRIE. What an adventure!

Cars pass, bristling with cannon, rifles and tommy-guns. Over the German camouflage is painted in big letters: "F.F.I." A French pennant whips in the wind.

The F.F.I. and the MILICES PATRIOTIQUES * of the ARRONDISSE-MENT occupied the MAIRIE three days ago with six revolvers and a few automatic rifles. Thanks to weapons "liberated" from the enemy, today they were able to arm more than four hundred and fifty men.

The new municipal staff is in permanent session. Calm, me-thodical, clear-headed, and straightforward men. Inside the strongly guarded barricades everything is order. Fighting is one thing, ad-ministration is another. The ARRONDISSEMENT has to live, eat and defend itself. The mayor thinks of everything, wood for the bakeries, milk for the children, precautions against pillaging, the service of supplies. While I was in his office, at the door of which stood an armed guard, the telephone rang. The Germans were advancing through Rue Boursault and the Boulevard des Bati-gnolles. I started out immediately with an F.F.I. detachment that moved along in single file hugging the walls to reach its combat position and re-inforce the advance posts of the F.F.I.

A tank preceded us. It was a Somua tank that still bore the serial number of the WEHRMACHT. The workers in the Somua factories, which worked for the Germans, had assembled this tank in haste—just in time for the F.F.I. of the Batignolles to capture it in the factory, in spite of a spirited resistance on the part of the Germans. The tank, manned by the F.F.I., had come from Saint-Ouen to assist in the defense of the MAIRIE.

* A secret para-military mass organization of the Resistance; not to be confused with La Milice. (Translator's note.)

An F.F.I. grenade man, a Negro,* slipped off the track of the tank. He was wounded. While the Germans were still firing, the stretcher-bearers carried him off. The blood flowed, bright red in the sun, against the white shirt and the black skin.

The German resistance was growing weaker. From the Rue de Rome an interpreter, cupping his hands, shouted a message to them. They replied in German. A bath towel waved from a window. A loud cheer broke out. The Germans were surrendering. The prisoners and the wounded were taken to join the other captives in the classrooms of the public school.

In the meanwhile, in the center of the city, the Germans had launched Tiger tanks and armored cars in an all-out attack on the HÔTEL DE VILLE and the PRÉFECTURE DE POLICE. But the vital centers of the insurrection were holding out. The Allied armies were closing their grip around Paris.

WEDNESDAY. I came out of the office of the COMITÉ DE LIBÉRA-TION DU CINÉMA on the Champs-Elysées. In the company of Jean Painlevé, Pierre Blanchar, Louis Daquin and their associates, I saw the first newsreels of the war in Paris being filmed by volunteer cameramen, who had started out on the first day in pursuit of pictures in streets swept with machine-gun bullets.

At the Rond-Point des Champs-Elysées shooting began again. In front of the American bar, L'ESCARGOT, I had barely time to drop flat on the ground. Four tanks, two Tigers and two Goliaths, were coming up through the bushes in the garden of the Champs-Elysées. Cannon and machine guns opened fire. The asphalt was

* A number of Senegalese, having hidden their uniforms after the débâcle, lived among civilians all through the occupation. They were most loyal to France (having heard about the Nazi race doctrines) and fought bravely in the F.F.I. One became a popular hero during the insurrection by climbing on a German tank and decapitating all the members of the crew. He first beheaded one man who was directing the progress of the tank. With obliging stupidity, the others stuck their heads out of the turret one by one to see what was happening, and he cut their chumps off too. The Senegalese, however, were sometimes embarrassing colleagues in the underground. A new Senegalese in a village was so conspicuous that even a German would know he was not a local boy. American or British aviators could get by pretending to be deaf and dumb, but that was not enough of a trick to protect a Negro.—L.

torn by the heavy caterpillar treads. Pedestrians dodged into PORTES-COCHÈRES that opened on a crack to admit them.

The Germans were attacking the police station at the corner of the GRAND-PALAIS. The F.F.I. holding the station were very inferior in number. They defended themselves fiercely. An ice wagon was pulled up at the curb a few meters from us. The horse was pawing the ground. A bullet struck him. He sank down between the shafts like a burst sawdust toy.

A great cloud of smoke went up from the GRAND-PALAIS. With a sound of bleating sirens the firemen arrived. I saw them trying to reason with the Germans, who refused to allow them to try to put out the fire caused by their incendiary shells. The firemen attempted to disregard their orders. The Germans opened fire on them. The bullets pierced the hose that the firemen had hurriedly strung. In the Avenue Victor-Emmanuel, ten little jets of water danced. Bullets whistled. An absurd thought passed through my mind. I thought of the jets of water in shooting galleries at a street fair with the little celluloid balls dancing on top of them.

Blinded by the smoke, the defenders took refuge in the cellar. In the meanwhile, the German tanks were shooting down passers-by in the Champs-Elysées. German grenades finally broke the desperate defense of the F.F.I. Some of the defenders escaped. Others were taken prisoner. The Germans rounded up without distinction both the combatants and the civilians who, surprised in the street by the outbreak of the fighting, had taken refuge in the GRAND-PALAIS.

The fire was spreading. The firemen got their hoses into play. There was still some shooting going on in the midst of the smoke, the torrents of water, and the roar of the flames under the immense glass roof. Through the noise and confusion, the stretcher-bearers picked their way, bringing out the wounded. The Germans kept their heads: they form a chain line to save the bottles of champagne from the refreshment stand of the HOUCKE CIRCUS established on the ground floor of the palace. Whinnying madly, their croups gleaming with sweat, rearing and stamping with all four hoofs, the horses, maddened by the smoke, flames and the play of the fire hoses, were led out. Volunteers formed a rescue line to save the exhibit of handicraft of French prisoners of war and the articles on display in the Museum of Science. Firemen, Germans, rescuers and prisoners all milled about together. The Germans seemed to be having trouble making up their minds whether to stop the rescuers or to help them. We waded ankle-deep in papers, fallen plaster, charred wood, water, empty shell cases and cartridges. A bramble of bicycles was burning. Horses whinnied and reared. The wooden timberwork was entirely consumed, as well as the wooden stands of the circus, the railings, and the straw in the stables. Fighting was still going on in the cellars. A girl carefully carried out a lacy paper tablecloth, the handiwork of the prisoners in some German STALAG. A photo of Pétain lay on the grass. Above the entrance of the circus, dangling trapezes swung in the smoke. The horses sniffed and snorted as they passed by the body of the horse that had been killed. From their windows people looked down on this madhouse spectacle while keeping an eye on the lunch that was cooking on the paper-burning stove. It was noon. The firemen had the fire under control.

THURSDAY—WITH THE HOSPITAL UNITS. I decided to pass the morning at the HÔTEL-DIEU * with the boys and girls whom I had seen for the past five days going out under the thickest of fire to bring in the French and German wounded and waving, as if to shoo bullets away, little white pennants with red crosses on them. They talked of their work as if it were the most natural thing in the world, as if there was nothing heroic about those civilians leaving their cashier's windows, offices, shops, stores, or schoolbooks, to live night and day in the full fury of an insurrection, in the odor of drugs and the blood of first-aid stations and hospitals.

Nobody here—professors, surgeons doctors, interns, nurses, stretcher-bearers, or blood donors—had slept for five days. The only thing that counted was that lives should be saved and pain spared or assuaged.

There had been times, I admit, when I lost faith in my comrades, in the youth of France. But I know today that I was wrong.

---

* A large public hospital on the square between Notre-Dame and the Préfecture de Police.

Anyone who looked into these weary but happy eyes will henceforth know the look of Hope itself: it is the never-to-be-forgotten look on the faces of the fighters, the stretcher-bearers, the whole Parisian insurrection—heroes with arm bands and heroes with white smocks, brothers-in-arms.

A SOLDIER SALUTES SOLDIERS. At noon two cars dashed into the courtyard of the HÔTEL-DIEU. The president of the C.N.R. and the prefect of the Seine had come to salute the wounded.

A pair of dark eyes, fervent and steady: this is Monsieur Georges Bidault,* president of the C.N.R. His is not one of those anonymous, official-looking faces. It was not a formal, uncommunicative mask that met the feverish gaze of the wounded.

The prefect of the Seine, Monsieur Flouret, slim, graying, attentive and silent, accompanied Monsieur Bidault.

The stretcher-bearers welcomed them. Monsieur Bidault's speech was short but from the heart.

"With an unflagging heroism, you have given your care to our soldiers and the enemy alike. The life of a German intact is an enemy life. The life of a German wounded is a human life. In the name of our nation, already liberated, already victorious, I thank you."

This man, who for four years had been one of the leaders of the daily underground battle, stooped for a moment over each bed.

One of the wounded was the young Maurice N., motorcyclist in the Fourth Motorized Group. He had been wounded, first by a shot fired by a MILICIEN on the Quai des Tournelles, and then by a German bullet on Avenue Daumesnil. Maurice made a vague attempt to sit up.

"Take it easy, my boy, and let me embrace you."

* A professor of history at the *Lycée Louis-le-Grand* before the war, Georges Bidault was active in a small political group, the Christian Democrats, which combined Catholicism with a fairly advanced social and economic doctrine. One of the early organizers of the *Conseil National de la Résistance*, he resigned from the C.N.R. after the liberation to become Minister of Foreign Affairs in the De Gaulle Government. The *Mouvement Républicain Populaire*, which has become since the liberation one of the three major parties in France, is the spiritual descendant of Bidault's little Christian Democratic party. Bidault, as leader of the M.R.P., has been one of the first "new" men to make an impression on French postwar politics.—L.

He moved on to the ward where the German wounded lay. One of them spoke French.

"Translate what I am about to say to your comrades." And Georges Bidault began:

"I am the chief of the French Resistance movement . . ."

The German translated.

". . . and I have come to wish you a prompt recovery . . ."

The German translated.

"May you soon return to a free Germany in a free Europe."

The German translated. Georges Bidault raised his hand in a salute and withdrew. A soldier saluting soldiers.

We were hardly up the stairs when an intense firing broke out. Cannon shots resounded in the corridors and wards and shook the windowpanes. There was fighting in the square in front of Notre-Dame.

Dr. D. had lent me a Red Cross arm band. I left the little party of officials and joined a team of stretcher-bearers under the command of Odette D., a student in liberal arts.

Completely unaware—because of the total breakdown of their liaison and communication systems (as we were to learn later from the prisoners themselves)—that Paris was in a state of insurrection, a German convoy of six trucks, a heavy prime mover, and a trailer had come up the QUAIS only to blunder into the trap of barricades between the PRÉFECTURE DE POLICE and Notre-Dame. One of the trucks was already afire. The Germans fought back stubbornly. There was bitter fighting. While the firing was still going on near the bridge of Notre-Dame, Odette D. and I were already on our way with a rubber-tired stretcher cart. Near the trailer were some wounded men. In the heat of battle, one of the F.F.I. was reluctant to hand over his wounded prisoner. We almost had to snatch him away by force. Odette was equal to the occasion.

The trailer was loaded with gasoline. Some of the cans had been pierced by bullets, and the ground was covered with an incongruous mixture of gasoline, blood and dirty rain. We loaded our patient, who was bleeding copiously from wounds in the shoulder and belly, onto the stretcher. My hands were covered with blood. We trundled our stretcher back to the hospital on the run. In the hospital yard, our patient was transferred to a hand stretcher and taken down to the first-aid station.

The doctors and nurses were hard at work. Frenchmen and Germans were undressed. A man whose wounds were being dressed groaned. The whole room smelled of sweat, disinfectants and blood. It took less than ten minutes for these men, naked and covered with blood, to be cleaned, bandaged, bundled up and evacuated, some to the operating room, some to the ward where shock cases were treated, and the rest to wards reserved for less serious wounds.

In the shock ward, everything possible was being done to save two lives, one German and the other French. Plasma and blood transfusions were given. Reflecting heaters were plugged in to warm these bodies that life seemed about to leave. Second by second, the battle of men against death went on.

A German on a stretcher, waiting for his turn to be taken into the operating room, was moaning. A secretary noted down his name and rank. He was a boy from the LUFTWAFFE. He bore a French name, the name of one of the Protestant families that the revocation of the Edict of Nantes had driven into Germany. A little nurse was dipping her hand in a pitcher of water and bathing his forehead. The wounded boy looked up with questioning eyes. She explained to him in his own language that he would not have to wait much longer.

The telephone rang. There was fighting at the ODÉON. Already the stretcher-bearers were on their way.

THE HARBINGERS OF VICTORY AT THE HÔTEL DE VILLE. The members of the C.N.R. were pacing back and forth with excitement. It was in this office that the hopes of four interminable years of anguish were to be fulfilled. We knew that shortly this door would open and that the incredible moment for which Frenchmen had lived and died, been tortured, shot, imprisoned and deported, would arrive. In the heart of Paris in arms, through a night when machine-gun fire clattered like a typewriter under the fingers of destiny, we waited for the gates of liberty to open.

O my friends dead or in exile, my friends deported to the death camps of Germany, I am here in your name. I am here to open my eyes, to see a man come in through this door, and to tell you what I saw—for you who hoped and for you who are hoping. The messenger of the tragedies of Aschylus is about to enter. My comrades, my only aim is to repeat to you his words and to listen—for you; to hear—for you; and, for you, to weep for joy.

The advance guards of General Leclerc's division had captured the LYCÉE LAKANAL. The French armored column was bearing down on the PORTE D'ITALIE. In the great office of the prefect * the telephone rang; the chiefs of the Resistance, these men who had proved their patience through four years of waiting, drummed nervously on the arms of their chairs, walked to and fro, peered out the windows. Night fell. On a stand was the bust of the Republic. On the high mantelpiece above the fireplace was a cheap photograph of General de Gaulle, draped with a tricolored ribbon. Bullets had drilled the mirror above it with star-shaped holes. On the sills of the high windows were sandbags and tommy-guns. Men of the F.F.I. were on guard, unshaven and dirty.

In the courtyard, in the midst of trucks, half-tracks, and anti-aircraft guns captured from the enemy, and the F.F.I. vehicles, panoplies of the Allied flags were being made up.

The Allied armies were reported at Sceaux, Bagneux, at the PORTE D'ITALIE.

In the corridors and the staircases, MILICIENNES and women militants of the P.P.F., their heads shaved, were sweeping the floors under the orders of the F.F.I. One of them still wore her earrings, two magnificent pearls whose sumptuous luster seemed strangely out of place against the close-cropped head.

At eight o'clock everyone except the guards on duty went to the refectory. The prefect and the members of the C.N.R. were eating noodles and bread from wooden trestle tables. Suddenly Bidault rose. There was a breathless silence. He shouted, he howled, his voice choked. "The first tanks of the French army

* Unlike most regions in France, Paris has two prefects: the Prefect of Police, whose office, as we have already seen, is located in the Prefecture of Police, and the Prefect of the Department of the Seine, whose office is in the Hôtel de Ville.

are crossing the Seine in the heart of Paris!" There was a thunder of cheers. Standing on the tables, a thousand men as one, from the Prefect to the F.F.I., sang "The Marseillaise" of deliverance.

Then there was a general rush to the doors. At the corner of the Place de l'Hôtel de Ville nearest the river, the tank ROMILLY came to a stop. It was 9:22 p.m.

Carried by a mob of armed men, weeping, laughing and shouting, two men entered the prefect's office.

"Captain Dronne and Private Pirlian, of the Route Regiment of the Tchad." *

The president of the C.N.R. had the bearded captain in his arms. "Captain, in the name of the soldiers of France without uniforms, I embrace you, the first French soldier in uniform to enter Paris."

I also embraced the captain, with his fringe of whiskers, his sweat-covered face, his crushed and filthy KÉPI. He said only: "I'm pretty dirty—filthy. . . . It was a long trek."

Captain Dronne had come from the Cameroon to Paris, via Marsa-Matrouk, Tobruk, Benghazi, Bir-Hakeim, the Tchad, London and Cherbourg. It had taken him forty-eight months.

Private Pirlian had the accent of Nice and a funny little round helmet that went so strangely with a French face, an American helmet.

Rockets streaked the sky. There was a series of reports. The salvos of victory!

Suddenly the windowpanes were shattered. The pendants of the chandeliers flew to bits under a burst of machine-gun bullets. The plaster fell from the ceiling. The Germans were attacking the HÔTEL DE VILLE.

We put out the lights. The F.F.I. returned the fire from the windows.

"Everybody without arms down on the floor!" ordered Major Stéphane, commander of the F.F.I. of the HÔTEL DE VILLE.

---

* Lake Tchad in Central Africa. Free French Forces, organized in French Equatorial Africa, marched from there to Tripoli to join the Allied North African campaign. The tank *Romilly* was named after a small city in the Department of the Aube. Leclerc's people had a whole regiment of tanks named after towns and regions.—L.

Flat on their faces under the devastating fusillade, the members of the C.N.R., the officials and the prefect passed the first minutes of French liberty.

I tried to get out of the HÔTEL DE VILLE. The doors, around which the fighting was intense, were out of the question. The MÉTRO was the only possible exit. Accompanying an F.F.I. patrol on its way to relieve the men on guard at the Châtelet station, I made my way, in a sullen silence, walking the tracks where the thundering trains of our daily MÉTRO no longer rolled. At the junction of each communication tunnel we stopped and listened for approaching steps. Could it be the enemy who had succeeded in making an infiltration?

"What's the password?" we challenged.

"Verdun."

We picked our way slowly through the labyrinth of tracks, tunnels and corridors that echoed to our tread.

A steel grating opened enough to let me pass, and I emerged into the opaque darkness of Paris. An enormous fire reddened the sky at the far end of the Rue de Rivoli. Church bells were ringing in the night. At a street corner there were voices and an accordion. Paris was singing its deliverance and victory:

"ALLONS, ENFANTS DE LA PATRIE,
LE JOUR DE GLOIRE EST ARRIVÉ."

FRIDAY. Friday morning, 8 o'clock. A wave of armored cars, jeeps and tanks rolled down the Rue Saint-Jacques. Painted on the plates of their armor, the tanks bore names wonderful to read after four years of Nazi parades: VALMY, D'ARTAGNAN, PORTE DE LA CHAPELLE, LE MORT-HOMME.

The crowd cheered, threw flowers and kisses to the dusty, bronzed and bearded soldiers. The morning was to bring an extraordinary mixture of triumphal processions and street fighting.

From the roof of the SORBONNE, a group of MILICIENS turned a machine gun on the crowd that gather to cheer Leclerc's Division. In the Rue des Ecoles women and children were killed. There was blood on the asphalt pavement.

The barricades opened, cautiously at first, and then, as if by a miracle, melted away.

All through the day the French tanks went about supporting the F.F.I. in mopping-up operations. At the Place de la République, the Senate, the KOMMANDANTUR, and in the Rue de Rivoli, the last islands of enemy resistance were surrounded, pounded by shell-fire, and obliged to surrender. As our armored vehicles penetrated ever deeper into the enemy defenses wild rejoicing sprang from the paving behind them. The stores of silk stockings, tobacco and bread found in the enemy trucks, the booty piled up by Nazis looting, were distributed to the crowd. Girls were in the arms of soldiers. Children played with the mysterious gadgets of armored cars and half-tracks. The soldiers told the crowds who gathered about them to listen to the fantastic tales of their odyssey—the escape from France, the fascist prisons of Spain, the drive from Lake Tchad across the Sahara with Leclerc's column, Tobruk, Marsa-Matruk, Benghazi, Bir-Hakeim, the fighting in Tunisia, the landing, the Battle of Normandy, the war in France. The Parisians listened, all ears.*

Frenchmen were talking to Frenchmen.

Success Story†

by CLAUDE ROY

Never will Paris forget those announcements that it found posted on its walls on August 19. The white paper, still wet with printer's ink and paste, bore the heading that had not been seen for four years, RÉPUBLIQUE FRANÇAISE. This order of general mobilization revealed the name, hitherto unknown to most Frenchmen, of the man who was to direct the final fight for Paris: "The commissioner delegated by the Provisional Government, in accord with the Paris Committee of Liberation, reminds all the organized

---

* They were surely getting an earful. Leclerc left Tchad, in 1942, with an "army" that included only 175 whites. He reached Paris in 1944 with an overstrength division of 17,000 white men. How many of these could have ever seen Tchad?—L.

† From *Les Lettres Françaises*, September 30, 1944.

groups of the Resistance movement that they, as well as the police force and the GENDARMERIE, are to consider themselves incorporated into the French Forces of the Interior and that these forces, in the Departments of the Seine, Seine-et-Oise, Seine-et-Marne, and Oise, are under the orders of the colonel commanding the region, Rol."

Rol? Who was Rol?

Henri-Georges-René Tanguy was born at Morlaix, Finistère, on June 12, 1906. His father was an officer in the merchant marine. His mother ran a small laundry. The Tanguys were poor, very poor. The little Breton's childhood was a wandering one. Successively, as his father's home port changed, the family lived at Brest, Cherbourg, Toulon and Nantes. At thirteen the boy left school and went to work in a factory to earn his living. His future was laid out for him. He would be a laborer all his life.

On Friday, August 25, 1944, three men signed their names to the articles by which the German garrison of Paris surrendered. For the vanquished, General von Choltitz. For the victors, General Leclerc * and Colonel Rol.

Colonel Rol was Henri-Georges-René Tanguy. He was thirty-eight years old. In spite of the hard life he had lived, the young colonel, blond and blue-eyed, scarcely looked thirty. He laid down the fountain pen. And perhaps Rol-Tanguy, this colonel of the "terrorists" who had just written his name into history between that of General de Hautecloque, alias Leclerc, and General von Choltitz—this colonel who, only a short time ago, had been a sheetmetal worker smiled to himself.

Yes, a worker. But let us have no romantic notions on that

---

* Many of De Gaulle's officers, although outside France, took noms de guerre so that the Gestapo would not harm their families at home. Among these was the Marquis de Hautecloque. Twice taken prisoner by the Germans during the campaign of 1940, he twice escaped, and joined General de Gaulle. Sent to French Equatorial Africa he organized the famous column which in the winter of 1942-43 came up from Lake Tchad in Central Africa, crossed the Sahara, fought its way through Italian territory and joined the British Eighth Army in Libya. That column, by the way, consisted of 3800 Negroes and 175 white men. The whites were officers and non-coms. Even the nurses in the field hospital were big elaborately scarified black men with pointed teeth. The doctors denied that they were cannibals. After the junction Leclerc's men were incorporated in the Fourth Indian Division, which had lost one of its brigades at Tobruk. A British brigade is roughly equivalent to an American combat team, and three of them make a division. "Four Ind

score. Nothing "picturesque." Rol does not speak argot. His hands
are not black. He does not curse or swear. He speaks in a clear,
even voice and with great precision in his choice of words. If it
were not that the word carries some connotation of preciosity
and overniceness, I should say that he expresses himself with
elegance. Rol is not precious. He is precise. His is a mind clear
and firm, formed by the double experience of a culture slowly
acquired through his own efforts, and a well-filled life. Rol ha:
been through all adventures including that of "those adventurers
of the modern world, fathers of families," as Péguy says. Somewhere in Paris are a six-month-old boy and a little three-year-old
girl who have their father's blond hair and blue eyes. Rol says
simply, "It is a great responsibility to have children when you
live like an outlaw, wanted by the GESTAPO and the police."

Rol was fifteen years old when he came to Paris in 1923. He
worked in garages and later in a factory. He read widely.

"I dipped into a little of everything. I even tried Kant's CRITIQUE
OF PURE REASON. My favorite reading was the poets—Baudelaire
and the Symbolists."

The young worker also wrote poetry. It was not from himself
but from Pierre Villon * that I learned this.

"The less said about it the better, it was pretty poor stuff,"
Rol protests. "At eighteen everybody tries his hand at poetry."

Rol studied at home after work. He read the philosophers, the
economists and the social theoreticians. At seventeen he was
slowly and patiently seeking the key to this cruel and confused

---

Div," at that juncture, looked like an anthropological exhibit at a world's
fair, with Sikhs, Gurkhas, Rajputs, Frenchmen, Englishmen from the home
counties, Punjabi Moslems and the tribes of Central Africa. Leclerc finished
that campaign as a forty-year-old brigadier general. He was promoted subsequently to general of division. By the time he reached Paris he was so
well-known as Leclerc that the soldiers would have been confused by the
interjection of a General de Hautecloque. He is a cocky little man with a brick-
red face and a notion that a general should command a division from a post
in advance of his own reconnaissance. This used to embarrass some of the
American and British officers sent to him with messages. Their first impulse,
when informed at divisional headquarters that the general was up ahead, was
to say that they would wait until he came back. But they were told that he
probably wouldn't be back until the end of the war.—L.

* French writer and poet, general secretary of the *Front National*. Member
of COMAC.

universe in which he lived. He thought that he had found it, and he had. The life of a radical trade-unionist, between 1933 and 1939, was not an easy one. This refined and pleasant-mannered young Breton who expressed himself frankly and directly was a "bolshevik"—one of the breed who were pictured on the posters of the time with a knife between their teeth. He was discharged and blacklisted. Renault, Citroën, Bréguet, he worked in all these plants. He changed jobs often. He was listed as a dangerous character. "To be watched," his dossier said.

"I imagine that there are some ill-informed Frenchmen," Rol said, "who still see us as demagogues, rabble-rousers, and trouble-makers responsible for the state of our armament in 1940. Some day that misapprehension should be cleared up. The public should be told how the trusts used the forty-hour week as cover for their sabotage. By way of discrediting the measures of social reform of those days, the coal-mining trusts of the Nord and the Pas-de-Calais began to exploit unproductive lodes to reduce production. War industries chose to close down rather than to give their workers vacations with pay. Our airplane constructors slowed down their production, pleading the shortage of aluminum, while behind the scenes they were selling our bauxite to Germany on credit. If Pucheu * thought that he had gotten rid of the incriminating witnesses by including Timbault, the secretary of the Metal Workers' Union, and Poulmarch, secretary of the Chemical Workers' Union, among the hostages at Châteaubriant, he was wrong. There are still witnesses alive. I am one of them."

Rol warmed to his subject. I brought him back to the topic of our interview (from which we had not perhaps strayed so far as one might think)—the liberation of Paris.

"How did you happen to become a soldier?"

"I did my military service like everybody else. 'A dangerous character' according to my dossier; 'sharpshooter' according to my

* Pierre Pucheu, the first prominent Vichy official to pay for his treason with his life, was tried and executed in North Africa in 1943. He had gone there after our landing in 1942, apparently with some idea of making a deal with us. Pucheu had been minister of the interior under Pétain in 1941 and had selected hostages to be handed over to the Germans for execution, mentioned just below. Timbault was Rol's old idol, his philosopher and guide.—L.

service record. In 1937, the 'dangerous character' remembered that he was a sharpshooter. 'Our frontier,' Mr. Churchill said in 1939, 'is on the Rhine.' In 1937 there were Frenchmen who believed that our frontier was on the Ebro and that, unless something were done about it, the great field maneuvers that the Germans and Italians were holding in Spain would prove to be in preparation for a great invasion of France."

"They weren't far wrong."

"As a matter of fact, they weren't. In February, 1937, I was in the Fourteenth International Brigade, the MARSEILLAISE, on the Ebro and in the Sierra Caballos. It was there that I stopped a German bullet. It came in through my arm and lodged between the shoulderblade and the third rib. It is still there. It is shifting around. Soon I can be operated to remove it."

A German bullet in one's body from 1937 to 1944 is a better reminder than a string around one's finger. Rol did not forget.

"When the International Brigades were dissolved in 1938, I returned to my position in the Metal Workers' Union, working with Timbault, who was shot at Châteaubriant. Then the war came along. I was in a Senegalese regiment. I received the CROIX DE GUERRE. But soon I heard the call of another kind of warfare.

"To fight the army of occupation that was stripping our country and bleeding it white, another army—the army of liberty—was needed. I had already fought in two wars; I enlisted in a third one—it was all the same war. But the conditions this time were very different. Of the three it was not the easiest. Far from it."

Future historians, for whom we can only take notes, will tell the epic story of the clandestine organizations that soon covered France with a tight network of heroism and defiance. They were many: CORPS FRANCS DE LA LIBÉRATION, CEUX DE LA LIBÉRATION, CEUX DE LA RÉSISTANCE, ORGANIZATION CIVILE ET MILITAIRE, LIBÉRA-TION-NORD, and F.T.P.

F.T.P.F., FRANCS-TIREURS ET PARTISANS DE FRANCE. It was of them that Rol spoke. Spearhead of the revolt of a people who refused to yield, it was of their fight that Rol told me, because it was as a leader of this organization that he had lived and fought before he became the chief of all the Resistance movements in the Paris region welded into a single army—the F.F.I.

"Our FRANCS-TIREURS came from pretty much everywhere, from every social class and age group: workers, students, teachers, craftsmen, technicians, business men. We had one idea in common: refuse to accept defeat, prevent the enemy from settling down quietly and peacefully in France. Already in 1940 we began to harass and annoy them. In 1941, 1942, and 1943, our aim was to drive them out. We succeeded."

As he talked, Rol showed me documents, letters, and communiqués covering four years. Four years! How quick it is said! Yet how long it is, counted day after day when you are fighting in silence and solitude—with always the idea that tomorrow you may be tortured, that you may die in silence and darkness, alone, so terribly alone.

"Our war was not like other wars. After each operation, our men went back to their homes and jobs, dispersed all over the city. They were open to all sorts of distractions, all sorts of influences and discouragements. We know what morale is to a military unit, what it means to stand shoulder to shoulder in the face of danger and death. It is a force that is multiplied by all the forces that surround it. Our men had nothing of the kind to sustain them, once the operation was over. It was up to each man to keep up his own energy and determination and turn his back on the temptations of ease and happiness."

There was one crisis in the existence of the F.T.P. that Rol discussed with admirable sobriety. It was the moment when, in answer to the attacks that were hampering their movements and preparations, the Germans resorted to their horrible and traditional measure, the murder of hostages. The consciences of these boys—even though they knew that they were the armed might of a nation that had no other means of expression—were filled with misgivings. It is always hard to kill and to risk being killed when one is not sustained by the ardor and excitement of battle. It is hard to be obliged to kill even an enemy, even a Nazi, in cold blood.

"When the first lists of the hostages who had been executed were posted on the walls of Paris," Rol said, "I saw many of our lads turn pale and hesitate. It was a bad moment for us. We were tortured by our scruples and uncertainties. In our imaginations we saw the sun rising for the last time for our comrades in the prisons, the firing squads at dawn at Mont-Valérien, the unpainted pine coffins. The only answer was to let our imaginations go further and replace these visions by others still more terrible. Imagine a France calm and complaisant, an easy prey, without reaction and without resistance. We had to envisage what we had so narrowly escaped: Germany mobilizing Frenchmen, millions of our compatriots thrown as cannon fodder into the fight against the enemies of the Reich, French corpses on the battlefields of a war that was not our own. That was a possibility. Even at the cost of the blood we could least afford to shed, the blood of our best friends—and our own—we had to show the Germans that France could be beaten by neither trickery nor terror. We did not give up."

No weapons? The only way to get them was to take them from those who had them—the enemy. No explosives? With the help of the quarry workers of Paris, an excellent gunpowder could be made of charcoal, saltpeter and sulphur. Add matches and a bit of fuse and you had a very effectual bomb for setting fire to an enemy forage car. A capsule of sulphuric acid and some chlorate of potash dropped in the gas tank of a German car, and a few minutes later it would burst into flames. Chemical laboratories and institutions of higher learning in Paris worked for the F.T.P.

A chemistry student would bring in the acids. A quarry worker provided the saltpeter. A student in the humanities contributed a text! It was by Victor Hugo and was as timely in 1940 as it was in 1870. "Let us organize the dread battle for our country. Go forth, O FRANCS-TIREURS, cross torrents, take advantage of twilight and darkness, worm your way through ravines, sneak, crawl, aim, fire, exterminate the invasion!"

There were F.T.P. MAQUIS. But it is with Paris that we are concerned in these pages. For the F.T.P. of Paris the darkness was the darkness of streets and the twilight the twilight of the city. They went out into the surrounding country for marches and field maneuvers.

Throughout the whole region there was no point where the F.T.P. did not carry the fight "with honor and loyalty," as their oath pledged. But the figures for the Parisian region alone are impressive. Between April 15 and July 31, 1943, the F.T.P. killed two German generals and six colonels. Among them was General von Schaumberg, the murderer of hostages. The bullets and grenades of the F.T.P. also accounted for 430 officers, noncommissioned officers and soldiers, among the German or Italian fascists. A bald transcription of the figures representing the results of only four months' fighting in the Parisian region alone, speaks for itself:

Wounded: 570 BOCHE or Italian fascist officers, noncoms or privates.

Executed: 2 anti-French police commissioners who had tortured members of the F.T.P.; 7 policemen, 1 gendarme (for his zeal in tracking down F.T.P. men); 10 traitors, collaborators and denouncers of patriots.

Derailed: 10 BOCHE trains (Paris-Cherbourg, Paris-Le Mans-Orléans, Château-Thierry-Beauvais, Brest, Dieppe, Versailles-Orly, etc.)

Attacked with grenades and tommy-guns: several BOCHE troop trains and AA batteries mounted on flatcars; numerous SOLDATEN-HEIMEN * and SPEISELOKALEN, as well as hotels and other premises occupied by the BOCHES.

Captured intact: from the BOCHES, many machine guns and pistols; from the police, pistols and bicycles.

"They were tough jobs all right," Rol said. "But even more wearing and difficult than the fighting itself were the arguments with patriots who thought that action was useless or premature. Many people weighed the overwhelming disproportion between our strength and the Germans' and let themselves be paralyzed

---

* One afternoon in March, 1943, for example, a long line of German soldiers was standing in front of the *Soldatenheim* the German Army social center, on the Champs-Elysées, waiting for admission to a free moving picture. There was a line at the same place and time every evening. A few lads came along the Champs-Elysées on bicycles and as they passed threw hand grenades among the movie fans. They inflicted fifty casualties. It was probably a terrible movie anyway. Some of the Germans ran after the cyclists, and three men with tommy-guns stepped out of a doorway and shot them down. The three men with tommy-guns ran down a side street, followed by some German M.P.'s. Three more tommy-gunners got the M.P.'s. A minute later the streets were empty of Frenchmen. The German casualties totaled 70. The F.F.I. suffered just one. That was a man shot at the tip of the little finger of his left hand, probably by one of his own comrades. This sort of thing required planning, rehearsals and timed "dry runs."—L.

by theoretical calculations that did not take into account all the military, technical and psychological aspects of the problem. Many, who later were to show plenty of courage and initiative, had a sort of superstitution about D-day and made a fetish of the Allied landings. But to count on Allied help did not justify our standing by and doing nothing in the meanwhile. The way to prepare for war was to intensify guerrilla warfare in order to try out our tactics and technics, harden our men, interefere with and slow down the enemy war machine, and undermine the morale of the Nazi soldiers.* The Committee of Military Action (COMAC) supported this view and helped us to win over those of our comrades who were blinded by a false concept of the situation to the doctrine of immediate action. These discussions also called for energy, determination and tenacity. Our doctrine led to the order of the day which was issued immediately following the landings and whose directives were obeyed to the letter all over France. This order set up three distinct zones: the advanced zone, the zone of the Allied armies and the zone of the interior.

These were the directives for the zone of the interior:

(1) Carry out the demolitions ordered by SHAEF;

(2) Intensify guerrilla activities in order to interfere as much as possible with the material life of the enemy;

(3) Wherever, in the course of operations, the weakening of occupation forces makes it possible, use reserve formations and the MILICE PATRIOTIQUE to take over and consolidate any territories that afford facilities for resistance.

"But that was toward the end," Rol went on. "In 1942 and 1943, we still had a long way to go. Our detachments, Bir Hakeim, Marseillaise, Stalingrad, Victor Hugo, FRANCE-ACTION, Guy Moquet, Galliéni, 1918, etc., were carrying on continuous warfare, openly against the enemy, under cover against the GESTAPO."

What Rol did not say was that, in addition to his heavy responsibilities as commander, he personally took part in this twofold combat. If he is still hale and hearty today, it is only because enemy bullets and the nocturnal visits of those callers with foreign

---

* An F.T.P. once said to me, à propos of a similar incident, "We just did it to give them a workout. We didn't want them to think this was a health farm."—L.

accents who took you to places from which you never returned, always missed him.

The losses of the F.T.P. were incredibly smaller than those of the enemy. In the course of ambushes, street battles and grenade attacks, careful preparation economized French lives to the maximum. The F.T.P. did, however, have its losses, its heroes and martyrs.

On June 12, 1943, members of the Jeanne d'Arc detachment, supported by a reserve squad, were cutting a railroad track in the Paris region. The object was to derail a German supply train. During the operation they were surprised by a guard patrol commanded by one of those individuals whom the F.T.P. called FLICS-PÉTAIN. It was the matter of a moment to disarm the FLIC-PÉTAIN and capture his men. The operation continued. In the meanwhile the reserve squad had captured a second guard patrol, which brought the count of their prisoners to twenty-four. They led them into a near-by woods and one of the F.T.P. leaders addressed them, explaining the reason for cutting the track. The German supply train arrived at full speed. Twenty cars were shattered to bits. The F.T.P. detachment came to attention and saluted their exploit with the cry of, "VIVE LA FRANCE!" The guard patrol joined in the salute. They and the FLIC-PÉTAIN, without his arms or uniform, were released. The track was blocked for seventy-two hours.

"Terrorists?" said the F.T.P. leader who told me this story. "A terrorist is a man who acts alone, cut off from humanity, in the solitude of despair and futility. WE had behind us the entire French nation, whose rage and revolt we were expressing and whom we were inspiring to follow our example eventually. When the Germans called us terrorists it was as much to reassure themselves as to discredit us. It was self-hypnotism on their part. The day was to come when they would wake from their trance to find not only the Allied armies but forty million French 'terrorists' at their throats."

October 6, 1943. Noon. It was a warm, golden autumn morning in the Place de l'Odéon. Under the arcades, book-collectors were thumbing over the volumes in the booksellers' stalls. In front of the CAFÉ VOLTAIRE a prospective client was consulting the menu.

At the corners of the Rue de l'Odéon, Rue Monsieur-le-Prince, and the Rue Condé, the perennial collectors of old books, autographs and stamps were window-shopping. Over the near-by Luxembourg Palace floated the swastika. This was Paris under the German occupation.

You can see for yourselves that we are not barbarians since we are so at home here in Paris, so comfortable and peaceful. We mind our own business. There are as many books in the bookstore windows as ever. And very fine books at that. See—Chardonne, Châteaubriant, Céline—and Hérold-Paquis.* The menus of the restaurants are a little shorter than usual; but what can you expect? There's a war on. Speaking of the war, the French are very understanding. There is already the Anti-Bolshevik Legion and compulsory labor in Germany. And we have hopes for even better things. It is best to try to get along together, isn't it? Our occupation isn't over yet by a long shot. Isn't it best to accept it without any fuss? . . .

A German detachment is marching up the Rue de l'Odéon. No matter how much at home they feel, it is wise to be on the safe side—which explains why the detachment has a vanguard, a rearguard and a guard on each flank, all armed with tommy-guns.

It came about so quickly—a volley of bullets and a few hand grenades—that nobody knew what had happened. Ten Germans lay dead in the Place de l'Odéon. There were fewer book collectors gazing into the windows of the bookstores. The gentleman who had been studying the menu of the CAFÉ VOLTAIRE had disappeared (perhaps he had gone inside).

Decidedly it is wiser never to go out unarmed. But it is rather a bore to go to the FOLIES-BERGÈRE with a rifle that you can't check at the cloak-room. And then too in the streets at night, the footsteps behind you! When shall we get back home? Oh, damn the war!

In every street of Paris, liberty is beginning to stir. And all over the world, inexorably, the noose is drawing tight. Stalingrad, North Africa, the defeats at sea and in the air.

* Chardonne, Châteaubriant and Louis-Ferdinand Céline were collaborationist authors. Jean Hérold-Paquis was a Vichy radio propagandist; he was shot as a traitor in 1945. (*Translator's note.*)

"National insurrection," General de Gaulle had declared, "is inseparable from national liberation." The formation of cadres and units went forward day by day in spite of losses, arrests and executions. Training went on feverishly.

"I spoke of these soldiers as men," wrote Alastair Forbes in THE DAILY MAIL. "I found it hard to remember that the great majority of them were still school children when the armistice of 1940 was signed. They have no military service behind them. Their training had to be carried on under the very noses of the BOCHES. Yet today they constitute a seasoned and disciplined army. It takes a really well-trained soldier to fight with no other weapon than a short-range rifle and so little ammunition that he cannot afford to miss a single shot."

I have before me one of the manuals published by the F.T.P. There is nothing striking about the cover. It bears no resemblance to the INFANTRY OFFICER'S MANUAL or the HANDBOOK OF FIELD MANEUVERS that we used to know. On the cover of this innocent-looking pamphlet is a boy waving his hat. In the background is a peasant plowing with his ox team. The title is SCOUT and the publishing house is given as EDITIONS DE LA NOUVELLE FRANCE. You turn the page: "Chapter I—German weapons. (a) The German pistol. (b) The automatic rifle. (c) The machine gun."

Yesterday's schoolboy, the victor of tomorrow, leaning over the same table where such a short time ago he used to do his homework, studies the diagrams and nomenclatures: "Grasp the automatic rifle in the right hand at the center of balance. With the left forefinger draw back the knob of the bolt and the safety-catch pawl. Using the left hand, insert the clip in the clip-holder and push home until the clip catches."

On May 13, 1944, the CONSEIL NATIONAL DE LA RÉSISTANCE appointed three delegates to the COMAC: Vaillant, representing the Resistance organizations of the North Zone; Valrimont of the MOUVEMENT DE LIBÉRATION NATIONALE, and Villon of the FRONT NATIONAL. Under orders from COMAC, the staffs of the F.F.I. were set up: the national staff, the regional and departmental staffs, each including the four usual bureaus, personnel, operations, supply and intelligence. On D-day everything was in readiness. It was Rol who was assigned the heavy responsibility of commanding the Paris region.

From then on, all over France, and especially in Paris, the conflict which had, so to speak, never ceased during four years, was to take on a new intensity.

At ten o'clock, after a conference between Colonel Rol and Boucher of the Police Committee of Liberation, the Parisian police force, which had been on strike for three days, received the following orders: all policemen were to remain in civilian clothes, put on their F.F.I. arm bands and divide up into small patrols in preparation for the forthcoming battle. The GARDE RÉPUBLICAINE would assure the defense of the bridges of Paris.

At eleven o'clock Colonel Rol received Monsieur Luizet, the new PRÉFET DE POLICE appointed by the Provisional Government. General mobilization was decreed. At that moment, the colonel and the PRÉFET received a visit from Monsieur Nordling, the consul-general of Sweden, who had already been in negotiation with the Germans for several days and who now intervened in the hope that the liberation movement would not resort to violence. The colonel and the PRÉFET decided to give "due consideration" to his views. Exit Monsieur Nordling.

The shortage of automatic weapons was already acute. To the requests that poured into the regional headquarters, there was only one possible reply: "Take them from the enemy."

But already the F.F.I. had gone into action. Tonight Paris would have weapons.

At one o'clock in the afternoon, the President of the COMAC, Villon, and Valrimont arrived at the PRÉFECTURE. From then on, the strategy of the Resistance was clear. To occupy official buildings was all right, but there was no sense in huddling there, empty-handed, to await the enemy's attack. It was necessary to go over to the offensive, capture arms and ammunition, harass the enemy, and do everything possible to hamper the retreat of the troops fleeing before the Allied armies. "National insurrection is inseparable from national liberation," General de Gaulle had said. "Unconditional surrender," Churchill, Roosevelt and Stalin had stipulated. The staff of the F.F.I. of the Paris region was to abide by these directives.

Villon and Valrimont requested Rol to move his command post from the PRÉFECTURE to a pre-arranged position at the LION DE BELFORT.*

Reality is always more imaginative than fiction. An insurrection with headquarters in an underground passage is all right for Walter Scott, Eugène Sue or Jules Verne. But no writer of our times who had to describe an insurrection in a great modern city would dare to put the command post of his insurgents in a spur of the catacombs twenty-six meters underground.

Reality has less false modesty. At two o'clock on August 19, two cars stopped in front of the Denfert-Rochereau MÉTRO station. Monsieur Tavès, chief of one of the services of water supply and sewers of the city of Paris, received Colonel Rol and the officers of his staff. He led them down a stairway of one hundred and twenty-eight steps cut in the living rock. This shelter, constructed in 1939 by the minister of war, was a veritable underground fortress, twenty-six meters below the ground level and protected by a layer of limestone eighteen meters thick. At the entrance were armored doors, gas-proof and strong enough to resist any attack. A huge ventilating plant pumped fresh air into this invisible stronghold. Since Paris was without electricity, the elevators were not working.

"Oh, well, we'll use the stairs," Rol said. "It's a mere detail."

A mere detail, but one which repeated twenty times a day for a week, began to mount up. Rol was to wear out his entire staff, including Lieutenant Rollin, the former trackman. He climbed the stairs four at a time. His big black automobile tore along the bullet-swept streets.

F.F.I. mounted guard at the armored doors.

"The password?"

"Duroc."

* The *Lion de Belfort*, a heroic statue of a lion, in the Place Denfert-Rochereau, symbol of the defense of Belfort in the Franco-Prussian War. A short distance from the statue and opening into the Place Denfert-Rochereau, is the entrance to the catacombs of Paris. The catacombs are a vast network of underground passages spreading out under the Left Bank of Paris. The part of the catacombs near the *Lion de Belfort* is a repository for bones dug up when the medieval cemetery of the Innocents, in the center of Paris, was abandoned. (*Translator's note.*)

The guards stepped aside. The heavy armored door swung open.

Diesel motors and eighteen storage batteries provided the lighting for the command post. A switchboard such as was used in the Maginot Line connected it with all parts of Paris. Two hundred and fifty employees of the Sewer Department were members of the F.F.I. of long standing. The men at the other end of the line could be trusted.

"Hello! Batignolles? Are you holding out?"

"German tanks are reported attacking in Rue Boursault."

"Keep us informed. Hello! Fifth ARRONDISSEMENT?"

"An armored car is out of action on Boulevard Saint-Michel. We are running short of ammunition."

"We'll send you some. . . . Hello! PRÉFECTURE?"

The command post was at the center of an immense subterranean network that winds its way under all Paris—a veritable labyrinth of quarries, catacombs, sewers and MÉTRO tunnels, more than three hundred miles of underground passages where only an expert could find his way about. You could come out in almost any part of Paris you chose or even in the suburbs as far away as Bourg-La-Reine. The couriers and liaison officers entered by the Place Denfert-Rochereau and left by Rue Schoelcher. After having traveled—with guides—through the underground maze for a while, when they first stepped out in the daylight, they stood there lost and blinking. As soon as you stepped out of the cement fortress itself a heavy dampness settled over your shoulders like a cloak. Arrows pointed the way to the catacombs and the Montparnasse cemetery. At the crossroads were signs corresponding to the streets above—Rue Boulard, Rue Froidevaux, Rue Schoelcher. (Shafts cut in the rock led down to a network on a still deeper level.) In the vaulted rooms of the C.P., telephones rang and typewriters clattered. German tanks were prowling in the streets above. The Gestapo would have given a lot to lay hands on the mysterious Colonel Rol.

In the course of Saturday evening, Monsieur Nordling appeared once more on the scene. He telephoned from the Swedish consulate to the office of the PRÉFECTURE DE POLICE. The Germans were asking for a truce until six o'clock in the morning to allow them to gather up their wounded. They also asked that parleys be started to arrange a prolongation of the truce.

The negotiations began on Sunday. In embattled Paris, the C.N.R. began trying to round up its members. Those in favor of accepting the truce pushed their case and for a while seemed to have the upper hand. Communications being uncertain and so many of the leaders of the Resistance being out on missions, there was some delay in getting them all together for this conference that was to decide the fate of Paris. At last everybody was located, and the crucial discussions got under way.

Monsieur Nordling was a peaceful soul. He did not believe in bloodshed. Neither did the Germans, it appeared. He stated his case. A week earlier he had begun conversations with General von Choltitz, military governor of Paris. Today the German general requested an armistice. If the request was refused, he threatened to lay waste Paris with planes and flame-throwers.

Monsieur Parodi, delegate-at-large of the Provisory Government, went to sound out the Germans directly. A German patrol arrested him on the way and locked him up. He was finally released.

From the beginning, the issue lay between those who saw the truce as a wise solution, on the one hand, and the COMAC, Colonel Rol, and the majority of the C.N.R., who favored continuing the fight to the end, on the other. At first Villon, Valrimont, and Varllant were almost alone in opposing the "pacifists."

"We lack arms and ammunition," the partisans of the truce argued. "Even in the public buildings that we still hold, like the PRÉFECTURE, our situation is becoming critical."

"The only way we can get arms," their opponents argued, "is not by a truce but by an offensive. As for the situation of the public buildings, it can only become desperate if we follow the mistaken tactics that the MAQUIS used at Glières, where all our forces were massed in a square only to be surrounded and massacred. We must use guerrilla tactics, organize our troops into skirmish detachments. We must defend the public buildings, of course, but we must also protect them by barricades and improvised hedgehog positions. After all, the possession of a building has only a symbolic value."

The course of events was to prove the soundness of this contention.

"Beware of German reprisals," the "pacifists" pursued. "They will wipe out Paris with its population and art treasures."

"War is war," the die-hards replied. "We don't want Paris to share the fate of London, Warsaw and Berlin. But we are at war, and the eyes of France and the entire world are on Paris. Paris must furnish the example of a successful uprising. Moreover, in their hurry to withdraw, the Germans will have neither the time nor the means to undertake reprisals against a city as large as Paris."

"And what about bombing?"

"It is not likely that they will resort to aerial bombardment. Their first result would be to block the streets—which is the last thing in the world they want." (As a matter of fact, the Germans did bomb Paris, but only after they had lost all hope of holding on to it.)

The "pacifists" pointed out that the F.F.I. prisoners in German hands would make ideal hostages.

"We also have thousands of captured or wounded Germans in our hands, if it comes to reprisals," was the reply.

Still the "pacifists" did not give up. "Could not the F.F.I. go outside of Paris to fight?"

"And let the suburbs and the outlying districts bear the brunt that Paris refused to bear?"

"After all," Monsieur Nordling suggested, "the Germans are only asking to be allowed to withdraw their retreating columns without damaging the city."

"So that they can devastate the rest of France after Paris has set the example of abjection and cowardice? After that, not a city from here to the German border could be blamed for trying to avoid fighting. And such spinelessness on our part would not prevent repetitions of savage massacres like those of Oradour and Ascq. No, we must call on the entire population to take an effective part in the fight, to do their utmost to hamper the enemy's movements, and to throw up barricades and road-blocks to cut them off from their bases."

While these discussions were in progress, certain unauthorized persons had given orders that the Parisians were to be informed that a truce had been signed. Loud-speakers mounted on trucks were sent out to make the announcement. Our combatants were seized with dismay. Had those who had already fallen died in vain?

The battle of France had reached one of its decisive turning points. Would Paris lay down her arms without having achieved a victory?

The discussion went on all day. Then Monsieur Nordling played his trump.

"Are there any Communists in the Resistance?"

"Yes."

Monsieur Nordling turned to the assembled company. "Then you understand why insurrection must be avoided at any price."

A strange argument. The COMAC, the staff of the F.F.I. and the majority of the C.N.R. did not follow it.

"It would be rank disobedience to the orders of the Allied High Command and General Koenig, which are to harass the retreating columns, use guerrilla tactics, capture weapons, including cannons and tanks, and do everything in our power to slow up the enemy and help to destroy him. In Paris, as everywhere else, the enemy must surrender unconditionally."

It was unanimously voted to continue fighting.

The "pacifists" tried one last argument.

"A temporary cessation of hostilities would not prevent our taking up arms again if we judged it necessary."

"A Frenchman's word is sacred," their opponents protested. "What kind of a war would it be if combatants could be manipulated like marionettes on strings. A movement begun must be carried through, and a victory followed up to the utmost."

The fighting began anew. Once more the combatants took up the arms that they had never laid down. Exit Monsieur Nordling.

The next morning the Germans found themselves entrapped. At every street crossing, in every street, and in every square, was a barricade.

"Right up to the end then," I said to Rol, "your victory was the triumph of sheer will power. But this question coming up so near the end . . ."

"It was so simple. Our duty was so clear."

And looking at Rol, it does seem simple. His keen eyes and forthright smile. Rol is the incarnation of clarity. As I looked at this man whose tranquil strength shows through, even in his moments of repose, I thought of the admirable lines from Claudel:

IL SE MEUT DANS SA SEIGNEURIE COMME UNE CHOSE NATURELLE
C'EST LUI QUI EST LE MAÎTRE, ET IL NE PERMET PAS AUX
    AFFAIRES DE LE DOMINER
HUMBLE ET FORT, ET CE PLI AU COIN DE LA LÈVRE SI BON,
    ET TOUJOURS SOURIANT ET VERMEIL
IL SAIT EN TOUT CE QU'IL A À FAIRE AUSSITÔT ET LES CHOSES
    S'OUVRENT À LUI COMME DEVANT LE SOLEIL.*

"While this discussion was going on at the C.N.R.," Rol went on, "and while the loud-speakers were still broadcasting the order to cease firing, we learned of a hundred instances of the Germans violating the truce. On the 21st, forty SS troops attacked the Porte d'Orléans with an armored car and artillery. At five o'clock they killed one of our men in the Rue de Seine. On the Boulevard Victor-Hugo, the SS fired on the Allied flags hoisted over a building.

"At ten-thirty, in the Place Clichy, the SS opened fire on the crowd without provocation. At Vitry on the Pont Mazagran they shot down without warning six F.F.I. on a supply truck."

"Did you have any precise information about the Allied advance? That was the great question all over Paris: where are they?"

"The first liaison officer who tried to establish contact with the Allied armies, Captain Truty de Vorreux—an old French name—was killed at Dourdan on August 18. Then on the 20th, Major Gallois set out and succeeded in getting through to Allied

---

* He moves in his Mastery as his natural element. It is he who is master, he does not let affairs dominate him. Humble and strong, with that line at the corner of his kindly, ever-smiling mouth, he knows what should be done and things open to him as before the sun.

headquarters. He got in contact first with General Patton and later with General Eisenhower himself. His mission was of inestimable value to us and to the Allied armies. During the whole insurrection, liaison and intelligence officers kept us accurately informed of the advance of the French and American armies. You know the rest."

"I do indeed! Those bright, pure days so mingled with our grim memories of a Paris now so peaceful with its streets and parks, and the children playing in the squares where the barricades had so recently stood. But I should like to hear your own story of the final scene of the uprising."

"On Friday, August 25, at eleven o'clock in the morning, General von Choltitz drove up to the PRÉFECTURE DE POLICE in an F.F.I. car. He was received in the PRÉFET's office by General Leclerc, Valrimont of the COMAC, and myself. The negotiations began. They were concluded, at noon, by the signature of the articles by which the German garrison of Paris surrendered unconditionally. The conditions stipulated that delegates and F.F.I. officers should be sent to all points of enemy resistance that were still holding out, to transmit the surrender order signed by the general commanding the Paris region."

"What was Von Choltitz like?"

"A man of about fifty, very fat and very calm. He was quite decent in the whole affair. From the PRÉFECTURE he was driven in an armored car with General Leclerc and myself to Leclerc's headquarters at the GARE MONTPARNASSE. In spite of his weight he jumped out of the car with a spryness that made the machine gunner say, "Say, he's still light on his feet, that big porker!"

"Is that all there is to tell?"

"Not quite. Here is what really tells the story."

Colonel Rol handed me a sheet of figures showing the achievements of the insurrection in the city of Paris alone. To this should be added the list of prisoners and supplies captured by the F.F.I. in the suburbs and the Parisian region as a whole. Here are the figures: more than 4000 prisoners (not counting those captured by Leclerc's Division); 35 tanks captured (among them 14 Tiger tanks) and an even greater number destroyed; 7 armored cars; 9 anti-tank guns; 13 field guns; 32 machine guns; 3 anti-aircraft guns; thousands and thousands of rifles, pistols, tommy-guns, and boxes of grenades and explosives.

"Enough to burn down all Paris," Rol said, "enough to destroy Notre-Dame and the SAINTE-CHAPELLE, the LOUVRE and the PALAIS-ROYAL. Imagine Paris defenseless, abandoned to the fury of some division like DAS REICH or the ADOLF HITLER Division. Imagine what it might have been like if Paris had been wide open, without barricades, without defenders—a Paris destroyed like Warsaw or London or Ascq or Oradour or . . ."

The list was too long. Rol paused.

You who love Paris and all its changing aspects, the QUAIS and the bookstalls, the antique shops in the Rue Bonaparte, the Flower Market, the Egyptian collection in the LOUVRE, the Poussins, the Cézannes, the stained glass of Notre-Dame and the shop windows of Rue Royale, the Tuileries, Parc Monceau, the Champs-Elysées, the art galleries of the Faubourg Saint-Honoré—you who love OUR Paris, happiness regained, the happiness of which that seventeen-year-old boy about to die before a firing squad wrote so touchingly: may I present Henri Tanguy, metal worker from Morlaix, Colonel Rol, commander of Paris-in-arms, into whose care was entrusted a captive Paris and who returned it to you victorious and free? Thank you.

I asked Rol how he came to choose this NOM DE GUERRE that sounds like a whip-crack of challenge and defiance, like a bugle call, a rallying cry.

He hesitated. With lowered voice he said, "It was the name of one of my comrades in the International Brigade. A friend. Killed at Sierra Caballos."

PART EIGHT

Summation

The Summing Up

The last three pieces in the book are the work of men equally illustrious in letters and in the Resistance when resistance was dangerous. Published in the legitimized LETTRES FRANÇAISES in the first weeks after the liberation of Paris, they express their author's first intellectual response to the attainment of what had been the immediate goal for four years. There is in each of the essays an allusion to the writers' further and higher goals for France. They had not been complacent in the years before the war. None of the three had thought that the illness of modern Europe began with the entry of the Germans into France and would end with their departure. I have already told of Mauriac's feeling that the years 1935-9 had been harder to endure than the occupation.

Jean-Paul Sartre, who wrote LA RÉPUBLIQUE DE SILENCE, the first of these essays, is famous in France as the author of HUIS-CLOS—a play first put on in the last year of the occupation that became the event of the theatrical season. It continued to hold the stage in the first year of liberation and to be the most discussed drama of its time. The Germans found nothing political in it. Sartre's detractors even discovered implications of fascism in what they denounced as its negative attitude toward life. Nothing happens in the play; the characters, who are dead, find they cannot escape from themselves. That is their punishment, not for what they have done (which, from their reminiscences, seems to have been plenty) but for what they are. Sartre is now identified with the doctrine of existentialism. Being, not doing, is important to the existentialist. Particularly, it would seem, being miserable. Sartre has adumbrated the idea in a seven-hundred-page book, BEING AND

NOTHINGNESS. A brief and vulgar summary of the position is this: man is lonely, everything is equally possible, you can't prove anything, but you can't escape because your responsibility is absolute. This would seem discouraging, but the exponent of the cheerless credo was fearless and active in the underground and continues so in French politics.

Sartre, to explain this apparent preoccupation with doing things instead of just concentrating on being somebody, wrote in 1945:

"—We assert emphatically that man is absolute. But he is absolute in his own time, in his own environment, on his own earth.— the absolute is Descartes, the man who escapes us because he is dead—; and the relative is cartesianism, that coster-barrow philosophy which is trotted out century after century, in which everyone finds whatever he has put in. It is not by chasing after immortality that we will make ourselves eternal; we will not make ourselves absolute by reflecting in our works desiccated principles which are sufficiently empty and negative to pass from one century to another, but by fighting passionately in our time, by loving it passionately, and by consenting to perish with it."

This is merely to indicate that even when Frenchmen are in accord on an action, in this case resistance, each reserves the right to furnish his own reason for the way he acts. No two Paris taxi drivers take the same route to a given destination. But they all get there. To the German soldier it probably made little difference whether he was extinguished by a Communist, an existentialist, a medievalist or just a marquis operating under a fictitious name.

In the flesh, I must note, Sartre is a very short, very jolly man to whom this existence is apparently not a cause of pain.

François Mauriac, a slender, delicately boned man with a pointy face and bright, intelligent eyes, once referred to himself as "LE SEUL VIEUX MONSIEUR" of the Resistance. VIEUX MONSIEUR has a connotation of respect tinged with fussiness and caution for which English has no exact equivalent. Old gent sounds too familiar and old gentleman too exalted. But Mauriac was making fun of himself. He is more properly a VIEUX MONSIEUR MANQUÉ, a man who by virtue of his family background, his wealth, and his earned but very conventional success, which came early in life, should *have developed into a* VIEUX MONSIEUR *but didn't. He even* LOOKS *like a* VIEUX MONSIEUR—*except for the eyes. Mauriac was born in 1886. His voice is a hoarse whisper, which always sounds as if he had a severe sore throat. It is a consequence of a throat ailment that nearly resulted in his death in 1934; an operation saved his life but not his speaking voice. The same illness resulted in his election to the* ACADÉMIE FRANÇAISE, *he professes to believe. The* ACADÉMIE *usually chooses new members from among illustrious men so old they are near death; Mauriac says they picked him while he was ill because they were sure he would die immediately. The French attitude toward the* ACADÉMIE *is to say the least ambivalent. All Frenchmen make fun of it, but they must consider it of great importance, or they could not become so emotional as they do when discussing its failings.*

Claude Morgan changed his name—before the Resistance!— because his father happens to be a rather dull academician. Mauriac says that he would like to get some of his young and brilliant Resistance colleagues like André Malraux and Louis Aragon into the ACADÉMIE, *but he is afraid that one of two bad things would happen. "Either they would lose their talent," he says, "or the* ACADÉMIE *would explode." It is symptomatic, however, that he has not resigned. He holds to the past as well as the future, as the conclusion of this brilliant essay indicates.*

Mauriac is a Catholic, by conviction as well as circumstance. Catholic intellectuals in France, while numerous, are in a minority among other intellectuals. He chooses to speak of France as a nation with a soul and a vocation—"being fully aware that certain words irritate Frenchmen in 1944." Sartre might speak of France's "responsibility" and Aragon of her "mission," without changing the argument of the piece.

Mauriac's fine-spun mind is hypersensitive to intellectual poison. It has a quality like the cuffs we wore on our arms on D-day, which were supposed to change color at the slightest trace of poison gas in the atmosphere. The arguments of Charles Maurras, Léon Daudet, Jacques Bainville and other editors of the newspaper L'ACTION FRANÇAISE *in the years between the wars had been more than an affront to Mauriac, they had been an affliction.* L'ACTION FRANÇAISE *was not only a newspaper but a movement and more* than either a state of mind. The state of mind was sustained by reading the paper. It pretended to be royalist, but had been disowned by the exiled French royal family, and Catholic, but had been disowned by the Vatican. Its royalism was in practice simply anti-republicanism, its religion anti-masonry, anti-semitism and an assertion of proprietary rights in Joan of Arc. Together they added up to nihilism, rationalized by a fake nostalgia for a past that the poison manufacturers consistenly misrepresented.

L'ACTION FRANÇAISE was violently anti-labor, anti-democratic and anti-Soviet. It made its readers feel that they were members of an élite which could not secure its due of deference and power in a democracy. One became a member of this élite by subscribing to the paper. The élite was left to assume that wealth would come with power. Explicitly L'ACTION had little to say about money. It implied that only Jews, politicians and labor leaders cared about that. Naturally it enjoyed the approval of the wealthiest men in France, who were neither Jews, politicians nor labor leaders. In both these details it resembled Westbrook Pegler's syndicated newspaper column.

In its ensemble the doctrine presents analogies with the late Huey Long's, or straight Hitlerism, but L'ACTION FRANÇAISE made no attempt to achieve a mass base for a political movement. It concentrated on reiteration of scathing assaults on the rottenness of all existing institutions. This was interpreted by its readers as a release from any social obligation and moral justification for every anti-social attitude. Because it demanded no positive action on the reader's part it was a comfortable as well as a fashionable cult. Its converts went out from the schools to exploit every angle of a system for which they felt no responsibility. Their submission to the conquerors was a natural corollary of their NATIONALISME INTÉGRALE, a pet term of theirs which might be idiomatically rendered as 100 per cent Americanism, in the isolationist sense. The defeat which they had done nothing to avert brought them a gratification of the ego, because they were able to say, "I told you so."

It was the editorial skill that went into L'ACTION FRANÇAISE that had made it so effective for evil throughout its half century of existence. Maurras and Daudet—the latter a son of the original

nanny goat man—were plausible, vitriolic, voluminous, and permanently immature. Their arguments were aimed at students in their
teens, and they convinced thousands of them. With many French
intellectuals L'ACTION was merely a phase associated with puberty.
With others it lasted. Particularly did it last with those whose
intellectual life ended at the college gate, when they went into
business or the routine exercise of a profession. For young men,
insecure like young men the world over, a group that assured them
of their own superiority had a great appeal.

In conflict with parental authority in their own homes, they
felt the attraction of a doctrine that not only defied the established
order but made it the butt of daily abuse. Extremely lax laws of
libel made it easy to keep the abuse varied and interesting. The
thesis that the French Revolution had been a mistake had the
same paradoxical attraction as American historical novels glorifying
the Tories of 1777 or the Confederates of 1863. But the thesis
was offered seriously, with a quack-doctor assurance and a parade
of mumbo-jumbo erudition. Jacques Bainville, who died in 1941,
was the "great historian" touted by L'ACTION. But he was a historian
of synthesis rather than method. Like the old colored cook who
would say only that her sauce contained "ingredients," Bainville
permitted no analysis. Léon Daudet died in 1943. In the first year
of the liberation Maurras was tried in Lyon and condemned to
life imprisonment for treason.

Charles Vildrac is best known in the United States as author
of PAQUEBOT TENACITÉ, a play produced here by the Theatre
Guild in the twenties. He is a poet as well as dramatist. IL FAUT
RESTAURER LA PERSONALITÉ is a pendant to Mauriac's LA NATION
FRANÇAISE A UNE AME. The chief problem of modern man, according to Vildrac and many others, is the conflict between the demands of the state and those of the individual. It is peculiarly
acute in France because the French are the most individualistic
people in the world and at the same time must work closely
together in order to survive. Vildrac speaks for the individual and
against French imitators of alien herd customs. General Giraud,
in a disastrous speech on his visit to America in 1943, said that
there were "some good things" about the Nazi system. He probably meant the marching, the discipline and the mass spirit.

Vildrac contends there is nothing good about it and the sooner the French forget it the better off they will be. As an individual, he feels, the Frenchman is inimitable. As a member of a youth organization he is a poor imitation of a German. The thing works two ways. Only fools conform without question, and a habit of conformity will make anybody a fool.

The Republic of Silence

by JEAN-PAUL SARTRE

We were never more free than during the German occupation. We had lost all our rights, beginning with the right to talk. Every day we were insulted to our faces and had to take it in silence. Under one pretext or another, as workers, Jews, or political prisoners, we were deported EN MASSE. Everywhere, on billboards, in the newspapers, on the screen, we encountered the revolting and insipid picture of ourselves that our oppressors wanted us to accept. And, because of all this, we were free. Because the Nazi venom seeped even into our thoughts, every accurate thought was a conquest. Because an all-powerful police tried to force us to hold our tongues, every word took on the value of a declaration of principles. Because we were hunted down, every one of our gestures had the weight of a solemn commitment. The circumstances, atrocious as they often were, finally made it possible for us to live, without pretense or false shame, the hectic and impossible existence that is known as the lot of man. Exile, captivity, and especially death (which we usually shrink from facing at all in happier times) became for us the habitual objects of our concern. We learned that they were neither inevitable accidents, nor even constant and exterior dangers, but that they must be considered as our lot itself, our destiny, the profound source of our reality as men. At every instant we lived up to the full sense of this commonplace little phrase: "Man is mortal!" And the choice that each of us made of his life and of his being was an authentic choice because it was made face to face with death, because it could always have been expressed in these terms: "Rather death than . . ." And here I am not speaking of the élite among us who were real Resistants, but of all Frenchmen who, at every hour of the night and day throughout four years, answered NO. But the very cruelty of the enemy drove us to the extremities of this condition by forcing us to ask ourselves questions that one never considers in time of peace. All those among us—and what Frenchman was not at one time or another in this situation— who knew any details concerning the Resistance asked themselves anxiously, "If they torture me, shall I be able to keep silent?" Thus the basic question of liberty itself was posed, and we were brought to the verge of the deepest knowledge that man can have of himself. For the secret of a man is not his Œdipus complex or his inferiority complex: it is the limit of his own liberty, his capacity for resisting torture and death.

To those who were engaged in underground activities, the conditions of their struggle afforded a new kind of experience. They did not fight openly like soldiers. In all circumstances they were alone. The were hunted down in solitude, arrested in solitude. It was completely forlorn and unbefriended that they held out against torture, alone and naked in the presence of torturers, clean-shaven, well-fed, and well-clothed, who laughed at their cringing flesh, and to whom an untroubled conscience and a boundless sense of social strength gave every appearance of being in the right. Alone. Without a friendly hand or a word of encouragement. Yet, in the depth of their solitude, it was the others that they were protecting, all the others, all their comrades in the Resistance. Total responsibility in total solitude—is this not the very definition of our liberty? This being stripped of all, this solitude, this tremendous danger, were the same for all. For the leaders and for their men, for those who conveyed messages without knowing what their content was, as for those who directed the entire Resistance, the punishment was the same—imprisonment, deportation, death. There is no army in the world where there is such equality of risk for the private and for the commander-in-chief. And this is why the Resistance was a true democracy: for the soldier as for the commander, the same danger, the same forsakenness, the same total responsibility, the same absolute liberty within discipline. Thus, in darkness and in blood, a Republic was established, the strongest of Republics. Each of its citizens knew that he owed himself to all and that he could count only on himself alone. Each of them, in complete isolation, fulfilled his responsibility and his rôle in history. Each of them, standing against the oppressors, undertook to be himself, freely and irrevocably. And by choosing for himself in liberty, he chose the liberty of all. This Republic without institutions, without an army, without police, was something that at each instant every Frenchman had to win and to affirm against Nazism. No one failed in this duty, and now we are on the threshold of another Republic. May this Republic about to be set up in broad daylight preserve the austere virtues of that other Republic of Silence and of Night.

The French Nation Has a Soul
by FRANÇOIS MAURIAC

If there be anything on which we may pride ourselves, it is our faith, which through four years of nightmare never waned. Even in June, 1940, though the Reich howled its joy to every microphone of the Western world and though—in a France drained bloodless by every tenacle, every sucker, of the octopus—the Vichy followers of Maurras, quivering with delight, at last were trying out their doctrines—yes, even then we were still drunk with hope.

It was not that we never felt the temptation to despair—especially during those last months when the claws tightened as if to strangle us and when, the blood of the beast flowing from innumerable wounds, we felt ourselves crushed in the last convulsions of its death throes. It may seem strange that, so close to liberation, we sometimes had to struggle against a mortal anguish.

Oh, I know . . . the throbbing motors of death against the sun or beneath the stars, the old house trembling in every windowpane, the youth of France hunted down by the jailers of Vichy as tribute to the Minotaur, the sudden disappearance of our friends,

the torture chambers where we knew they had refused to talk,
the volleys of firing squads saluting every dawn of these radiant
springtimes and those summers when it never rained, and twice
a day, ringing out above our infinite shame, the voice of Philippe
Henriot exhorting us, in Vichy's name, to every turpitude. . . .
But no, even all these horrors would not have been enough to dis-
hearten us. Under the blows, what ancient hack, no matter how
decrepit, would not, in one last effort, have struggled to its unsteady legs?

And we did rise up! We never doubted, God be thanked, that
France would live again. But what, we wondered, when the storm
had passed, would be her place? To what rank might she be
relegated? And whatever rank might be accorded to her, would
she even then have strength enough to maintain herself in it?
The cleverest minds among those who betrayed us were well
aware of this anxiety of ours. All their speeches and all their
writings did their best to foster it. If they had succeeded in persuading us that, henceforth, what had been a great nation would
be only an accessory in the clash of empires, by the same token
they would have been absolved in their own eyes and in ours:
when a nation no longer exists, the word treason has no meaning.
How happy they would have been if they could have made it
appear that France was really dead! For it is impossible to betray
a thing that is dead. To believe them, they had crawled to the
conqueror's feet only because there was no other country for
them to serve. We watched from afar these false orphans pretending that they no longer had a mother.

Shall we still search our hearts gnawed by hesitation and doubt?
We were not so particular in the early days of our enslavement.
Little did we worry then about the place that France might later
hold among nations! We had other concerns than her lost prestige
as a power. In those days, France's only dilemma was to be or
not to be. That she should not die before she could be liberated,
that she should survive at all, that she should exist—this was the
anxiety that had our hearts in our throats. But today her existence
is no longer at stake! Covered with wounds that are still bleeding,
but alive among other living nations, she rises before the eyes
of Europe, clasping to her breasts her sons who delivered her.

Shall we forgo the joy of this resurrection and, with a Drieu de la Rochelle,* give ourselves up to reckoning the number of inhabitants of each empire, comparing the areas in square kilometers and, figures in hand, conclude that France will never be more than a puny satellite of the triumphant mastodons?

At a time when those who hope to capitalize on our despair are incessantly rubbing our noses in figures showing the economic might of each nation, I admit that there is no use in our closing our eyes to them. Yes, even the reconstructed France will find herself relegated to a fairly modest position; and, on a materialistic plane, there is no chance of our regaining the first place among nations. Undoubtedly we could take a Machiavellian point of view and argue that none of these dominant powers has received any promise of eternity, that each of them has within itself potential causes of disintegration and germs of its eventual decay, that the conflict of their interests will set them up against each other and that a France occupying the leading place among nations of second rank could use their rivalries to further a world policy of her own. . . . We MIGHT take such an attitude, but we shall not! The concepts of Machiavelli are not ours. It is our ardent desire that a grateful France shall look her noble and powerful allies in the eyes without any trace of an ulterior motive. We shall never abandon our hope, with their help, to deliver humanity from its cruelest scourge. From the midst of the bloody shambles, we proclaim our faith in a world in which all the power of the mind and all the vigor of young hearts shall no longer be devoted to collective murder, the destruction of cathedrals that are the houses of God and cottages that are the homes of the poor.

We believe that it is to a greatness of this order that France resurrected should aspire. Though those who hope to profit by our humiliation and exhaustion retouch from day to day the pictures of our country that they would force upon us—the carica-

* Drieu de la Rochelle, collaborationist writer—of talent—who consented to replace Jean Paulhan as editor of the Nouvelle Revue Française, when that periodical was made the official show window for intellectual solidarity with the New Europe. He resigned when it became apparent that the Allies would win, attempted suicide, was stopped from doing so, but after the liberation made another try and succeeded in killing himself.—L.

ture of us as an old agricultural land, backward and broken down, from whom the masters of this world in both hemispheres expect only cheeses, wines and dress fashions—tirelessly we shall remind them of what they pretend to have forgotten, what it is to their interest to forget: that the French nation has a soul!

Yes, a soul. I am quite aware that Frenchmen of 1944 are irked by certain words.

When a great nation has known the depths of misfortune, when, trodden under foot by her conquerors for four long years, she has been treated like the tribes that the slave-holding powers decimated and deported—when, in short, a people has reached such a point of shame that it has even recruited lackeys and hangmen for its masters, it is not a seemly moment to speak to it of its soul and to meet the cold figures that attest its economic ruin with outbursts of eloquence and emotion.

Yet what the collaborationists tried to make us forget, in order to keep us in despair, was a real and tangible fact: the spiritual wealth of France survives, and it has paramount bearing on her temporal power. P.-J. Proudhon wrote in 1851: "As for me, the least mystic man alive, the most realistic and the least given to imaginings and enthusiasms, I think that I am already in a position to affirm, and I shall prove, that an organized nation like ours constitutes a being as real, as personal and as endowed with a will and an intelligence of its own, as the individuals who compose it." It is also Proudhon who protests in another letter that a nation "is a being SUI GENERIS, a living person, a soul consecrated before God." A person, a consecrated soul, manifests itself by its vocation. Here again I am on guard against choosing a word for a mere effect of eloquence. But nevertheless when in September, 1939, France, divided against herself, unarmed, and already tottering, rose up to defend Poland and to take a step that the rape of Prague had not been enough to persuade her to risk, everyone—even those Frenchmen who reproach her with it today—must know what obligations of her vocation she was fulfilling. And when the government of Monsieur Pétain subscribes to the Nuremberg Code and turns over to the GESTAPO foreigners who had trusted the word of France, when the Nazi executioners find, in the Vichy police and among the followers of Doriot and

Darnand, so many lackeys and helpers that they are not obliged to soil their own hands—when these things happen, who can pretend not to see that it is with treason—or more accurately, with apostasy—that these wretches have burdened the conscience of the living soul that is the French nation? A soul so living, in spite of this disgrace, that it was against this soul that the accomplices of her torturers leveled their attacks first of all, as soon as the disaster was an accomplished thing and as long as they continued to believe in the triumph of the FÜHRER. Later, when they could not help seeing his approaching defeat, it was our economic exhaustion and the inevitable domination of the U.S.S.R. or the Anglo-Saxon countries that they began to stress. But in the early days of our subjection, only this mattered to them: that France should not discover in her glorious past or in what remained of her virtue of old, the strength to withstand her German masters. They had to block her ears to keep the insistent and untiring voice of General de Gaulle from raising her from the mud where Vichy kept her kneeling and prostrate. We must do this justice to the collaborationists: they were proof that this flame still burned, by their very fury in trying to extinguish it. I hope that Monsieur Bernard Faÿ,* whom Vichy made master of the BIBLIO-THÈQUE NATIONALE, carefully preserved in its files the newspapers and magazines that were published after June, 1940, in the occupied zone. What hypocritical commiseration! What scarcely veiled jibes! And at times what insults to defeated France! Between June, 1940, and June, 1944, one unanimous jeer at our motherland, gagged and tied to the stake, went up from every editorial room in the land. "YOU ARE DONE FOR!" was the single theme of their chorus. Ah! it is not enough to say of the second-rate and third-rate journalists who held the limelight then, that they were heavy-handed! Only one real writer, Monsieur de Montherlant,†

---

* Faÿ, professor in France and America, historian and critic. His anti-Semitism made him a natural-born collaborationist. He was one of the very few prominent men in French university circles who actually went over to the Nazis, heart and soul. (*Translator's note.*)

† Henri de Montherlant, a contemporary writer who made a literary fashion of virility and tough-mindedness. He proved a fake when the test came and mild-mannered men like Paulhan and Mauriac demonstrated their courage. In an article of transparent allegory he once compared the patriots to worms blinded with urine, who refused to die.—L.

poured forth, not without art, his spittle and excrement upon those whom he called "the worms of France."

I beg you to believe THEM, if you will not believe me: these Frenchmen in German service. . . . (No, it was more than that —in the service of the inhuman lust of Nazi Germany.) These Frenchmen directed their fury not against a phantom, but against that part of ourselves which protested, resisted, against that soul, weakened, it is true, profaned, sullied—but nonetheless living, and that is essential. Behold this martyred nation, abused by her conqueror, a gag in her mouth! Watch how her head never ceases moving from right to left, through nearly five years, to make the gesture of refusal.

It is to feed this flame that I invite you. Here again I mistrust the metaphor, but I beg you to fix your minds on the reality that it represents. We have nothing else to do than to become ourselves as rapidly as possible. For in this universe given over to the great triumphant empires, very little time is allotted us to assure our indivisibility. The more so since, in this land already riven by dissensions before the war, we know that circumstances have raised up new barriers and dug fresh chasms even within parties and classes. Fortunately, the Resistance first rallied around General de Gaulle, and then joined and amalgamated in a single urge Frenchmen of all classes and conditions. May this alloy prove strong. May it resist all disintegrating forces. Therein lies our only promise of salvation.

But a great turn in the course of our internal political situation leads me to believe that this hope will not be in vain: the mortmain that the eternal ÉMIGRÉS laid on the concept of nation has been lifted.* The collusion on the part of a certain number of nationalists—not all of them, thank God, it must be said—and particularly of those who are proud to call themselves the ad-

* The reference is to the émigrés who during the French Revolution left France and often served in the armies of her invaders. Their descendants, the Royalists ("eternal," in their obstinate refusal to accept the fact of democracy), still held to the émigrés' views. While trying to establish a monopoly on the word "nation" and preaching a doctrine of fanatic nationalism, their first enemy was the French Republic. The slogan of the Royalist party and of its organ, L'Action Française, was, "Everything that is French is ours!" (Translator's note.)

herents of total nationalism—the treason of L'ACTION FRANÇAISE in short—came as a shock to the very people who entertained the least illusions concerning that publication. It SHOULD, above all, have filled them with joy; for henceforth nothing stands in the way of all loyal Frenchmen—Gaullists of the right, trade-unionists, or Communists—joining together in devotion to the nation, a term which for half a century has been the monopoly of the men who had confiscated our country.

The course of events unmasked these self-styled nationalists who hated the nation. Some of them were dumb-struck: they had never before seen themselves in their true light. It was in good faith that they had made their country a monopoly for the benefit of their class, and they had succeeded in persuading themselves that a citizen has the right to stop—to set back—the history of his country to some given moment in the past, and that a man can at the same time love his country and hate everything that, in the eyes of the entire world, is inseparable from it.

It must be said in justice to them that until the end of the first World War nobody cast any doubt on their sincerity. Thousands of boys whose ideologies were shaped by Barrès * and Péguy, but also by the Maurras † of the early years of the twentieth century, laid down their lives. What else shall we grant Charles Maurras? As many another man had done before him, but with a persistent and daily fury, for almost half a century he denounced the iniquities of a degenerate parliamentary régime; he worked out, from experience, some of the conditions necessary to our national life. But why go on? Alas, everything that might be put forward in his defense breaks down before the awful outcome of his doctrine. Without having wished it, he and his disciples awoke one day to find themselves in the enemy camp, on the same side as the German executioners and their French assistants.

* Maurice Barrès (1862-1923), French novelist, critic and politician. A rather transcendental aesthete and dilettante in his beginnings and a snob to the core, he became a rabid nationalist at about the time of the Dreyfus case. Charles Péguy (1873-1914), French Catholic writer and nationalist who adhered to a mystic, rather medieval, form of socialism and inspired fanatic patriotism in his followers. Both of these writers exert considerable posthumous influence in French political thought today. (*Translator's note.*)

† Here Mauriac concedes that Maurras had been honest early in the century—which is charitable.—L.

How did total nationalism come to end up in treason? What took place between the two armistices of 1918 and 1940—the one of glory and the other of shame? Simply this: the principles dear to the French nationalists, whose triumph they had not been able to bring about in their own country, swept the lands beyond the Alps and the Rhine. Their dream came true—but in enemy countries. The crushing of the Socialists and Communists and the much-hated Jews, the destruction of labor exchanges and trade-unions, the primacy of force proclaimed and practiced at home and abroad, the working-class left defenseless and humiliated, the individual enslaved by an all-powerful party incarnated in a man, and, lastly, a police force ruling, "beyond good and evil," over consciences and hearts by means of torture and murder—this fine dream, that for fifty years so many Bonapartists without a Caesar * and Boulangists without a General had cherished in France, they now saw with their own eyes. Mussolini left them wonderstruck. The rise of Hitler dazzled them with joy. By contrast, the state of things in France seemed all the more detestable.

Thus they came to side with the adversary! Yes, there is only this to say: it was inevitable. France remained linked forever with parliamentarian government and democracy. The nation and the principles that she served would perish together; they knew where they stood. In the ordeal by combat in Spain, the judgment of God had been handed down, and, under other stars, thousands of Abyssinian corpses bore witness to the triumph of force.

Let me cite the shocking phrase of a certain Laubreaux at the beginning of the war: he wished his country "a short and disastrous war." Not all of them dared to voice their thoughts so freely, but this was nevertheless the heartfelt hope of at least some brands of French nationalism.

In their eyes, the enemy was the sole possessor of the formula of life. How beautifully the ideas of Sorel and Maurras, choked

* Bonapartists after the overthrow of Napoleon III, i.e., partisans of a dictatorship instead of the Republic. Earlier in the nineteenth century—between the restoration of the Bourbons in 1815 and their overthrow in 1848—Bonapartists were apt to be rabid republicans, democrats and even communists. The Boulangists were the supporters of General Boulanger (1837-1891), the original "man on horseback," who attempted to overthrow the Third Republic in 1889. (Translator's note.)

out in France by the tares of democracy, had sprung up and flourished in Italy and Germany! And at their radios, they followed from afar the tramp of those processions before the idol. They bowed down with all those young men in uniforms, well-muscled, blank-faced, unthinking, obedient to the gesture and the voice. They hailed as saviors these millions of robots to whom the kingdom of the earth was promised.

Nights when I cannot sleep I think with satisfaction of the survivors of those throngs that we used to see in the photographs in L'ILLUSTRATION in 1936, forming immense geometric figures at Nuremberg around the high seat of the human object of their fetish worship. They have now learned this truth: that no force in the world exists that cannot meet its match. They chew this bitter cud amid the smoking ruins of their great Reich. I never weary either of thinking of that other photograph in L'ILLUSTRATION—of Ciano, his head flung back in broad laughter, on his return from a raid in which he had massacred, with no danger to himself, tribes of peasants and shepherds. But behind him, on his plane was painted a death's-head, laughing with the same expression.

Henceforth then, nothing prevents Frenchmen of all parties, united in the same resistance to the invader, from rallying together about the idea of nation, which a handful of so-called "nationalists" no longer monopolize. Out of the working class, which believed itself won over to internationalism, the nation saw innumerable defenders arise. They stood by the country while many who professed nationalism betrayed it. Paris freed herself and, like so many other old French cities, gave a magnificent symbol to the world that the sense of nation was roused in a militant people. The spirit of 1793 lived again! But I hereby pledge that we shall not allow any further confusion as to what "nation" means. The Fourth Republic will not be the easy-going dupe whose unworthy leaders learned Bainville's editorials by heart and unwincingly, beatifically, accepted the bucket of filth that Léon Daudet emptied over their heads each morning. They had even lost the protective reflex that the instinct of self-preservation gives to animals. The autopsy of the murdered Republic reveals a deep cancer gnawing within her. The impotence, or rather the

non-existence, of the ACTION FRANÇAISE at the ballot-box * kept
most democrats from noticing the havoc these termites of Maurras
were working in the heart and brain of the nation.

Today we know that liberty must be defended. We shall no
longer be confused by a contradiction that used to paralyze us.
We shall not hesitate to use force to defend liberty against its
eternal enemies. Today we understand the meaning of the revolu-
tionary slogan from which the timid republicans of the Second
Empire lopped off the essential word: Liberty, Equality, Fraternity,
or DEATH. Yes, or death. Not that we have any intention of considering opinions as a crime or of setting up scaffolds, but we
SHALL mount resolute guard around the Republic.

From the moment that peace is restored, we shall be able to
measure, according to the attitude our leaders take toward the
supporters of L'ACTION FRANÇAISE and all those who, directly or
indirectly, are its spiritual descendants—even though their lips
deny it—what the chances of the resurrected Republic are to be.
Of course there will be other touchstones too, such as the answers
given to simple questions like, "Who owns the newspaper LE
TEMPS?" † But first of all, it is impossible to overrate the symbolic
importance that the survival or death of the spirit of L'ACTION
FRANÇAISE will have. We need seek no pretext: we had before
our eyes every morning right up to the dawn of the liberation the
proof of what "nationalism" leads to: the copy of L'ACTION FRAN-
ÇAISE published under German control, the daily article by Maurras approved by the KOMMANDANTUR.

Of those who shared in this guilt, the least that the Republic
can demand is retirement and silence. It would be folly on our
part to forbid them to think what they think and believe what
they believe. But they shall never again, as they did with im-
punity for half a century, turn against liberty the arms put into

* For many years before the second World War, even under proportional
representation, and in spite of the huge number of deputies, not a single
royalist collected enough votes to hold any national elective office.

† A well-known conservative paper which supported Pétain and was therefore suppressed after the liberation. Le Temps was for years considered the
semi-official spokesman of the government. In its latter days it was said to be
owned by the French members of the European steel cartel.—L.

their hands by the Marianne * that they caricatured as a droopy-breasted slattern puppet in a street show and whom their "nationalist" press made the favorite butt of their gibes.

All governments are alike when it comes to scandals. This is one point they all have in common. The devil alone knows what the inside history of the dictatorships was like. The tone of Saint-Simon's memoirs † lends dash and even a sort of glamour to crimes that make the trivial skulduggeries of democratic régimes seem very innocent indeed. But alone among all the governments in history, the Third Republic gave complete license to its enemies to single out and magnify the most insignificant episode, to slander brazenly the men in power, and to persevere in their patient enterprise of defamation which, in June, 1940, culminated in collaboration with the enemy.

The truth is that the defense of the Republic depends on our determination and on a sound organization of justice. But first a problem of quite another nature, and one that at first glance seems difficult to solve, will confront us. What shall be the relations between the political parties revived within the nation? United as they will be in their loyalty to the nation, the causes of divison among them will nevertheless continue to exist. And, for example, the discussion dating from the eve of the war concerning the "outstretched hand" extended by the Communists to the Catholics will be reopened, but with what imperious urgency!

Perhaps the secret of our destinies is linked with the occult intentions of certain men whose names are not yet known but who, in time to come, will call the tunes. Throughout four long years, the interests of their ideology were one with those of the defense of the nation. The Communist martyrs could not die for their party without at the same time dying for France, and it is to France first of all that they belong. But the return of peace changes the factors in the French situation.

Communists, Socialists, Gaullists, let us remember Maurras' ghastly error. Let us not discard from our national heritage those elements for which we may be tempted to believe our party has

---

* Symbol of the French Republic. (Cf. Uncle Sam for the U.S.A.)

† Louis, Duc de Saint-Simon (1675-1755), chronicler of the reign of Louis XIV. (Translator's note.)

no further use or whose charm may no longer appeal to us. We know today that no political party, even an international party, can continue to live in a nation that is dead.

A Plea for Personality *

by CHARLES VILDRAC

In a masterly article that appeared in this publication, François Mauriac denounced the work of the "termites of Maurras" in the heart and brain of the nation. As Mauriac implicitly points out, their work was particularly baneful in that it opened the way in France for the epidemic of fascism which, originating in Italy, swept over most of the rest of Europe, after having reached its greatest virulence in Germany.

For our country, like almost all other countries, was infected with this black, or brown, plague—less so than some countries but still enough for us to know what it cost and still costs us. It spread into all social spheres and even into those where Maurras was never read.

The ground was not therefore prepared by Maurras alone. There was no Maurras in Spain to conjure up a Franco, nor in Belgium to give rise to a Degrelle.† And in Switzerland, where Maurras did have readers, the murky ideology of total nationalism never spread beyond Geneva, where a few intellectuals, ridiculously enough, joined the CAMELOTS DU ROY.‡

I believe that everywhere the rise of the fascist phenomenon coincided with the state of undernourishment and anemia of so-

---

* From Les Lettres Françaises, September 30, 1944.

† Léon Degrelle, Belgian leader of the Rexist ("Christ the King") movement, a fascist group which originated some years before the outbreak of World War II. When Hitler invaded Belgium, Degrelle was appointed Gauleiter for his country. (Translator's note.)

‡ The royalist youth movement, affiliated with the Action Française. Aside from their activity in hawking the Action Française at the doors of churches after mass, these well-bred young thugs usually formed the nucleus of reactionary demonstrations and were adepts with bludgeons and blackjacks. (Translator's note.)

ciety between two wars. From 1920 to 1939, the social organism was more or less sickly. It suffered from fatigue after so much blood-letting, the fever of false prosperity, the fatty degeneration of inflation which left it short-winded and incapable of any spontaneity, and which could not be banted off. There were also those gastric attacks which were nothing other than the digestive troubles of a plutocracy that was already doomed—attacks during which the patient beheld in a cold sweat the hallucination of the surgeon of his nightmare—the Man with the Knife Between his Teeth.* Quacks and adventurers of every hue exploited this scarecrow, that only yesterday Berlin and Vichy were still trying to patch up.

Finally, there were the first symptoms of that universal malady: a decline and abdication of the personality, a mania for gregariousness, a falling-off of the critical sense, sinking into a state of blind and tutelary conformism.

All of this could not make serious inroads into the rich individualism that is a part and parcel of the genius of France and with which every régime had been, and should be, obliged to reckon. But, just the same, how many adolescents, how many young men, we saw preferring to march in step and follow the first guide that presented himself rather than to set their own pace and choose their own paths!

The desire of many of them was not to have to think: to have a leader to do it for them, to hand them a ready-made creed, rituals, slogans, and if possible, a uniform and arms. For it is one of the characteristics of a fundamental weakness to affect the external trappings of strength; and a sentimental yearning for creative activity makes vacillating minds easy prey for any sort of ideological claptrap.†

Remember those leagues that used to ape Nazi methods. Remember the "punitive expeditions" of the gentlemen in little BÉRETS who rolled about the country in trucks, with blackjacks

---

* The conventional caricature of the Communists, dear to reactionary newspapers.

† Colonel Casimir de la Roque's *Croix de Feu*, Doriot's *Parti Populaire Français*, Maurras' *Camelots du Roy*. This was the period when the French industrialists were still looking for a home-bred *Führer* to back. But they didn't find one worth backing.—L.

and revolvers, twenty of them against one opponent. Remember the delirious rag-tag battalions that put themselves at the disposition not of some great ideal but of some little adventurer.

A FÜHRER-mania, fortunately not widespread, expressed itself in the GRAFFITI scrawled on billboards and the slates of street urinals: "So-and-so for dictator!"

Scatterbrained veterans' organizations yearned for colored shirts and the goose step. Young toughs practiced with tommy-guns. And under the nose of a spineless government, the agents of Mussolini controlled Southern France, while the Nazis were establishing their Brown House in the very heart of Paris.

The German occupation authorities—including Vichy—while spreading this malady, at the same time roused the organism of France to a healthy and magnificent reaction against it. We know what heroes the revolt produced. Tomorrow we shall know all those exploits in which, in a framework of concerted action, they displayed the highest kind of individual qualities. Thus, while among the prisoners and deportees and slave laborers, the human personality was more downtrodden and enslaved than it had been before, in the Resistance it recovered all its value and all its dignity.

But, among those who played no active part, among the least oppressed of all the people in France, how many there were who were contaminated to one degree or another—and usually without being aware of it!

In the "legions," "militias," and youth organizations set up by the Marshal, a nauseating "corporalism" copied from the occupying forces prevailed. The only thing about it that seemed to be a distinctively Vichy contribution was the element of masquerade. I am thinking of those comic opera Tyrolean hats, the white stockings, chamois vests spangled with trinkets and fobs and tricked out with ribbons and lanyards, and those voluminous capes of a size and luxury that were indecent at a time when little children lacked clothing.*

* When we got to North Africa, the S.O.L., the Légion des Anciens Combattants, the Chantiers de la Jeunesse (Vichy youth camps) and the Compagnons de France (fascist boy scouts) seemed to be in a fancy dress competition with the Arab Four Hundred. There was, as Vildrac says, something peculiarly absurd about these proto-military organizations because they

During the summer of 1942 I passed a few weeks in a region where several summer camps for schoolchildren had been set up. There was splendid scenery to look at, there were trees to get to know, flowers to pick. At every step there were worth-while objects for observation, discovery, contemplation. In amazement I saw these groups of boys march through the meadows and woods in close-order drill formation, braying inanities from the musical repertory of the LÉGION, that needed only the accompaniment of boots to make them complete.

The young priests who supervised these children were probably decent and guileless patriots who never for a moment suspected that they were suffering from, and inoculating their charges with, the Nazi virus.

During more than four years and in obedience to the orders of the oppressor, our rulers, after having abolished our liberties and dissolved our labor unions and associations, did their best to set up a guardianship, that is to say, a close supervision, over all categories of Frenchmen. Youth organizations, vigilance societies, professional corporations, employers' associations were so many parasitical—and paralyzing—nuisances.

At last, all these inventions have been liquidated or are in process of liquidation. The windows are wide open to the fresh air and the light. It remains for us to recover, with a deep breath, our facility of thought, along with our freedom of motion. And it is not in a single day that all the traces of the infection and the ankylosis will disappear.

Too many of us have become accustomed to speaking in lowered voices and in ambiguous terms, to fearing to make a move or take an initiative or a responsibility without consulting the authorities, seeking official support, showing papers (authentic or forged), without being covered by a permit or a decree. It has gotten so that some people are so accustomed to restrictions that they have come to mistake their shackles for crutches. Let us liberate them—from shackles and crutches alike—even though they may feel unsteady on their feet at first. Let them go their

were French. Dress as they would, the men looked out of character. It reminded me of a convention of those frolic boosters, the Tall Cedars of Lebanon.—L.

own ways without travel orders or AUSWEIS * and accept hence-forth no other discipline than that of free men.

If, as I believe is the case, the disease from which we have suffered is more or less due to a decline of personality, it is individual worth and character that we must first of all restore, cultivate, and re-establish in a place of honor—beginning, of course, by imposing respect for the human person.

* Nelly de Vogüé, driving an automobile between Paris and Orléans a couple of weeks after the liberation, was stopped by a gendarme who asked her for her *Ausweis*, or permit from the German *Kommandantur*. Habit had been too strong for him.—L.

own ways without travel orders or konvois,* and accept henceforth no other discipline than that of her spirit.

If, as I believe is the case, the disease from which we have
suffered is more or less due to a decline of personality, it is individual worth and character that we must first of all restore,
cultivate, and re-establish in a place of honor—beginning, of
course, by imposing respect for the human person.

*Actis de Vogüé, driving an automobile between Paris and Orléans a
couple of weeks after the liberation, was stopped by a sentinelle who asked
him for his Ausweis, or permit from the German Kommandatur. He'd had
been too strong for him....

In Lieu of Epilogue

In Lieu of Epilogue

The publishers of this book had the idea that I should round it off by an epilogue. But an epilogue is a speech at the end of a play, and history has no end. Artistically, the liberation might seem a good place to round off the story of France. There have been, in the course of that same story, a dozen other aesthetically satisfactory places to write Finis and Epilogue. One was the coronation of the Dauphin Charles VII at Reims in 1429 which marked the completion of Saint Joan's mission; another the coronation of Henry IV which marked the end of the Wars of Religion and in the opinion of the contemporary world the triumph of common sense. The fall of Robespierre, the battle of Waterloo, the triumph of 1918, all offered good opportunities for a narrator to draw his threads neatly together, tie a knot and then snip off the loose ends. Unfortunately, from the point of view of the amateur of certainties, history is not composed by playwrights. This is lucky, from mine, since I do not desire any ending to the story of France, even a happy ending. That is of course inconceivable in the case of a nation anyway. Not even Father Divine has ever promised a heaven for dead nations.

France was threatened with a death that besides being death was as squalid and humiliating as suffocation in the arms of a Yahoo. Her predicament puts me in mind of Gulliver's when, while he was bathing, the Yahoo, "which smelled very rank," embraced him "in the most fulsome manner." France resisted and escaped. And with her there escaped from the hairy and ill-smelling arms of the bleary beast all hope for the continuity of civilization. But people in France are not living happily ever

519

after, any more than are people in the United States, or Norway, or the United Kingdom or Russia. I do not think this cause for disillusionment. Escape from extinction is a pretty good thing in itself. As a cross-grained Irish waiter in a grim restaurant once said to me: "What do you expect for two dollars?—a gold watch?"

Jean-Paul, the Armored Division soldier who wrote to me from the front on May 10, 1940, when he saw the refugees from Luxemburg, was demobilized in the Vichy "free" zone after the Pétain armistice. He went back to Paris, found little to do, and after a while drifted to Orléans, where he started a small trucking business. With his unfailing gift for tinkering with motors, he repaired a couple of venerable vehicles and converted them to run on charcoal. He then got into the Resistance and used his trucks to retrieve and haul to safety Sten guns and other arms parachuted by the R.A.F. He found a fine, merry woman in a town near Orléans and married her.

When the Americans approached Orléans in August, 1944, Jean-Paul, who speaks American well, went out to meet them and formed the liaison between them and the F.F.I. His guidance was at least partially responsible for the capture of Orléans with a loss to us of only fourteen men. After the liberation he returned to Paris and got a place as manager of a big garage, an appointment which carried with it a fairly comfortable apartment above the garage and the right to raise chickens on the roof. But the government requisitioned the garage for military vehicles and Jean-Paul found himself doing the same chores he had performed with the Armored Division in 1940.

When I last heard from him he and his wife still had the apartment, however, and during the cold winter of 1944-5, when they could keep only one room heated, they were raising fifty small chicks in the living room. "DES VRAIES POULES DE LUXE," he wrote. "POULE DE LUXE," literally a luxury chicken, means colloquially a luxuriously kept woman. So LE PETIT SOLDAT FRANÇAIS with his DEBROUILLARDISE CARACTÉRISTIQUE continues to make himself a little life of his own.

My friend Louis Pavageau, of whom I haven't said anything before, a big square-jawed aviator I met in Alsace in 1939, went back after the Pétain armistice to Dombasle in Lorraine, his home, and there lived out the four-year agony of that eastern province. He was in the Resistance there, and his great day came in September, 1944, when, with the Americans approaching, the F.F.I. men could come out into the open and fight. "We had only one automatic rifle and one sporting rifle for a hundred and fifty men," he wrote to me, "but what a relief it was to fight." He sent me news of other men I had met in Alsace.

One of them, a Major Bourgon, I had remembered during the dark years with mixed feelings. He was a sanguine, thick-necked, middle-aged survivor of the first World War who looked like Henry VIII and had similar tastes. He had commanded a battalion in a forest near the Rhine and had set the best table in Europe, having managed to snare a roast-chef from one great Paris restaurant and a pastry cook from another. There had been a wartime order against hunting, but there was always plenty of venison on Major Bourgon's table. "Can we help it if the deer strangle themselves in the barked wire?" he once asked me. "And the pheasants?" I said, with a rapturous glance at three fat, redundant birds that soldier waiters had just carried in. "The battalion surgeon runs over them on his bicycle," Major Bourgon replied. At the time I had thought this magnificent, but after the débâcle I had wondered if such concentration on the good life was compatible with relentless war.

Pavageau wrote me that Bourgon had been killed "SUR PLACE," in 1940, defending his deer forest.

Pavageau had had a Belgian brother-in-law, also a flier, Jean Demay, who had escaped to the United States in 1942. He returned to Europe as a soldier in the American Army, made first lieutenant, and was killed at Metz.

Pavageau thought that things were slowly, very slowly, getting better. Jean-Paul thinks so too. And Georges Adam, the man who used to carry the LETTRES FRANÇAISES copy to the secret printer, and who was in the United States last winter, is sure France will "get out of the dough trough" eventually.

Personally, I believe that France has a great future, because France is full of great people. This is an old-fashioned, romantic point of view for which I have recently been taken to task by a young friend who has never been anywhere but who reads all the ieaviest political, economic and literary magazines to be obtained in Brentano's basement. "It's interesting," he said to me the other day when I had been talking about the efforts of the individual men and women who had found each other to form the Resistance —"but in this atomic age it's dated already."

Courage, however, has no date.

It outlasts "Thousand-Year Empires."

It is a little white goat on the hills.